Color and Culture

color & culture

Black Writers and the Making of the Modern Intellectual

Ross Posnock

Harvard University Press
Cambridge, Massachusetts, and London, England

Copyright © 1998 by the President and Fellows
of Harvard College
All rights reserved
Printed in the United States of America

Library of Congress Cataloging-in-Publication Data

Posnock, Ross.
    Color and culture : black writers and the making of the modern
intellectual / Ross Posnock.
        p.   cm.
    Includes bibliographical references and index.
    ISBN 0-674-14309-4 (alk. paper)
    1. American literature—Afro-American authors—History and criticism.
2. Language and culture—United States—History—20th century.
3. Du Bois, W. E. B. (William Edward Burghardt), 1868–1963.
4. American literature—20th century—History and criticism.
5. United States—Intellectual life—20th century.
6. Afro-Americans—Intellectual life.   7. Locke, Alain LeRoy, 1886–1954.
8. Afro-Americans in literature.   9. Blacks—Intellectual life.
I. Title.
PS153.N5P68   1998
810.9'896073—dc21   98-11604

Designed by Gwen Nefsky Frankfeldt

This book has been digitally reprinted. The content
remains identical to that of previous printings.

To Richard Poirier

Acknowledgments

I wish to thank the John Simon Guggenheim Memorial Foundation for a fellowship in 1993 which was of great benefit to my work. A number of people offered useful provocations of various kinds, witting and unwitting: Charles Altieri, Martha Banta, Thomas Bender, Sara Blair, Robert Boyers, Hazel Carby, Stephen Cox, Morris Dickstein, Mary Esteve, Jonathan Freedman, Susan Glenn, James Gregory, Charles Johnson, Eric Lott, Walter Michaels, Mark Crispin Miller, Marc Posnock, David Shields, Brook Thomas, Priscilla Wald, Kenneth Warren. Gregg Crane deserves special thanks for his painstaking reading of various drafts and for making so many valuable suggestions. At Harvard University Press the advice of Lindsay Waters and the scrupulous manuscript editing of Camille Smith have been much appreciated. My gratitude as well to Suzanne Hyman, managing editor of *Raritan,* for nearly a decade of support.

Parts of this book appeared in different form in *American Literary History, Critical Inquiry,* and *Raritan.* Quotations from *Atlantis: 3 Tales* by Samuel Delany are used by permission of the author and his agent, Henry Morrison, Inc. Quotations from *People Who Led to My Plays* by Adrienne Kennedy are used by permission of the publisher, Theatre Communications Group.

As always, and as in everything, Karen Shabetai has been indispensable, not least because her skepticism—"loving, rapid, merciless"— enacts the truth of Blake's wisdom that "opposition is true friendship." One eight-year-old, curious about what I was spending too much time on, wondered aloud, just who is this www.Du Bois? For that, and much more, I am delighted to thank my daughter Sophie.

Contents

Color and Culture

Introduction:
Culture Has No Color

They "never expected to see a black intellectual and did not know one when they saw one." Not too long ago this moment of nonrecognition from Richard Wright's *The Outsider* (1953; 557) might have been enlisted as an apt epigraph for a study of black intellectuals. The quotation concisely renders the theme of invisibility that Wright and Ralph Ellison made famous and that is present in the works of many other authors. The last ten years, however, have banished any possibility that Wright's words might serve such a purpose. If, by the end of the eighties, the public intellectual had been declared lost in the jargon-infested groves of academia, his return in the nineties is largely a continuing black achievement. This is news only to those who have not read any of the countless sagas that have recently filled magazines and newspapers. But Wright remains worth quoting if only to mark the distance between then and now.

If Wright summed up *then*, what sums up *now*? A bookjacket blurb will do as a bit of raw data. It is from a 1996 book by a prominent black intellectual: an academic, a preacher, a writer, "and a black American who chooses to speak across the color line, he embodies the ideal public intellectual for our time: translator, boundary breaker and healer of a war torn culture."[1] The journey from invisibility to ambidextrous "ideal public intellectual" has been the stuff of myriad articles in the mainstream media, often rendered with at least a note of self-congratulatory triumphalism of the "look how far we (white liberal readers) and they (the black intellectuals, and by extension the black bourgeoisie) have come" variety.[2]

In this book I turn on its head this tidy scenario of the black intellectual as a late-twentieth-century invention or discovery. Rather than latecomers, black writers circa 1900 were arguably the first modern American intellectuals. The very word "intellectual" entered political discourse only a century ago, in 1898 when Zola (among other professionals) left his study, interrupting his novelistic labors to enter the political maelstrom of the Dreyfus Affair. Zola and the Dreyfusards saw themselves as giving voice to humankind's sense of justice and humanity against the anti-Semitism of French nationalists. For intruding where they did not belong and for invoking universal values, the Dreyfusards were scorned as *déracinés* and branded with the imprecation of *Les Intellectuels.*

Apart from their ultimate success in winning Dreyfus's freedom, the Dreyfusards' most valuable legacy was their challenge to a dichotomized social configuration that kept mind and power, culture and politics, static and separate realms. As Jürgen Habermas has observed, the emergence of the modern intellectual depends on, and is simultaneous with, the making of a political public sphere. This space must be won against the opposition of two camps who share an anti-democratic bias: on the one hand, mandarin proponents of high culture who regard it as the private preserve of an elite; on the other, an administrative class who designate politics as the sole province of experts. "Both sides fear from the intellectual a mixing of categories that would do better to remain separate" (Habermas 78). Thus from its historical origins the modern intellectual is born of a crisis of categories and an assault on the exclusionary and proprietary.[3]

A young social scientist with a love of art and literature (before long he would publish poetry and fiction) had followed the Dreyfus Affair as he visited France in the 1890s. At the turn of the century W. E. B. Du Bois began organizing a cohort of black professionals to agitate for equal rights. By 1910 he had created a base of support to help make possible a more inclusive voice: the interracial NAACP demanded justice and opened a public space for discussion. The instrument of the latter achievement was a journal of politics and arts called *The Crisis,* sponsored by the NAACP and edited by Du Bois. Implicitly Du Bois was guided by the Dreyfusard ideal of protest founded on a rejection of culture and politics conceived as private domains ruled by vested interests. For instance, Du Bois refused to fetishize (even while respecting) the autonomy of art. To inculcate in the masses appreciation for the integrity of aesthetic experience was, to Du Bois, a political responsibility, not its evasion. Instead of segregating culture from politics, Du Bois (and the intellectuals he influenced) sought to develop a "higher and broader and more varied human culture," a project he described as the "main end of democracy" (*Writings* 1063–64). I will call this effort cosmopolitan. Though often misconstrued in our own time as a synonym for elitist privilege, the cosmopolitanism of modern black intellectuals presents a democratic challenge to the obdurate belief that high culture is a private citadel of white privilege.

Despite its historical myopia, the contemporary media hype heralding the black intellectual is on to something. The time *is* ripe for the study of black intellectuals. But not only for the obvious reasons noted above. What makes the current moment opportune is that postmodernism is waning, including its tribal conception of politics founded on a romance of identity. This atomized, essentialist politics has always coexisted uneasily with postmodern theory's preference for a dispersed self of pastiche. Whether postmodernism's successor will be called post-identity, post-ethnic, trans- or post-national, or trans-American (to note some contenders), it will express a left-liberal skepticism of cultural pluralism, better known as identity politics.[4] This skepticism is particularly salutary for the study of African American intellectual history, especially the history of black intellectuals. For here identity politics (practiced by whites and blacks alike) has long dominated, fixated on racial difference and the question of what and who is authentically black. The demand of authenticity is always conformist and enforces homogeneous norms, for instance rigid masculinism and rooted regionalism, while suppressing the cosmopolitan recognition that one lives as a "mixed-up self" "in a mixed-up world" where ancestral imperatives do not exert a preordained authority (Waldron 95).

Cultural purism has been rejected by a growing chorus of thinkers busy writing postmodernism's obituary. Although nationalism has been resurgent since the end of the cold war, there is also a renewed sense of convergence and commonality among the world's regimes in the wake of recent transitions from communism to emerging market capitalism. Universalism, according to the social theorist Jeffrey Alexander, has now become the positive half of a binary whose other (polluted) term is nationalism, a dualism poised to replace the postmodern and modern as the defining binary code of the present. Anthony Appiah, Julia Kristeva, Tvetzan Todorov, Edward Said, Martha Nussbaum, and Alain Finkielkraut are among those who have engaged the possibilities and the limits of the postmodern politics of difference. Instead, they have chosen cosmopolitanism.[5] The symmetry is striking: the century's end returns us to its beginning.

This book commences with a brief visit to "The American Museum of Unnatural History." It is built, Zora Neale Hurston says of her imaginary edifice, on the "folk belief" that all "non-Anglo-Saxons are uncomplicated stereotypes." The main target of Hurston's barbs in the essay "What White Publishers Won't Print" (1950) is the WASP American reading public, whose "indifference, not to say skepticism, to the internal life of educated minorities" has made the "unnatural history museum" a flourishing enterprise. It encourages white publishers to accept from black writers only work that reflects what is already found on exhibit (951). In addition to displays of the "typical" "Oriental, Jew . . . and Latin," visitors to the museum would find two figures in the "American Negro exhibit." One is "seated on a stump picking away on his banjo and singing and laughing. The other is a most amoral character before a share-cropper's shack mumbling about injustice. Doing this makes him out to be a Negro 'intellectual' " (952).

Hurston consistently mocks those who appropriate "intellectual" to describe their principal activity, which is to "stand around and mouth the same trite phrases, and try their practised-best to look sad" while rushing "around seeking for something [they] can 'resent,' " as she wrote in a 1938 essay, "Art and Such" (908). In their belief that "no Negro exists as an individual" but "only as another tragic unit of the Race," these "champions of 'Race Consciousness' " have had a deadening effect on literature, Hurston laments, especially on "the universal oneness necessary" to it (908, 911). Given its skepticism that "minorities do think, and think about something other than the race problem," the white public is only too happy to honor the race champion as "Negro 'intellectual' " with a place in "The American Museum of Unnatural History."

Hurston's mordant wit reveals that the "Negro 'intellectual,' " as distinct from the race champion, is at best an inferred, shadowy presence, a figure all but eclipsed both by her American museum and by the grip of "race consciousness." Yet she retains the hope, at least in 1938, that a "weakening of race consciousness, impatience with race champions and a growing taste for literature as such" are imminent in African American culture and that a less encumbered black intellectual will emerge (911). In these two essays Hurston implicitly casts herself as this emergent counter-figure, an artist who writes "Negro" stories "offered without special pleading." She represents "the Negro's poetical flow of language" not as a lecture on the race problem but as a way to create "verisimilitude . . . by stewing the subject in its own juice" (910).

In this book I examine how literary artists devised ways to exit the "American Museum of Unnatural History," to make *black intellectual* mean more than race man or woman. Leaving the museum required dissolving the seal of isolation and idiosyncrasy that kept them objects under glass, a seal composed of invidious race distinction. In a society as obsessed with race as the United States the effort could never be entirely successful, the seal never fully broken. The American Museum still stands, most recently renovated and repaved with the good intentions of multiculturalist identity politics. But what has generally been unrecognized, misunderstood, or undervalued is the effort made to lift the burden of being a group representative or exemplar. To escape the pressure to conform to the familiar and recognizable, to stereotypes, is to be free to delete the first word or to accent the second in the phrase *black intellectual* or to vary one's inflections at will or as circumstance dictates. To impart something of this lability and this ambition to interrogate the very category of race, I use the term *antirace race man or woman.*[6]

This vexed personage of "complex double vision" (to borrow Ralph Ellison's version of "double consciousness") moves from the shadows of Hurston's discourse to the center of this book (*Shadow* 131–132). Hurston dramatizes what is seldom acknowledged with such clarity— the conflict between race champion and intellectual. But her satiric exaggerations simplify by splitting the roles into separate people; even her own double stance is left unaccounted for. Hurston's simplifications are especially apparent given that much of her ridicule is directed in all but name at the most famous race man of the day. One would never know from Hurston's remarks that Du Bois also happened to be the preeminent black intellectual of his era and, furthermore, that he shared Hurston's frustrations. From the age of twenty-five Du Bois accepted the personal sacrifice involved in race work and pledged himself to uplift—the struggle for racial and political (civic and social) equality. But he did not stop there; as an antirace race man, he also sought to ventilate the psychic and intellectual constriction imposed by racial identity. "What is a Negro anyhow? He is just human": this is the unsettlement that "true Art" creates, says Du Bois at the end of a famous essay, as he suggests his ultimate aim, to dispense with race classification (*Writings* 1002).

The black intellectuals to be discussed in this book believe in the promise of aesthetic freedom—that art and culture can be practices resistant to racial identity.[7] Struggling to assert the freedom of art while laboring for race uplift, they enact "two unreconciled strivings, two warring ideals in one dark body," to borrow Du Bois's famous words defining "double consciousness" (*Souls* 364). This struggle was a virtual given for such early figures as Pauline Hopkins, Charles Chesnutt, and Du Bois, as it was for the next generation of Alain Locke, Jessie Fauset, Wallace Thurman, Nella Larsen, Jean Toomer, and Hurston herself. The effort continued with, among others, Richard Wright, Ralph Ellison, and James Baldwin. Some ended the conflict peremptorily, opting for a cosmic universalism (Toomer), or dying early (Thurman), or suffering various forms of oblivion, self-induced and/or culturally inflicted (Hopkins, Larsen, Fauset, and Hurston). But whatever their final fates, they all turned unreconciled strivings into a source of expressive energy and often into their subject matter, none more so than Du Bois. A "fiercely sunny" "strife" kept him productive for nearly three-quarters of a century (364). As Emerson says, "the mind goes antagonizing on" (483).

Du Bois manifests creative strife in a penchant for simultaneity; as *The Souls of Black Folk* discloses, he celebrates and contests racial identity, for he both works within the "Veil" of black America and seeks to move beyond it to what he called "the kingdom of culture" (365). A catalyst of Du Bois's mobility, I will argue, is the pragmatism imparted by his mentor William James. Although the standard intellectual histories tell us that the prodigious career of John Dewey defines pragmatism after William James, this neglects the great flowering of pragmatism in the careers of prominent twentieth-century black intellectuals, specifically Du Bois and Alain Locke. Although of different generations at Harvard, both men received Harvard doctorates. They revered James, absorbed his pragmatism, and, in good pragmatist fashion, revised it each in his own way. Key figures in the antirace race lineage, Du Bois and Locke were inspired by James's pragmatist pluralism (which is crucially distinct, we shall see, from what became known as cultural pluralism), by his openness to the excluded, and by his critique of the primacy of identity.

The interracial exchange sketched above has been a missing chapter in American literary and cultural history.[8] The omission is partly the result of the way this history constructs (and constricts) "black" and "intellectual." For instance, "New York intellectuals" designates neither the black writers and critics of the Harlem Renaissance of the twenties and thirties and the Harlem-based Black Arts movement of the sixties, nor New Yorkers of the twenties who influenced black thinkers (Dewey, Franz Boas, Kenneth Burke, for instance), but only the postwar Manhattan literati centered in and around *Partisan Review* and Columbia University. Composed largely of WASPs and Jews, this group remained distant from African American life, although Ralph Ellison and James Baldwin were occasional contributors, the latter given important early support by the magazine. Daniel Bell dubbed them "cousins" in the *Partisan Review* "family." More than any other single group, the "New York intellectuals" defined for several generations the image of the public intellectual as a freewheeling cultural and literary critic upholding high modernism, Enlightenment (and Marxist) universalism, and urban (and urbane) cosmopolitanism. Not by accident, black intellectuals have consistently been characterized, until very recently, by the absence of these values. They are typically depicted as particularists, bent on creating a nationalist, vernacular folk culture of uplift. In short, to be a black intellectual is by definition to labor in an ethnic province, to accent the *black*, to be a race champion.

This impoverished scenario perpetuates an historical blindness by ignoring that Du Bois is virtually the first American to turn "intellectuals" into a force for "justice and humanity" after the word emerges from France in 1898.[9] The morally impassioned universalist perspective of *Les Intellectuels* coincided with Du Bois's early-twentieth-century effort to disseminate values and ideals unbounded by the color line. Nearly a generation before the "Young Intellectuals" of 1910 led by Randolph Bourne's vision of "trans-national America," and over thirty years before the New York intellectuals, Du Bois crafted a cosmopolitanism that only now is being recognized. The profound irony that a black thinker, himself a New Yorker for most of his last fifty years, imported the tradition of modern intellectuals into the United States, should confirm the suspicion that some of the basic categories of American literary and cultural history are terminally sclerotic.[10]

Where the keynote of the black intellectual as race champion is group loyalty, the New York intellectual is, above all, said to be "sophisticated in . . . grappling with complexity" (Cooney 355). What constitutes this complexity is the rejection of both particularism and assimilation (these are "simplistic extremes" that attract the "ideologist of commitment" with his weakness for the orthodoxies of "formulaic identity") and an embrace of the "*voluntary* aspect of modern identity" that enables the "balancing of multiple claims" (355). This ideal type bears a striking, if ultimately superficial, resemblance to the description of Du Bois, for instance, in the following pages. While "complexity" is a familiar value term for such midcentury liberal intellectuals as Lionel Trilling, it remains for them largely an aesthetic category, expressing cautionary skepticism of, and an alternative to, political commitment. But for a black intellectual like Baldwin, complexity—resistance to racial identity—is, say in *The Fire Next Time,* precisely the means to achieve more nuanced modes of political engagement. For the antirace race men and women I will discuss, then, there is always more at stake in the "balancing of multiple claims" than intellectual sophistication.

Often this balancing is a matter of life or death, literal or psychic, never less than an experiment in enacting unprecedented modes of being that are automatically under suspicion in a white supremacist world. "Our life is a war," the grandfather in *Invisible Man* tells his grandson; "live with your head in the lion's mouth" (16). Charles Chesnutt would have concurred. Writing in his private journal in 1880, the twenty-two-year-old North Carolina schoolteacher notes that "the subtle almost indefinable feeling of repulsion toward the Negro, which is common to most Americans, . . . cannot be stormed and taken by assault; the garrison will not capitulate: so their position must be mined, and we will find ourselves in their midst before they think it." Chesnutt faces his task and fuses the literary and political: "the Negro's part is to prepare himself for social recognition and equality; and it is the province of literature to open the way for him to get it" (*Journals* 140). Du Bois speaks of the "dogged strength alone" that keeps one from being "torn asunder" as one tries to be both an American and a Negro, a race man and an intellectual, "without being cursed and spit upon" (*Souls* 365). These hostile responses were precisely those of rabid Southern whites in the 1950s and 1960s to the lone young black men and women, books in hand, whom they forced to run gauntlets to enter and desegregate Southern schools and colleges.

We shall see that bringing black and intellect together has, historically, been an incendiary coupling. And the making of black intellectuals occurred for most of this century within a condition of public unease. One consequence for this book is that familiar questions that tend to frame discussions of literary intellectuals—calibrating the relation of aesthetics and politics and the political responsibility of the intellectual—are curiously moot. For these questions presume the availability of choice. And the unique public glare in which black intellectuals have worked makes all their artistic projects already political. Thus a tension stressed in this book—between race champion and intellectual—neither reduces to nor expresses a tension between the political (the race figure) and the aesthetic (the intellectual). Indeed, a distinctive aspect of the antirace race lineage under scrutiny is how richly entangled the aesthetic and political become, an entwining that stands as an implicit alternative to the tendency of high modernism to oppose them.

The black American novelist most self-consciously affiliated with modernism, and hence the black writer most often accused of political quietism or conservatism, suggested this entanglement as the condition of his career. In response to a critic puzzled by his seeming lack of political engagement, Ralph Ellison remarked (in 1964): "no Negroes are beating down my door, putting pressure on me to join the Negro Freedom movement, for the simple reason that I am enlisted for the duration" (*Shadow* 142). Ellison's firmness that he is "enlisted for the duration" in the struggle for freedom is treated skeptically by critics for whom "political" functions as little more than a litmus test of moral (read ideological) virtue.[11] Ellison's notion of the political, as I will show, recovers an almost classical sense of the word.

This book, a mix of literary criticism and intellectual history, is neither comprehensive nor inclusive. Instead, I study the evolution of a particular cultural formation over the course of a century. Ranging among five generations, Chapters 1 and 2 are an overview, while Chapters 3 through 8 are more tightly focused. In place of expected groupings and writers (the obligatory chapter, say, on Wright, Ellison, and Baldwin), some less familiar figures and texts are presented in unexpected juxtapositions and contexts. For instance, I discuss Du Bois's novel *Dark Princess* (1928) as a remarkable window on his relation to modernity in the tumultuous years from World War I to the Harlem Renaissance. And the novel fantasizes an escape from race responsibility by way of erotic obsession. In other chapters I bring together writers whom critics often set against one another: Locke, Hurston, Toomer, and Ellison in one, Baldwin and Amiri Baraka in another. In the final chapter I examine two avant-garde contemporary black writers—Adrienne Kennedy and Samuel Delany—who not merely accept but relish the poetics of division and "double consciousness" that in earlier figures reflected ambivalences and conflict. Kennedy and Delany remake the antirace

race lineage by abolishing the obligation to represent the race. Disrupting conventional coherence, they favor the paratactic disorientations of collage as a thematic and structural principle. Their collages frustrate the demand of identity and anticipate (and in one instance register) the current decline of identity politics.

This decline, suggested by a near blizzard of straws in the wind—international and domestic, cultural and political—will be discussed in Chapter 1. But a literary straw will be noted here. Richard Wright is now being reevaluated; his late books are back in print after forty years, and the remarkable last decade of his career is being examined with wider lenses. Ever since *Native Son* (1940), critics had made Wright into the sacred totem of genuine blackness, a canonization that left little or no room for the expatriated, proudly "rootless" internationalist ("I can make myself at home almost anywhere on this earth") who looked forward to the day when "those conditions of life that formerly defined what was 'Negro' have ceased to exist" and "Negro literature as such" would disappear. Then the "basic unity of human life" would be affirmed (*White Man* xxix, 108–109). Wright's critical cosmopolitanism and its interrogation of race belong to what has been called an "eclipsed tradition in black intellectual culture."[12]

In this book I recover and reconstruct this lineage of black intellectual history and argue for its currency in a contemporary moment that seems especially propitious. One reason the cosmopolitanism found in, say, Du Bois and Locke has never been appreciated is that they defamiliarize the word, turning it from its typical connotations of an apolitical leisure class with "essentially a tourist's view of the world" (Lasch 6).[13] Above all, for Du Bois and Locke cosmopolitanism means that "culture has no color." Nor do individuals, groups, or nations possess "special proprietary rights" to culture (Locke *Philosophy* 233). To end "the vicious practice" of exclusionary ownership of "various forms of culture" would be to abandon a practice that undergirds imperialism and that "has been responsible for the tragedies of history" (203). Deracializing culture leaves us free to "face the natural fact of the limitless interchangeableness of culture goods" (203).

Enunciated in 1930, Locke's ideal of "cultural reciprocity" and of civilization as a "vast amalgam" of "composite" cultures pays implicit tribute to William James (73, 203). Locke's thinking was evolving in 1908 when he heard James in a lecture on radical pluralism evoke how experience, when "concretely taken, overflows its own definition . . . nature is but a name for excess; every point in her opens out and runs into the more." James was seeking to liberate us from the "vicious intellectualism" of the Western philosophic tradition that rules by imposing "names" that suppress "the more" (James *Writings* 728, 760). In effect, James's recovery of "overlap" in a fluid world where "all is shades and no boundaries," offered Locke metaphors for understanding cosmopolitanism as "limitless" interchange (760–761). Locke in 1930 echoes inadvertently what the socialist Du Bois had celebrated two years before in his novel *Dark Princess*. There he describes as "Divine Anarchy" the "great and final freedom" of an unbounded social order that nurtures "Talent served from the great Reservoir of All Men of All Races, of All Classes, of All Ages, of Both Sexes" (*Dark Princess* 285).

Locke and Du Bois could both be said to remain in touch with the original cosmopolitan ideal. Greco-Roman Stoics developed the notion of a world citizen and stressed human interconnectedness, ideas that would come to influence Kant's Enlightenment ideal of cosmopolitan law as the basis of permanent peace in a world comprising a federation of republic states. Kant's Stoic cosmopolitanism includes the right of all human beings to "communal possession of the earth's surface."[14] Something of this communalism is apparent in Locke and Du Bois as they envision an entrance to a "new era of social and cultural relationships" (Locke *Philosophy* 203). That era would seek, said Locke, to offset "our traditional and excessive emphasis upon cultural difference" and identity with a counter-paradigm of "equivalence" and "reciprocity" (73). Deflating the possessiveness of identity claims, this new model would stress "commonality" as a way to end "the idea of race as a political instrument." This invidious use of race inherently breeds exclusionary relations to culture, thus fueling history's "huge struggles for dominance and supremacy" (203–204). As Locke knew, "the best chance for a new world lies in a radical revision of this root-idea of culture, which never was soundly in accordance with the facts, but which has become so inveterate that it will require a mental revolution to change it" (204).

Nearly seventy years after Locke's statement this revolution in thinking about color and culture remains to be enacted as a "practical necessity." Locke's "radical revision" is founded on a logic of disarming clarity: "culture-goods, once evolved, are no longer the exclusive property of the race or people that originated them. They belong to all who can use them; and belong most to those who can use them best" (206).[15] In emphasizing the primacy of use rather than identity, Locke makes the pragmatist move that conceives identity not as antecedent essence but as an effect of action.[16] The demotion of identity has liberating consequences, the crucial one being "that there is no room for any consciously maintained racialism in matters cultural." All "we should be sanely concerned about is freer participation and fuller collaboration" (233). This liberation is the distilled lesson that antirace race men and women teach, each in their own idiom. Though in a Jim Crow world the effort to abandon "the idea of race as a political instrument" was doomed from the start, this fact must not be an excuse to discredit or forget the ideal that guided the struggle. Out of that struggle emerged a new social presence—black intellectuals.

"Culture has no color": Locke's phrase suggests a deracialized ideal that, to postmodern ears, sounds suspicious—the rhetoric of a liberal humanism by now synonymous with a (pseudo) universalism that was actually the property of white men. The phrase also summons the notion of color-blind jurisprudence, which, as critical legal theorists have shown, is often in practice a formalism that erases material conditions and constraints. Skepticism is useful to the extent that it reminds us that color-blind rhetoric and discourses, legal and cultural, have long been a favorite ideological camouflage to affirm the status quo. Such camouflage abounded in the cold war era. For instance, a critically esteemed Howard University production of Ibsen was invited to tour Scandinavia at around the same time that Paul Robeson was quoted as saying that "only in Russia could the Negro artist straighten his shoulders and raise his head high." Journalists exploited the coincidence to rebut Robeson. Declared the *Washington Post:* "The Howard Players . . . appeared not as representatives of their race but as representatives of theater art. They served their country very well."[17]

Given that color-blind ideals are appropriated routinely for conservative political use, it is easy to distrust the ideal and even regard it as inherently bankrupt. But this reflex debunking can end up perpetuating the very ahistoricism it intends to challenge. For in fact black intellectuals historically have used deracialized discourses as weapons *against* the status quo of white supremacy. The preeminent recent example is the Christian universalism of Martin Luther King. Two principal color-blind discourses and ideals were prominent at the turn of the century: democratic citizenship, founded on the ideal of universal suffrage, and the "kingdom of culture," which Du Bois names the "end" of black "striving."

Democratic culture and citizenship grounded in common humanity are pillars of the cosmopolitan Du Boisian lineage. Its universalism is neither "a mask worn by ethnocentrism" nor a code word for imperialism, as Tzvetan Todorov has remarked of contemporary abuses of the concept (387–388). Du Bois insisted on a dialectic between (unraced) universal and (raced) particular: "Failure to recognize the Universal in the Particular," he wrote in 1921, breeds "the menace of all group exclusiveness and segregation" (*Writings* 1194). The reality of particularity would be affirmed by the mediation of the universal and vice versa.[18] In the rest of this introduction I will examine some of the contexts and the consequences of black intellectuals' investment in universal ideals.

Democracy and art are entwined, complementary realms of value. Like his mentor the Reverend Alexander Crummell and his contemporary Charles Chesnutt, Du Bois locates them above the "Veil of Race" (*Souls* 418). In 1888 Crummell declared that the "democratic idea is neither Anglo-Saxonism, nor Germanism . . . but HUMANITY, and humanity can live when Anglo-Saxonism or any class of the race of man has perished" (*Africa* 53). Twenty years before, in the early years of post–Civil War Reconstruction, much of the nation had seemed poised to live this idea. Then, said Du Bois, "a majority of thinking Americans in the North believed in the equal manhood of black folk." The "days of distinction between colors is about over in this (now) free country," wrote a black man in his diary (qtd. Foner 127). Du Bois was moved by the glory of this moment in American history and pained by its fragility. For this "human faith" in equality soon faded and remains to be recovered, he noted in *Black Reconstruction* (1935; 726). His monumental study of the era commemorates the grandeur and tragedy of the failed utopian experiment in creating, in Eric Foner's words, a "collective national identity" founded on a "society purged of all racial distinctions" (Foner 122, 127). A simple stubborn fact, said Du Bois, stymied this noble ambition—the inability of Southerners to conceive Negroes as ordinary human beings. This is the fatal germ, he believes, that has left democracy in America forever stunted.[19]

Leavening Du Bois's despair are two great figures of "American courage," Senators Thaddeus Stevens and Charles Sumner, prime architects of Radical Republican efforts to win black suffrage and exponents of "impartial . . . universal suffrage" as a "universal right" (*Reconstruction* qtd. 193–194). Both men sought to at last make good "those early promises of the Fathers" (qtd. 193). To keep their ideals of pure Democracy alive, Du Bois quotes copiously from their speeches ("This is not a white man's Government . . . This is Man's Government," declared Stevens), and one quotation in particular, from Sumner's final plea for the civil rights bill, sounds a strikingly Du Boisian note: "There is beauty in art, in literature, in science, and in every triumph of intelligence, all of which I covet for my country; but there is a higher beauty still" in "making the rights of all the same as our own" (qtd. 266, 592–593). For Du Bois, aesthetic experience (exemplified in his famous remark "I sit with Shakespeare and he winces not") and democratic principle (all shall be equal before the law) are forms of freedom founded on release from particularity, from preordained identity *(Souls* 438). This release is implicit in something Sumner was fond of saying: "what is universal is necessarily impartial" (*Reconstruction* qtd. 195).

Charles Chesnutt would have concurred with Sumner, for as a fledgling writer he came to experience the generosity of the impartial. In 1882 Chesnutt was isolated and desolate, teaching in rural North Carolina, burning with the ambition "to become a *man* in the highest sense of the word"—an author. He confided in his diary: "What a blessing is literature . . . Shut up in my study, without the companionship of one congenial mind, I can enjoy the society of the greatest wits and scholars . . . [and] find myself in the company of the greatest men of earth" (*Journal* 167, 172). In 1903, having known the "blessing" of literature's impartial embrace and become a man in the highest sense, Chesnutt in effect renewed Sumner's universalism. In an essay pleading for black suffrage, he sought to help redeem the failed hopes of Reconstruction.

That era had ended after the removal of federal troops from the South in 1877. Unprotected, blacks saw their political gains dissolve, as Southern governments fell back into the hands of former slaveholders. The Negro, predicted *The Nation,* "will disappear from the fields of national politics. Henceforth the nation, as a nation, will have nothing more to do with him" (qtd. Foner 245). As Du Bois points out, blacks did not easily surrender the ballot, and held on to "remnants of political power" in houses of legislature until 1896. "But it was a losing battle, with public opinion, industry, wealth, and religion against them. Their own leaders decried 'politics' and preached submission . . . From 1880 onward, in order to earn a living, the American Negro was compelled to give up his political power" (*Reconstruction* 692–693).

Chesnutt found the situation worsening in 1903. He saw the "revival of slavery" in reports of a growing system of peonage in the South. In his essay Chesnutt urged no compromise on the question of the Negro's franchisement in the South, parting company with his friend Booker T. Washington's temporizing on the matter. Washington urged his usual caution, believing that a heritage of enslavement had diminished black capacity for citizenship. Blacks will eventually secure their political rights and win white respect, Washington maintained, once they increase their "knowledge and wealth and character."[20] But in a letter to Washington Chesnutt declared that considerations of "color or origin" or "condition" were irrelevant. The question we face "is not the question of the Negro race" or "what the black race has or has not been able to do in Africa." Rather, we are "directly concerned with the interests of some millions of American citizens of more or less mixed descent, whose rights are fixed by the Constitution and laws of the United States" (*To Be an Author* 182, 186). In 1904 he reiterated: "There can be but one citizenship in a free country; if the laws make or recognize any distinctions, then that country is not free" (216). Clearly Chesnutt, like Du Bois, was inspired to revive the promise of radical-democratic suffrage that flickered in Reconstruction.

The divergence between Washington and Chesnutt, like the public clash of Du Bois and Washington, registers the imperiled status not only of the political but also of the possibility that the cultural might provide access to the political. Faced with little choice in the matter, the "Wizard" of Tuskegee Institute in Alabama surrenders universalism for racial identity as the horizon of life. In submitting to Jim Crow separatism, he withdraws the demand for equal rights of American citizenship and urges industrial education as preparation for contented utilitarian toil in the agrarian South. This becomes defined as the black lot in life. Washington's position, in short, posits tacitly a racial ideology of authenticity that is prepolitical in its bias toward the private and the tribal and against a public world of citizenship where one would be judged by word and deed rather than "color or origin" (Chesnutt). The Du Boisian civic construction of politics, while demanding recognition of black consciousness, pressed for a radical program of agitation and reform. This position eventually prevailed with the creation of the NAACP in 1910. But for more than another half-century black suffrage in the South remained an empty pledge. And the Bookerite forces, it is fair to say, won the battle over "authenticity," that is, the right to legislate who and what counts as truly black and white. As we shall see, Washington stigmatized *black intellectual,* making it a locus of racial, sexual, and economic anxieties. In the late 1960s, Washington's contempt of the intellectual as inauthentic was revived by Black Power and Black Arts nationalism. In our own day, the ideology of authenticity is enshrined as identity politics, the dominant form of multiculturalism.

In this contemporary light, to link affirmation of racial/ethnic identity with a retreat from the political sounds anomalous; indeed, the political seems precisely to entail this affirmation. Chesnutt and Du Bois imply something nearly opposite: an idea of the political as civic participation by those whose qualifications are severed from family, tribe, class, and caste. This understanding of citizenship recalls a Hellenistic sense of the political. The *politikos* referred to those men permitted and willing to leave the private household for the *polis*, where men of various origins and social standing engaged in rational debate as they attempted practical problem solving for the community, an activity requiring intellectual improvisation in the face of uncertainty. In the polis one had to cope with *pragmata*, the contingencies of unsettled circumstances.[21] According to one commentator, those outside political life, excluded from speaking the language of politics, were called *ethnos*, the root of ethnic. These provincial *idiotes*, also known as *barbaros*, are embedded in nature, confined to a tight circle of blood relations, reliant on the habits and folkways of forefathers, and resigned to the monotony of time endlessly unfolding.[22]

In the United States the black American was forced to the ethnic province in the wake of Reconstruction's collapse. The effacement of blacks from public political life froze them in the ghetto of group identity. Embedded in nature, they were Negroes as distinct from Americans. After 1877, noted Ralph Ellison, "the whole focus upon the relationship of black people and their culture to the broader culture was sort of shut down. Not much light could come through" (*Collected* 376). Not until the cultural efflorescence of the 1920s and 1930s, when "Aframerica" and "Aframericans" circulated as emancipatory terms of hybrid identity, did the veil of separatism begin to be pierced culturally, if not politically.

Ellison described Alain Locke as a catalyst of this cultural liberation from the *ethnos*. "He did point a direction, he did act as a role model" by making a "conscious assessment of the pluralistic condition of the United States" (442). Locke's anti-purist pluralism helped Ellison and his friend Albert Murray see that "all blacks are part white, and all whites part black" (442). Locke came to the fore in that 1920s moment of "turbulent transition," just "when we were far enough away from the traumas of Reconstruction" to broaden perspectives (447, 444). As early as 1916 Locke had argued that when "modern man talks about race" he is really talking about ethnic groups, which Locke labeled "ethnic fictions" to expose the "fetish of biological purity" animating such terminology. In fact, ethnic groups are "the products of countless interminglings . . . the results of infinite crossings" (*Race Contacts* 11). By 1925, as editor of *The New Negro,* Locke had sponsored a collective cultural practice that enacted his dismissal of purity.

In the 1960s and 1970s Ellison watched with dismay the retreat to purism, to the ethnic province of "blood magic and blood thinking" (*Territory* 21). We shall see in Chapter 6 that Ellison's critique of black nationalism implicitly posed *ethnos* against *politikos:* he regarded the reemergence of the *ethnos* as a regrettable reduction of politics, an abrogation of civic responsibility to participate in the "fluid, pluralistic turbulence of the democratic process" (*Territory* 16). Given that, for Ellison, the impurity of "pluralism is the air we breathe . . . the ground we stand on," separatism was tantamount to suffocation (*Collected* 443). "My identity as Western man, as political being," Ellison says, is inseparable from his self-understanding as a black man and as an intellectual (*Shadow* 117).

Ellison's stance is comparable to Bayard Rustin's, who in the mid-sixties urged a move "from protest to politics."[23] Rustin, the activist/ intellectual and crucial strategist of the civil rights movement, had schooled Dr. King in Gandhian nonviolence and had masterminded the 1963 march on Washington. Soon after, he began to argue that militant protest had done its job and that a broader-based progressive coalition with labor and liberals was needed.[24] Not only would exclusive advocacy of a black economic program be a mistake, but preoccupation with racial identity, Rustin argued, would be equally ineffective politically. As he would warn in the next decade, black nationalism seeks "refuge in psychological solutions to social questions" and produces a "politics of escape" (Rustin 304, 294). Of his own activism, Rustin remarked late in life that it "did not spring from being black. Rather, it is rooted fundamentally in my Quaker upbringing and the values instilled in me . . . Those values were based on the concept of a single human family." He fought against racial injustice because it challenged his belief in "the oneness of the human family" (qtd. Anderson *Rustin* 19).

Rustin once described his move from protest to politics as parallel to Ralph Ellison's devotion to "portraying human reality in all its complexity" (Rustin 332). Predictably, both men were branded as race traitors, a judgment that vividly reveals how entrenched is the *ethnos* over the *politikos*. While Rustin assessed the political damage caused by the forfeiture of complexity inherent in racial chauvinism, Ellison weighed the intellectual damage. Black Power seemed regression to 1877 when the "relationship of black people and their culture to the broader culture" had been erased. In his 1974 essay on Locke he expounded on this isolation: "during the decade [the sixties] these linkages between people on the basis of ideas and experience were automatically, arbitrarily thrown overboard. That is disastrous for writers; it is disastrous for any sort of human enterprise because we live one upon the other; we follow, we climb upon the shoulders of those who have gone before" (*Collected* 446). Ellison's words remain urgent, and they are the premise of my tracing of an intricate tradition of American intellectual history.

His words recall Du Bois's own sense of overlap as the condition of culture. With his preternatural receptivity to multiple cultural and disciplinary traditions, Du Bois responded to predecessors with exceptional energy and creativity, the source of which was his passionate feasting at the remarkable intellectual banquet that was his international education. His plasticity took the impress of a score of thinkers, and he inveterately turned them to his own complex purposes. Alexander Crummell and William James might be regarded as his principal mentors because they encouraged in Du Bois this propensity to remake and refashion. Beyond the transmission of particular intellectual doctrine, Crummell and James (to adapt Whitman) taught Du Bois the freedom and the virtue of straying; in effect (if not in intention, at least Crummell's), they urged not veneration but their own overcoming. "He most honors my style," wrote Whitman, "who learns under it to destroy the teacher."

As is well known, Crummell's Pan Africanism, romantic racialism, and emphasis on creating an intellectual vanguard of race leadership all shaped Du Bois. And Jamesian accounts of consciousness, pluralism, action, and anti-imperialism left their mark on his student. Yet Du Bois came to remake the legacies of both men. He turned from the political limitations of James's liberalism; indeed, some have argued that Du Bois influenced the social turn of James's late thought. In his most Crummellian discourse, "The Conservation of Races" (1897), Du Bois regarded history as composed of groups and races and decried "the individualistic philosophy of the Declaration of Independence" (*Writings* 817). But even by the end of this text (in speaking of "personal liberty") Du Bois began sounding a note he would play consistently in the new century—that American democratic modernity must at last make good on its promise to secure for all "the real freedom toward which the soul of man has always striven: the right to be different, to be individual and pursue personal aims and ideals" ("Evolving" 69). In other words, even as Du Bois was establishing his credentials in the late 1890s as a stern, moralizing race man in the manner of Crummell, he was also opening his Victorian stance to the beckoning new possibilities of modernity.[25] And after 1906, under the impact of Boasian anthropology, he began to revise his race essentialism.

The revisionary act of turning from and toward, is, we shall see, the imperative of the Jamesian pragmatist. An analogous teaching was enacted in Crummell's restless life—he extolled "flexibility" and eclecticism as indispensable to cultural creation, a teaching born of "the world-wandering of a soul in search of itself," as Du Bois described the clergyman's twenty-year pilgrimage from New York to England to Africa and back to America (*Souls* 518). Both Crummell and James encouraged in Du Bois a disposition skeptical of any intellectual or cultural edifice which claims absolute originality and purity. Such claims are inevitably exclusionary, in the service of erecting boundaries. To examine Greek and Roman civilization, noted Crummell, is to encounter not discrete, self-contained worlds but, rather, monuments to man's capacity for "eclectic" imitation: "they seized upon all the spoils of time. They became cosmopolitan thieves. They stole from every quarter. They pounced, with eagle eye, upon excellence, wherever discovered and seized upon it with rapacity" (*Destiny* 201–202).

Like Martin Delany before him and Hurston after, Crummell believed in blacks' natural genius for imitation. Indeed, for Crummell, the potential greatness of African civilization is founded on the "fact" that black people are endowed with a "mobile and plastic nature, with a strong receptive faculty" (201).[26] Crummell's enthusiasm for the heterogeneous and mimetic could (at least theoretically) threaten his rigid racialism, a tension also found in Du Bois.[27] But whereas Crummell leaves the contradiction unremarked, Du Bois uses it and others to stimulate his hyper-receptive "double consciousness"—his gift of "second-sight" (*Souls* 364). What outlives Crummell's racialism is his praise of imitation as the motor of civilization. Banishing the exclusionary rhetoric of origin and authenticity, he implies that culture is public property available for appropriation and refashioning.[28]

Irony, of course, emerges when Crummell's metaphor of cosmopolitan thievery is set against the historical fact that without white plundering of black talent, American popular art, especially music and dance, would be radically impoverished. Yet Crummell's anti-proprietary perspective, however idealized, yields a valuable distinction: the scandal of white plagiarism resides not in violation of black ownership but in the refusal to acknowledge indebtedness. White America's acknowledgment of cultural dependency has, until recently, been muted at best to protect the fiction of cultural segregation. The actuality of overlap and linkage inspires the cosmopolitan thievery that animates Du Bois and the other intellectuals discussed in this book.

1

After Identity Politics

To recover the intellectual is to recover a cosmopolitan universalism that has been held under suspicion during the reign of postmodernism. With its bias toward the local, the particular, and the relative, postmodernism favored the "organic" (Gramsci) and "specific" (Foucault) intellectual. In the wake of these prestigious icons, universalism returns not in nostalgic defiance but chastened, neither positing a "view from nowhere" nor seeking to bleach out ethnicity and erect a "color-blind" ideal. Rather, it stands in reciprocal relation to the particular.[1] In other words, many contemporary understandings of universalism are strikingly reminiscent of Du Bois's a century earlier. In this chapter, moving freely within this hundred-year span, I selectively examine some significant efforts to escape the reductionism of the ideology of "authenticity," which fixates upon particularity or difference. The Dreyfus Affair is a catalyst in this effort to find alternatives, for it generates a cluster of terms to designate what violates the authentic and is deemed deracinated and artificial: the cosmopolitan, the universal, and the intellectual.

The emergence of these last three as a nexus during the Dreyfusards' campaign for Justice is generally a known if not a familiar fact of intellectual history. Generally unknown and unfamiliar is how "Les Intellectuels" was imported to American shores. It was William James, the leader of philosophical pragmatism, and a Dreyfusard, who proudly inserted "intellectual" into American popular vocabulary in 1907. The college-educated, he reasoned, are "the only permanent presence that corresponds to the aristocracy in older countries," and "we ought to have our own class consciousness" (*Writings* 1246). But James's call for "class consciousness" had been anticipated by another Dreyfusard, a former student of his at Harvard. In 1903 Du Bois called for a black "aristocracy of talent and character," which he dubbed "the Talented Tenth" (*Writings* 847).

In addition to the Dreyfus Affair, another spur to Du Bois's effort to organize a vanguard of intellectuals was the formation of the American Negro Academy in 1897 by Alexander Crummell in Washington, D.C. The first black learned society, at a time when less than three percent of the black population was educated, the Academy sought to inculcate race pride ("race feeling" in Crummell's words) by being a showcase for lectures and debate (Moss 11, 60). But particularism was not an end in itself. As Du Bois noted in his address "The Conservation of Races" (1897), the "Academy Creed" was two-fold: to encourage "race solidarity" as a means to "the realization of . . . broader humanity." Specifically, Du Bois urged black Americans "to maintain their race identity until . . . the ideal of human brotherhood has become a practical possibility." And in conclusion he insisted on "greater respect for personal liberty and worth, regardless of race" (*Writings* 822, 825–826). Six years later in *The Souls of Black Folk* Du Bois implicitly conceived the black intellectual (a "co-worker in the kingdom of culture") along Dreyfusard lines as one who embodies and helps promote in others the "sovereign human soul" and the "higher individualism" of universal values (365, 437).

In sum, by 1903 the full transatlantic concatenation turns out to be not only the cosmopolitan, the universal, and the intellectual but pragmatism and the antirace race figure as well. These formations are historically entwined, indeed symbiotic in the case of Du Bois and James. Yet this remarkable constellation has often been overlooked. In particular, the entwinement of the universal and the cosmopolitan with the black intellectual has eluded the attention of intellectual and cultural history.

Not only does this nexus seem bizarre, but its incongruity has become thoroughly naturalized. Note the words of a sympathetic observer in 1965 who wonders: "is it traitorous for a Negro to try to be as broadly human and humane as possible? Is it even relevant?"[2] More recent is the warning from a prominent black intellectual in 1991 that "the idea that there is no meaningful connection between black experience and critical thinking about aesthetics or culture must be continually interrogated."[3] What has bred this segregation? Postmodern identity politics is one explanation. But this contemporary reductionism incarnates the logic of an older one known as cultural pluralism.

Cultural pluralism believes in ethnic or racial or religious group solidarity as valuable intrinsically, not merely tactically or provisionally. Such a belief, says the political philosopher George Kateb, "only serves to validate the desire of people to think in categories and stereotypes" (Kateb 535). This is precisely the kind of thinking to which pragmatism presumes to be the antidote. John Dewey once described the pragmatist "spirit" as a revolt against "that habit of mind which disposes of anything by tucking it away in the pigeon holes of a filing cabinet" (qtd. Kaufman-Osborn 12). But intellectual history reminds us that it was a loyal Jamesian pragmatist, Horace Kallen, who invented cultural pluralism as a plea for tolerance of hyphenated (ethnic) identity amid nativist and progressivist pressure to Americanize the immigrant via a thorough soaking in the melting pot. While he counted himself a disciple of James, Kallen was a less than careful student of the philosopher. Had he been careful, he would not have linked James to a notion of cultural pluralism as an array of irreducible differences.[4]

As will be discussed in Chapter 6, the birth of cultural pluralism was quickened when Kallen and Alain Locke heard James give his Hibbert Lectures (published as *A Pluralistic Universe*) at Oxford University in 1908. But only Locke engaged what is radical in pluralism—skepticism of what James calls identity logic (whose twin beliefs are that "what a thing really is, is told us by its *definition*" and that reality "consists of essences, not of appearances") (*Writings* 728). Although James is famous for revering the individual, his is not a philosophy of the sovereign subject. His pluralism imagines experience unanchored to an a priori self. Rather than already in place, authentic, and originary, the self is an "affair of relations," or a "mere echo" as he once called consciousness. Like all pragmatists, James distrusts the appeal to identity as a grounding category, for it violates the "inextricable interfusion" of "our immediately-felt life" (778, 761). Hence his concern in *A Pluralistic Universe* is to reveal what escapes the grid of identity and difference (which is built into the logic of identity). Any point of view that imagines itself complete and definitive betrays a commitment to identity that suppresses the stubborn crudity of experience which remains inassimilable to or denigrated by philosophy's closed systems

(particularly rationalism and intellectualism). James values this residuum ("the more") as proof that "nothing includes everything, or dominates over everything . . . Something always escapes" (760, 776).

In using James's thought to sanction multiple, discrete ethnic
groups, Kallen stayed within the identity logic that James had repudiated, and did so while proudly proclaiming himself a Jamesian pluralist.
But actually Jamesian pluralism protested the deforming effect of segregation. And though James confined his critique to the history of
philosophy, Locke found it suggestive for his own efforts to reject "cultural purism" and to construct a cosmopolitanism founded on the capacity to use "culture-goods" instead of owning them. Giving urgency
to Locke's project was the racism he encountered at Oxford as the first
black Rhodes scholar. His cosmopolitanism, fashioned with other minority students at Oxford, became a survival strategy.

Locke's elective affinity with James's critique of identity logic rather
than with Kallen's cultural pluralist celebration of identity is important
for two reasons. It places him, as Chapter 6 will show, at the center of
an underappreciated pragmatist cosmopolitan tradition whose currency
may now be renewed amid the decline of identity politics. This lineage
includes Du Bois, Locke, Zora Neale Hurston (whom Locke knew at
Howard University), Ralph Ellison, Albert Murray, and James Baldwin
(whose relay to pragmatism was Henry James). But Locke's attune-
ment to the implications of James's refusal of coercive, closed systems
of thought has another significance. Locke makes vivid that identitarianism in whatever form—as essentialist philosophy, as cultural pluralism, as Jim Crow segregation, as imperialism—was a disciplinary regime
to be avoided, especially by those racially marked. And one of the few
intellectual weapons one might wield was Jamesian, and later Deweyan,
pragmatism. This philosophy pursued a critique of identity logic not
only in Western thought but in its sociopolitical instruments—imperialism and racism.

Refusing the paradigm of identity/difference, pragmatist pluralism
escapes the circular logic of cultural pluralism: becoming a mirror image
of what it sets out to repudiate—racialist, nativist thinking.[5] These alleged enemies both fetishize difference. This is one reason pragmatist
pluralism has remained marginal: both right and left, nativists and cultural pluralists (now multiculturalists), make culture a matter of blood
inheritance, of ownership ("ours"), rather than something achieved,
such as citizenship.

In *Our America* (1995) Walter Benn Michaels reveals how in the twenties the entwined logics of nativism, pluralism, and modernism thwarted efforts to move beyond race. Because Americanness was constructed as a fact of racial inheritance and not as a political ideal, identity itself was made into what Michaels calls "an object of cathexis, into something that might be lost or found, defended or surrendered" (141). Michaels's thesis helps explain why the pragmatist pluralism theorized by black intellectuals has been overshadowed, their aspirations for a deracialized, universalist approach to culture unfulfilled. Ironically, *Our America* perpetuates this absence by leaving the anti-identitarian lineage unmentioned and unaccounted for. Yet Michaels exposes the identity logic of cultural pluralism by, in effect, making a Jamesian pragmatist critique. There are no "anti-essentialist accounts of identity," according to Michaels, because "the essentialism inheres not in the description of the identity but in the attempt to derive the practices from the identity—we *do* this because we *are* this" (181).

A sign that identity politics is at last losing prestige in the academy is that the glamorous provincialisms that congregate under the names multiculturalism and Cultural Studies are revising their tendency to absolutize ethnicity and race. Hence there is greater awareness of "the contradiction we are caught in whenever we claim an identity . . . that we reaffirm the differences we are seeking to challenge."[6] Nevertheless, postmodern fascination with hybrids, cyborgs, mestiza consciousness, creolization and the transnational, tends to make identity only more fluid and complex, but no less secure and foundational. Thus each option, though it deploys a rhetoric of anti-essentialism, depends on the identity/difference model of cultural pluralism. Each new rubric represents "just another turn of the essentialist screw," to borrow a phrase from Michaels.[7]

Grounded in group identity, cultural pluralism makes membership fate. As Appiah has noted: "The large collective identities that call for recognition come with notions of how a proper person of that kind behaves . . . Demanding respect for people as blacks and as gays requires that there are some scripts that go with being an African-American or having same-sex desires. There will be proper ways of being black and gay, there will be expectations to be met, demands will be made." Appiah concludes that between "the politics of recognition and the politics of compulsion, there is no bright line," and, he avers, "I would like other options" ("Identity" 159, 162–163).

Appiah's words resonate. They express the desire of black creative intellectuals for options other than race responsibility. With a rare bluntness and candor, Hilton Als in his memoir *The Women* (1996) poses and pursues the question: What does it mean to be a "disgrace to the race"? To become a disgrace is, says Als, one way of "reacting against the dead and deadening ideology (inspired by Booker T. Washington by way of W. E. B. Du Bois)" known as uplift—"being made to feel, intellectually, that one was emotionally responsible for other blacks simply because they were black—a thought process that involves no thought at all, but a dull reaction." Stripping off the "mask of piety," Als, who describes himself as an "auntie man—what Barbadians call a faggot," seeks to turn disgrace into a mode of sexual and creative freedom (72–73, 57, 9). Als's book crystallizes what has usually been kept implicit or unspoken: that the very notion of black intellectual has been entangled in the "disgrace" of effeminacy at least since Washington, *the* black voice of his era, opposed the black intellectual to what is natural, manly, and virtuous. Later chapters take up this matter.[8]

Whether they opt for disgrace or not, black intellectuals tend to fall outside categories and lose visibility when they are untethered from the race work that typically defines them. This is confirmed in a small but telling moment in *Who Speaks for the Negro* (1965), Robert Penn Warren's brilliant deconstruction of the notion of "speaking for," of being a race representative. After talking with the prominent black judge William Hastie, whose mind, says Warren, "is steeped in an awareness of human complexity," Warren wonders, "is it traitorous for a Negro to try to be as broadly human and humane as possible? Is it even relevant?" (277). What prompts this question is Warren's realization that Judge Hastie would be dismissed as a race traitor, as mere "window dressing," by black nationalists, and as irrelevant, as statistically insignificant, by sociologists. With his New Critical respect for particularity, Warren refuses to dismiss the judge. Instead, he finds that Hastie's "candid will to look at the complexities of a situation" is an effort to "eschew what William Blake thought of as the great evil, 'the single vision and Newton's sleep'—a mechanical, schematic, dehumanizing vision, that violates the density of experience" (277). Warren, like his friends Ralph Ellison and Albert Murray, shares Jamesian pragmatism's suspicion of Enlightenment rationalism as intolerant of the wayward particular.

An analogous intolerance appears in what Cornel West calls the "racial reasoning" that animates the discourse of black authenticity. Racial reasoning conceals "behind a deceptive cloak of racial consensus" the varied political and ethical commitments of individuals in relation to communities, black and white. Yet, as West notes, "racial reasoning is seductive because it invokes an undeniable history of racial abuse and racial struggle." Claims to black authenticity "feed on the closing-ranks mentality of black people" (West "Black" 394–395). One result is that distinctions of gender, class, and sexuality are lost.

But the assumption of a monolithic black community is becoming harder to maintain. One reason is the increasing recognition accorded biracial and multiracial heritage. Another is the impact of events such as the Anita Hill/Clarence Thomas hearings. It heightened public recognition in white America both of black middle-class identity and of an array of internal differences within that identity. This was dramatized in the hearing and its aftermath as judgments formed and reformed and predictable gender, class, and racial alliances unraveled. If one indisputable thing emerged, says Toni Morrison, it is that "the time for undiscriminating racial unity has passed" ("Introduction" xxx). The confrontation between Hill and Thomas, noted Angela Davis, "symbolically represented the passing of a conception of community with which many of us have lived. I experienced it both as a loss and as an emancipation. I used to be able to talk about 'my people.' " Davis notes the "historical obsolescence of the particular sense of community we once found so necessary"—a community that "no matter what . . . was racially all-embracing" (Davis 328). The internal fissures revealed by Hill-Thomas reflect a larger divide—between the black underclass and the black middle class, both of which are larger than ever.

How does one lift the burden of expectations and demands preordained by race? For at least a century black writers have explored this question in fiction and nonfiction. In the endless fight against racialized, proprietary notions of culture, black intellectuals had to devise, with varying degrees of self-consciousness, their own counterlogics to ventilate the suffocating demands of the ideology of racial "authenticity."[9] Du Bois's cultural kingdom is only the best-known and most influential alternative. Whatever their particular inflections, these countermoves attempt to reconcile what James Baldwin, late in his career, called the competing claims of "inheritance" and "birthright," the former limited and limiting, the latter vast and boundless. To unlock the "conundrum of color" he found it a "necessity" to try and locate himself "within a specific inheritance and to use that inheritance, precisely, to claim the birthright from which that inheritance had so brutally and specifically excluded me" (*Notes* xii).

The "struggle to stare down the deadly and hypnotic temptation to interpret the world and all its devices in terms of race" was, for the young Ralph Ellison, a perpetual one: "I learned that nothing could go unchallenged; especially that feverish industry dedicated to telling Negroes who and what they are" (*Shadow* xix–xx). Eluding the coercive expectations of identity logic, the novelists Dorothy West and Ann Petry, both born to prosperity, negotiated the tensions of color, culture, and class. Petry, from a privileged family in an exclusive Connecticut town, in the late thirties moved to Harlem, where she transmuted her observations of urban bleakness into the unsparing naturalism of her powerful novel *The Street*.

To generalize broadly, but from some suggestive evidence, it seems fair to say that a number of figures in the post–Harlem Renaissance generation—Petry and West, Ellison and Baldwin, and also Saunders Redding, Bayard Rustin, Owen Dodson, and Gordon Heath—made their way to the "kingdom of culture" more easily than their predecessors. Doubtless the fact that most of them in this cluster, save Ellison and Baldwin, were middle-class Easterners facilitated the move.[10] While class differences partly account for Baldwin's more difficult passage, this difficulty perhaps forced him to articulate a belief many of his generation would embrace: that "one cannot claim the birthright without accepting the inheritance."

Important contemporary black writers construct a significantly different relation to culture. Charles Johnson, for instance, has said that "all knowledge, all disclosure, all revelation from the past, from our predecessors, black, white, and otherwise, is our inheritance . . . Any sense that other human beings have made out of the world . . . all that is what we have inherited as human beings" ("Interview" 166). For Johnson, as for Samuel Delany, there is no striving to enter the kingdom of culture, one is already in residence. Hence Baldwin's dialectic is irrelevant.[11]

Johnson's universalism would seem virtually utopian to earlier figures. "To do something memorable in literature" would require becoming a "Prometheus" to "break the chains" that hold one to "the racial rack," muses Wallace Thurman's fictional surrogate in *Infants of the Spring*, a 1932 novel of Harlem Renaissance literary life (145). Thurman's protagonist expresses the ambition of his generation and the preceding one. The effort to elude, escape, or abandon what Du Bois candidly called "group imprisonment within a group" became inseparable from creativity itself (*Dusk* 651).

Few have felt that black identity and aesthetic freedom were as starkly in conflict as did the writer Anatole Broyard. In 1996, six years after his death, the fact that Broyard had been born black and had lived white was made public. Broyard was a well-known book reviewer who spent many years blocked on his long-awaited novel. The paradox of Broyard's life, as Henry Louis Gates reports, was that he wanted to be respected as a writer, not for being black, "even though his pretending not to be black was stopping him from writing" ("White Like Me" 76). A friend of Broyard's summed up his dilemma: "he felt he had to make a choice between being an aesthete and being a Negro. He felt that once he said, 'I'm a Negro writer,' he would have to write about black issues, and Anatole was such an aesthete' " (76). Broyard's assessment of his situation was, says Gates, "perfectly correct. He *would* have had to be a Negro writer, which was something he did not want to be . . . We give lip service to the idea of the writer who happens to be black, but had anyone, in the postwar era, ever seen such a thing?" (78).

Without Broyard's option to pass but facing a similar choice, the young James Baldwin expatriated to Paris to prevent himself, he said, "from becoming *merely* a Negro; or, even, merely a Negro writer" (*Price* 171). In Chapter 7 I will discuss how Baldwin in Europe resolved the choice between aesthete and Negro by finding ways not to choose. One way was to become an intellectual, that is, to craft an essayistic voice that seemed unraced, a voice whose detachment and authority and literary cadence sounded neither black nor white but closer to that of a cosmopolitan sensibility. After all, Baldwin's literary hero, Henry James, had cultivated an analogous "ambiguity" ("I aspire to write in such a way that it would be impossible to an outsider to say whether I am at a given moment an American writing about England" or vice versa) as a sign of being "highly civilized" (qtd. Matthiessen 302). Baldwin communicated an intriguing elusiveness to a number of readers of his early essays in *Partisan Review* and *Commentary.* "My friends and I at Columbia fell to wondering whether or not he was a Negro," recalls Norman Podhoretz. "He was a Negro intellectual in almost exactly the same sense as most" of the *Partisan Review* crowd "were Jewish intellectuals"—moving in "the broader world of Western culture" rather than an "ancestral ethnic" one (123–124). Although Podhoretz simplifies Baldwin's relation to Western culture, he evokes something of what Baldwin (at least early in his career) achieved and Broyard did not—a power to bewilder categories, to elude all definitions by becoming himself, as Baldwin said of Bessie Smith (*Price* 181).

If Broyard, in passing, affirmed race classifications and Baldwin bewildered them, Jean Toomer dismissed racial categories as comprising "the entire machinery of verbal hypnotism." By the mid-twenties, he had decided that his goal would be to "liberate" himself and "ourselves" from this hypnotism and be "simply of the human race" (qtd. Kerman and Eldridge 341). Whereas most of his generation insisted on the interplay of universal and particular, Toomer folded the latter into the former. Toomer called race a "hurdle" that he must jump, a "false factor" and a "constriction" that he would "clear up and cut away" (340). But, ironically, Toomer ended up spending "a lot of time expounding his theory of racial irrelevance in order to get on with more important things," his biographers note (340). But irrelevance is not quite precise. Encouraged by Toomer, many critics mistakenly assume race was unimportant to him. But in fact a major subject of his unpublished (now posthumously published) writing is his theory of an emergent "American race," a new mixed and higher race consciousness that would abolish the stalemate of white versus black and bring a human world. At last Toomer's day has come. He has been hailed by one contemporary political analyst as a visionary prophet of a "trans-racial American identity."[12] In Chapter 6 I will examine his revived status in the course of discussing the cultural meanings of the oblivion that engulfed both Toomer and Zora Neale Hurston once they resolved to reject the dominant terms of classification.

Toomer's is perhaps the most radical abandonment of "group imprisonment within a group" and for that very reason has been perceived by some as a threat to be defused. Here I will sketch how Toomer's profound disturbance of orthodox views of racial identity as white or black, and his contempt for racial uplift, tended to be ignored or explained away, as if it were traitorous for a Negro to be as broadly human as possible. Toomer's relation to the Harlem Renaissance is a case in point. Although he is regarded as one of its leading lights, he had already rejected "the label 'Negro' " before the movement got under way (*Wayward* 133). Toomer disliked the movement's "over-play and over-valuation of the Negro" and claimed that Alain Locke reprinted parts of *Cane* in *The New Negro* (1925) without his permission (*Reader* 102). Adding insult to injury, *The New Negro* hailed Toomer as "the very first artist of the race" (44).[13]

By 1925 Toomer had begun the "revolution" that left him indifferent to labels—one was of "no more consequence than any other"—and had decided to devote his life not to writing but to a "search for a whole way of living . . . the creation of a human world" (*Wayward* 129, 133, 128–129). After *Cane* in 1923, he issued one other significant work in 1936 and died in 1967, leaving voluminous unpublished self-reflections. These included no fewer than six attempts at autobiography. "I felt I should write a book stating who and what I actually was," Toomer once said. But he confessed that he was "not equal to the handling of it. It would be a difficult book to write" not least because he felt he had no nonracialized language to express his views of post-identity (*Wayward* 133).[14] But if language was inhospitable, so were other instruments of identity. In the 1920s the melting pot and Jim Crow reigned, both in different ways erasing all racial or ethnic minglings. After 1920 the mulatto category was dropped from the U.S. census as the one-drop rule tightened its grasp.

In 1925 Toomer had attempted to spread the cosmic consciousness of his spiritual master, the émigré Russian mystic Gurdjieff, to Harlem. It was not a happy fit. Because the Gurdjieff regime demanded inordinate amounts of solitary contemplation by which one's "evolved soul" grew oblivious to time, the working people of Harlem found it difficult to find time to join. Yet for a year he attracted a small group of writers and artists including Wallace Thurman and Nella Larsen. Both were drawn to Toomer not only by *Cane* but by its author's effort to "alone determine" his "racial composition . . . and position in the world," as he once told his publisher by way of rebuking him for publicizing *Cane* as a novel by a "colored genius" (*Reader* 94). In an essay of 1927 Thurman would extol Toomer for writing a book "above the heads" of the two main audiences for the Harlem Renaissance—"sentimental whites" who overrate and patronize black writers, especially primitivists, and bourgeois "Negroes with an inferiority complex to camouflage" who disdain black writers if they lack the requisite "refinement or race pride." Toomer managed to confound both audiences because, explained Thurman, "as Waldo Frank forewarned in his introduction to *Cane*, Jean Toomer was not a *Negro* artist, but an *artist* who had lost 'lesser identities in the great well of life' " (Thurman "Negro Artists" 111).

Frank's distinction, which Thurman so cherishes, suggests Toomer's deracialized aesthetic. But this has been overshadowed by the reflex racializing of most critics. They subscribe to some version of Toomer's friend Gorham Munson's theory which explained Toomer's artistic decline as the result of "no longer drawing on the strength of his roots in Negro life." He had "abandoned his lyrical vein" (qtd. Kerman and

Eldridge 390). Hence Toomer has been allegorized as a tragic mulatto whose deracination strangled his gift of racial expression. His life and art are read as a cautionary tale: the price of betraying one's genuine black identity is to drift in the vacuous abstractions of mystical consciousness.

But this morality play was tenuous from the start. It ignored not only the interracial desires suffusing *Cane* but what Waldo Frank's introduction to it implied—that Toomer as *artist* (not as Gurdjieffian mystic) was already challenging fixed racial identity. Frank was the decisive influence on Toomer in the early twenties and in effect prepared him for Gurdjieff. A transnationalist, Frank conceived art as communicating spiritual, not racial, meaning. "The gifted Negro was too often thwarted from becoming a poet because his world was forever forcing him to recollect that he was a Negro," Frank wrote in his introduction to *Cane*. When Sherwood Anderson started forcing Toomer, the latter wrote to Frank: "Sherwood limits me to Negro. As an approach," as part of a larger whole, "Negro is good. But try to tie me to one of my parts is surely to lose me. My own letters have taken Negro as a point, and from there have circled out. Sherwood . . . ignores the circles" (qtd. Kerman and Eldridge 97). Here Toomer, unwittingly, predicted what literary history would make of him.

A few recent critics have heeded Toomer's protest about Anderson and have attended to the circling out of his quest for an American future. Darryl Pinckney, for one, is skeptical of the tragic mulatto allegory. He finds it symptomatic of an investment, by white and black critics alike, in mandating that the black writer remain an exemplar of the race. Pinckney has described the allegory of race betrayal woven around Toomer as suggesting critics' "tainting wish for retribution, a neurotic alertness to the wages of treason among black artists, to what offends the carefully monitored collective black conscience." To those who moralize over Toomer, says Pinckney, "example is everything and nothing must be allowed to threaten the idea of black history as a heroic drive up Jacob's ladder" ("Phantom" 36).

One of the frankest confessions of disgust with exemplarity and the "obligations imposed by race" begins Saunders Redding's *On Being Negro in America* (1951). Described on the paperback edition as "a book which takes you inside the Negro world as no book ever has before," Redding's memoir turns out to be less a testament to authenticity than to being its prisoner. The book, he tells us at the outset, is written to purge himself once and for all of an "unhealthy" arrest in "ethnocentric coils." "I hope this piece will stand as the epilogue to whatever contribution I have made to the 'literature of race.' I want to get on to other things . . . I think I am not alone" (14). He recounts that a famous singer once told him she was weary of the obligation to perform spirituals on every program, as beautiful and as artistically challenging as they were, "tired of trying to promote in others and of keeping alive in herself a race pride that had become disingenuous and peculiar. The spirituals belong to the world, she said, and 'yet I'm expected to sing them as if they belong only to me and other Negroes' " (14).[15]

Du Bois in 1933 had voiced analogous complaints about the patronizing response of the white music critic of the *New York Times* who praised the Fisk Choir spirituals for expressing the "sacred spirit and the uncorrupted manner of their race." Calling this "unadulterated nonsense," Du Bois added, "what it really means is that Negroes must not be allowed to attempt anything more than the frenzy of the primitive, religious revival." Any effort to sing Italian or German music, said Du Bois, "leads them off their preserves and is not 'natural.' To which the answer is, Art is not natural and is not supposed to be natural. And just because it is not natural it may be great Art" (*Writings* 1239).

Or the refusal of the natural may chain one to another obligation— to represent the exotic. In *The Alchemy of Race and Rights* (1991), Patricia Williams wittily describes the work of turning this obligation into profit. She is acutely aware of her own marketplace status as a luxury, an exotic commodity: Williams is not only a black female law professor but, in the eyes of a racist society, a credit to her race, an "experimental black," as she calls herself. Being this "sleek product" is endless work and she narrates the arduous labor of becoming such a self: "when I get up in the morning I stare in the mirror and stick on my roles: I brush my teeth, as a responsibility to my community. I buff my nails, paving the way for my race . . . I glaze my lips with the commitment to deny pain and 'rise above' racism . . . When I am fully dressed, my face is hung with contradictions; I try not to wear all my contradictions at the same time. I pick and choose among them; like jewelry" (196). And all the while she is assembling herself she is haunted by the opposite impulse—to refuse to "compose" herself "properly," to "split at the seams" and return to the womb (196). Stripped of its irony, Williams's insistence on dressing herself in contradictions, her experience of her "blackself as an eddy of conflicted meanings . . . in which agency and consent are tumbled in constant motion," sounds strikingly Du Boisian (168). "Crucified on the vast wheel of time, I flew round and round with the Zeitgeist," begins Du Bois's autobiography *Dusk of Dawn* (555).

As a great race man and an intellectual of genius, Du Bois more than anyone felt viscerally the "conflicted meanings" of upholding the burden of representation and having the "spiritual desire to be oneself without interference from others; to enjoy that anarchy of the spirit which is inevitably the goal of all consciousness" (*Dusk* 652). Simultaneously finding and failing to find ways to reconcile the burden and the desire affirmed his root conviction that "two-ness" is the condition of the African American. His "unreconciled strivings" became the spur of torrential productivity across a stunning range of genres and disciplines. Sociologist, historian, novelist, editor, essayist and poet, romantic racialist as well as universalist, Du Bois spent nearly a century strategically adapting, revising, and resisting a panoply of stances—nationalist, assimilationist, integrationist, segregationist, Pan-Africanist, Marxist socialist, and Communist.

Generating all this activity, paradoxically, was a man who felt "kept in bounds" by a white world that, with "sleepless vigilance," made him "limited in physical movement and provincial in thought and dream" (653). In 1934, six years before he made that statement, Du Bois respectfully disagreed with James Weldon Johnson's "genial" claim that he would not let prejudice blight his life. "And yet the fact is," said Du Bois, Mr. Johnson and I "are quite helpless in the matter . . . whether we will or no, color prejudice in America sears our souls; it shrivels up our finer qualities and provincializes our outlook . . . I am perfectly aware that Negro prejudice in America has made me far less a rounded human being than I should like to have been" (*Book Reviews* 174). Not the least constriction inflicted by race prejudice was the constant temptation to invert white supremacy into black.

As a young man, Du Bois had weighed the threat of provincialism as he dedicated himself to a life of race service on his twenty-fifth birthday in 1893. "I am striving to make my life all that life may be," he grandly declares in his journal, even as he is "firmly convinced" that his "own best development is not one and the same with the best development of the world." The world's best development would be "the rise of the Negro people." And as he pledges himself to the role of race man he twice describes his decision as a "sacrifice"—"to the world's good" (*Autobiography* 171). In 1903 he would commend the "Gospel of Sacrifice" preached by the talented tenth (*Souls* 420). In *Dusk of Dawn* (1940) he spoke of this sacrifice again, this time less personally, when he described the " 'race' man" as a "prisoner" of the "group," condemned to provincialism (651). Indeed, by the mid-thirties younger black intellectuals were rejecting what they called Du Bois's black chauvinism and provincialism.[16] Sacrificing himself to group identity, hostage to Jim Crow's mania for frozen classification, Du Bois's lifelong challenge becomes to find a margin of freedom, a way to mitigate, if not evade, the twin sacrifice demanded by the repressions of coerced identity—as race man and as "a colored man in a white world" (653).[17] Little wonder that Du Bois found inspiring Jamesian pragmatism's esteem for the unclassified and insouciance toward alleged necessities. "God be praised," he said in *Dusk of Dawn*, that I "landed squarely in the arms of William James of Harvard" (578).

Du Bois himself offers ample testimony of James's impact both personally and intellectually. Yet commentators have tended to neglect or minimize this evidence.[18] Here one can cite two important but seldom mentioned instances: in a 1944 career retrospective Du Bois notes that by 1910 he had evolved from the constraints of a positivist model of social science to adopting "Jamesian pragmatism" in order to "measure the element of Chance in human conduct." From then on, his work "assumed . . . a certain tingling challenge of risk" ("Evolving" 58). And in a 1956 letter Du Bois recollected that "the Jamesian pragmatism as I understood it from his lips" had, by 1896, inspired him to study "human action in exhaustive detail by taking up the Negro Problem" (*Correspondence* 3: 395).

Du Bois embraced risk as one way to mitigate the constraints of both race responsibility and provincialism imposed by segregation. He contrived to enjoy an "anarchy of the spirit" both in life and in art, in political practice and in the domain of fiction. For Du Bois, anarchy is nearly synonymous with the aesthetic and both sponsor freedom: "living in the fuller and broader sense of the term is the expression of art," a belief he shares with John Dewey (*Writings* 1061). Pragmatism, I contend, encouraged the anarchic, aesthetic impulses that fueled Du Bois's revisionary project. Pragmatism is a kind of philosophic anarchy in its skepticism of any authority or institution that believes itself grounded in necessity or in acontextual ideals. Du Bois shared his esteem for anarchy with his mentor James. The philosopher was a self-described "anarchistic sort of creature" who cherished "a world of anarchy . . . with an 'ever not quite' to all our formulas, novelty and possibility forever leaking in" (*Pragmatism,* 124; qtd. Perry 2: 700).

To claim that pragmatism orients Du Bois's career would seem to reduce it to the tidy dimensions that any single label imposes. Yet because pragmatism makes the classifying impulse itself a prime object of critique, it is a label that functions not to arrest but to lead (in James's word). What it leads to is heightened understanding not only of Du Bois's commitment to simultaneous and multiple forms of inquiry but of the freedom this affords him.[19] What anchors Du Bois's career of course is unwavering activism on behalf of equality for black Americans. But this anchorage functioned as the pivot from which he "flew round and round . . . waving my pen . . . to see, foresee and prophesy" (*Writings* 555). Du Bois's career is one of turnings and transitions, of going astray and taking chances. As I will show in Chapter 5, his political conduct deliberately courted risks: he ignited bitter controversy in 1917, when he urged blacks to "close ranks" behind America's entry into the world war, and in 1934, when he tried to force the NAACP to change its defining mission of integration.

And yet mention pragmatism in black intellectual history and the name likeliest to come to mind is Booker T. Washington's. The self-made "wizard," with his genius for accommodation and compromise, has long been regarded as a consummate pragmatist. As head of the white-funded "Tuskegee Machine," Washington not only spread the gospel of industrial training but maintained an iron grip over black media and political patronage. Incensed at Washington's repression of all dissent, Du Bois and his "talented tenth" cohort rebelled. The rest is history, or, rather, that familiar historical set piece Washington versus Du Bois, which is usually painted in dramatic polarities: the steely pragmatist schooled in slavery pitted against a Harvard- and Berlin-educated Hegelian idealist who scorned Washington's mammonism, his counsels of submission, and his philistine intolerance of book education.

This scenario requires at least two qualifications, and both hinge on the insufficiently recognized disjunction between the colloquial and philosophical senses of pragmatism. A masterly organizer and disciplinarian, Washington was a pragmatist in the colloquial sense but the virtual antithesis of a philosophical pragmatist. Du Bois inverts these distinctions; as a political strategist he seldom acted with pragmatic efficiency but often with chronic "incongruity" (as Harold Cruse says) that usually left him "either too far ahead or too far behind, but out of step with mass thinking" (Cruse 176). But Du Bois's missteps are the very imprint of philosophic pragmatism's esteem for experimental action.[20]

Du Bois prided himself on lacking "that singleness of vision and thorough oneness with his age" that he noted in Washington's career, and disdained as submission and compromise (*Souls* 393). His skeptical mind made such "singleness" impossible for Du Bois. One consequence was his wariness of political dogma of any stripe. This is important to recall in considering what seems to contradict it—Du Bois's notorious admiration for Stalin. Yet his regard for Stalin is without any illusions that the "dictator [who had built] a socialistic state at any cost" had created a democracy. Stalin was a bloody beginning of a great project, and "the death of Stalin brought opportunity and demand for change" (*Writings By* 4: 280–281). Always reverent of Karl Marx, Du Bois consistently spoke against Marxism as an instrument of black liberation since it preached violent revolution while reducing race to economics. Indeed, to remedy this defect in Marxist thought is one aim of his fictional *Black Flame* trilogy written near the end of his life.[21] Du Bois joined the party in 1961 after a lifetime of expressing unbridled contempt for it and only after Communism had long ceased to be a live option in the United States. Once again he was true to his impeccably bad timing. For in the twenties and thirties, when Communism was a tempting option for black Americans, he urged them to resist the party's entreaties. Du Bois also cut against the grain in his relation to the two other ideologies he most valued—socialism and democracy. He was consistently skeptical of embracing them as a panacea because their American incarnations were deformed by racism.

Du Bois's refusal of single vision was also manifested in a self-conscious ambivalence about race representation. Whereas Washington did all he could to make himself an ascetic exemplar seamlessly fused with the group, Du Bois, as I have suggested, refused any such transparency as a way to make problematic the role of exemplar. Yet it is Washington who stands as the "direct progenitor" of today's black public intellectuals. And therein is the problem.

So argues the black political scientist Adolph Reed in a probing if unduly harsh critique. Writing in 1995, Reed looks beyond the fact that in the past dozen years the terrain of American intellectual life has been permanently enlarged because of the collective ferment in black intellectual production, as a surge of activity has produced new journals, publishing projects, film and television companies, endowed chairs, and disciplinary innovations. Reed is not interested in applauding this new chapter in the more-than-thirty-year growth of the black bourgeois professional class. What he attends to is a less uplifting dimension. The heart of Reed's complaint is not simply that a number of prominent public black intellectuals (Gates, West, hooks, Robin Kelley, Michael Eric Dyson) are "unalloyed products" of the "academic celebrity system" ("What" 35). As in his book on Jesse Jackson, Reed probes the political content of celebrity or charisma and finds that, at least since Booker T. Washington, it has played a dangerously inflated role in black life. "Beneath all the overheated academic trendiness . . . the black public intellectual stance merely updates" the role of "Black Voice" that Washington perfected. Unelected, unaccountable, Washington was the "first purely freelance race spokesman" and flourished in the civic void mandated by Jim Crow. His function as the representative of black authenticity for white elites was, says Reed, a "pathological" product of segregation's disfranchisement of blacks (32). Today's "children" of Booker perpetuate the flight from the political to the *ethnos* that Washington affirmed.

Thus Reed's dismay at the current resurgence of the Black Voice. He finds the preference among black academics for "cultural politics" a "quietistic alternative to real political analysis," one that encourages passivity in black citizenry and an empty civic life (36). In this void, the superstar Voice performs for white audiences, and inevitably a minstrel quality seeps in. In sum, Reed implies that black public intellectuals, the new minstrelsy, remain trapped in a kind of time warp, forever stunted by the historical circumstances of their birth—an *ethnos*-centered anti-politics of appeasement dictated by the disfranchisement which, in turn, it helped maintain. Still wanting is "black proprietorship of the institutions of governance and policy processes on an identical basis with other citizens" (36). How might black public intellectuals escape Washington's legacy? Reed recommends a "principled self-consciousness in negotiating" their dual responsibility of addressing white and black audiences. Each audience has different needs, interests, expectations. To continue to provide merely a single "all-purpose message" whose terms are dictated by the white audience is a moral and political failure (34).

Another way of saying this is that the grip of Washington might be loosened if the Black Voice were decentered. Du Bois accomplished this with his inveterate propensity for making double moves. He engaged in the difficult project of balancing universal and particular, political and racial, without subordinating one to the other. In 1920 he summarized his role as talking "freely to my people and of them, interpreting between two worlds" (*Darkwater* 23). This addresses the dilemma Reed has identified. As does Du Bois's effort to destabilize the race-man imperative of authentic blackness by rejecting charismatic authority—he despised "the essential demagoguery of personal leadership"—and by flaunting his multiracial lineage (*Dusk* 775). A 1926 essay described Du Bois as resembling "a sunburnt Jew," a Turk, an Italian, a Cuban, "anything but what you are: A Negro." Du Bois found this sufficiently accurate, Arnold Rampersad contends, to accept it for publication in *The Crisis* (Rampersad 16). The allegedly "natural" identity of "you are a Negro" is what Du Bois repeatedly complicates and contests.

Yet I do not mean to imply that the impasse Reed identifies might be resolved by replacing a Washington model with a Du Bois model. To do so risks turning the latter into an exemplar. And Du Bois's power is his ability to contest this landlocked role. While I will argue that Du Bois speaks urgently to the contemporary moment, exemplarity is not the source of that urgency. But there are other reasons that replacing Washington with Du Bois is a mistake. It presumes that strategies developed in response to historical crises of seventy to eighty years ago can be imported intact into the present. And to believe this implicitly grants legitimacy to the most problematic dimension of Reed's analysis—his continuity thesis: the claim that there is a straight line from Washington to West, a line stunted from the start and doomed to repeat endlessly the original deformity. But this continuity thesis ignores the specific and unprecedented conditions within which contemporary black intellectuals are created and work. The elements of the public sphere that intimately shape intellectuals and their discourses—institutions, technologies, classes, audiences (mass and high culture, white and black, urban and suburban)—are radically different from two decades ago, let alone nearly ten. Thus an approach that insists on continuity without assessing discontinuity is bound to be historically deficient.

Du Bois's challenge to the "gods of the pigeonhole" (to borrow a phrase of Hurston's) remains potent, evident in how he still evades the labels invoked to resolve his paradoxes. The journalist Murray Kempton vividly imparts this. He had attended a lunch given by Gannett newspapers dedicated to the memory of Du Bois:

The eye could not see that name without being flooded with the puzzle of which Du Bois our master proposed to salute. Was it the Du Bois who sits with small company on the peak where there abide those who have supremely described the world? Or was it the Du Bois who assembled the evidence that got poor Marcus Garvey, the black nationalist, in jail for mail fraud? Or was it perhaps the Du Bois who strayed too far in the direction of Marxism and Leninism to be tolerated by the NAACP, was expelled from the editorship of *The Crisis*, the NAACP magazine he had founded, was harried by grand juries, and died at last self-exiled in Ghana, scarcely noticed and even less mourned by the organ of enlightenment that polished his laurels yesterday? (297)

To engage the provocative "puzzle" of Du Bois might help revise the coercive terms that historically define the role of black public intellectual. In this context, Cornel West's recent portrait of Du Bois in *The Future of the Race* is a missed opportunity. Far from being a puzzle, West's Du Bois is monochromatic, a naively optimistic Enlightenment rationalist and New England Victorian, a black Matthew Arnold whose elitist aesthetic idealism promotes "highbrow culture" to "civilize and contain the lowbrow masses" (*Future* 65). Black folk at a Baptist revival, claims West, "frightened this black rationalist . . . because they are out of control" (60). West's Du Bois blindly subscribes to the Enlightenment values of autonomy, progress, education, high culture, and, above all, to an icy rationalism manifested in an "inability to immerse himself in black everyday life" (58). "Nor was he intellectually open enough to position himself alongside the sorrowful, suffering, yet striving ordinary black folk. Instead, his own personal and intellectual distance lifted him above them even as he addressed their plight" (57–58).[22]

While one may grant that all of the aspects West mentions are present in Du Bois, they are not purely present. Instead, they are intermixed with other, contrary elements. Obviously I have been sketching a different portrait of Du Bois, on which I will elaborate in later chapters. But West's critique raises larger, if implicit, questions about the contemporary figure of the intellectual that are worth engaging at this point. One question concerns West's standard of judgment. He measures Du Bois by the Gramscian "organic" model, which posits as normative the intellectual rooted in the native soil and at one with the worker. Hence West's regret of Du Bois's distance and autonomy. But given his care in adopting denaturalizing strategies of incongruity, Du Bois did not wish to be limited to any single role. Instead of defusing differences and contradictions, he cultivated them, making productive use of tension to stimulate his creative negotiation among "unreconciled strivings."

For instance, he used elitist means to tap democratic populist potential. Du Bois regarded the emergence of exceptional black men as proof that "down among the mass, ten times their number with equal ability could be discovered and developed," if effort were exerted (*Dusk* 713). Thus he turns elitism toward possibility, and by 1940 he turns against an earlier strategy—the "flight of class from mass." Now "mass and class must unite for the world's salvation" (712–713). In 1896–1897 alone he espouses a Herderian racial nationalism in "Conservation of Races" and an aesthetic Eurocentrism in "The Art and Art Galleries of Modern Europe."

In sum, Du Bois sets the organic and cosmopolitan, the mass and elite, the particular and universal, into a deliberately unstable synthesis that enables him to move among positions as warranted by historical circumstance and exigency.[23] Ironically, West suggests Du Bois's unstable synthesis when, in an earlier account in *The American Evasion of Philosophy* (1989), he dubs him a "Jamesian organic intellectual." West's phrase is unintentionally discordant given that the universalism and cosmopolitanism of James and Du Bois qualify and complicate their "organic" stance. But the phrase is precise not despite but because of this discordancy.

In *Dusk of Dawn* Du Bois wrote that the American Negro faces "an intricate and subtle problem of combining into one object two difficult sets of facts" (qtd. Cruse 564). Harold Cruse quotes this twice in his landmark work *The Crisis of the Negro Intellectual* (1967), for it "was truly the first theoretical formulation of the historic conflict" that, for Cruse, defines black American history in this century: the conflict between two difficult sets of facts—"integrationist and nationalist forces in politics, economics and culture" (564). "The pendulum swings back and forth, but the men who swing with it always fail to synthesize composite trends" (564). Alone among the three major leaders, Washington, Du Bois, Garvey—whose "amazing, historic triangular feud" generated "everything of . . . value to the American Negro"—Du Bois came closest to constructing a synthesis that would move beyond these oscillating poles (334). One reason that Du Bois came closest was his double-agent status. As Arnold Rampersad declared in his groundbreaking 1976 study, Du Bois "was spy and counterspy; he knew two worlds and felt that he was therefore doubly powerful . . . he lived at least a double life, continually compelled to respond to the challenge of reconciling opposites" (18, 292).[24]

But West's organicism does more than deny Du Bois sufficient intricacy. It denies Du Bois's status as a cosmopolitan intellectual in the modern Dreyfusard sense. For the modern intellectual, as Fredric Jameson reminds us, "is necessarily and constitutively at a distance, not merely from her or his own class of origin, but also from the class of chosen affiliation" (279).[25] The context of Jameson's 1993 remarks is germane; he is discussing the embarrassed status of the classical (Dreyfusard) intellectual in American Cultural Studies where "the desire called the organic intellectual is omnipresent," especially in the veneration accorded group identity and populism (260). The latter's "negative symptom . . . is very precisely the hatred and loathing of intellectuals as such" (280). The promise of the organic is that "reimmersion in the group" will "cleanse" one "of that particular original sin which is the crime of being an intellectual" (280).

Though organic intellectuals believe in their own exemption from this sin, they are self-deceived. Jameson points to those

> who were able to feel that because they were women, Blacks, or ethnics, as intellectuals they counted as members of those "peoples," and no longer had to face the dilemmas of the classic intellectual with his Hegelian "unhappy consciousness." But we now know this is impossible particularly since the question of the intellectual has been rewritten in the new paradigm as the problem of representation as such, about which there is some agreement that it is neither possible nor desirable. (279)

Jameson here arrives at the nuclear contradiction between postmodern theory and practice. The power of the theory is its critique of representation (part of its critique of identity), which contests the deluded practice of intellectuals speaking for and seeking solidarity with the marginal and dispossessed. This solidarity is premised on a naive chain of beliefs: representation can be made transparent, the distance that constitutes intellectuals erased, and intellectuals dissolved into the group. Jameson emphasizes "the class and blood guilt" of a situation in which left intellectuals who practice identity politics make "a desperate attempt . . . to repress their condition [as intellectuals], and to deny and negate its facts of life" (280).

Like the present effort, Jameson challenges postmodernism's devaluation or erasure of the modern intellectual. That the preeminent American Marxist critic urges the return of the intellectual testifies to the flux of a moment when Cultural Studies pieties of organic solidarity are breaking apart from pressure within the left itself.[26] Always distrustful of nationalism and tribalism, Marxism has the authority to urge a broader, cosmopolitan perspective. Even Baraka, perhaps the most adamant and influential organic black literary intellectual, started in the seventies to inflect his organicism with a Marxist internationalism. More recently, he has been guided by a Du Boisian premise that "you can learn from anything and anybody . . . the whole of world culture is at your disposal" (*Baraka Reader* 249–250). Thus within the contemporary moment of postmodernism's demise, West's complaint that Du Bois is insufficiently organic seems regressive.[27] For it confines black intellectuals to their traditional place of preordained group identity. But, as Baraka's memoirs attest, even when the confinement is chosen, the choice is not without ambivalence and unintended consequences.

Seldom has the turn from modern to organic intellectual been more vividly drawn than in *The Autobiography of LeRoi Jones/Amiri Baraka* (1984). Baraka in the 1950s led the life of a bohemian intellectual, a glamorous icon in that epoch. The fifties intellectual contested the gospel of careerism and conformity preached by the white and black bourgeoisie both. "A writer! what a thing to be . . . so outside of the ordinary parade of gray hellos and goodbyes" (119). One of the most poignant moments in Baraka's memoir is the epiphany he has at twenty-two of the "*beauties* the absolute *joy* of learning" (104). While drifting around Chicago in 1956, now in the air force after having left Howard University, he stumbles across a literary bookstore, its window filled with philosophy, art, poetry ("Pound, Eliot, Thomas"). "Something dawned on me, like a big light bulb over my noggin. The comic strip *Idea* lit up my mind at that moment as I stared at the books." He buys some of the books, going home "in a daze, having leaped past myself, to myself. All kinds of new connections yammered in my head. My heart beat faster my skin tingled . . . At that moment my life was changed" (103–104). Before long, he realizes: "I wanted to become an intellectual" (115).

Becoming an intellectual, Baraka discovers, involves a leap past oneself and administers a shock to origins and roots, in particular to the familiar moorings of "Howard University and its brown and yellow fantasy" of the "readied-for-the-slaughter Negro pursuing his 'good job' " (115). Rejecting this life of "prepared sheepdom" for a life as "an intellectual" means dispensing with fixed identity: " 'Who was I?' was going through my head. Who was I? Where did I fit in?" (115). An acute sense of "class consciousness" as an intellectual now separates Jones from the "careerist Negro" of the Howard ideal (115–116).

But as he tries "to become an intellectual," Baraka finds himself "becoming haughtier and more silent. More critical . . . more specialized . . . more abstract and distant" (120). And this affect, which originally seemed an alternative "class consciousness," begins to seem complicit with bourgeois elitism. Baraka feels reluctantly drawn into the very world for which Howard had prepared him—one ruled by "blunt elitism" and whiteness as the measure of all things. In a retrospective passage that summarizes what was unacknowledged in the fifties but reached painful consciousness by the mid-sixties, Baraka racializes his intellectual epiphany and traces its upsetting consequences:

> My reading was, in the main, white people. Europeans, Anglo-Americans. So that my ascent toward some ideal intellectual pose was at the same time a trip toward a white-out I couldn't even understand. I was learning and, at the same time, unlearning. The fasteners to black life unloosed. I was taking words, cramming my face with them. White people's words. Profound, beautiful, some even correct and important. But that is a tangle of nonself in that for all that. A nonself creation where you become other than you as you. Where the harnesses of black life are loosened and you free-float. (120)

The threads binding him to black life would continue to unravel and his distance increase until Baraka ended his free-float in 1965. That year he stitched up all the loose seams of selfhood, leaving the integrated bohemian art world of the Village to move uptown to Harlem, where he became a central figure in the Black Arts movement of cultural nationalism. The move was a shift of primary colors. Baraka describes it in the third person: "Having dug, finally, how white he has become," the "middle-class native intellectual . . . now plunges headlong back into" blackness, "charged up with the desire to be black, uphold black" (202). He ended the year by plunging even deeper—returning home to Newark. In *Home* (1966), where he collected the nationalist essays that memorialize his return to roots, intellectual seems definitively rejected, now made synonymous with white men and with homosexuality—in short, with an abject betrayal of genuine blackness (*Home* 219). But, as I will argue in Chapter 7, Baraka's brutal repudiation of intellectual hides an ambivalence that entangles him in what he would renounce and becomes the source of the imaginative density of two of his most successful works of the sixties—*The System of Dante's Hell* and *The Toilet*.

Until his recent turn to Marxism and international socialism, Baraka's career starkly dramatized the two swings of the pendulum of African American history: integrationism/nationalism, the primacy of whiteness/the primacy of blackness. Synthesis is absent. In the oscillation of mirror-image polarities, white to black, is inscribed the futility of the "supremacy game." Two thinkers—Du Bois and Frantz Fanon, the Martinican theorist of revolution—devised ways to end the game by fashioning a dialectic of universal and particular. But "supremacy game" is Baraka's phrase and refers to what he now regards as the essentialist error enshrined in his black nationalism, an error he says he might have avoided had he read Fanon more carefully (*Autobiography* 323). For those shut out from "the kingdom of culture," *Black Skin, White Masks* and *The Souls of Black Folk* can be used as tool-kits to gain entrance. For both texts suggest that to end the "supremacy game" ("there is no Negro mission; there is no white burden," says Fanon) requires introducing invention and action into existence; this is "the real *leap*" that will turn one from resentment and reaction to the "actional" (*Black Skin* 228–229, 222). Du Bois and Fanon, prophets of black nationalism, will be recontextualized in Chapter 3 as champions of post-ethnicity *avant la lettre*.

When he entered "the kingdom of culture" (to borrow Du Bois's phrase), Baraka experienced a "daze," a vertiginous moment of "free-float," of leaping beyond himself, "unloosed" from racial boundaries, open to "all kinds of new connections." Even though Baraka would eventually halt his free fall by returning to roots, his exhilarated experience of being uprooted enacts the primal scene of the modern intellectual's birth when Dreyfusards were condemned as *déracinés*. And Baraka's dispersal of self prefigures the rebirth of the modern intellectual in the nineties, a rebirth born out of a death—"the end of the innocent notion of an essential black subject." This phrase of Stuart Hall's points to the working premise of a number of contemporary writers working within, or coinciding with, the postmodern critique of identity ("What" 32). Samuel Delany and Adrienne Kennedy enact this end of innocence by favoring the palimpsest or phantasmagoric collage to express a post-ethnic embrace of simultaneity.

Delany's aesthetic is perched upon that refusal to be caught in the net of predictable expectations attached to racial and gender markers. As Delany says of his experience as a black gay man in "racist, sexist homophobic America": it "colors and contours every sentence I write. But it does not delimit and demarcate those sentences, either in their compass, meaning, or style. It does not reduce them in any way" (*Silent Interviews* 73). Valuing the diffuse, permeable, and fleeting, Delany's epistemology (adapted from the topologist René Thom) perceives "the significance of 'white,' like the significance of any other word, [as] a *range* of possibilities." Color and significance fade "quite imperceptibly . . . toward every other color," and areas of significance "intermesh and fade into one another like color-clouds in a three-dimensional spectrum. They don't fit together like hard-edged bricks in a box" (Delany *Triton* 58–59).

Delany turns this fascination with blurred boundaries, described in his science fiction novel *Triton* (1976), into a structural and thematic motif of simultaneity that he names "suspension" in *The Motion of Light in Water* (1988) and *Atlantis: Model 1924* (1995). In these two works, the first an autobiography subtitled "sex and science fiction writing in the East Village 1957–1965," the other an historical novel set in twenties Harlem, the prime inspiration and site of this suspension is the world's first suspension bridge. The Brooklyn Bridge prompts Delany unconsciously to mime it when, alone in Central Park, in an epiphany of his own Whitmanïan expansiveness, he spreads his "arms out on the back of a bench" and takes stock. Mulatto, bisexual, and "that most ambiguous of citizens, the writer," Delany seeks neither the closure nor security of an identity: "So, I thought, you are neither black nor white. You are neither male nor female." Instead, he realizes, he incarnates a "pivotal suspension . . . a kind of center, formed of a play of ambiguities, from which I might move in any direction" (*Motion* 52). In short, his self becomes a bridge, an open, traversable locus of "sensation-saturated fragments" in motion (*Silent* 198). In the novel, where Hart Crane and Sam, the central consciousness, meet on the bridge—"this miraculous suspension above the brilliant river"—the density of the allusive surface is at times heightened to disorientation as Delany creates a collage by running two different but related strands of narrative in two parallel columns on the same page.

If Delany equates freedom with meanings that are simultaneous, intermeshed, and in suspension, and Appiah, a self-described "rootless cosmopolitan," equates freedom with the unscripted, Stuart Hall links it to the "unguaranteed." In an exploratory passage in a 1988 essay, "New Ethnicities," Hall looks at what is in store for one willing to dispense with the props of essentialism: "Once you enter the politics of the end of the essential black subject you are plunged headlong into the maelstrom of a continuously contingent, unguaranteed, political argument and debate . . . You can no longer conduct black politics through the strategy of a simple set of reversals" that replace evil whites with virtuous blacks.[28] Hall's maelstrom, like William James's pluralist world of overlapping edges and transitions, offers little in the way of familiar bearings. Instead, it suggests the freedom of experiencing the "unguaranteed" in a messy world where the ground rules of identity politics—that, for instance, nonwhites possess an inherent oppositionality—no longer apply. If the maelstrom sponsors a regulatory ideal it might be: all the moral cards are neither marked in advance nor held by one group. This book on the conundrum *black intellectual* is written from within this moment of the "unguaranteed" and "unscripted," as the epoch of postmodern tribalism wanes.

2

The Unclassified Residuum

A t the opening of *The Souls of Black Folk* (1903) Du Bois tells us of a question "ever . . . unasked": "How does it feel to be a problem?" Well-meaning white people "flutter round it," but it dies on their lips for fear of insult (363). They avoid asking directly, as if intuiting that to be a problem is to be less a human being than an entry in an "endless cataloguing" of "statistics, slums, rapes, injustices." Thus noted James Baldwin in 1951, echoing Du Bois's own sense of how the particularity of black humanity is kept at bay (*Price* 66). At the outset of *The New Negro* (1925), Alain Locke reanimated Du Bois's question and framed the birth of the New Negro as simultaneous with an end to being a problem. "Until recently, lacking self-understanding, we have been almost as much of a problem to ourselves as we still are to others" (4). The Negro for generations "has been more of a formula than a human being," not a person but "a something to be argued about, condemned or defended," perceived by others and himself through "the distorted perspective of a social problem" (xi, 3–4). The "unusual outburst of creative expression" in Harlem that Locke sought to publicize represented, to his fervent optimism, a decisive liberation from being a "problem." Yet twenty-five years later Zora Neale Hurston noted that to Anglo-Saxons "a college-bred Negro still is not a person like other folks, but an interesting problem" (950).

To regard the black American as a problem, says Baldwin, is to feel "virtuous, outraged, helpless, as though his continuing status among us were somehow analogous to disease—cancer, perhaps, or tuberculosis—which must be checked, even though it cannot be cured." Such concern masks a patronizing passivity that puts black people at a certain human remove and indirectly contributes to their "invisibility and namelessness," as Cornel West in 1996 describes what he finds still to be the "fundamental condition" of black culture (*Future* 84). Citing Du Bois's "seminal" passage, West sums up the components of this anonymity: "Black people as a problem-people rather than people with problems; black people as abstractions and objects rather than individuals and persons" (84).

If a problem with being treated as a problem is effacement or suppression of individuality, Du Bois's immediate antidote is *The Souls of Black Folk*. It brings before a white public the results of his experiment in excavating the "unknown treasures" of the "inner life" of black folk. Black psychic interiority, the "rich and bitter depth of their experience," had long been repressed under the weight of racist stereotype and exclusion (438). In a 1904 assessment of his book he speaks of the "intimate tone of self-revelation" and the "distinctively subjective note that runs in each essay" (*Book Reviews* 9). To achieve this intimacy and subjectivity required that Du Bois leave "the world of the white man" and step "within the Veil" of segregation. Only by speaking from within and raising the veil to show us "its deeper recesses"—the struggles and passions of black folks' sorrow and souls—will he redeem the clinical detachment that inheres in being treated as a problem.

"Being a problem" has another reference and context: in 1900 Jim Crow America, *black intellectual* embodies with particular force the "strange experience" of "being a problem" (363). "All wrong" is the reflex judgment that is branded upon the black intellectual and artist in a society of caste segregation: "He should never have been born, for he is a 'problem.' He should never be educated, for he cannot be educated" is how Du Bois summarized the dismissal. Writing of the black British composer Samuel Taylor-Coleridge, Du Bois notes that his very existence disturbed assumptions: rather than being trained as a "musician,—he should have been trained for his 'place' in the world" (*Darkwater* 201–202). More charitable responses were even more humiliating. Paul Laurence Dunbar's late-nineteenth-century dialect verse, noted Langston Hughes, elicited the kind of "encouragement one would give a sideshow freak (a colored man writing poetry! How odd!) or a clown (How amusing!)" (Hughes 307). In 1920 Bernard Shaw earnestly remarked to Claude McKay: "It must be tragic for a sensitive Negro to be a poet. Why didn't you choose pugilism instead of poetry for a profession?" (McKay *Long* 61). When condescending reviews of his first volume of poetry appeared, McKay realized that Shaw's point was confirmed. Summarizing an attitude widespread in the twenties, when the "Negro was in vogue," Dorothy West calls "Negro writing" an "elephant's dance . . . remarkable not so much because it was writing, but because it was Negro writing" (216).[1]

Eventually we will probe the unspoken assumptions that account for the condescension and contempt that *black intellectual* stimulates. Here it is worth noting that *black intellectual* is a disturbance that encloses another, prior one—the very fact of black literacy. This was a specter that filled white Southerners with consuming fear throughout the nineteenth century. "To stamp out the brains of the Negro!" said Alexander Crummell in 1898, was the South's "systematized method" of subjugation (*Destiny* 291). If caught reading, a slave might have fingers or hands chopped off. "For coloured people to acquire learning in this country, makes tyrants quake and tremble," declared David Walker in his *Appeal* of 1829 (31). "Educating the coloured people," he implies, ignites a train of dire consequences: not only does it spell the end of submission and the publicizing of slavers' "infernal deeds of cruelty," but, most important, it explodes the white image of blacks as "talking apes, void of intellect, incapable of learning" (61–62). On all these counts, Walker's *Appeal* is a nightmare, its very existence shocking proof of prodigious black intellectual capacity. Little wonder that to distribute it was a crime of sedition (one white sailor was convicted) or that it had to be sewn into the coats of sailors for surreptitious distribution. "Why are the Americans so very fearfully terrified respecting my Book?" Walker asks in mock wonder. "Is it because they treat us so well? . . . Why, I thought the Americans proclaimed to the world that they are a happy, enlightened, humane, and Christian people" (72). He took furious delight in being a problem.

As the preeminent black thinker, Du Bois was acutely aware of the affront inherent in *black intellectual.* He faced the challenge of representing in his own life and in art a figure that seemed to resist every way of making sense of black identity. In dramatizing in "The Coming of John" (a short story that is the penultimate chapter of *The Souls of Black Folk*) the black intellectual as an antirace race figure, a living conundrum, Du Bois joined other turn-of-the-century writers, including Charles Chesnutt and Sutton Griggs. In Chapter 3 I explore how they devised aesthetic strategies to represent a new social category.

In this chapter I examine how a contemporary of this cohort, Pauline Hopkins, in her novel *Of One Blood* (1903), depicted a fantasy of escape from being a race champion which anticipated the preoccupations of a number of novelists of the next generation. Harlem Renaissance writers, including the ubiquitous Du Bois, Nella Larsen, Jessie Fauset, and others, sought to enlarge the field of black intellectual endeavor beyond race uplift. In their fiction, all three variously imagined a release from "race" into "life." These are Du Bois's terms to describe Helga Crane of Larsen's *Quicksand*. We shall see that his admiring response to her includes an identification with black female intellectuals as having a distinctive opportunity for experiencing and dramatizing such a release.

If problems are to be patronized, freaks are to be exhibited. Both responses ensure that detached spectators survey static objects. At least since the attestation affixed to Phillis Wheatley's book of poems in 1773, the black intellectual had been deemed a freak to be carefully monitored. Wheatley appeared before a board of eighteen Boston examiners, who inquired into the veracity of her authorship. Upon being certified, her status shifted from problem to freak; soon she became a favorite society curiosity. "Phillis in her day was a museum figure who would have caused more of a sensation if some contemporary Barnum had exploited her," remarked Wallace Thurman in 1928. Thurman suggests Wheatley's continued currency in the 1920s: "She was exhibited at the Court of George III, and in the homes of nobility much as the Negro poets of today are exhibited in New York drawing rooms" ("Negro Poets" 98–99). More recently Amiri Baraka has noted that Wheatley reflected the "ideology of Charlie McCarthy in relation to Edgar Bergen" (*Reader* 314).

The most famous black exhibit of the nineteenth century was the young Frederick Douglass. In 1841 he appeared at abolitionist conventions "introduced as a '*chattel*'—a '*thing*'—a piece of Southern '*property*'—the chairman assuring the audience that *it* could speak" (Douglass 366). Objecthood attested to authenticity. But Douglass soon fractured this equation. He grew restless with the injunction of his handlers to stick to reciting the same facts night after night while letting them "take care of the philosophy." As they explained, " 'tis not best that you seem too learned" (367). Instead, just "be yourself . . . and tell your story." The irony of this advice is pointed (if unwitting), for the authentic self they imagined him to be—a compliant self of "mechanical" repetition—was one that Douglass was rapidly becoming unwilling to perform. "I was now reading and thinking," he recalls, and "it did not entirely satisfy me to *narrate* wrongs; I felt like *denouncing* them." A black talking object doing a "mechanical" task was the kind of freak to excite curiosity; a black thinking subject was a threatening freak pushing at the outer limits of credibility and coherence. "People doubted if I had ever been a slave. They said I did not talk like a slave, look like a slave, nor act like a slave." And, what is more, his education made him a "contradiction" of all known facts about slaves (367). Blatant here is the clash between Douglass's insistence on personal authenticity and an ideological construction of authenticity.

Eventually Douglass "resolved to dispel all doubt" by setting down in 1845 a narrative of the basic facts of his life. He enacted this practice again ten years later and again in 1881, as if each time repeating the original act of disobedience toward his abolitionist advisers. Each new version of his life testified to the fact that he "was growing, and needed room," that he would not be satisfied with knowing his place as "mechanical" object reciting the bare facts. Not only was disobedience inscribed in both subsequent autobiographies, but collectively they deepened the "contradiction" of being an educated slave. For with each book Douglass affirmed and enlarged his authorship and thus his stature as a black intellectual. Intending to narrate his life and to resolve the contradiction, he only succeeded in strengthening it.[2]

The Douglass depicted here exemplifies the "problem" Du Bois will explore: the black intellectual as embodied "contradiction," one who does not know or keep his or her "place." Like David Walker before him and Du Bois and his cohort after him, Douglass has ceased being merely a problem to be patronized or a freak to be exhibited. Rather, as a thinking black subject he could be said to initiate a crisis in established ways of making sense. As such, he is someone "we do not know what to do with . . . if he breaks our sociological and sentimental image of him we are panic-stricken and we feel ourselves betrayed" (*Price* 66). I have borrowed James Baldwin's words that describe white reaction when a black individual emerges from the "jungle of statistics" and is revealed not as a "problem or a fantasy" but as a "person" (181). When that person is a black intellectual, anxiety is heightened. The response of alarm and betrayal is at the center of "The Coming of John." Returning home to rural Georgia full of his "education and Northern notions," the black intellectual protagonist is accused by blacks of acting "monstus stuck up" and by whites of wanting to "reverse nature" (*Souls* 531). Nearly a century later, a residue of panic and bewilderment remains, however sublimated and displaced; witness the media fascination of the mid-nineties with the existence of contemporary black intellectuals.

We have seen that as a black intellectual Douglass inevitably challenges the way a white supremacist culture understands black identity. More precisely, he contests the ideology of authenticity, which is grounded in the absolutist metaphysics of rationalist and intellectualist thought. Pervading these discourses is a rhetoric of the natural, of origins, of organicism, and of immutable identity. These essentialist tenets provided the intellectual armature of white Anglo-Saxon supremacy and its instruments of nationalism and imperialism, as well as orienting positivist science (scientism) and affirming the pervasive exceptionalism of American social science. By the end of the nineteenth century the ideology of authenticity was contested—by philosophical pragmatism in the United States, led by the anti-imperialist William James, and, in France, by the Dreyfusards, foes of rabid French anti-Semitism and nationalism. What emerged from the crisis of authenticity was the modern notion of intellectuals.

In 1907 when William James imported "Les Intellectuels," he used it as an honorific standing "for ideal interests solely": " 'Les Intellectuels'! What prouder club-name could there be than this one, used ironically by the party . . . of every stupid prejudice and passion, during the anti-Dreyfus craze, to satirize the men in France who still retained some critical sense and judgment!" (*Writings* 1246). His student Du Bois had witnessed the craze close up. "I followed the Dreyfus case," Du Bois notes in his *Autobiography,* and remarks that the year he traveled in France (1894) was the year Dreyfus was arrested and tried for treason (122, 177). Du Bois was in Paris again in 1900 when the scandal was raging anew, for the year before Dreyfus had been convicted a second time. Yet the Dreyfusards eventually achieved the acquittal of the unjustly accused captain. Du Bois had ample reason to be impressed: not only had the Dreyfusards achieved justice but they also had established the "specific function" and domain of the modern intellectual. As Habermas has noted, the Dreyfusards create a "political public sphere" in which to "intervene on behalf of rights that have been violated and truths that have been suppressed, reforms that are overdue and progress that has been delayed . . . they count on a recognition of universalist values" (75, 73).

In the first decade of the twentieth century Du Bois would be preoccupied with the work of creating a public sphere in which to be heard.

In 1903 he calls for a "Talented Tenth," a critical mass of trained black professionals, businessmen, teachers, as well as "leaders of thought and missionaries of culture" (Du Bois *Writings* 861). This elite becomes the basis of his effort to articulate a collective public voice for justice, which culminates in 1910 with the formation of the interracial, multi-ethnic NAACP. A Dreyfusard logic informs the premise of both this group and the "Talented Tenth": an "educated person acting without a 'political mandate' " makes use of "the means of his profession outside the sphere of his profession—that is, in the political public sphere" (Habermas 73).

In France in 1898 those who refused to know their place and instead strayed out of the study, the library, and the laboratory to pronounce upon political matters were scorned as *Les Intellectuels*. As one anti-Dreyfusard noted of Zola: "the intervention of a novelist—even a famous one—in a matter of military justice seems to me as out of place as the intervention, in a question concerning the origins of Romanticism, of a colonel in the police force" (qtd. Bredin 277).

Inevitable, then, is William James's esteem for these overreachers, *the intellectuals*. For they, along with pragmatists and black intellectuals, mount a revolt against the ideology of authenticity by calling in question what it holds sacred—"neat schematisms with permanent and absolute distinctions, classifications with absolute pretensions, systems with pigeon holes . . . all [that is] 'classic,' clean, cut and dried, 'noble,' fixed, eternal" (qtd. Perry 2: 700). This is James's enemies list, a summary of what he despised emotionally and philosophically. To counter it, James urged immersion in the "vulnerable" world of pragmatist pluralism, where one lives "without assurances or guarantees . . . for some part may go astray" (*Writings* 940). James honored what he called "wild facts, with no stall or pigeon-hole . . . which threaten to break up the accepted system" (*Will* 224).

As historians of the Dreyfus Affair have pointed out, the clash quickly transcended the fate of one innocent convict. It became, in part, a battle between those who construed human rights and justice as beholden to no particular interests and those demanding a totalizing nationalism, which "consists in resolving every question in terms of its relation to France," said Maurice Barrès, the virulent anti-Dreyfusard (qtd. Bredin 295). The figure of the Jew, particularized in Dreyfus, is identified as radically out of place, unassimilable to the nation. Rather than a member of the true Nation, Dreyfus, says Barrès, "is nothing but an uprooted plant . . . in our French garden" (296). Barrès's metaphor names the

Jew as *déraciné*, a homeless cosmopolitan, cut off from any organic unity with France.[3]

The equation is unmistakable: Jew = intellectual = *déraciné*. If an intellectual is a symbolic Jew, for the black intellectual this identity is complicated. As fellow pariahs, black and Jew are brothers in misery, as Fanon says. Yet they embody different threats: "the Negro symbolizes the biological danger; the Jew the intellectual danger" (*Black Skin,* 122, 165). And there is an additional difference: "the Jew can be unknown in his Jewishness . . . he can sometimes go unnoticed," whereas the black is "overdetermined from without," the slave of his "own appearance": "I am *fixed*" (116). Thus the Jew as pariah, as intellectual, possesses a freedom to pass that is denied the black. *Black intellectual* is itself a status that undermines stereotype and shares with the Jew the danger of intellect. However, the black intellectual does not share the Jew's liberty, which is grounded in nothing more than "his actions, his behavior." They are "the final determinant" (115).

Small wonder, then, that black intellectuals look to the Jew as an attractive figure of unrooted mobility. "Make me a Jew" is how James Weldon Johnson answered his own imaginary request to choose another race (*Along* 136). James Baldwin's "Jewish" identity (as mediated through that other Jew Henry James) has already been mentioned. Two other great black cosmopolitans affirmed affinity with Jewish models. "As with the Jew, persecution is making the Negro international," remarks Alain Locke of the global character of the "wider race consciousness" animating the Harlem Renaissance. The "Negro mind has leapt, so to speak, on the parapets of prejudice and extended its cramped horizons" ("New" 14). And in Chapter 5 we shall see that Du Bois's identification with Jewish cosmopolitanism was profound because mediated by his special friendship with the Jewish aristocrat and literary critic Joel Spingarn, his colleague at the NAACP. In "The Shadow of Years," an autobiographical sketch first delivered at a testimonial banquet organized by Spingarn, Du Bois declared himself one of the "Lord's Anointed," thus memorializing this kinship.

In France, "Les Intellectuels" emerges as a marker of identity that puts in question identity as rooted and fixed. Thus the intellectual is a figure *contra naturam*. And a figure of enviable freedom. The intellectual, says Pierre Bourdieu, is a "paradoxical synthesis of the opposites" of "pure culture and engagement" ("Corporatism" 99). The epochal nature of Zola's political intervention, Bourdieu has explained, is that his authority was based on the relative autonomy of the artistic and scientific disciplines with their core values of ethical integrity, impartiality, disinterestedness, and skepticism. These values reject the mercenary objectives of money and power which dominate in politics and economics.[4] Upholding "ideal interests solely," as William James put it, the intellectual practiced what Bourdieu calls an "antipolitical politics," a "*politics of purity*—the perfect antithesis to the Reason of State" (101). With Zola's "J'accuse," intellectuals were no longer content simply to assert their anti-commercial values

> by extending the limits of their inverted world. They now affirmed their antivalues in ordinary social life, ethics—notably sexual matters—and politics . . . Intellectuals asserted their right to *transgress* the most sacred values of the collectivity—most strikingly, those of patriotism and nationalism— by supporting Zola's criticism of the army . . . in the name of values transcending and superseding parochial ones. They derived their authority from the unwritten laws of ethical and scientific universalism. (101)

Bourdieu's incisive summary of the genesis of "Les Intellectuels" is worth recording not least because of its relative unfamiliarity in the postmodern epoch. But, more important, to resurrect the intellectual reanimates the context in which figures such as William James, perhaps the most eminent American public intellectual of his day, wielded a profound moral authority for people like his student Du Bois, for his admirer Randolph Bourne, and for the generation of 1910 which Bourne dubbed the "young intellectuals."[5] The turn-of-the-century birth of the modern urban intellectual created a momentous charge of freedom and responsibility—"the right to *transgress* the most sacred values of the collectivity"—which exhilarated those who came of age at this historical moment. Indeed, in his famous series of essays in 1917 protesting American entry into world war, Bourne would enact in near-heroic terms this transgression against patriotism and nationalism, the sacred values of the State.

Generally regarded as the founder of the twentieth-century tradition of the urban public intellectual, Bourne developed an ideal of the intellectual as the quintessential modernist, a "malcontent" and radical skeptic. He derived his model by bringing James together with another of his heroes—Nietzsche (Bourne 347). The pairing was a shrewd one and reminds us of the profound conjunction between the two thinkers, most readily evident in their shared love of Emerson. While all three contest the utilitarian temper of rationalism, they seek not to abolish but to deepen and broaden the Enlightenment (see Lampert 360).[6]

James's freethinking intimately aligned him with the powerful icon-oclasm of the modern Dreyfusard intellectual. His skepticism of the authority of origin, essence, and identity is one reason pragmatism was compelling to Du Bois and later to Bourne. These writers found in pragmatism, along with Franz Boas's anthropology, a tool that, virtu-ally alone among turn-of-the-century behavioral and social sciences, could oppose the theory and practice of white supremacy. Pragmatist pluralism, like Boasian contextualism, dismissed "all the great single-word answers to the world's riddle, such as God, the One . . . Nature" and "*The* Truth," as "perfect idol[s] of the rationalistic mind!" (*Prag-matism* 115). Bourne would add White Anglo-Saxon Protestantism to the list of idols. A student of Dewey's (whose pragmatism he would critique in 1917), Bourne used his and James's teachings to lambaste the WASP ideal and promote cultural and ethnic pluralism. His ideal was a "trans-national America" that would serve as an alternative, more democratic model to the coerciveness of the melting pot.

James's anti-imperialist defense of the dark-skinned alien reflects his pragmatism's refusal of absolutist systems and purified essences, the modes of thought often employed to defend racialist assumptions and racism. A remark that James makes in *The Principles of Psychology* can be read as a summary of the logic that animates his pragmatism, his psychology, and his social activism. He speaks of his effort to "restore . . . the *vague* to its psychological rights . . . The passing and evanescent are as real parts of the stream [of consciousness] as the distinct and comparatively abiding" (I: 452). His consistent effort is to reinstate what prevailing orthodoxies overlook, fear, and despise.

At the same time it should be noted that even James, Dewey, Boas, and Bourne had definite limits in their thinking about African Ameri-cans. To extend George Hutchinson's judgment of why the advances in understanding race made in the Harlem Renaissance were "too easily submerged" in later generations, even progressive intellectuals "never really understood the importance of black history and culture to the United States" and did not regard "the relationship between whites and blacks as central to the story of the republic. The idea of their own 'race' was unexamined; to them, the white immigrant and frontier ex-periences were central to Americanism . . . One could say that their Americanization was incomplete" (*Harlem* 446–447).

Yet it remains the case that James's legacy encouraged black thinkers to interrogate the orthodoxy of whiteness, to revise that which goes without saying. Pragmatism encouraged not only tolerance but historicist thinking and linguistic skepticism. Open to the hazards of change and contingency, to a reality that "is still in the making," pragmatists immerse themselves in the "tangled, muddy, painful and perplexed" mess of experience. They risk getting dirty, a prospect William James welcomed as the antidote to philosophic rationalism's shallow world, where all is "simple, clean, and noble" (*Pragmatism* 123, 17–18). James eventually renounced the instrument of this simplicity—rationalism's "logic of identity"—for it devours "wild facts" and the "irregular phenomena" which he collectively calls the "unclassified residuum" (*Will* 222).

The very notion of a "talented tenth" of black people of distinction was a wild fact defying Jim Crow identity logic, which froze blacks in racist stereotype. As Du Bois noted, "so long . . . as humble black folk [are] voluble with thanks" for any handouts from white philanthropy, so long as they know their place, "there is much mental peace and moral satisfaction" (*Writings* 925). White supremacy's identity logic was underwritten, said Du Bois, by "Nature's law" which decreed that "the word 'Negro' connotes 'inferiority' and 'stupidity' lightened only by unreasoning gayety and humor" (*Black Reconstruction* 726).

But Nature was not only an ally of white power. Booker T. Washington, implacable opponent of Du Bois and his talented tenth, enlisted Nature in his cause. His white-funded "Tuskegee Machine" naturalized blackness as cheerful submission to agrarian labor. In *Up from Slavery* (1901) Washington recalled the early plans for Tuskegee and sympathized with white anxiety about starting a black college. He remarked that those who had questioned the wisdom of creating Tuskegee had in their minds pictures "of what was called an educated Negro, with a high hat, imitation gold eye-glasses, a showy walking stick, kid gloves, fancy boots and what not—in a word a man who was determined to live by his wits" (92). The men and women of Tuskegee stood in merciful and stark contrast to this effeminate urban fop borrowed from the minstrel tropes of black dandy lore. He described Tuskegee itself as serene, rooted "upon the solid and never deceptive foundation of Mother Nature, where all nations and races that have ever succeeded have gotten their start" (77). In making Mother Nature his staunch ally, Washington stigmatized any opposition. To be against Booker was to be against Nature; hence black intellectual became a repugnant oxymoron, a corrupt and decadent monstrosity.

In 1903 Washington assailed those who disrupted a speech of his in

Boston as "artificial" men, "graduates of New England colleges" (qtd. Lewis *Du Bois* 301). And in his 1911 recounting of the incident, which had become known as the Boston riot, Washington gave a name to his unnatural enemies—"people who call themselves 'The Intellectuals.' " They live "at a distance," in a world of "theories, but they do not understand" people and things (*Education* 113, 120). In depicting the intellectual as unnatural Washington not only lashed out at his arch rival Du Bois as one of the "artificial" men of the New England colleges, but in effect reclaimed the French nationalist sense of the word. And he also wrested the term away from William James. Neatly disguised in Washington's power play to stigmatize *intellectual* was his own status as an intellectual. The shrewd Kelly Miller exposed this embarrassment in his critique of Washington's discouragement of black intellect. In his "Brief for the Higher Education of the Negro" (1908) in a section pointedly called "Dr. Booker T. Washington . . . an Example of Higher Culture," Miller observes that Washington built Tuskegee on the force of his "intellect and oratory. If Mr. Washington had been born with palsied hands, but endowed with the same intellectual gifts . . . Tuskegee would not have suffered one iota by reason of his manual affliction" (Miller 283–284).

Washington's success rested in no small part on his ability to address and assuage what David Walker had inflamed—white terror of black literacy. Working hand in glove with Northern philanthropists (including Rockefeller's General Education Board), Washington made Tuskegee into an instrument that would resolve what one of them, Robert Ogden, called "our great problem . . . to attach the Negro to the soil and prevent his exodus from the country to the city" (qtd. Anderson 89). Such an exodus would spell economic catastrophe for Northern investments, as it meant the drying up of a steady supply of cheap, nonunionized, black farm labor to keep the cost of cotton profitable. Washington's path was clear: he was "careful not to educate" his students "out of sympathy with agricultural life" and risk having them abandon physical for mental labor—what he called living by one's wits. Washington supported college education only for those who would teach the black masses the supreme value of industrial training and a life of contented subordination. Tuskegee's goal was to provide "such an education as would fit a large proportion of them to be teachers, and at the same time cause them to return to the plantation districts" (*Up* 96–97). To ensure this return, Tuskegee would keep book learning to a minimum, devoting itself to making the Negro humble and useful to

the community. To that end students were discouraged from even being seen carrying books because, as Franklin Frazier personally remembered, "white people passed through the campus and would get the
impression that Tuskegee was training the Negro's intellect rather than
his heart and hand" (Frazier 203).

So firm was Washington's control that even black educators in other
parts of the country who dared offer an alternative to the Tuskegee
regime met swift retribution. A most notable case involved Anna Julia
Cooper. The author of *A Voice from the South* (1892) and a mulatto
scholar of Latin and Greek, Cooper was principal of M Street School
in Washington, D.C., the largest and best black high school at the turn
of the century (in 1916 it was renamed Dunbar High School). In 1906
Cooper was fired from her post on dubious charges and exiled to four
years in a Missouri college. Her crime was having initiated a classical
humanities college preparatory curriculum to complement, not replace,
vocational training. But worse, a number of Cooper's students, mostly
from the working class, graduated with scholarships to Harvard, Yale,
Oberlin, Amherst, and Radcliffe, among others. The academic excellence of M Street School became an embarrassment and a threat to
ideologues of industrial education, who depended on strict adherence
to the fiction of black inferiority.

Cooper's challenge to Washington preceded Du Bois's. *A Voice from
the South* (1892), with its emphasis on the necessity of "leisure" as the
condition in which "the untrammeled intellect of the Negro, or any
other race, can truly vindicate its capabilities," had obvious affinities
with and probably influenced Du Bois's thinking (Cooper 261). Cooper came to know him at meetings of the American Negro Academy,
where she was the single woman in the organization. When Du Bois
lectured at M Street in 1903, and "called attention to the tendency
throughout the country to restrict the curriculum of colored schools,"
Cooper aligned herself with Du Bois, a move that made her position
still more vulnerable (Louise Hutchinson 67–68).[7]

Although, as the historian James Anderson has shown, the influence
of the Tuskegee model of industrial education waned after 1914, its
contempt for black intellect was a legacy not easily evaded, for it was
often internalized.[8] As we will see in Chapter 7, in the 1960s Washington's contempt acquired a nastier, nationalist edge in the work of black
cultural militants. Ironically, in deriding the black intellectual as the
locus of all that betrays genuine blackness, they affirmed not the radical
Du Bois, a hero of black nationalism, but the conservative Washington.

With James Baldwin in mind, Eldridge Cleaver dubbed the black intellectual not only an oxymoron but a monstrosity, "a white man in a black body." Cleaver and Amiri Baraka would also revive and elaborate the latent homophobia in Washington's ridicule and his insinuation of effeminacy. The "white man in a black body" is a castrate and "homosexual," the "tool" of whites who have deprived him of his masculinity (Cleaver 101).[9]

Closer to Washington's own era, Richard Wright lived the Tuskegee legacy, lived the visceral pain (which he turned to pride) of being an alien species: "My environment contained nothing more alien than writing or the desire to express one's self in writing" (*Black* 116). Reflecting in *Black Boy* on his grade school experiences in Mississippi in the late teens and twenties, Wright felt as if exiled to the "No Man's Land into which the Negro mind in America had been shunted" (253). Wright survived this desolation by dreaming of what "had no relation whatever to what actually existed"—"going North and writing books, novels." "By imagining a place where everything was possible, I kept hope alive in me" (161). An emblem of possibility was the short story he published in a local black paper. Though it met with harsh bewilderment from nearly everyone he knew—it was "the most alien thing conceivable to them"—the story sustains the dream he is "building up" (159). Wright's dream is one that

> the entire educational system of the South had been rigged to stifle. I was feeling the very thing that the state of Mississippi had spent millions of dollars to make sure that I would never feel; I was becoming aware of the thing that the Jim Crow laws had been drafted and passed to keep out of my consciousness; I was acting on impulses that southern senators in the nation's capital had striven to keep out of Negro life . . . In me was shaping a yearning for a kind of consciousness, a mode of being that the way of life about me had said could not be, must not be, and upon which the penalty of death had been placed. (161–162)

Wright summons the specter of the State using all its apparatuses to imprison him within the generic object labeled "black boy." Would that it could be dismissed as paranoid fantasy. Wright here is self-dramatizing, an effect created out of the disproportion between the minuscule "I" and the forces arrayed against him. But he is also offering a sober overview of what segregation and its loyal servant, the Tuskegee Machine, had wrought. Somehow, in the emotional isolation he endures, Wright finds himself daring to slip the tentacular grasp of an infrastructure designed to ensure that *black intellectual* would remain a stillborn fantasy, as ephemeral as "The Voodoo of Hell's Half Acre," his publishing debut, of which no copies survive.

Black Boy/American Hunger of course narrates Wright's near miraculous escape from the designs of white supremacy, as he becomes Booker T. Washington's nightmare. Yet Washington might have enjoyed the irony when Wright is "classified as an *intellectual*" by the only group that has ever inspired him to hope (314). The Communist Party he joins in Chicago has "classified" him. The word is ominous, the clue that the Party is as suspicious of *intellectual* as Tuskegee or his own family. All three regard him as incorrigible, a cipher lost in thought, addicted to solitary contemplation and thus incapable of action. Before long Wright feels that "an invisible wall [is] building slowly between" himself and the Party. "Officially accused of nothing," he is treated as an "open enemy." When he is with his comrades, working beside them, "they always looked straight ahead, wordlessly" (315, 361, 358). The condition of invisibility is hardly new to him; it repeats and reaffirms his sense of having been assigned "the role of a nonman" in the South, of being "emotionally cast out of the world" and "made to live outside the normal processes of life" simply because he "wanted to talk and act like a man" (233, 195, 191).

While little could be more familiar to Wright's readers than his sense of being an outsider, an invisible "non-man," the intellectual ancestry of his anonymity is less well known. Yet in 1945 he made it explicit. In introducing *Black Metropolis,* the groundbreaking urban sociology of St. Clair Drake and Horace Cayton, Wright sought an image to sum up the dehumanized status of the "American Negro," his near-total "rejection" by white Americans. To make vivid this exclusion, he quoted a passage from William James's *Principles of Psychology:* "No more fiendish punishment could be devised, were such a thing physically possible, than that one should be turned loose in society and remain absolutely unnoticed by all the members thereof . . . if every person we met 'cut us dead,' and acted as if we were non-existent things, a kind of rage and impotent despair would ere long well up in us" (Drake and Cayton xxxii).

Saunders Redding calls this quotation "the ground of all Wright's works, fiction and nonfiction . . . [it] revealed, as it were, him to himself. It can scarcely be doubted that from the moment he read it . . . Wright became a man with a message and a mission" (*Scholar* 158). James had supplied the terms of how it felt to be a problem.[10] But also the terms of its solution. Wright read William James at fifteen or sixteen, says Redding, evidently securing a copy by "subterfuge" of the sort he practices in *Black Boy*—perhaps forging a note from a white man to get books from the library. Redding implies that Wright's necessary "denial of his *self*" was one reason James's passage spoke directly to him (157). But James's words not only confirmed for Wright his dilemma but suggested his survival strategy. He turns the form of his alienation—the suffocating anonymity imposed by white racism—into a weapon. Rather than seeking to overcome self-erasure, he uses it, devising a studied "deadpan" "neutrality" in public to maximize his inner freedom for thought and to create a pathway for expanded intellectual activity: "writing or reading . . . were ways of living" (267, 266). To be "classified as an *intellectual*"—to be fixed in an identity—arrests his intellectual way of living (162).

The autobiography ends with Wright, having just been literally thrown out of the Party during a May Day parade, returning to his "narrow room" in utter aloneness, bereft of any "examples of how to live a human life" (365). But Wright's solitary "non-self" is not the nadir of futility and alienation but instead the condition of doing intellectual work: "writing had to be done in loneliness" (355). This fact, he had come to realize, was what made him intolerable to the Party's declared "war on human loneliness." Unconcerned to discover his own authentic identity, in the tradition of American individualism, Wright keeps faith with writing as an act, literal and symbolic: "I picked up a pencil and held it over a sheet of white paper . . . I would hurl words into this darkness and wait for an echo" (365).

In giving primacy to action, not identity, Wright enacts an eminently pragmatist stance. But his literary reputation inverts his stunning indifference to the ideology of authenticity. It is a disturbing irony that, until very recently, Wright remained for white critics the canonical icon of "the genuine article, the authentic Negro writer, and his tone the only authentic tone." Which is to say, his work allegedly testifies "that unrelieved suffering is the only 'real' Negro experience." This is Ralph Ellison's famous and contemptuous summary of the terms of Irving Howe's influential celebration of Wright (*Shadow* 111). In making " 'Negroness' a metaphysical condition, one that is a state of irremediable agony," Howe presented Wright as the exemplary sufferer, an image as securely policed and classified as the generic pigeon-hole "black boy" (130).

Howe, like many others, fetishized the raw poverty of Wright's Southern class position (his father was a "black peasant" sharecropper) as his essence. This ignored Wright's passionate class warfare against Baptist fear and loathing. The war commences on page one. The fire Wright sets to his house at the book's opening emblematizes his obsession to uproot himself by any means necessary to achieve the deracinated freedom of modernity. "I like and even cherish the state of abandonment, of aloneness," he would say later in life, but his conviction is born in childhood (*White Man* xxix). With their gaze fixed on race and class as fate, connoisseurs of authenticity were blind to the obvious: that *Black Boy* records the coming of age of a quintessential modernist intellectual. H. L. Mencken, one of Wright's intellectual heroes, could have been describing Wright when he began his book on Nietzsche (another of Wright's heroes) by saying "let a boy of alert, restless intelligence come to early manhood in an atmosphere of strong faith, wherein doubts are blasphemies and inquiry is a crime, and rebellion is certain to appear with his beard" (3).[11]

Wright fashions a forbidden "mode of being," a set of tactics, which turn anonymity into a "protective mechanism" that permits him to stay a marginal figure of "self-sufficiency" inexplicable to the white South with its blind certainty that "it knew 'niggers.' " "Well, the white South," said Wright, "had never known me—never known what I thought, what I felt . . . my deepest instincts had always made me reject the 'place' to which the white South had assigned me" (879). And, for that matter, he rejected the place assigned by the black South and by the Communists. Flying under the radar of conventional terms of intelligibility, those dictated by group thinking, Wright embodies one of those "wild facts, with no stall or pigeon-hole" revered by William James (*Will* 223).

The opening scene of *Of One Blood* (1903), Pauline Hopkins's quasi–science fiction novel, presents a brilliant Harvard medical student alone in his rooms absorbed in a just-published treatise entitled *The Unclassified Residuum* (442). Reuel Briggs, melancholy, solitary, suicidal, is of unknown origin but passes as white and is regarded by his peers as a scientific "genius." He has devoted his studies to what "the ordinary medical man dismisses"—such "irregular" phenomena as "divinations, inspirations, demoniacal possessions, apparitions, trances" (442). When rumors of his mixed racial identity begin to impede his career, he leaves America to join an archaeological expedition bound for Africa and an ancient Ethiopian site where they will "unearth buried cities and treasure" (494). Eventually Reuel is revealed as the incarnation of

Ergamenes, an ancient Ethiopian king who has been destined to "return and restore the former glory of the race" (535). He is crowned ruler and, with his beautiful Queen Candace, rules from a throne in the splendid "hidden city" of Telassar.

The Unclassified Residuum grips Briggs because on one level it is his own biography. Its subject matter—"unaccountable phenomena"—mirrors his own "irregular" status as black genius, albeit one who hides his racial origin. That his reading triggers identification in Briggs is implied by how fully the book absorbs him: "he was thinking deeply of the words he had just read . . . the book suited the man's mood" (442). Putting it down, he remarks, "I know the truth of every word" (443). "Unclassified Residuum" is a direct borrowing from James. In the same essay in which this phrase appears, James writes that in its ideal of achieving a "closed and completed system of truth," science regards the "unclassifiable within the system" as "paradoxical absurdities, and must be held untrue" (*Will* 222). In one case study, Briggs reads of a "non-hysterical woman who in her trances knows facts which altogether transcend her *possible* normal consciousness, facts about the lives of people whom she never saw or heard of before" (443). Like *black intellectual*, this woman falls outside the "closed and completed system" of science. Both therefore are "untrue" because their knowledge violates the limits of what science deems "possible normal consciousness." What Hopkins's opening tableau suggests, then, is that *black intellectual*, legislated by science as outside the realm of normal existence, is an alien life form. Thus to represent such "absurdities" is to create science fiction fantasy.

Hopkins not only borrows "unclassified residuum" from James but quotes from the essay in which it originally appeared—"The Hidden Self" (1890)—which was reprinted as part of "What Psychical Research Has Accomplished" in *The Will to Believe* (1897).[12] Another source is Du Bois, whose 1897 *Atlantic* essay had theorized a "double consciousness" unique to black Americans. (In *The Souls of Black Folk* Du Bois would revise and republish this essay in the same year that Hopkins published *Of One Blood*). Du Bois, in turn, drew in part on James's notion of a "hidden self," "subconscious" and "buried." This also inspires Hopkins's Africanist fantasy. James speaks of a " 'subliminal' self" that "we all have potentially," as capable of making "at any time irruption into our ordinary lives. At its lowest, it is only the depository of our forgotten memories; at its highest, we do not know what it is at all" (*Will* 237). It is accessible by hypnosis and manifests itself telepathically. Hopkins turns James's notion of a hidden self (actually a notion that James himself shared with psychologists such as Alfred Binet, author of *On Double Consciousness* and mentioned by Hopkins) into a metaphor of the recovery of "forgotten memories"—the black American's buried African self. She also literalizes the metaphor; at one point Briggs speaks of "the undiscovered country within ourselves—the hidden self lying quiescent in every human soul" (448). Africa is at once the "undiscovered country" and the "hidden self" to which Reuel Briggs finds his way back. This originary self is essentialist, testimony to the contradictions, noted below, that hamper Hopkins's attempts to escape race.

Of One Blood is particularly dramatic proof that James's sponsorship of the unclassified residuum spoke directly to black intellectuals. But Hopkins does not simply use James as a source. Rather, she takes the various strands that make up the intellectual genealogy of double consciousness—its psychological (Binet), philosophical (James), and Africanist (Du Bois) constructions—and weaves them together. And this act of weaving, what amounts to Hopkins's ingenious meditation on intellectual history, is itself represented in the novel. It is present metaphorically, refracted through the entanglements generated by an incest plot that entwines the three main characters and carries the burden of the novel's moral—that we are all "of one blood." In her multiple foregrounding of the fact of mixing, Hopkins seeks to explode the racialist epistemology that grounds Jim Crow: "the slogan of the hour is 'Keep the Negro down!' but who is clear enough in vision to decide who hath black blood and who hath it not? Can anyone tell? No, not one" (607).

But Hopkins undermines the monogenetic argument of her title. As Walter Benn Michaels points out, "one blood is turned into two," for her hero, heroine, and villain all bear a lotus-shaped birthmark "that, despite their whiteness, 'proves' their 'race' and 'descent' from ancient kings of Ethiopia and that guarantees a racial identity no amount of miscegenation can obscure" (Michaels 59–60). Despite pervasive amalgamation, African identity remains pure. But Hopkins's lingering essentialism, her commitment to blood, evident also in the fact that Reuel reigns not by consent but by hereditary right, does not cancel her commitment to ending race. Together both efforts compose Hopkins's antirace race project.

Amalgamation—the fact that "no man can draw the dividing line between the two races"—reverberates without and within *Of One*

Blood. It begins with what inspires her fiction—the late-nineteenth-century effort, of James, Binet, and Du Bois, to loosen the hold of identity logic by opening up the constricted boundaries of the white Western psyche to the alien, to "the subconscious something," in James's phrase (237). All three men hope to blunt the edge of the phobic rationalism that conceives science as a "closed and complete system of truth" (*Will* 222). Instead of the "peremptory denial" that has become the reflex of science frozen in "fixed belief," James urges recognition that "science, like life, feeds on its own decay. New facts burst old rules; then newly divined conceptions bind old and new together" (240, 239, 236).

In creating a novel that concatenates contemporary discourses skeptical of the discrete and bounded, the closed and complete, Hopkins replicates the binding together that James takes as the hallmark of an emancipated science. By the novel's end she has woven a synthesis of universalism and racialism that at once celebrates the races "united" in one blood and raises pride in African consciousness. Our final view of Reuel shows his double stance: he has "returned to the Hidden City" of Telassar (after resolving matters in America) without renouncing Western knowledge—"he spends his days in teaching people all that he has learned in years of contact with modern culture" (621). But Reuel is no missionary uplifting the benighted; earlier he had learned first-hand that "in the heart of Africa was a knowledge of science that all the wealth and learning of modern times could not emulate" (576).

Appropriately, Hopkins's acts of binding or weaving—as subject, theme, and technique—create a hero who is a composite, and not only racially. Briggs blends aspects of James and Du Bois. Like James, Briggs is a charismatic Harvard scholar whose fondness for the wayward and the marginal cuts against the grain of scientific orthodoxy. Like Du Bois, he is a Harvard-educated "Afro-American" (Hopkins's phrase) genius who, in theorizing about double consciousness, wishes neither his American nor his African self to be lost. Briggs finds impossible what Du Bois strives for—the freedom to "be both a Negro and an American . . . without having the doors of Opportunity closed roughly in his face" (*Souls* 365). Briggs knows that passing is the price for his prospering at Harvard. And this cost, as we see from the opening scene, is driving him to suicidal despair. Once rumors of his racial origin are planted, the doors of opportunity close in the United States, and so Briggs joins the expedition to Ethiopia, hoping it will be a temporary solution. At this point he is a universalist, desiring "above all else the well-being of all humanity" (473). He is about to discover his hidden Africanity and thereby redeem his "shame" at having "played the coward's part in hiding his origin" (560). Yet the achievement of redemption turns out to be contingent on becoming a permanent exile; thus Hopkins bleakly implies that in the United States being black and being an intellectual cannot unfold together.

She had drawn this moral three years earlier in *Contending Forces,* where Will Smith, another Du Bois–inspired paragon, a graduate of Harvard and Heidelberg, seeks to establish an alternative to Negro industrial education. Late in the novel he mentions his plans to Dr. Lewis, the Booker T. Washington figure who earlier has recommended that the Negro be content with manual labor and leave "to the white man the superiority of brain and intellect" (251). When Will Smith confides his goal to put black students "on equal terms with men of the highest culture," Lewis scoffs: "Chimerical and quixotic . . . It can't be done" (389). And Smith concedes that he probably will have to build his school "abroad . . . across the water" (389). There is no more mention of his plans, but the novel ends with Will and his family aboard a Cunarder bound for Europe. Thus if Will Smith is to have a career and fulfill his educational mission, escape from America is imperative. And Hopkins has outfitted him accordingly: she describes him as a "wealthy cosmopolitan" of "grace, ease, elegance, and an imposing well-developed intellectuality" (385). Philosophy, she tells us, "was a mania with him" (167).

As we shall see in the next chapter, fiction by Hopkins's contemporaries Griggs, Du Bois, and Chesnutt, depicts the black intellectual not as resourceful or self-possessed in the mode of Will Smith, but as a doomed, enigmatic figure, searching for a place. Unlike the main characters in this group, Reuel Briggs is depicted as a flourishing survivor who finds a place, indeed a throne.[13] But Hopkins has resolved the problem of *black intellectual* at the price of escapist fantasy. Reuel may fulfill his genius only in the "hidden city." However, any hint of compromise is absent when he is crowned King Ergamenes. He reflects that his old "dreams of wealth and ambition" are "about to be realized . . . it seemed the most natural thing in the world to be sitting here among these descendants of the ancient Ethiopians" (570). Yet Briggs might also be rationalizing his exile, a possibility suggested when he wants to settle affairs in America. He realizes that "virtually he was a prisoner" in Telassar (579). To leave he has to obtain special permission from a "Council" and his closest friend must accompany him as "surety for

Reuel's safe return" to the "hidden city" (594). This constraint is symbolized in the crown on Reuel's head, an emblem of black intellect shackled to communal responsibility.

The sense of imprisonment is a sharp edge that lurks within the fantasy of escape without puncturing it, akin to the "shadows" of guilt and moments of melancholy memory that "darken" Reuel's life even on his throne (621). If these intrusions suggest the precariousness of the fantasy, they also affirm its willfulness. It is hard not to concur with one critic's remark (Claudia Tate's) that "Telassar the fantastic underground city seems in part like an external projection of Briggs's desire for suicidal release from his racial anguish" (207). He ultimately assuages the shame of passing in America by burying himself in his Africanity, as if this second effacement atones for the first. Finally, shame and atonement seem to give way to a kind of bliss. To spend the rest of one's days sealed inside the womb-like "hidden city," camouflaged by mountains and swamps, "secure from the intrusion of a world that has forgotten," is to live a fantasy of invisibility, of soothing oblivion, precisely of the sort Briggs has been yearning for since we first saw him in his solitary room (547). Early on it is noted that "in the whole category of live issues" of the day, Briggs is silent on only one—"the Negro problem" (449).

In sum, *Of One Blood* presents two fantasies. The more familiar one is of Pan-African uplift that literalizes the African American recovery of the "undiscovered country" within. But the novel also discloses a latent one—of release from "the Negro problem." While her uplift fable reflects its historical moment (the Pan-African movement had formally begun in 1900), in dramatizing the latent fantasy of release Hopkins's text is prescient. *Of One Blood* is germinal, for it can be considered the seed of antirace race texts all published in the generation after her own: James Weldon Johnson's *The Autobiography of an Ex-Colored Man* (1912, rpt. 1927), Du Bois's *Dark Princess* (1928), Nella Larsen's *Quicksand* (1928), Jessie Fauset's *Plum Bun* (1929), and Wallace Thurman's *Infants of the Spring* (1932). Two later works can be read as a kind of coda to this cluster—Ellison's *Invisible Man* (1952) and Wright's *The Outsider* (1953).

Hopkins's novel harbors a yearning, in Reuel Briggs's early universalist aspirations and later hidden life, that is shared by a number of later black writers: to have black intellectual mean more than race man or woman. The above lineage generates its deepest imaginative energy in the act of contesting, at times even abandoning, the traditional, often heroic, role of the race paragon. While a source of political power and spiritual communion, the role is also a cross to bear. For it requires ceaseless self-vigilance and sacrifice. What spurs rebellion against the obligation of race responsibility is the chance of freedom (however elusive or limited for black people) promised by cultural modernism and urban cosmopolitanism. Most of these characters lead bohemian lives as they struggle, with limited results, for artistic and literary success. At its most unconditional, modern freedom courts the risk of self-annihilation. Death, emotional and literal, marks the denouement of a number of these works.

These antirace race texts can be said to engage creatively the "dilemma of the Negro author." In 1928 James Weldon Johnson defined the dilemma as a set of twin pressures: white America's "hard-set stereotypes . . . as to what the Negro is" and black America's "taboos" erected to police black art that might "betray" the race. The effect was to make black artistry "defensive and exculpatory" as it urgently, if unconsciously, sought white approbation ("Double" 411–412). Black taboos, says Johnson, are "blighting" in their discouragement of "everything but nice literature." Johnson proposes to solve the dilemma by being obedient to neither set of expectations but rather by making "a common audience out of white and black America." While "standing on his racial foundation," the Negro author "must fashion something that rises above race, and reaches out to the universal in truth and beauty" (412). Johnson's dialectic of universal and particular produces an aesthetic experience where race is held in abeyance.

Another way to rise above race is to lift the burden of representation, as James Baldwin described the "necessity thrust" on Richard Wright to be "the representative of some thirteen million people." It is, said Baldwin, "a false responsibility (since writers are not congressmen) and impossible, by its nature, of fulfillment" (*Price* 71). Many have noted the mordant irony in this admonition to Wright, for Baldwin went on to become the foremost intellectual exemplar of his generation while knowing full well the costs of doing so. In vain seemed to be Baldwin's oft-repeated distinction between his intellectual stance as "witness" and his political activism as "spokesman." The burden may be unavoidable, as Toni Morrison suggests: a "black author . . . is at some level *always* conscious of representing one's own race to, or in spite of, a race of readers that understands itself to be 'universal' or race-free" (*Playing* xii).

To be representative depends on taking for granted a "unitary blackness." This is a fiction, as Isaac Julien points out, one required for the business of racial uplift, whose goal is to produce "positive images" or "nice literature" in Johnson's phrase (Julien "Black" 271). This project is an impossible one, notes Julien: "Though it may have the best intentions of redressing balance in the field of representation," the propagation of positive images "is bound to fail as it will never be able to address questions of ambivalence or transgression" (261). The working through of just such questions constitutes the common ground of these antirace race novels.

No one explored questions of ambivalence and transgression more creatively, across more genres, and for a longer time than Du Bois. In 1928 he created what was then unprecedented in black fiction: a hedonistic, black, cosmopolitan intellectual hero. In contemptuous rebellion against the United States, which he regards as provincial in its racism, Matthew Towns travels to Europe as a self-styled "exile," his expatriatism joining him to one of modernism's most glamorous icons. Whether in a Harlem club, where he meets a prostitute with whom he spends an enjoyable night, or suavely sipping tea with an Indian princess at a Berlin café, or excelling in the classrooms of the New York medical school where he is a leading student, Towns embodies the vertiginous class mobility of urban modernity's romance of possibilities. *Dark Princess*, as I will show in Chapter 5, is a fantasy of release on a number of levels, including a liberation from stereotype.

The provincialism that Towns flees is the race leader's lot. In a remarkably candid passage in his autobiography *Dusk of Dawn*, Du Bois calls the race man self-effacing, unselfish, and loyal. Yet, he adds, these very virtues "congeal," making the exemplar "provincial" and embittered, isolated from the "environing race" and a "prisoner" of the group (*Dusk* 651). In Du Bois's life and art the roles of race man and intellectual overlap but are not identical. They jostle against each other, providing a source of creative tension throughout Du Bois's career. He makes this tension the very subject of his two most important works of fiction, "The Coming of John" (1903) and *Dark Princess*.

If Matthew Towns feasts at the banquet of modernity, John Jones is permitted a few crumbs. On a visit to the city from a black college in rural Georgia, the sight of the "streets of New York" "brilliant with moving men" arrests John Jones (*Souls* 525). "He scanned their rich and faultless clothes, the way they carried their hands, the shape of their hats; he peered into the hurrying carriages. Then, leaning back with a

sigh, he said, 'This is the world.' " Later, at the opera house, Wagner's
Lohengrin electrifies his aesthetic consciousness, stirring him to "rise
with that clear music out of the dirt and dust of that low life that had
held him prisoned and befouled" behind the veil, a world of "cringing
and sickening servility" where he is the "slave and butt of all" (527).
But this abruptly ends when he is asked to leave; a Southerner in the
audience objects to his presence. After this humiliation, John resolves,
with a certain fatalism, to accept his "manifest destiny" and fulfill his
promise to return to "the choked and narrow life of his native town"
and become a race man. Yet, as if to preserve his New York epiphany,
John decides that the goal of his race work will be to bring his people
into the modern world. But of course this precipitates hysteria among
white and black. That John's double initiation—into urban modernity
and aesthetic bliss—is abruptly terminated makes clear how precarious
is the black American's relation to these freedoms at the turn of the
century.

A dozen years later the start of the era of black migration North
begins to create the conditions that will make more accessible the romance of urban freedom and the means of attaining it. For the migration brings masses of black people (50,000 to Chicago alone between
1910 and 1920) into the metropolis, the crucible of modernity, the
theater of self-invention. The color line remains but is not static; in
1920 Chicago "it bends and buckles and sometimes breaks," note
Drake and Cayton in *Black Metropolis*. That the line wavers, and even
the "violence that sometimes results, is evidence of democracy at work"
(101).

"She was in a new world and with new people," muses Angela, heroine of *Plum Bun*, referring to the 1920s Greenwich Village milieu
which she comes to know (107). Her comment inadvertently echoes
John Walden's announcement that "we are new people" in Chesnutt's
The House Behind the Cedars (1900).[14] Walden calls himself "new" to
hide his African heritage. But to live his newness, he must pass not only
out of the South but out of the novel, presumably to head North.
Angela too uproots, but her trajectory, not its absence, is the subject
of Fauset's *Plum Bun*. Tired of "discussing the eternal race question"
with her sister and friends, she leaves her native Philadelphia and moves
to a "new world" (67). In New York she passes, inspired by her late
mother's "old dictum . . . 'Life is more important than color' " (333).
A life devoted to art proves the truth of this. In New York, where the
novel unfolds, she lives in bohemian freedom and makes painting her

vocation. Fauset's heroine chooses art as a way to make good on her belief that "the matter of blood seems nothing compared with individuality, character, living" (354). Her choice implies that the freedom of art and culture is founded upon their indifference to "blood." Eventually, spontaneously, she announces her color but continues to pass.

That "the kingdom of culture" is uncolored is a sustaining faith for writers in this lineage. They drew on the rival legacies of the assimilationist Douglass and the Pan-Africanist Crummell, who concurred in the belief that "universality is the kernel of all true civilization" and its products are the common property of all (Crummell *Destiny* 297).[15] The "one thing of real value" that America is teaching the world, says Matthew Towns, is "that ability and capacity for culture is not the hereditary monopoly of the few" but a possibility for the "majority of mankind if they only have a decent chance in life" (*Dark Princess* 26). Kelly Miller, the anti-Bookerite race man and Howard University professor, argued that the key to awakening the power and dignity of black self-reliance is to learn that "primary principles" of knowledge—found in philosophy, mathematics, science, art—"have no ethnic quality." Instead, they are "the common possession" of all who apply them (Miller 275–276).

"Of one blood," a pledge that foresees not only equality but an end to race itself, is an apt title for the mother text of this lineage. The phrase, ubiquitous in sermons by nineteenth-century black preachers, is invoked by William Dean Howells in his famous 1896 review of Paul Laurence Dunbar's first book of poems. Significantly, his "imaginative prophecy" connects common humanity to the domain of art. Howells ventures that "the hostilities and prejudices which had so long constrained his [Dunbar's] race were destined to vanish in the arts; that these were to be final proof that God had made of one blood all nations of men. I accepted them as evidence of the essential unity of the human race" (qtd. Miller 257).[16]

Most race men or women tend to defer talk of "essential unity" or aesthetic education. Their concerns are narrower, more particularist, reflecting their commitment to uplift and to being an exemplar, a "credit to the race." To represent the race requires that one be representative, that is, stand for the whole. Thus representation works by a synecdochic (or identity) logic which unwittingly replicates the ontology of Jim Crow: in caste segregation's master trope of "blood" as identity—the "one-drop" rule—part invariably stands for whole. A logic of substitution structures race representation and Jim Crow to produce homogeneity. That enemy and opponent share the same logic assures a disturbing circularity: racist assumptions and practices are affirmed by the very forces combatting them. (As noted in Chapter 1, an analogous circularity occurs in cultural pluralism, the discourse that aims to champion rather than repress ethnic and racial difference.) Thus considered philosophically, if not historically, the changes we have been tracing—from problem to freak and now to exemplar—are not progressive but only variations on a static condition of objecthood.

Being representative requires repression both outward and inward. Because exemplars are "forever on display," they must be models of "rationality and decorum," not permitted to "make the mistakes of normal men or democratic leaders," in the words of the historian Nathan Huggins. The racial "paragon," says Huggins of Douglass, Washington, and Du Bois, presents himself "as living proof that blacks could perform as citizens in ways that were above reproach" (*Revelations* 212–213, 223). All this makes an exemplar's life profoundly constricting. An additional burden is the uneasy relation between the elite and the mass. This unease is inherent in the notion of the representative; achieving this status, after all, requires not simply being one of the people but being exceptional (213). To inquire into the political basis of this exceptionalism further opens the contradiction: the race leader usually is unelected, and depends on a charismatic rather than democratic or electoral mode of representation. This breeds the belief, says Adolph Reed, that "standard principles of political representation do not apply among Afro-Americans" (*Jackson* 109). In historical context, "the idea of the free-floating race spokesman was a pathological effect . . . specific to the segregation era" (Reed, "What" 32).[17]

"They were me and I was they; that a force stronger than blood made us one" is how James Weldon Johnson describes in his autobiography the awakening of his race consciousness in 1891. But this unity will be belied when he soon notes that "we of the vanguard" look with "despair" at some of the "characteristics of the masses." The vanguard/masses hierarchy makes oneness precarious at best. One of the most distinguished "race men" of his time, Johnson describes this solidarity as a "deepening, but narrowing experience; an experience so narrowing that the inner problem of a Negro in America becomes that of not allowing it to choke and suffocate him" (*Along* 78).

The unnamed narrator of Johnson's *The Autobiography of an Ex-Colored Man* gives vent to the same frustration. He laments that "the ever-present 'Negro question' " has a "dwarfing, warping, distorting influence . . . on each and every colored man in the United States." Johnson's protagonist must see not as a citizen, or a man, "or even a human being, but from the viewpoint of a colored man" (55, 14). Like Du Bois, Johnson turns to the privacy of fiction to explore forbidden impulses of transgression. Racial erasure is Johnson's particular fascination. In recalling the novel's genesis, he spoke of the "exhilaration" of freely creating an experiment in prose fiction masquerading as an autobiography narrated by someone nameless and passing, which he then published anonymously in 1912. Most reviewers in 1912 treated the book as nonfiction. In 1927 Knopf reissued the novel under Johnson's name with an introduction by Carl Van Vechten that (inverting the usual point of an attestation) vouched for its fictive status. In his actual autobiography Johnson admitted, "I did get a certain pleasure out of anonymity" (*Along* 238). Given his crafting of an elaborate maze of imposture, Johnson's is a remark of no small understatement.

But the novel suggests that this pleasure in anonymity exacted a heavy price. To escape the ubiquitous "Negro question," Johnson's fictive solution is to pass. Yet passing is an attenuated option that emerges from the ashes of what he abandons—a plan to translate black vernacular idioms such as ragtime and slave songs into "classical musical form" (108). This cosmopolitan project that would have bridged cultures, classes, and races was to be the narrator's life work. But sustaining it proves as fugitive as the opportunity black novelists have to leave behind stereotypes and to represent "respectable" black people of "culture" (123). Both efforts to enlarge the domain of representation and thus "to give the country something new and unknown" must be deferred. But there is a vanguard, the narrator notes, "striving to break the narrow limits of tradition," and he regards *The Souls of Black Folk* as displaying this innovative energy (123). The brave attempts by Du Bois and others to interrogate racial divisions cast a mocking light on the narrator's submission to them.

By his novel's end the narrator/protagonist's life of successful passing fills him with shame and self-laceration ("I have been a coward, a deserter"). On the final page he recalls the acclaim that greeted Booker T. Washington during a Carnegie Hall address. The Wizard of Tuskegee was impressive "not because he so much surpassed the others [speakers] in eloquence, but because of what he represented with so much earnestness." Next to Washington, the narrator feels "small and selfish" (154). What began for Johnson as a way to achieve an "exhilarating" anonymity free from race representation ends in shame-faced affirmation of its dignity. With solemn biblical finality the ex-colored man recognizes his betrayal of race: "I have sold my birthright for a mess of pottage" (154). Left unmentioned is his other betrayal—of antirace, cosmopolitan projects. Johnson's own life of interracial race work and mastery of multiple art forms, high and popular, resolved and redeemed contradictions that his novel would not.

Despite caving in to a cycle of guilt and atonement, Johnson's experiment in anonymity was lastingly evocative, certainly for Ellison. Given his synthetic, integrative imagination, Ellison absorbs into *Invisible Man* William James (via Wright), Johnson, and Wright. "Irresponsibility is part of my invisibility," declares the narrator, who, we will recall, ends up hibernating in his hole after having been groomed by the Brotherhood to be "the true interpreter of the people . . . the new Booker T. Washington" (14, 307). He has been training for the role ever since his graduation speech on "humility" as the "essence of progress" made him the pride of the black community and the choice to address the leading white citizens. Surviving the bloody humiliation of the "battle royal," he manages to make his scheduled speech on "social responsibility" and wins a prize, a "badge of office" (17, 31). After hearing him lead an impromptu protest rally in Harlem, Brother Jack senses the birth of a new Booker: "he came out from the anonymity of the crowd and spoke to the people," says an admiring Jack, who now has a new pawn (307).

In short, visibility, distinction, responsibility, the coming out from anonymity, are all linked to objecthood, to being the instrument of white power. Invisibility will eventually be the antidote, a form of power that seems mere "irresponsibility" to those invested in keeping blacks tied to fixed identity, to knowing their place. Such fixity Ellison images as "ice," the "emotion-freezing ice which my life had conditioned my brain to produce" (259). And at a pivotal moment of dawning awareness, the ice of " 'self-control,' that frozen virtue, that freezing vice," starts "melting to form a flood" (259–260). Eventually realizing the "possibility of being more than a member of a race," and by the end willing to risk his own humanity, Ellison's protagonist vows that he is "coming out" from underground, though "no less invisible." But "even an invisible man has a socially responsible role to play," he realizes, referring to his vocation as an intellectual, which he has discovered in the act of putting his life down on paper (355, 576, 581).

Thus Ellison revises his earlier equation, ultimately affirming invisibility *as* responsibility. This revision signals his working through to an embrace of ambivalences or "division": "so I denounce and I defend and I hate and I love" (580). Working through ratifies the novel's synthetic, assimilative economy and replicates the narrator's own act of creation. Though invisible man remains in a hole and only says he is coming out, he provides us a glimpse of a possible way to resolve the dilemma of artistic vocation, race responsibility, and freedom conspicuous in the cluster of texts under discussion.

If *Invisible Man* is an affirmative coda, *The Outsider* is a negative one. Wright's novel, published the year after Ellison's, is a demonic Nietzschean work that represents a disturbing limit case; it can stand as the virtual epitaph of this group of antirace race works. In *The Outsider,* Wright's self-declared love of "abandonment, of aloneness," breeds the fantasy of a self-immolating triumph of the intellectual as a figure of radical (and unraced) interiority. "Being a Negro was the least important thing in his life," reflects the outsider, Cross Damon (read Demon), whose "upbringing" has "somewhat shielded him . . . from the more barbaric forms of white racism" (525, 679). His relative indifference to "racial consciousness" affirms Wright's view that "the word Negro in America means something . . . purely social" rather than biological. Or in his starker formulation: "Negroes are Negroes because they are treated as Negroes" (*White Man* 83, 108).

Damon is absorbed in his mental life. Once a devoted student of continental philosophy at the University of Chicago, where "ideas had been his only sustained passion," Damon's is a life of consuming inwardness: "the insistent claims of his own inner life had made him too concerned with himself to cast his lot wholeheartedly with Negroes in terms of racial struggle. Practically he was with them, but emotionally he was not of them . . . his character had been so shaped that his decisive life struggle was a personal fight for the realization of himself . . . What really obsessed him was his nonidentity" (419, 525).

Damon's aesthetic taste reflects his inwardness. He favors "the pure creation" of abstract art that expresses the artist's own projections. "Why let objects master us?" or nature? he says to his friend Eva, a painter, as he affirms her own "nonobjective" art. But Eva is shocked at his love of abstraction. "I'd not have thought that a colored person would like nonobjective art. Your people are so realistic and drenched in life . . . so robustly healthy" (589–590). "*Some* of us," he dryly responds. Having condescended to him, Eva now pities his "aloneness." His solitary passion for the nonrepresentational extends from art to race politics, where Damon refuses the responsibility of racial representation. To these negations, the exchange between Cross and Eva adds yet another—the conundrum of the black intellectual. "They didn't understand me . . . And they shoot what they don't understand," says Damon as he is dying (838).

Yet he has deliberately made himself opaque to others. As a self-styled martyr to his nonidentity, Damon has devised and lived a fantasy of absolute autonomy. He seeks, in short, to become an intellectual unbound not only to race but to anything that would threaten a purity of mental and emotional freedom indistinguishable from a Godlike power of authorial execution. After being presumed dead in a train wreck, he has the opportunity to invent a new life, "like a writer constructing a tale." His willed "homelessness" manifests his "perfect freedom," which he ensures and affirms by multiple acts of murder (456–457). His first killing ensures that his invention will continue. His next murders are unplanned and affirm his exultant sense of Godlike liberty. Like his invented life, Damon's murders are also his works of art, which express his "choosing to make his own world" rather than accept the given one, which he finds a "static dreamworld" (526). Cross Damon never seeks forgiveness ("I'm *innocent*" are two of his last words) for enacting his rigorous project—the "contemptuous repudiation of all the fundamental promises that men live by" (772). Expressed here is the outer limit, the suicidal terminus, from which the texts in this cluster could be said to draw back in fascinated disgust (490).

Nella Larsen's *Quicksand* is most fascinated. Indeed, for most of the novel the opaque Helga Crane lives at the outer limits, only reluctantly recoiling. Like Cross Damon, she is "incapable of containing herself," but her rage does not turn homicidal (110). Helga's tendency is toward "the impetuous discharge of violence" directed at all projects of control (5). *Quicksand* begins with Helga, a striking mulatta aesthete, young and unmarried, abruptly quitting her teaching position at Naxos (read Tuskegee, where Larsen had worked for a year in the nursing school). Its disciplinary regime has turned the school into a "machine . . . cutting all to a pattern . . . it tolerated no innovations, no individualisms" (4). Helga feels herself suffocating under ceaseless talk of "race consciousness," which she finds hypocritical for it conceals an imperative to adopt a uniform code of drabness in clothing and thought as a way to acquire white bourgeois gentility. Disgusted by those who "yapped loudly" of "race pride, and yet suppressed its most delightful manifestations, love of color, joy of rhythmic motion, naive, spontaneous laughter," Helga wishes someone would write "A Plea for Color" (18).

While she despises conventional race uplift as an assimilative project of whitening, Helga's own version of uplift is hardly a corrective affirmation of black pride. Helga is as ambivalent about black people as she is about everything else. Rather, her "plea for color" is at once purely aesthetic and purely racial, founded on her "unanalyzed, driving spirit of loyalty to the inherent racial need for gorgeousness" (18). Her racial need for the gorgeous produces in Helga anarchic passion for uncensored excess. Thus her own plea for color finds expression not in solidarity but in moments of imagined self-exposure. Helga regards herself as an "obscene sore," an "ugly mutilated creature" on the immaculate "clean white linen" surface that race uplift requires (20, 29, 22). She wonders if there is "some peculiar lack in her," what the Dean of Naxos calls a "protective immunity, a kind of callousness" that productive members of "every ordinary community" possess (20). The Dean has inadvertently described precisely what Helga's "plea for color" wars against—the bleached, bounded, fortified structure of repression that produces identity. Naxos is a factory in the business of reproducing that structure as racial exemplarity.

If anything rules Helga it is an "unreason in which all values were distorted or else ceased to exist" (4). Hence she finds intolerable whatever imposes order and coherence and is addicted to "aimless strolling" among crowded city streets, moving in circles like the drifting, "tremulous clouds" above her, spun by desire's amoral oscillations.[18] Perhaps her life is most accurately described as ruled by a "vagrant primitive groping," a phrase used to describe the feeling she arouses in others (95). Helga's gropings are primitive because so intensely immersed in the present moment of doing. Her gropings are not in the service of survival but for their own sake: they are implacable and instinctive, like movements of a "jungle creature." This phrase comes to her after she experiences the delirium of a Harlem jazz club. Dancing there brings a pleasure of release: the music makes her feel "blown out, ripped out, beaten out . . . The essence of life seemed bodily motion" (59). What may be most compelling about Helga is the degree to which she submits to this loss of control; though she is ashamed of it at times, and frustrated by its "uncontrollable violence," it moves her, no matter how destructive the consequences.

After having scorned both the black folk and the bourgeoisie as without aesthetic taste, Helga discovers the "irresistible ties of race" (92). In short order, and with volition supplied by the blind force of a rainstorm, she meets and marries a black Baptist preacher, moves back to the hated rural South, and bears four children in three years. She is last seen depleted and exhausted. The ties of race, in other words, ensnare the nearly illegible Helga in the plainly readable plot of return. But Larsen encases her in a return-to-roots saga replete with tragic mulatta trappings not to validate these tropes but to highlight Helga's estrangement from any prefabricated structure of meaning. Although her second tour in the South is not as race rebel but as race leader (the preacher's wife), she remains as enigmatic and bizarre to others and herself as she was at Naxos. At the end, bedridden, still defiant, vowing to leave, Helga finds it "pleasant to think about freedom and cities" (135). Before she is brought low in the South, Helga's anarchism makes her a descendant of Cross Damon. What propels their furious passage is, as Wright says of his outsider, "a sharp sense of freedom that had somehow escaped being dulled by intimidating conditions. Cross had never really been tamed" (774). They both live the "frightened ecstasy of the unrepentant" (457).[19]

One striking quality of these works as a cluster is that they disrupt some of the alignments first created by those embroiled in the fiercely contested literary politics of the Harlem Renaissance. Such alignments should be viewed skeptically. For, as in any literary marketplace, rivalry promotes distortion and exaggeration among those jockeying for position. Yet, unfortunately, critics and historians have tended to take these boundaries at face value, and hence they remain in place. The easiest battle line to draw was generational: for reasons good and bad, Du Bois and Johnson, as senior race men, often were condescended to or disparaged by younger intellectuals like Thurman, Hurston, and Hughes.[20] But the major boundary in relation to which authors and texts were situated was the black bourgeoisie, perhaps because, historically, it has been the arena where racial anxieties about authenticity, often in the form of citizenship and suffrage disputes, are played out.

As Ann duCille has cogently argued, our own cultural moment, like earlier ones, privileges the vernacular and constructs " 'authentic' blacks [as] southern, rural, and sexually uninhibited. 'Middle-class,' when applied to black artists and their subjects, becomes pejorative . . . less than authentically black" (71). These dichotomies, duCille notes, have especially stunted critical understanding of Fauset and Larsen, whose works too often are reduced to symptoms of apolitical bourgeois gentility. This reductionism was apparent early on. In Wallace Thurman's sweeping judgment of 1927, Fauset's fiction, like *The New Negro* anthology and much else produced during the "Negro art fad," was written to "prove to the American white man" that blacks were also cultivated. This vindicationist appeal was "soothing" to black "self-esteem and stimulating to his vanity" ("Negro Artists" 111–112).

The cluster of texts we have been examining tell a different story from Thurman's. These works make visible that, from various class positions and across generations, writers were launching powerful, inescapably political critiques of the received, genteel images of black (literary and self-) representation. Larsen's *Quicksand* savagely mocks the plot of rural return, and Fauset's *Plum Bun* is an anti-tragic mulatta urban romance. Both are written from within the bourgeoisie but are hardly acts of class solidarity. Rather, these authors, like Thurman, seek to participate in the interracial intellectual culture of urban modernity.

Thus Fauset in *Plum Bun* makes passing itself less a betrayal of race than a mode of modernist being, a version of Greenwich Village Nietzschean individualism, a "joke upon custom and tradition" (108). And it is a joke whose spirit is shared by Angela's bohemian Village circle, in which the New Woman ideal presides. A feminist friend, for instance, boasts that "there is a great deal of the man about me," and she refuses to "let her femininity stand in the way of what she wants" (105). Mixing gender roles, destabilizing racial markings: both are modes of modern freedom that permit one to "live . . . life as an individualist" (207). Angela views passing not as "inherently wrong" but instead as a "joke" dependent on context (332). And ending passing is not an inherent good. When Fauset's heroine opts late in the novel to announce her color publicly, it is spontaneous, a "whim" to expose an injustice done to a black friend. Rather than now lead a "black" life, Angela will enjoy "the benefits of casual whiteness in America when no great issue was at stake" (333). Her decision consorts with her distrust of "grand gestures" of renunciation, whether of passing or of outing. "Casual whiteness" nicely imparts the dismissal of authenticity which is her answer to those who would make color "the one god . . . to whom you could sacrifice everything" (333, 44).[21]

"I'm sick of discussing the Negro problem . . . I'm sick of whites who think I can't talk about anything else, and of Negroes who think I shouldn't talk about anything else" (215). This is Raymond Taylor, the voice closest to Wallace Thurman's in *Infants of the Spring*. A scourge of uplift, Thurman was a self-styled bohemian aesthete who made a frontal assault on philistinism black and white. Apart from his acid tone, Thurman's attitude is not far from that of the elders—Johnson and Du Bois—whom he devoted much of his brief literary career seeking to outrage. When Raymond, who hopes to be a "Nietzschean," says he wants also to lose "racial identity as such" and "do something memorable in literature," he articulates the spirit of Johnson's haut bourgeois "passing" novel, Du Bois's depiction in *Dark Princess* of the private life of an international power elite, and Fauset's and Larsen's urban fiction (145, 200).

What is Thurman's own is his corrosive contempt. Dorothy West notes that he was "equally hard on the nationalists and miscegenists, but he had no theory which he could substitute for those which he rejected" (220). Complementing his refusal to racialize the aesthetic is his rejection of all standard political options, right, left, and center, be it "wholesale flight back to Africa or a wholesale allegiance to Communism or a wholesale adherence" to NAACP integrationism. "Individuality is what we should strive for. Let each seek his own salvation" (59, 145, 240).[22] In his novel he saddles his cast of black intellectuals with his own brilliance and frustrations. Raymond's friend Paul Arbian is the particular vehicle for Thurman's fears and also idealizations. A light-skinned bisexual aesthete ("I think that Oscar Wilde is the greatest man that ever lived"), Paul "sits around helpless, possessed of great talent, doing nothing, wishing he were white, courting the bizarre" (24, 59). The novel concludes with Arbian's major work: an elaborate suicide ritual. Donning a "crimson mandarin robe," wrapping his head in a "batik scarf," he slashes his wrists with Chinese dirks in the bath. The overflowing tub soaks to illegibility the manuscript of his only novel (282–283).

All dressed up and no place to go: Thurman's final tableau sees no way out save the art of death. Paul is proof of Raymond's theory that "the more intellectual and talented Negroes of my generation are among the most pathetic people in the world today" (225). Given that Paul articulates a number of his creator's fondest beliefs, Thurman's bitter self-contempt here is striking. Regarding himself as a "citizen of the world," Paul, like Raymond, mocks the call that the "young Negro artist must go back to his pagan heritage for inspiration." "I'm not an African," says Paul, "I'm an American and a perfect product of the melting pot" (24, 236, 224, 238). This articulates Thurman's belief in the compatibility among fin-de-siècle decadence, European modernism, and multi-ethnic America.

Dorothy West calls Thurman, who drank himself to death at thirty-four, the "most symbolic figure" of the Harlem Renaissance (227). But it is hard to say just what he symbolized. Rage and frustration certainly, but who or what was the target? Was it the patronizing whites and blacks who made it impossible, in Raymond's words, to surmount racial identity and be acclaimed for "our achievements"? Or was his bitterness also directed at himself, the result of realizing that one obstacle to achieving the deracialized ideal he aspired to was his own inability to believe in it. Perhaps he could not quite trust in Du Bois's "kingdom of culture," which required that one stop believing the old genteel lie that intellectual heritage was the private property of the white European and the Protestant American.

Thurman's terminal individualism stands in stark opposition to group membership, in which the individual's capacity to choose or devise affiliations is discouraged, for one lives representatively, "expressing in everything one does the spirit or essence of one's race."[23] Booker T. Washington, of course, was the exemplar's exemplar—a leader transparently at one with the group. So seamless and sanitized was the life of this paragon that an offstage Washington is hard to imagine. But Du Bois did imagine it, in a remarkable passage from the second volume of his *Black Flame* trilogy of autobiographical novels (1959). As he does throughout the trilogy, Du Bois blends historical fact and fictional rendering.

The narrator reconstructs the night in 1911 when Washington was chased down and beaten on a New York City street by a white man who was convinced Washington was making an assignation with a white woman. Since Washington was attacked near a red-light district, rumors flourished that he had been attempting to visit a brothel. Du Bois was certain the rumors were true.[24] Thinking back to 1914, the narrator notes that as "the world lapsed into universal murder," Booker Washington "lost his grip on complete reality" (*Mansart* 34). Always a lonely man, "he had no recreations; no field of escape. For fifteen years he had been acclaimed but also cruelly attacked and blamed. Of the thousands whom he met he really knew few and believed in fewer. He was tense and full of fears and suspicions. He had few close friends and did not trust even them." Wandering alone in New York one night after a speech, "suddenly he wanted the companionship of women. He wanted to sit beside somebody he did not fear, somebody who was not spying on him, who had no complaints . . . [who] could not take him to task for not helping all the black folk of the world" (35). He fondly recalls an earlier visit: "it was a small gay group . . . it was so quiet and homelike."

This is perhaps the most sympathetic portrayal of Washington that Du Bois ever wrote.[25] Surely, not a small amount of self-projection suffuses his entry into Booker's psyche. It brings to life Du Bois's own sharp sense of confinement in the role of exemplar. But, most strikingly, it reveals that the burden of exemplarity is so heavy because it is bound up with the burden of masculinity. Women become a realm of freedom, a "field of escape." In imagining a scene in which the embattled male warrior is soothed by maternal/erotic tenderness, Du Bois suggests the primal fantasy that nourishes his own desire for release from race work. Matthew Towns, the hero of the novel that dramatizes this desire, is not a warrior but rather an aesthete, one willing to cede power of his own and stand to the side as his lover, an Indian princess, triumphantly takes the public stage. For Du Bois, in sum, the fantasy of abandoning race responsibility, whether mediated through his vision of Washington or in *Dark Princess,* seems inseparable from surrendering the discipline of masculinity.[26]

Du Bois's glimpse into the brothel, then, finds not only a sexist space of male privilege. As male armor is loosened, defenses relax, and an unconscious miming of the feminine occurs. Something of Du Bois's vicarious identification with the feminine as freedom is evident in his admiring response to Larsen's Helga Crane in a review of *Quicksand.* His response is, in a sense, anticipated in the text, in the Naxos Dean's reaction to Helga. Her relative indifference to the repressions that identity demands, her attraction to urban pleasures of "circling aimlessly" and drifting, make her powerfully seductive to those, like the Dean, who have renounced such freedom and have submitted to the Naxos machine's "ruthlessly cutting all to a pattern." The Dean, proud of his "protective immunity," nevertheless feels "sheer delight" at "mere proximity to Helga," for she arouses "a vagrant primitive groping toward something shocking and frightening to the cold asceticism of his reason" (95). This locates the source of Helga's power in her "shocking" contempt not simply for imposed "pattern" but for rationalism's fear of unmastered experience.

Du Bois admired Helga's experiment; after all, in her revolt against

Naxos she in effect carries on his own fight against the "Tuskegee machine." But, ironically, Du Bois erects Helga into an exemplar. This is not to say that he calls her a tragic mulatta. Quite the opposite: Du Bois's reading is adamantly (and refreshingly) anti-tragic. He extols Helga as "still master of her whimsical, unsatisfied soul" even when she sinks. "She never will utterly surrender to hypocrisy and convention." But then he typifies her: Helga is "typical of the new, honest, young fighting Negro woman—the one on whom 'race' sits negligibly and Life is always first . . . White folk will not like this book" (*Book Reviews* 114). Evidently Du Bois found so compelling what Helga embodies—the fantasy of release from race into life—that he ignored the extremity and risk of her primitivism and turned her, in effect, into an antirace race woman. Thus she scorns obligation, overrides preordained categories, and eludes white folks' stereotypes. As Du Bois remarks, this makes her a threat.

If Du Bois is guilty of idealizing Helga, not least because he identifies with her, his canny sense of her importance is undeniable. Du Bois's Helga Crane, antirace race woman, is a virtual Dreyfusard intellectual whose "antipolitical politics" assert the right "to transgress the most sacred values of the collectivity," including racial uplift (Bourdieu "Corporatism" 101). Du Bois's response to Larsen's novel is an implicit tribute to the distinctive power and opportunity of the black female intellectual and indirectly suggests why black women writers are conspicuous in opening up the field of endeavor to "Life."

Wallace Thurman's friend Zora Neale Hurston directly suggests why when she speaks of herself as becoming the "eternal feminine" as a condition of being unraced (829). Belonging "to no race nor time," Zora the "eternal feminine" dubs herself at such moments "cosmic Zora." She trumps everyone by expressing a fantasy of release that leaves behind both Race and Life to embrace the universe: "the stuff of my being is matter, ever changing, ever moving, but never lost; so what need of denominations and creeds . . . I am one with the infinite and need no other assurance" (764). Du Bois would probably envy this exuberant declaration of nonidentity, what in *Dark Princess* he calls "divine anarchy."

Hurston scorned "Race Champions" for obstructing the freedom of artistic creation. "Can the black poet sing a song to the morning? Upsprings the song to his lips but it is fought back." In Hurston's scenario what intrudes is the Negro past. The poet "mutters, 'Ought I not be singing of our sorrows? That is what is expected of me and I shall be considered forgetful of our past and present. If I do not some will even call me a coward. The one subject for a Negro is the Race and its sufferings and so the song of the morning is choked back. I will write of a lynching instead.' So the same old theme, the same old phrases get done again to the detriment of art" (908). The effect of the dominance of "Race Champions" "has been to fix activities in a mold that precluded originality and denied creation in the arts" (909).[27]

Hurston has Du Bois and Johnson (among others) in mind when she lambastes the "Race Man" in "Art and Such" (1938), the essay quoted above, and, more famously, in her autobiography *Dust Tracks on a Road* (1942). As is characteristic, Hurston's mockery exaggerates to dramatize her own salutary insouciance. "I cannot accept responsibility for thirteen million people," she remarks, explaining why she refuses the "solace of easy generalization" (*Dust* 238–239). But her own scathing estimates of "Race Champions" show her dependence on precisely this solace. If taken at face value, her generalizations make it hard to discern that Johnson and Du Bois might well have concurred with much of her own critique, if not its caustic tone. What they probably would have asked for was a bit more empathy. After all, they were antirace race men who had to explore their ambivalences from within an immanent position, whereas "cosmic Zora" flew free of any impediments.

Du Bois would certainly agree about the risks to art posed by race responsibility. We will see that he devotes a key essay of the twenties, "Criteria of Negro Art" (1926) to negotiating the relation between artistic freedom and race struggle. And *Dusk of Dawn,* published two years before *Dust Tracks,* is a work that not only addresses the frustrations inherent in race representation but also devises strategies to mitigate them. In sum, it makes great sense that Du Bois and Hurston have much to say to each other, not least because pragmatism and Boasian anthropology influenced them both.

But silence has largely reigned between Du Bois and Hurston, abetted by literary history's uncritical acceptance of the combative polemics of the Harlem Renaissance as definitive. But the central obstacle to fuller, more integrated knowledge is that conventional African American literary history often reflects and enforces the unexamined assumptions that racial authenticity is the standard of value and the black bourgeoisie its negation. What this binary tends to leave out is *black intellectual,* the unclassified residuum whose telling is this book.

3

Black Intellectuals and Other Oxymorons: Du Bois and Fanon

he goal of the "American Negro" is to be a "co-worker in the kingdom of culture" (*Souls* 365). Thus at the beginning of *The Souls of Black Folk* Du Bois challenges Booker T. Washington's dominion of utilitarian toil. But Du Bois's larger aim is to "make it possible for a man to be both a Negro and an American without being cursed" (365). Becoming a "co-worker in the kingdom of culture" secures this possibility in a paradoxical but decisive way: by making claims of particular identity, be they racial or national, Negro or American, irrelevant. The "kingdom of culture" has neither color nor country. Thus to the extent that African Americans are striving to "rend the Veil" of segregation they aspire to be "co-workers in the kingdom."[1] Du Bois typically couched the struggle for equal rights in universalist terms: "Our enemies," he wrote in 1906, "triumphant for the present, are fighting the stars in their courses. Justice and humanity must prevail" (*Reader* 369).

Les Intellectuels of 1898 heroically affirmed what Du Bois himself was seeking—ethical and cultural ideals unbounded by nation or race. That same year Du Bois spoke enthusiastically of how technological modernity dissolves boundaries in creating a transnationalism that makes "life broader." "For the first time in history," he told Fisk graduates, "there is one standard of human culture as well in New York as in London, in Capetown as in Paris, in Bombay as in Berlin" (*Writings* 831). He added: "Is not this, then, a century worth living in?" If the "problem" of the twentieth century is the "problem of the color line," its amelioration would seem to lead (at least in part) to the freedom to enjoy cosmopolitan, international modernity. John Jones, in the penultimate chapter of *The Souls,* tastes this freedom and in a sense dies of it. And Du Bois warns the Fisk graduates, as we shall see, that their relation to the new century will be fraught with peril if they fail to develop strategies that will take the ambiguity of their position—still within the veil while seeking to rend it—into account.

Du Bois's theorizing of the black intellectual as an antirace race figure was and is usually ignored or overshadowed by his simultaneous and overlapping work of creating a "talented tenth" of race men.[2] Thus to link the universal and black intellectual sounds discordant, as strange as asserting that the souls of black folk are uncolored or that Du Bois understands *black intellectual* as an oxymoron. The arguments for each of these assertions organize this chapter into two parts. In the first I construct historical and thematic contexts, including a reading of Du Bois's famous collision with Washington as an instance of a larger historical pattern in the late nineteenth century both in the West and in West Africa, a pattern that reveals the social role of the intellectual as founded on a dream of deracinated freedom, a severing of roots.

This severance has rarely, if ever, been enacted and articulated more strenuously than in the life and work of Frantz Fanon. Against origins and starting from them, Fanon and Du Bois fashion a performative cosmopolitanism that anticipates the contemporary moment of postidentity.[3] The extremity of Fanon's turn from Negritude to universalism sets in relief Du Bois's own efforts to negotiate the racial particular and the unraced universal. In moving beyond authenticity, they both displace the originary Cartesian subject by deriving identity from action. In Fanon this shift is analogous to his plea that anti-colonial nationalism move rapidly from national consciousness (preoccupied with who people are) to political and social consciousness (focused on people acting in relation to others).[4]

The contexts developed in the first half of the chapter situate the subject of the second half—how a figure who had been deemed a freak of nature requiring containment (at least since the Phillis Wheatley tribunal of 1773) managed to emerge as a social category. The emergence of black literary intellectuals depended on their devising an aesthetic of deferral, vagueness, and open margin, modes of literary representation that simultaneously became political strategies of denaturalization in a society where racist stereotypes reigned serenely as "Nature."

That the souls of black folk are uncolored seems flatly contradicted by the fact that Du Bois is the father of the black soul movement. But *The Souls of Black Folk* gives a more complicated answer. It is double, like everything in Du Bois. Within Jim Crow America's color line, within the "Veil of Race," black people are judged by their skins and not by their souls; their lives often grow "choked and deformed" (*Souls* 510). But "above the Veil," in the "kingdom of culture," souls walk "uncolored," enjoying "freedom for expansion and self-development" (509, 437).[5] Faith that this freedom will one day "rend the Veil" constitutes the very "meaning" of the sorrow songs of the slaves. These ancestral voices, the greatest expression of American art, says Du Bois, herald "a truer world" where "men will judge men by their souls and not by their skins" (544). In *The Souls,* then, Du Bois sets himself a double project: he works both within and beyond the veil, celebrating the "Negro soul" in the former, while preparing black Americans for the "chance to soar" "above the Veil" where the "sovereign human soul" expands, protected by "the centres of culture" (365, 437–438).

The fact that Du Bois tends to be confined to the familiar role of talented-tenth race activist within the veil attests to the presiding ideology of authenticity. It anchors identity to an immutable race or category as decisively as the one-drop rule of white supremacists, and it makes paramount the essentialist question of who and what counts as truly black. Even Frederick Douglass's attempt at an answer is dictated by the question's constricting terms. Douglass remarked of Martin Delany, his one-time *North Star* colleague and rival: I "thank God for making me a man simply; but Delany always thanks God for making him a *black man*" (qtd. Harding 149). A measure of Du Bois's significance is that he in effect positions himself outside the Delany and Douglass polarities. In a characteristic self-representation he boasts of his Negro, French, and Dutch ancestry (and adds: "thank God! no 'Anglo-Saxon' ") (*Darkwater* 9). By flaunting his own hybridity, his cosmopolitan multiplicity, he renders incoherent a need to be true to a prior essence—be it abstract humanism or unalloyed blackness. Neither "a man simply," nor only a black man, Du Bois exceeds categories.

Du Boisian hybridity is indifferent to white or black fantasies of purity; indeed, the famous start of *The Souls* stages what could be called a primal scene of inauthenticity. African American vision is forever mediated, "born with a veil" and "gifted with second sight" in an American world that yields one "no true self-consciousness" (364).[6] The impossibility of true self-consciousness—the "sense of always looking at oneself through the eyes of others," in Du Bois's phrase—would become normative, part of the self's ontology, for the pragmatist psychologist George Herbert Mead. Since 1900 he had been developing a socialized conception of self that has some striking affinities with Du Bois's formulation. However, Mead's mediated self is not racialized, whereas the Du Boisian self is double because it perceives itself "through the eyes of [white] others" who look on in "amused contempt and pity" (364).[7]

The veil of racial difference descends upon Du Bois not as the implacable verdict of biological determinism but because of the chance presence of the "tall newcomer" whose rejection of Du Bois's greeting card ignites—"with a certain suddenness"—his race consciousness (364). Once he has been "shut out," Du Bois's first concern is not to affirm his racial identity but to maximize his capacity for decisive action. He rejects both "sycophancy" and "hatred" as different forms of stasis. Du Bois seeks a "better and truer self" but does not desire to dissolve his "double self" into unitary identity. His priority is to resolve the paralysis of black agency, of "turning hither and thither in hesitant and doubtful striving," by making it possible to be black and American (365).[8] How to maintain this doubleness is the explicit question, one itself doubled by what Du Bois calls "ever an unasked question": how is it possible to be both black and a literary intellectual (363)? To devise an answer in 1900 would require carving out an interstitial space within a social order partitioned by color, where the dominant class had "epidermalized Being" (Charles Johnson *Oxherding Tale* 52).

But "my black skin is not the wrapping of specific values," Fanon would remark half a century later, challenging the equation produced by an ideology of authenticity (*Black Skin* 227). Fanon reveals how authenticity is wielded as a weapon of colonial control that propagates fantasies of regression, through stereotypes and nostalgia, twin devices of imperialism. They seal Fanon in a "crushing objecthood" that weighs him down with a triple burden of responsibility—for his body, race, and ancestors. When he examines his objecthood, he finds it composed of an internalized montage of stereotypes: "I discovered," says Fanon, "my blackness, my ethnic characteristics; and I was battered down by tom-toms, cannibalism, intellectual deficiency, fetishism, racial defects, slave-ships" (*Black Skin* 109, 112). Colonizers circulate such imagery of the authentic while encouraging "the traditions of the indigenous society," defending "the native style," and urging intellectuals to "go native" and busy themselves preserving an "arrested image" of primitive black artistic genius (*Wretched* 220–221, 242). Du

Bois, in *Color and Democracy* (1945), notes the colonialist strategy of "sudden interest . . . in the preservation of native culture" and the vernacular as a way to keep the natives from "modern cultural patterns" (42). The production of nostalgia, says Fanon, helps distract intellectuals from joining with the colonized in the present, "that fluctuating movement" and "zone of occult instability," that houses the "seething pot out of which the learning of the future will emerge" (*Wretched* 225, 227).[9]

To live in the present demands a radical act of deracination. And Fanon's career compels because it actually met the demand. His life of willed exile and self-invention may be unprecedented; Albert Memmi has judged it "impossible" in its lavish indifference to origins or limits, be they of homeland or of "blood" (Memmi 9). Fanon's most famous books conclude with pleas for upheaval. *Black Skin, White Masks* urges a "leap" that would introduce "invention into existence" (229). And in *The Wretched of the Earth* his goal is nothing less than establishing a "fundamentally different set of relations between men . . . a new humanity" that will come to define a "new humanism" and a "new man" (246–247, 316). Despising the pseudo-universalism of European humanism, which functioned to disguise imperialism, Fanon embraced "the universality inherent in the human condition" (*Black Skin* 10).

Admittedly, to stress the universalist commitments of Du Bois and Fanon may seem surprising, even perverse, in the face of substantial racial grounds of comparison. To traverse them quickly: declaring in *The Souls of Black Folk* that the Negro is "sort of a seventh son" with "a message for the world," Du Bois reaffirms the romantic racialism he had inherited from Hegel, Herder, and Alexander Crummell, and becomes the father of the international black soul movement. Celebrating the beauty of blackness and black African culture, he helped create Pan-African solidarity as a defense against what he called the "logic of the modern colonial system" that fueled the global aims of European imperialism (Du Bois *Reader* 677).[10] In the thirties, *The Souls* served as a founding text of the black Francophone Negritude movement of Senghor and Cesaire. The latter was an influential teacher of Fanon, who, in turn, was the posthumous mentor of black power nationalists in America.

But the contemporary turn from identity politics has made it easier to discern that neither Du Bois nor Fanon regarded nationalism or Negritude as an endpoint or a fixed identity; instead they were moments, critical stages, to be worked through to reach a telos of the universal. This perspective sponsors a raceless society without erasing the historical experience of racism that unites all black and colonized people. In other words, Du Bois and Fanon would decline Sartre's Hegelian invitation, in his seminal essay on Negritude, to look "to the end of particularism in order to find the dawn of the universal" ("Black Orpheus" 329).[11] In contrast, they insist on a dialectic that preserves the interplay of universal and particular rather than liquidating them in an optimistic teleology. Fanon, for instance, speaks of a "two-fold emerging": "it is at the heart of national consciousness that international consciousness lives and grows" (*Wretched* 248).[12] And Du Bois describes the battle for equality as waged on three fronts simultaneously: it is "not for ourselves alone but for all true Americans" as well as for "the divine brotherhood of all men" (*Reader* 367, 369).

At the start of *Black Skin, White Masks,* Fanon describes his project as "nothing short of the liberation of the man of color from himself," the exchange of racial for human identity (8, 10). For Fanon, the native intellectual turns toward the possibility of this freedom when he discovers that he "cannot go forward resolutely unless he first realizes the extent of his estrangement" from the people (*Wretched* 226). Thus he resists the plunge into authenticity encouraged by imperialists and grasps the paradox that achieving transparent oneness with the masses is not a basis for revolution but a "blind alley," ending in a "banal search for exoticism" (220–221).

Fanon replaces authenticity with the imperative of making oneself a "new man" in the present. Invention is especially urgent because the colonized black intellectual embodies a contradiction in terms in a white society where the "Negro is fixated at the genital; or at any rate he has been fixated there" (*Black Skin* 165). To whites the sight of a "black man who quotes Montesquieu" is anomalous and alarming : he "had better be watched" (35). Surveillance is required because the black intellectual seems a walking category mistake, one that eludes the control of stereotype. As colonialism's prime instrument of identity, stereotype serves to disavow the threat of difference by reactivating, as Homi Bhabha points out, the primal fantasy of fetishism—the subject's desire to restore "originality" and "pure origin" to an object and thereby arrest the play of difference (Bhabha 75). In this light, the black intellectual is a threatening oxymoron, immune to the stereotype's regressive fantasy of authenticity.

Significantly, when Fanon does invoke the possibility of moving beyond the fetish of stereotypes to reach "authentic" exchange between white and black it is on condition that both renounce authenticity's flight to origins and identity: "The Negro is not. Any more than the white man. Both must turn their backs on the inhuman voices which were those of their respective ancestors in order that authentic communication be possible" (*Black Skin* 231). Fanon inverts the trajectory of authenticity by defetishizing it and stripping it of foundations, thus (unwittingly) reanimating the crisis of origins that perennially attends the figure of the intellectual. To this motif we will briefly turn.

When the radical French nationalist Maurice Barrès hurled the imprecation *déracinés* at the intellectuals during the Dreyfus Affair, his indictment was historically resonant. For the charge of deracination names the primal sin of the intellectuals. And not just Western intellectuals. The people who have been called the first "literate intellectuals of early colonial Africa" were the famous "recaptives" or "liberated Africans" of Sierra Leone's Freetown on the coast of West Africa, those whom Basil Davidson has called a "unique community." Except in neighboring Liberia, "there was no other people like them." Rescued by British naval patrols raiding slave ships bound for the Americas (from 1807 to the 1860s), recaptives had been saved from a life of enslavement yet "at the same time, they were now cut sharply adrift from their own homeland cultures . . . They had to build a new life for themselves" (Davidson 25–27). This included devising a new language called Creole that also became their collective name. Upper-class Creoles became famous for the degree to which they modeled themselves on their saviors. Their literary culture was Anglophilic, and they lived "with as much Europeanized elegance as they could afford," favoring heavy British woolens, collars, and high hats even though they were unsuited to the climate (Fyfe 40).[13] Their weddings were particularly grand and ostentatious displays, and a cult of the dandy flourished in Freetown.

Such behavior outraged African cultural nationalists like Edward Blyden, who worked with Crummell in Liberia and lived in Sierra Leone in the early 1870s. Although himself the "most Westernized of West Africans," in the words of his biographer, Blyden's object of special animus was the "Europeanized Africans" who populated Freetown. He sought to Africanize the recaptives, including a failed attempt at creating a Dress Reform Society. Condemning Creoles as "unnatural and artificial," he called them "apes" and parasites (Lynch 242; Blyden 224; Spitzer 113). Blyden's friend Booker T. Washington would have heartily concurred. In regarding the intellectual as *contra naturam*,

Washington sought to stigmatize his arch rival Du Bois, one of the "artificial" men of the New England colleges.

Those colleges sponsored the Brahmin ideal of one's civic responsibility to maintain, in William James's words, the "critical sense, the sense for ideal values" in a democracy that is permanently "on its trial," always capable of a "self-poisoning" that would enthrone mediocrity and greed (*Writings* 1245). Du Bois agreed; in 1903 he warned that a democracy without the college-bred would lack "yeast," an image James repeats in calling the college-bred "the yeast-cake for democracy's dough" (Du Bois *Writings* 847; James *Writings* 1247). In his 1898 Fisk commencement address Du Bois praised college for providing "a glimpse of the higher life, the broader possibilities of humanity" (827).

In depicting a black aristocracy in his Fisk speech, Du Bois avoids racial essentialism by creating a dialectic of the universal and particular. He enunciates "three universal laws"—of work, sacrifice, and service—that "in each age" differ in application (830). You will misunderstand the age and risk despair, Du Bois warns the Fisk graduates, if these universals are left abstract, not threaded with racial particularity. Only a double perspective balances the fact that late-nineteenth-century modernity is unprecedented in its "human opportunity" and "in the broadness of its conception of humanity" with another fact: that as "American Negroes" "upon the threshold of the twentieth century," his listeners live in a "strange environment and unusual conditions"— the medieval caste system called Jim Crow (831). A productive life will depend on negotiating the universal through the particular and vice versa. Du Bois concludes by reminding Fisk graduates to cherish their membership in a "dark, historic race" and in "that vast kingdom of culture that has lighted the world from its infancy and guided it through bigotry and falsehood and sin" (830, 840). To live in the ideal of "service" makes attainment of the "broadest, deepest self-realization" simultaneously the way to make life "broad and full and free for all men and all time" (832).

Du Bois's dialectic, in short, does not make culture a code word for Anglo-Saxonism. This equation is made, understandably, by the recaptives of Sierra Leone, and, ironically, by their would-be redeemer, Blyden. And it is made also by William Ferris, the Yale- and Harvard-educated, fiercely anti-Bookerite, itinerant black intellectual whose nearly thousand-page work *The African Abroad* (1913) takes as its frontispiece a photograph of a splendid reception at the governor's manse in Freetown. Ferris's book articulates what the photograph announces—his sense of affinity with the refined Anglophilia of Sierra Leone's Creole upper class. Despising the term "Negro," Ferris pleads for "Negrosaxon" as a replacement (*African* 1: 297). His neologism is meant to stress the mixed blood of a majority of American blacks, their lack of "ethnological integrity" and nationalist spirit. But the word most clearly suggests Ferris's Anglophilia, which ultimately vitiates his obsessively repeated point (and plea) that the Negro is a "full-fledged man" and demands to be treated as a human being (329).

It turns out that for Ferris *human being* has not a universal reference but a racial one—Anglo-Saxon—and the Negrosaxon "must become a black white man." Then "he can hope to be made over into the image of God" (304). One reason Du Bois does not equate humanity and whiteness is that he considers America's "religion of whiteness" to be little more than a desperate disavowal of the fact that the country is miscegenated, born of a "blood-brotherhood" between black and white (*Writings* 924; *Souls* 545). This leads him at the end of *The Souls of Black Folk* to scoff at Protestant America's pride of possession: "Your country? How came it yours? Before the Pilgrims landed we were here" (545). With "mingled . . . blood" his premise, Du Bois erects the "ideal of human brotherhood" as his telos.

Ferris's solution—becoming a "black white man"—is Fanon's dilemma. Given that the colonized becomes whiter "in proportion to his adoption of the mother country's cultural standards," whitening is inscribed as the very condition of becoming a black intellectual (*Black Skin* 18, 192). Fanon speaks of Martinicans who steep "themselves in Montesquieu or Claudel for the sole purpose of being able to quote them" because "they expect their color to be forgotten" through "their knowledge of these authors." The effort succeeds on condition that the Negro be "forever in combat with his own image" (194). This is the price exacted by a society whose "collective unconscious" (Fanon borrows and alters Jung's term) produces an ethics that says "one is a Negro to the degree to which one is wicked, sloppy, malicious, instinctual. Everything that is the opposite of these Negro modes of behavior is white" (192–193). Hence Negrophobia becomes normal for the native black, who "lives an ambiguity that is extraordinarily neurotic" (192).

Such neurosis was encouraged in Fanon's birthplace, the French West Indian colony of Martinique. Until the Second World War, the middle class there considered itself (white) European rather than (black) African, and erected its self-identity upon this "fundamental difference" (*Toward* 20). But eventually Martinicans made the painful discovery that their whiteness was merely a mask. Fanon's was torn from him on his first extended visit to France, when the whites he encountered in Paris fixed him in blackness. In recoiling from France, Fanon briefly turned to the flourishing Negritude movement led by his former teacher Aimé Césaire. But Fanon neither lost himself in Negritude nor returned home to his people. Instead, he embraced the cause of a country he had never set foot in—the white North African French colony of Algeria, a population composed largely of Muslims whose religion the Christian Fanon did not share, and whose main language (Arabic) Fanon did not speak. He required a translator for his many Muslim psychiatric patients who spoke no French.[14] Routinely he would speak of "we Algerians," just as later he would speak of "we Africans." By then his political engagement went beyond Algeria to embrace all of Africa and, near the end of his life, oppressed peoples everywhere. When he died in 1961 he was buried in Algeria, and his fellow revolutionaries saluted him in Arabic: "the late brother Frantz Fanon finds himself, today, in the midst of his brother martyrs" (qtd. Gendzier 237).

Ten years after his death the official Algerian reaction sought to minimize Fanon's role, to "de-Fanonize Algeria, and to de-Algerianize Fanon," in the words of one official. In short, "although he helped with 'our cause,' he was not 'one of us' " (qtd. Gendzier 244). This attitude, notes Irene Gendzier, betrays a desire to "lay aside the ghost of a too-powerful Fanon" and to "protect the authenticity of the Revolution as an all-Algerian phenomenon" (243). Authenticity is precisely what Fanon endangers, for he destabilizes the identity logic of us/them, identity/difference, inside/outside, native/stranger. Because it eludes these binaries, Fanon's life seems incoherent, an "impossible life" of no return and harrowing self-estrangement to those, like Albert Memmi, who judge by the Cartesian terms of existential humanism.

These terms are blind to how Fanon's allegedly impossible life enabled him to introduce "invention into existence" and challenge the disciplinary logic of identity thinking (*Black Skin* 229). We have seen that Fanon reverses the trajectory of authenticity to instigate a crisis of origins. Analogously, he turns identity from the ground of being into an effect of practice: what we do determines who we are. The West Indian is buried an Algerian "brother." Fanon describes his leap of invention as Nietzschean in its effort "to educate man to be actional" rather than reactive (222), and it approximates Nietzsche's dissolution of the subject into action: "The deed is everything—'the doer' is merely a fiction added to the deed" (*Genealogy* 45). Making the deed everything, in Nietzsche and Fanon, demands the past be evacuated, for history's humiliations still live in the present. The Negro "is the slave of the past," says Fanon, and "like it or not, the past can in no way guide me in the present moment" (*Black Skin* 225).

The extremity of Fanon's Nietzschean solution responds to the extremity of alienation endured by a black colonial subject. Du Bois's alienation under Jim Crow is palpable—as "a colored man in a white world" he felt "kept within bounds," neither an American nor a man (*Dusk* 653). But for Du Bois it would be unthinkable to jettison the past, since to work in the kingdom of culture is the very "end" of "striving." Yet Du Bois's cultural embeddedness does not paralyze his will to invent. After all, the Jamesian pragmatism he imbibed was a kind of American version of the Nietzschean philosophy of action that C. S. Peirce initiated in his 1868 deconstruction of the a priori Cartesian subject. In this light we can place Du Bois's controversial claim that it was only at Fisk that "a new loyalty and allegiance replaced my Americanism: henceforward I was a Negro" (*Autobiography* 108). He replaces biology with will, thus turning a statement of identity ("I was a Negro") into a declaration of practice. At Fisk, recalls Du Bois, "I became a member of a closed racial group with rites and loyalties . . . I received these eagerly and expanded them" (*Dusk* 627).

Du Bois displays a similar will to invent in the way he constructs his Africanity in *Dusk of Dawn* (1940). He notes the difference between posing the question "What is Africa to Me?" today in 1940 and in 1897 when he asked it in "The Conservation of Races." "Once I should have answered the question simply: I should have said 'fatherland' or perhaps better 'motherland' because I was born in the century when the walls of race were clear and straight; when the world consisted of mutually exclusive races; and even though the edges might be blurred, there was no question of exact definition and understanding of the meaning of the word" (639). That certitude has faded in the light of twentieth-century debunkings of race as a scientific concept. Now his relation to Africa, Du Bois claims, is founded more on feeling than on anything else. His "one direct cultural connection" with Africa was the melody his grandmother used to sing. Otherwise his upbringing was in a family culture whose speech, customs, and mores were not African but Dutch and largely New England. And out of this American soil grew his allegiance to Negritude. Like his decision at Fisk henceforward to be Negro, what he calls his "African racial feeling" was rooted not in biology but in choice: it was "purely a matter of my own later learning and reaction; my recoil from the assumptions of the whites; my experience in the South at Fisk. But it was nonetheless real and a large determinant of my life and character" (638).[15]

Du Bois's insistence on choice denaturalizes his racial identity and thus anticipates the "end of the innocent notion of an essential black subject," to recall Stuart Hall's remark. But even though opposition to a rhetoric of authenticity now flourishes, this viewpoint, it seems fair to say, depends on its object of critique; that is, authenticity remains the given, the framework, in which debates and dissents are enacted.[16] A vivid instance of the orthodoxy of authenticity is the celebrated Harvard sociologist Sara Lawrence-Lightfoot's 1994 book *I've Known Rivers*. It comprises lengthy interviews with six black professionals—"African-Americans of privilege"—among them a professor, a scientist, an artist, an executive. The thread binding these self-narrations is a shared recognition of the "power of ancestry," a power that has inspired most of the speakers to make time in their busy lives for the journey home (*Rivers* 10). The imperative of "reconnection with family origins" is at once the leitmotif of Lawrence-Lightfoot's book and the sine qua non of "growth and creativity" for her respondents, who otherwise, they claim, would feel emotionally desolate with their professional success (604). In her summation, Lawrence-Lightfoot declares: "I would say that each of these storytellers has grown 'blacker' as they have matured, stronger, and less ambivalent in their identity as African-Americans" (604).[17] Ironically, a hundred years ago, such adamancy about identity, about return, loomed as a threat to those seeking to deracialize their relation to culture.

At approximately the same time as Booker T. Washington was stigmatizing *black intellectual* as an oxymoron, a similar disgust was being expressed on the other side of the world, but with different consequences. In Nigeria, the first generation of Western-educated elite were former slaves who returned from British missionary schools eager to uplift the unlettered majority. They had imagined themselves "*the hope . . . the catalyst,* of a new Nigerian society" but before long discovered they were despised by the indigenous population as "moral and cultural lepers" and were refused recognition as "authentic members of society" (Ayandele 11). Such contempt took its toll, and by the early 1880s many members of the elite "began to perceive that they were rootless deluded hybrids" who had been educated out of the Nigerian milieu by British colonialism. In response, they "had to throw off the incubus of Western culture before they could be in a position to . . . develop into authentic Nigerians" (46–47). These are the words of a leading contemporary Nigerian historian—E. A. Ayandele—with a decidedly Bookerite take on Nigerian intellectuals. What Ayandele wants to emphasize is that the deluded hybrids successfully repented of their Western ways, discarded their English names and dress, swallowed a healthy dose of self-hatred (reproaching themselves as "mongrels of humanity") and campaigned for the vernacular as the proper language of teaching. Some became devout preachers of the racialist doctrine of African Personality.

Fanon has described another, more general, instance of the abrupt oscillations of authenticity. By 1945 West Indians, humiliated by French racism, had come to realize the fraudulence of their European identity and had embraced Negritude. The Africa they had so long despised became the locus of "truth . . . of an incorruptible purity" that West Indians now worshipped with all the passion they had once reserved for France. In making black "the virtuous color," says Fanon, light-skinned West Indians were unwittingly "dancing on the edge of a precipice. For after all, if the color black is virtuous, I shall be all the more virtuous the blacker I am!" The "precipice" is the polarizing logic of authenticity that entrapped West Indians in guilt and despair, "haunted by impurity." As Fanon says in his famous concluding words to "West Indians and Africans": "Thus it seems that the West Indian, after the great white error, is now living in the great black mirage" (*Toward* 23, 26–27). That "mirage" is a delirious fantasy of origin: imagining oneself a "transplanted son of slaves," feeling "the vibration of Africa in the very depth of his body," the West Indian "aspires only to one thing: to plunge into the great 'black hole' " (27).

Having experienced first-hand the futility inscribed in the pendulum swing of mirror-image opposites, Fanon vowed to recover neither a white nor a black identity but, instead, to "reach out for the universal," the racially unmarked, by granting primacy to action rather than identity (*Black Skin* 197). What this reaching out makes possible is the intellectual. A number of black American intellectuals around 1900 shared Fanon's logic if not his circumstances.

At the turn of the century, Du Bois, Charles Chesnutt, and the novelist Sutton Griggs faced the challenge of representing figures who seemed neither to know their place nor to have a place and who seemed to affront every way of making sense of black identity in Jim Crow America. All three authors depict the black intellectual as synonymous with enigma: one, humming Wagner, falls into a deathly trance (John Jones); another suddenly improvises a new identity and gender (Belton Piedmont in Griggs's *Imperium In Imperio,* 1899); and a third proves unrepresentable altogether (John Warwick, né Walden, the mulatto protagonist of Chesnutt's *The House Behind the Cedars* [1900], who heads North to pass and abruptly passes right out of the novel, leaving his sister to enact a tragic mulatta martyrdom).

In *The Souls of Black Folk* Du Bois's role as black intellectual involves an uneasy, imposed distance from virtually everyone, including the illiterate black masses. This tension is evident when he narrates his return to the rural South. Yet he returns not as a native but as a visitor, a summer teacher from Fisk, itself a far remove from his home state of Massachusetts, to which he will go back when he departs from Fisk for Harvard. Late in the book Du Bois uses fiction to confront anxieties latent in "The Forethought"—the precarious position of the black cultural worker ministering to his people. The painful question becomes, In what sense are they "his" at all? Indeed, "The Coming of John" narrates the shattering of this connection. The story explores how one's identity as an embodied "problem"—that is, a black intellectual—is further complicated once, in moments of aesthetic transport, one tastes "the free air" of life beyond the veil of the color line (*Souls* 527).

After such knowledge, what forgiveness? What place does aesthetic bliss have in a black bourgeoisie devoted to racial uplift? It has none in the one socially sanctioned scenario of black intellectual activity—the "journey home," the return to rural Southern soil as one's base for Christian race work. In this arena the exemplary "tragic mulatta" Iola Leroy (the titular heroine of Frances Harper's 1892 novel) will prosper as what we would now call, after Gramsci, an "organic" intellectual. Du Bois's acid comment on this approved ideal is discernible in the fate of his John Jones in "The Coming of John." After his intoxicating, if foreshortened, evening at the opera in New York City, he returns to his provincial roots to teach school in a world not unlike Iola Leroy's North Carolina plantation. Disaster quickly ensues: "every step he made offended someone," black or white (531). Before long, John Jones abruptly takes his suicidal leave. "I'm going—North," he tells his mother. Those are his last words. And mentally he does go North. Lost in aesthetic reverie, John thinks of the "gilded ceiling of that vast concert hall" in New York and hears again "the faint sweet music" of *Lohengrin.* "He leaned back and smiled toward the sea," again in "dreamland," his eyes closed, beyond the claims of white and black, as he sits with Wagner who winces not (535, 526). John is barely aware of the onrushing mob come to lynch him for killing the white man named John who molested his sister.

Whereas Du Bois disposes of the killing in a dozen words, he dilates upon John's experience of being lost in thought. Indeed the final scene culminates three previous moments of trancelike absorption: his college initiation into the "queer thought-world" of intellectual life; his being carried along the crowded streets of New York with "no time for hesitation"; and his "sitting so silent and rapt" in response to Wagner's music (525–526). He winds up at the opera house to purchase a ticket "to enter he knew not what" only after having been "pushed toward the ticket-office with the others" in a throng (526).

Lost in thought, lost in urban modernity, lost in aesthetic bliss: John Jones's inward appropriation of experience is at the center of the tale. Most remarkable is Du Bois's richly imagined rendering of John's journey as a college student into a world of intense intellection:

> He sat rapt and silent . . . or wandered alone over the green campus peering through and beyond the world of men into a world of thought. And the thoughts at times puzzled him sorely; he could not see just why the circle was not square, and carried it out fifty-six decimal places one midnight,—would have gone further, indeed, had not the matron rapped for lights out. He caught terrible colds lying on his back in the meadows of nights, trying to think out the solar system; he had grave doubts as to the ethics of the Fall of Rome . . . he pondered long and hard over every new Greek word, and wondered why this meant that and why it couldn't mean something else, and how it must have felt to think all things in Greek. So he thought and puzzled along for himself,—pausing perplexed where others skipped merrily . . . Thus he grew in body and soul. (524–525)

In attending so minutely to John's "world of thought," Du Bois dramatizes the formation of "that higher individualism which the centres of culture protect," a nurturing that earlier in *The Souls* he had named as the crucial task of the Negro college (437). Colleges must promote "a loftier respect for the sovereign human soul that seeks to know itself and the world about it; that seeks a freedom for expansion and self-development; that will love and hate and labor in its own way" (437). This last phrase, with its suggestion of an interior labor that escapes the instrumental and becomes autotelic, is the chord that resonates in the above passages that depict John thinking. What Du Bois's elaborations immerse us in is the life of the mind. In her book of that title, Hannah Arendt writes that the one precondition for thinking is

> withdrawal from the world of appearances . . . When we start thinking about a still-present somebody or something . . . we have removed ourselves surreptitiously from our surroundings and are conducting ourselves as though we were already absent. These remarks may indicate why thinking, the quest for meaning—as opposed to the thirst for knowledge, even for knowledge for its own sake—has so often been felt to be unnatural, as though men, whenever they reflect without purpose, going beyond the natural curiosity awakened by the manifold wonders of the world's sheer thereness . . . engaged in an activity *contrary to the human condition.* Thinking as such, not only the raising of the unanswerable "ultimate questions," but every reflection that does not serve knowledge and is not guided by practical needs and aims, is . . . *"out of order."* It interrupts any doing, any ordinary activities . . . All thinking demands a *stop*-and-think. (78)

As if to honor the arrest of thinking, Du Bois halts his narrative to elaborate John's inward expansion before his inevitable coming "back to a world of motion and of men" (*Souls* 525). The pause that Du Bois makes to enact the pause of thought, his lingering over the mesmeric power of sheer speculation that holds John, rebuts those, like Washington, who argue that blacks should be kept from a "classical" humanities curriculum for it would fill them with useless learning. And if, as Arendt says, all thinking flouts the practical by being out of order, "unnatural," and "contrary," to represent in 1903 a black man thinking pushes the perversity of intellection to an extreme.

What is more, John's addiction to thinking corrodes his passive acceptance of Jim Crow; having tasted life above the veil he now for the first time despises the "servility" that is the condition of life within the veil. As Arendt says, "thinking inevitably has a destructive, undermining effect on all established criteria, values, measurements" (175). John's return to a world of motion and of men bears this out: he will never obediently keep his "place" again. Arendt speaks of the "dazing after-effect" of thinking as a kind of "paralysis." And by the end, as John leans back and smiles, eerily indifferent to his imminent demise, his inwardness seems entwined with the deathly intimations that lurk in the imperative to "stop and think" (175).

John has been accused of wanting to "reverse nature" by "givin talks on the French Revolution, equality, and such like" (531–532). This accusation speaks more than it knows: John's life of inwardness has been a sustained assault on what his culture deemed natural. To reverse nature, one might add, also includes not making the journey home, not returning to Southern gardens and Southern mothers, not speaking black vernacular, but, instead, severing roots and going North. Such reversals at worst risk death, at best flirt with being unintelligible.

Belton Piedmont temporarily reverses nature in Sutton Griggs's *Imperium In Imperio* when he leaves Virginia for New York, where he dons a woman's wig and a "well fitting" dress to pass as a nurse to a leading white family. His strategy may be postmodern but his mission is earnestly empirical—to discover from the inside what "precautionary steps the white people were going to take" in the event of a potential black "insurrection." A self-styled "new Negro, self-respecting, fearless," Belton is part of a class of "educated malcontents" without professional prospects (62, 131). Alarmed at this frustrating impasse, which he fears may be breeding possible clandestine revolt, Belton has undertaken his mission. But all he learns is "that the white man was utterly ignorant of the nature of the Negro of today . . . He felt that the Negro was easily ruled and was not an object for serious thought" (133). The white complacency Belton discovers may be insulting, but it provides the room Belton and other "New Negroes" need for forming the secret black shadow government—the Imperium—that is taking shape "unnoticed and unseen" by indifferent whites.[18]

Although a nation within a nation, the Imperium, as Belton conceives it, is in an important way anti-separatist. For Belton regards the Imperium as the fruit of the universalist principles of liberty created in Western culture and also as a challenge that they in fact be extended to people of any color. Throughout, Griggs's fixation is skin color, but it operates as a mark less of race than of epidermal differences within the "whole human family" (2). This universalism is one way to escape the "vicious circle" of self-revulsion earlier described by Ayandele and Fanon.

Griggs, and other anti-Bookerite "deluded hybrids" like Du Bois and Chesnutt, emancipated themselves from the imprisoning rhetoric of authenticity with its inevitable racializing of culture. Kelly Miller shows how this was done. In his 1905 "open letter to Thomas Dixon," Miller rebuts the familiar claim that "the Negro lives in the light of the white man's civilization and reflects a part of that light." The Negro, says Miller, "has advanced in exactly the same fashion that the white race has advanced, by taking advantage of all that has gone before . . . The white man has no exclusive proprietorship of civilization. White man's civilization is as much a misnomer as the white man's multiplication table. It is the equal inheritance of anyone who can appropriate and apply it" (Miller 55–56).[19] As Alain Locke will do in the next generation, Miller deracializes culture by making one's relation to it a matter of present action not prior identity. What becomes pivotal is the capacity for practice, for appropriating and applying.[20]

If, for Washington, *black intellectual* is an oxymoron, Kelly Miller agrees, but for different reasons. For Miller, *black intellectual* is an oxymoron in the same way *white intellectual* is an oxymoron: to be an intellectual in the twentieth century (and in the wake of the Dreyfus Affair) is implicitly to offer a critique of the racializing of identity. Du Bois discovered this during his aesthetic awakening in the art galleries of Europe as a graduate student in Berlin (1892–1894). He was initiated not into the privilege of living in the light of the white man's civilization but into the practice of aesthetic contemplation, an initiation that in his *Autobiography* he depicts as concurrent with the "opportunity . . . of looking at the world as a man and not simply from a narrow racial and provincial outlook" (159). "I sit with Shakespeare and he winces not" is Du Bois's most famous expression of how fused for him are aesthetic experience and the erasure of the color line.

Some regard Du Bois and Kelly Miller's attitude to Western culture as smacking of genteel accommodationism or an assimilationism that whitens blacks. But such labels ignore the power of their position. For Du Bois and Miller, one's relation to culture and one's capacity for aesthetic experience are indifferent to the claims of an ideology of the authentic, with its fixation on origin, race, and ownership, the exclusionary mechanisms of an imperialist logic of identity.[21] That logic, according to the anti-racist anti-imperialist William James, carves up experience into static concepts and categories, tools that form the stereotypes on which a racially segregated social order depends. The concern of Jamesian pluralism is not merely tolerance of multiplicity but, more precisely, the recovery of what James calls the "unclassified residuum," that which slips the concept's grasp and encourages the "reinstatement of the vague" (*Will* 222; *Principles* 246). In *The Souls* Du Bois carries on this reinstatement of the vague as a political and aesthetic project.

In a seldom-examined assessment of *The Souls* he published in 1904, Du Bois speaks of the "penumbra of vagueness and half-veiled allusion" that he has spun around "a clear central message" (*Book Reviews* 9). While he notes that this vagueness has made some readers "impatient," it is "the nature of the message" that is at least partly responsible. That message is summarized in "The Forethought" to *The Souls:* "Herein lie buried many things which if read with patience may show the strange meaning of being black . . . I have sought here to sketch, in vague, uncertain outline, the spiritual world in which ten thousand thousand Americans live and strive" (359). To excavate meanings long repressed under the weight of racist stereotype, Du Bois must step "within the Veil" of segregation and raise it so that the reader "may view faintly its deeper recesses." Hence his immanent stance requires that vagueness be a condition of perception. Du Bois also assimilates the veil of vagueness into a serpentine prose style that dissolves the stark rigidities bred by Jim Crow. In its elaborate delicacy and deliberate fusions and confusions of pronoun references, his style blurs divisions and grants respect to the intricacy of black experience. It demands the reader's openness to complexity. Vagueness becomes a tactic (admittedly risky) to frustrate stock responses by arousing the reader's sympathetic patience. The patience Du Bois urges was another practice he acquired in his aesthetic initiation in Europe: "I had been before, above all, in a hurry. I wanted a world, hard, smooth, and swift" (*Dusk* 587).

By embroidering his first non-academic book with the aesthetic textures he had absorbed first-hand, Du Bois signals his intention to make *The Souls* a modernist artifact and not a collection of magazine articles. Difficulty and indirection become his chosen modes, the only ones flexible enough to do justice to the "strange experience" of "being a problem." To speak from within this experience is to achieve a kind of authenticity inimical to the kind mandated by Tuskegee's rhetoric of transparency. The authenticity Du Bois will pursue is founded on intimacy and vagueness, the subjectivity that is the hallmark of the modern.

Du Bois is thoroughly aware that his experiment is modernist. In his 1904 statement he speaks of renouncing "the usual impersonal and judicial attitude of the traditional author" as a loss "in authority but a gain in vividness." He mentions the "intimate tone of self-revelation," the "distinctively subjective note that runs in each essay" (*Book Reviews* 9). The epistemological decentering Du Bois describes aligns him with modernism as it exchanges what might be termed an imperial mode of authenticity for a liberated modernist one. He topples the Olympian assumption of authorial omniscience for the new authenticity of vulnerability. The impersonal clarity of the imperial mode is replaced by freely confessed ambivalences and uncertainties, what he calls in 1904 "abrupt transitions of style, tone and viewpoint," all leading to a "distinct sense of incompleteness and sketchiness." But Du Bois sought more than to represent modernist subjectivity. He ends his self-assessment saying "in its larger aspects the style is tropical—African. This needs no apology. The blood of my fathers spoke through me and cast off the English restraint of my training and surroundings" (9). Du Bois's mention of "blood" bespeaks a rhetoric of racial authenticity, but it does not take control of his discourse. Rather, he turns modernist and African aesthetics into twin sources of iconoclastic energy that overflow and intermix. Together they produce a hybrid text that casts off the restraints of the color line.

The Nigerian Nobel laureate Wole Soyinka describes "Authenticity" as one of "the most vulgar frontiers ever raised against the creative impulse." It is used as "one of the main parameters of proscription which African writers and artists have to undergo even at the tail-end of the twentieth century!" (*Art* 219). He further condemns African "apologists for regimes which, waving the opportunistic rag of 'authenticity' as a banner, suppress forms of literature, or other art forms, that may present a reality outside the glossy brochure" of state-controlled imagery dedicated to celebrating "the purity of African creative genius" (219, 221). Not only contemptuous of the political uses of authenticity, Soyinka is suspicious of its philosophical prestige: the "lure of tragic existentialism" saps the "re-assertion of will" and celebrates the "snare" of "spiritual in-locked egotism." As if echoing Fanon, he declares: "let actions alone" manifest "authentic being" (*Man* 87–88).

In a combination worthy of Du Bois, Soyinka is a member of the Nigerian Western-educated elite (he writes in English) who has managed to remain an unrepentant "deluded hybrid" while also being a leading democratic activist against Nigeria's totalitarian regimes.[22] His contempt for the proscriptions of state-mandated authenticity, directly influenced by Fanon, is inseparable from his fondness for the perverse indirections of the aesthetic as it faces the imperative to communicate. Granting that the "artist's primary frontier" is "communication," Soyinka asks "why do we encounter loiterers at its frontiers . . . fragmenting and recomposing, or operating 'through a glass darkly'? . . . delaying, suspending, or augmenting direct apprehension through a barrier of communication strategies" (*Art* 217).

Ambivalence about the instrumentality of direct communication and a preference for loitering and deferral characterize Soyinka's sense of the creative process and help explain his admiration for "Art for Art's Sake" of "the last *fin de siècle*," which produced, he says, an "unprecedented" "liberation of the human imagination" in Europe, resulting eventually in modernism's "celebrated encounter with African art" (*Art* 218). As I shall discuss in the next chapter, Du Bois came to maturity in that time of liberation in the aesthetic nineties. He loved art as an enemy of what is purported to be "natural": "Art is not natural and is not supposed to be natural" (*Writings* 1239). Home from Berlin, he lectured rural blacks about European art, for he realized that to promulgate respect for aesthetic autonomy was a social and political responsibility, not its evasion. Du Bois's insistence on aesthetic education is one way he renovates the role of race man, ventilating its inherent constrictions. As a wedge against "group imprisonment," Du Bois (like Soyinka) constructs the aesthetic as deferral and opposes it to the disciplinary yoke of authenticity.

Something of this urge for release helps explain, I think, why the Du Bois, Griggs, and Chesnutt texts are strikingly equivocal about pulling "the veil from before the eyes of the Anglo-Saxon that he may see the New Negro standing before him" (Griggs 244). This is Griggs's Belton Piedmont articulating a goal that these authors are at once committed to and ambivalent about. Their works do indeed inform white America that "he has a New Negro on his hands" (245). But rather than set him at center stage, and thereby risk being bound by the conventions and constraints of imperial authenticity, they preserve the black intellectual as an oxymoronic figure of racial inauthenticity. An "unclassified residuum" leading an impossible life, he is subject to abrupt narrative disruptions or terminations.

Equivocation is expressed in Du Bois's unveiling his "New Negro" John Jones while sending him silently to his rapid doom and in Griggs's informing us of the vast black Imperium hidden on the margins of white America while having his hero Belton executed because he insists that the Imperium go public and abandon its plans to overthrow the U.S. government. There is equivocation also as Chesnutt has John Walden describe himself and his sister Rena as "new people" but disappear North before giving that newness much enactment. Left behind to hold together *The House Behind the Cedars* is Rena, cast as tragic mulatta in the appointed script of the "old Negro."[23] In all three texts, ambivalence about representing the New Negro produces enigma and secrecy both thematically and as narrative modes of maintaining power in reserve, a way of both representing and deferring representation. Thus illegibility becomes a source of potent possibility in Jim Crow's identitarian regime.

Chesnutt's figuration of the illegible is profoundly and creatively equivocal about representing the black intellectual. And in his last published story, "Baxter's Procrustes" (1904), Chesnutt offers a haunting allegory of this ambivalence. There the blankness that is John Walden's unrepresented Northern future becomes "the wide meadow of margin" that is Baxter's unwritten poem *Procrustes* (274). If *The House Behind the Cedars* is a book that does and does not represent a black intellectual (by depicting him as a man who decides to pass—both racially and from the novel), "Baxter's Procrustes" pivots on an analogous riddle: how does one publish a book without publishing a book? His protagonist, a melancholy, enigmatic aesthete who over the years has occasionally read brief passages of a poem to friends, devises an answer: he publishes a "sealed" edition of his blank verse poem that, in reality, is nothing but blank pages—"all margin."

A publication of the Bodleian Club, where genteel collectors are dedicated to the art of exquisite bookmaking, the poem is actually Baxter's practical joke on a world that this gloomy cynic finds "so uniformly monotonous as to be scarce worth the living" (270). The joke mocks the pretensions of his smug fellow club members who act as if they have "read" the poem (before it was sealed) and are fully confident that now they "are so much the more intimately acquainted with Baxter—the real Baxter" (273). But Baxter, who is praised for having "written himself into the poem," is as elusive as his "Procrustes"—that is, both are "all margin." No one knows what, if anything, is behind his mask of indifference. His joke mocks both the presumption that we can know the "real Baxter" and the belief that we can confidently possess anything more than margin. Papering over this gap is the habit of certitude produced by the procrustean pressure of a society bent on uniformity, which catches "every man born into the world and endeavour[s] to fit him to some preconceived standard" (269).

Though the story's manifest content has nothing to do with race, Chesnutt's plea is for a margin as a defense against Jim Crow's procrustean one-drop demands of identity. In this light, Baxter's blank pages prove a pregnant image of anonymity, emptiness, and freedom to improvise. They are also a metaphor for the freedom of "pure Art" (Flaubert's phrase for his desire to write "a book about nothing"), for fin-de-siècle insouciance as a saving escape from the burdensome weight of imposed authenticity, of "preconceived standards." The blank pages evoke, as well, the blankness in *The House Behind the Ce-*

dars, created by John Walden's passing to the margins, to the space of his impossible life that eludes Southern doom for Northern possibility.[24]

Escape from the suffocating fatalism of the South preoccupied the young Chesnutt; a virtual obsession of his journal is the desire to go North and become a writer: "I pine for civilization, and 'equality' . . . I will go to the Metropolis" (*Journals* 172, 106). Before moving North, he worked in North Carolina, pursuing a precociously brilliant career as an educator, all the while turning himself into an intellectual. Chesnutt rigorously educated himself in classical and European languages and literature; indeed few people have more tenaciously applied and appropriated the riches of "what has already gone before," to borrow Kelly Miller's words. Like Miller and Du Bois, Chesnutt understood *intellectual* as a nonracialized term ("it is the dream of my life— to be an author!"); and as an intellectual in the rural South he felt "neither fish, flesh, nor fowl, . . . Too 'stuck up' for the colored folks, and, of course, not recognized by the whites" (154, 157–158).

Rather than letting his sense of marginality paralyze him, Chesnutt turns it into a source of creative energy, as his earliest story, "Lost in a Swamp," reveals. It is a page-long story in his journal about a young man whose father tells him to ride five miles to get seed-corn from a neighbor. He takes a "wrong turn" and gets lost in a swamp: "Instead of getting out of it, I was getting deeper and deeper into it." Eventually he extricates himself, gets his corn, and, in the tale's last words, returns home, "to the great relief of my parent, who didn't know what was become of me." The journal's next line suggests what has become of him: "The above is my first real attempt at literature" (47). What the tale stages is a creative birth wherein the act of writing is figured as immersion in a swamp, a losing of one's way, a wrong turn taken, a severance from roots. He returns to home and father the same but different—his father doesn't know "what was become" of him.

Chesnutt will later describe his solitary life of unceasing intellectual labor as a continual "working in the dark. I have to feel my way along . . . I have become accustomed to the darkness" (92). His intellectual life thrives as subterranean, liminal, as if in the midst of his community he is adrift, present but not present. In daylight he is a teacher, at night a writer engulfed in a kind of swamp—not of jungle oblivion but of consuming mental hunger, uncertainty, possibility, ambition. Chesnutt's fertile swamp of open margins is precisely the opposite of the terminal place that Rena stumbles into when "she . . . realized with a horrible certainty that she was lost in the swamp." In panic she has retreated deeper into the forest, to rejoin nature. She is found at "the edge of the swamp," next to a "well-defined path which would have soon led her to the open highway" (*House* 182–183). Rena, dying, is returned to home, fixed in her procrustean fate, forever denied the open highway, the exit from nature, the margin of possibility.[25]

A century later the ubiquity of the black intellectual would seem to spell a new era of hyper-visibility. But if this development—in a sense from oxymoron to tautology—does not also entail renouncing pursuit of an essential black subject, black intellectual life risks entrapment in polar oscillations of authenticity. In this light, the efforts by Du Bois and others at extrication around the turn of the century bear inspection. As does Fanon's impossible life. In reassessing these legacies, in turning Fanon and Du Bois, two prophets of sixties black nationalism, into prophets of nineties post-ethnicity, I take seriously what animates their projects—the leap, be it Nietzschean or pragmatist, from authenticity to invention. This leap revises the notion of legacy from serene repository to site of action. Otherwise one risks becoming "a prisoner of history" and exalting the past at the expense of the present and future (*Black Skin* 229). Fanon refused to be imprisoned, as did Du Bois: "No idea is perfect and forever valid," Du Bois told the NAACP in 1934 when its founding mission of integration was stalled. Although he had been present at its creation a quarter-century before, Du Bois had no impulse to fetishize origins: "Always to be living and apposite and timely, [ideas] must be modified and adapted to changing facts" (*Writings* 776).

Du Bois's lability encouraged his turn from the ascetic anti-modernist scenario of the "return" to Southern roots. Just as decisively, he turned from that equally static icon of black identity—the race champion. As we will see in the next chapter, the act of turning or troping is itself at the heart of pragmatism's stance toward experience. Turning becomes the counterpressure that Du Bois exerts against various demands of identity. He entwines the political and the aesthetic in the matrix of unsettlement that is the realm of *pragmata*, the slippery etymological ground of pragmatism, wherein Du Bois finds a measure of freedom.

4

The Distinction of Du Bois: Aesthetics, Pragmatism, Politics

"The fact of racial distinction based on color," Du Bois wrote in *Dusk of Dawn,* "was the greatest thing in my life and absolutely determined it." The white American and European worlds were "settled and determined upon the fact that I was and must be a thing apart" (653). But as his career attests, this source of constraint spurred Du Bois to ceaseless work and prodigious accomplishment. He threw in the face of oppressive racial distinction the contemptuous, unsettling challenge of impeccable black intellectual and personal distinction. In turning his being a "thing apart" from a condition of abjection into one of compelling originality, Du Bois appropriated a weapon of racist control and classification—the weapon of "distinction"—for his own use.

Du Bois's sense of distinction is often described as elitism, a word that typically alludes to his discarding of the proletariat and championing of an educated and cultured "talented tenth" as the collective agent of social change. David Levering Lewis's commanding biography focuses both on this political expression of Du Bois's elitism and on its personal embodiment in his dandyism: his carefully sculpted appearance, his aloof bearing, his love of beauty and the art of living.[1] In his forthright attention to Du Bois's elitism, Lewis is admirably nonpolemical; rather than lament elitism, he treats it as a condition of his genius, a fact of his nature that is not inherently retrograde politically, though it at times produces naivete and isolation.

One of Lewis's most important claims is that Du Bois's "marrow deep elitism" both fueled and "circumscribed . . . his racial militancy" for an "as-yet-undetermined time span" (149). While the span evidently covers the period of Lewis's first volume, 1868 to 1919, the claim pertains to 1894. The occasion was a diary entry made during the return by boat to America after two years on a fellowship in Europe. In his notebook Du Bois differentiates himself as one of three mulattoes from "two full-blooded Negroes" who are also passengers. "We do not go together." Herbert Aptheker, when he edited the posthumously published *Autobiography,* revised this passage to read: "There are five Negroes aboard. We do not go together." Lewis provides the original text to preserve Du Bois's distinction. For Lewis, that distinction indicates a "subtext of proud hybridization . . . so prevalent in Du Bois's sense of himself that the failure to notice it in the literature about him is as remarkable as the complex itself" (148). In probing Du Bois's notebook entry, Lewis wonders if there is not a "deeper culpability," "a willfully arrogant . . . standing apart as a different breed from the great majority of the people of the race he believed it his destiny to uplift?" (149).

By showing the tension in Du Bois between elitism and uplift, Lewis brings to light what some have preferred to leave in shadow. The urge to suppress Du Bois's elitism and inconsistency has been most evident in the Marxist Aptheker, Du Bois's literary executor, who influenced Manning Marable's 1986 book on Du Bois as an unwavering "radical democrat," a heroic man of the left. Cornel West acknowledges Du Bois's elitism, but laments it as characteristic of "the American pragmatists' obsession with critical intelligence" that breeds a feeling of superiority from and distrust of ordinary people (*Evasion* 179). West's comment that Du Bois "did not fully overcome" this aloofness suggests, however, that Du Bois indeed sought to overcome it.

With its stress on "double aims" and "double consciousness" and "the double life every American Negro must live," *The Souls of Black Folk* confirms Lewis's focus on Du Bois's ambivalences (364–365, 502). For instance, he depicts the talented tenth as "servants" to the masses, but also as "a dictatorship of intelligence" that demands obedience (qtd. Young 26). Such typical Du Boisian ambiguity blurs his political and moral identity and nurtured his fascination with "being a problem" (*Souls* 363). This investment determined his turbulent relations to institutional authority, especially to the NAACP, which he helped create.

One particular "problem" I will address in this chapter is a seeming anomaly: the pivotal roles of both elitism and aesthetic experience in the life and thought of one of the century's great democratic socialists and engaged intellectuals. "The truth of Art tampers," says Du Bois, "that is its mission"; it unsettles what the status quo pretends is settled (*Book Reviews* 66). And his political activity enacts an analogous mission that he once likened to reopening an old and bleeding wound. When they are creative, political and aesthetic practice are both interrogative and improvisational. They tap potentiality by cutting against the received idea of experience as primarily cognitive, a "knowledge affair" (Dewey *Experience* 21). This last phrase is John Dewey's. For both Dewey and Du Bois the aesthetic and the political are experimental modes of conduct that delve into "gross experience," thriving on risk while insinuating, says Dewey, "possibilities of human relations not to be found in rule and precept" (*Art* 349). Du Bois adumbrated an aesthetic politics in the late 1920s just as John Dewey was preparing his major work of pragmatist aesthetics, *Art as Experience* (1934).

I will explore how Du Bois's construction of pragmatism encouraged elitist, aesthetic, and activist impulses to overlap in his remarkably hybrid sensibility. While his efforts to reconcile the aesthetic and the political have long been noted, they have invariably been written off as the work of a self-confessed propagandist. A close reading of his essay "Criteria of Negro Art," in which Du Bois boldly defamiliarizes propaganda, will make clear the error of this received wisdom. Du Bois, in effect, shows how pragmatism can mediate between the aesthetic and the political and help move contemporary intellectual debate beyond constricting dichotomies. In particular, his career prompts a rethinking of current portrayals of aesthetic value as elitist and apolitical.[2]

Reexamining Du Bois is invaluable for the above reasons, but also because it helps revise pragmatism's image as inimical to the aesthetic and as the earnest champion of Enlightenment reason. But pragmatism, especially James's, has a strong "counter-Enlightenment" impulse, to borrow Isaiah Berlin's famous phrase for a lineage that begins with Vico's critique of Cartesianism and includes Hamann, the eighteenth-century German opponent of Enlightenment rationalism and a key influence on German romanticism.[3] The projects of Du Bois and Dewey would renew a venerable theme of that tradition—the aesthetic education of man, to borrow Schiller's famous phrase of 1795. Du Bois read Schiller during his intense study of German idealism in Berlin in the early 1890s (Lewis 139).[4] Schiller's powerful influence upon Hegelian Marxism—discernible not only in Hegel and Marx, but in Max Weber, Lukács, Marcuse, and Adorno—helped initiate what can broadly be described as a romantic expressivist critique of Enlightenment rationalism. To argue for Du Bois's pragmatism inevitably entails reassessing his relation to Hegel, the preeminent German idealist, who is usually regarded as a crucial influence on Du Bois.

To grasp how Du Bois is a pragmatist, it is necessary to return to his sense of distinction. I replace elitism with distinction not because the former is inaccurate but because it is inflexible: the word is too loaded with a pejorative burden to be easily available for troping. Resisting stability or closure, the act of troping creates new meanings by turning predetermined ones in various directions.[5] Du Bois played with both the social and diacritical meanings of distinction: possessing distinction and making and contesting distinctions were intimately related for him. Du Bois called himself a "devoted follower of William James at the time he was developing his pragmatic philosophy," and a propensity for troping constitutes a crucial part of James's legacy (*Autobiography* 133). Because scholarly work on Du Bois's relation to James has largely been confined to the latter's possible influence on the notion of "double consciousness," what has been missed is that Du Bois seems to have internalized pragmatism as a method and style of thinking.[6]

By inwardly appropriating pragmatism, Du Bois grasps it in precisely the spirit James intended. The instilling of a temperament, a mode of conduct, "is what the pragmatic method means," says James. Though most readers ignored him, James often stated that his pragmatism was not a philosophy but an "attitude of orientation" that "stands for no particular results" (*Pragmatism* 33). A method for conducting a career, for creating a literary style, for living "the strenuous life," Du Boisian pragmatism is creative revisionary practice. Thus, in good pragmatist fashion, he interrogated the limits of James's thought, pressing beyond his mentor's attenuated historical understanding and naive faith in "the New England ethic of life" (*Writings* 1315).[7]

Du Bois's predilection for the mobility of troping received philosophical coherence and direction from his favorite Harvard professor: "The turning was due to William James." In recalling that James encouraged him to move from studying philosophy to history and social problems, Du Bois also neatly distills the philosopher's catalytic impact (*Dusk* 582). To be fermentative, a favorite Jamesian word, was precisely the point of pragmatism. The pragmatist "turns his back resolutely . . . upon a lot of inveterate habits dear to professional philosophers. He turns away from abstraction . . . from verbal solutions, fixed principles, closed systems, and pretended absolutes and origins. He turns towards facts, towards action and towards power" (*Pragmatism* 31). Thus pragmatism, James declares, is "less a solution . . . than a program for more work, and more particularly an indication of the ways in which existing realities may be *changed*" (32). In this light, we can redescribe more precisely Du Bois's response to invidious racial distinction as thoroughly pragmatist. Faced with the "pretended absolute" of race, he turned it into a "program for more work," a challenge to the "ready-made compartmentalization" (to borrow Dewey's phrase) that racial distinction inflicts on psyches and on society.

Various modes of Du Boisian distinction converge in his classic of urban sociology *The Philadelphia Negro* (1899). At an historical moment when even educated whites regarded blacks as a lumpen homogeneous mass, Du Bois made visible the internal differentiation of the urban black population. "Colored people [are] . . . seldom judged by their best classes, and often the very existence of classes among them is ignored." Du Bois went on to argue that "in many respects it is right and proper to judge a people by its best classes," by its people of distinction, for "the highest class of any group represents its possibilities rather than its exceptions, as is so often assumed in regard to the Negro" (316). Revealing and having distinction were ways of thinking and living beyond the given of racism, and thus were forms of hope. Perhaps ironically, these forms also nourished the pursuit of a distinctly democratic possibility. The "real promise of democracy," said Du Bois, mines "the great possibilities of mankind from unused and unsuspected reservoirs of human greatness" (*Against Racism* 242). Democratic freedom thus breeds the potential not only to abolish material poverty but, more important, to create a world where "living is not for earning, earning is for living" and "giving rein to the creative impulse" becomes possible. For Du Bois, freedom marks "the path of art, and living in the fuller and broader sense of the term is the expression of art" (*Writings* 1060–61). We shall see that Du Bois shares Schiller's belief in the aesthetic as the condition of human freedom.

Du Bois's conjoining of possibility, democracy, and the freedom of art recalls Dewey, his colleague in 1929 in the short-lived socialist League of Independent Political Action. Dewey finds possibility inscribed in the open-ended, experimental thrust of pragmatism and democracy. By the twenties, Dewey's notion of democracy was staunchly participatory and resisted Walter Lippmann's argument that creating a technocratic power elite was essential to the efficient functioning of democracy. Both Lippmann and Du Bois were students of William James and George Santayana, and both sought to reconcile democracy and elitism. Thus Du Bois's desire that a black aristocracy would guide and elevate the masses places him somewhere between Dewey and Lippmann, for he used elitist means to nurture democratic populist potential. He regarded the emergence of exceptional black men as proof that "down among the mass, ten times their number with equal ability could be discovered and developed," if effort was exerted (*Dusk* 713). Thus Du Bois turns elitism toward possibility.

We will see that Du Bois performs an analogous democratizing of the aesthetic, whose embattled contemporary status deserves some mention here. A tendency of some work in Cultural Studies is to regard the aesthetic as a tool of hegemony and thus as inherently opposed to a progressive politics. But this view ignores the status of art in Western Marxism, one of the formative influences on Cultural Studies. Many of the most prominent figures in the Marxist tradition—Lukács, Benjamin, Adorno, and Marcuse—found in the aesthetic a paradigm of ethical behavior and cultural critique. Helping to devalue the aesthetic, notes John Guillory, is the critique of canon formation "which reduces that process to conspiratorial acts of evaluation" and is thus "compelled to regard the discourse of the aesthetic as merely fraudulent, as a screen for the covert affirmation of hegemonic values." The "effect of an openly progressive critique of aesthetics" says Guillory, "is to position the 'aesthetic' and the 'political' as the discursive antitheses of current critical thought, and thus to enjoin a choice between them" (270, 273).

Du Bois (and Dewey) avoids such dichotomies by turning the aesthetic into a form of praxis, thus making pragmatism compatible with Marxist cultural critique. What results is a pragmatist aesthetics animated by acts of troping that leave his relation to modernity unresolved. Yet this irresolution is overlooked in most accounts of Du Bois's politics. For instance, Wilson Moses and Adolph Reed have separately shown that Du Bois's socialism, both domestically and in his Pan-African vision, is anti-capitalist and anti-bourgeois. But Du Bois, they go on to say, is neither radical nor democratic in his technocratic confidence in expertise as the motor of modernization's administrative rationality. This view neglects Du Bois's pragmatism, which in effect complicated his socialism, making it more democratic by encouraging a creative ambivalence toward modernity's instrumentality and cult of efficiency.[8] Pragmatism as a method can be said to turn (or trope) ambivalence itself into a productive skepticism of the primacy of identity. And we shall see how this skepticism orients Du Bois's political practice.[9]

To construe pragmatism as skepticism rather than affirmation deserves some elaboration at this point. Far from being the philosophical expression and rationalization of America's triumphant capitalism, pragmatism's "workings are paralyzed here," said Dewey in the early twenties; "pragmatic faith walks in chains" (*Characters* 1: 546–547). To abide in the pragmatist spirit of creative making commits one to a "supremely difficult task . . . Perhaps the task is too hard for human nature" (545). One reason we are inadequate to the temptations of dogma and of "already made things" is that American commercialism degrades the nobility of commerce—"intercourse, exchange, distribution, sharing"—into the narrow confines of private interests. Modern American business "arrests, diverts and perverts" our creative pragmatic makings (545).

For Dewey (at least the Dewey whose faith in positivist science was shattered in the aftermath of having supported American entry into the war in 1917), fidelity to making involves accepting the ineradicable existence of chance. It loomed as the nagging, humbling fact from which modernity was still in flight. In 1925 he noted that we love "to mumble universal and necessary law . . . the uniformity of nature, universal progress, and the inherent rationality of the universe." But such positivist mumblings are mere "magic formulae" designed "to deny the existence of chance" (*Experience* 40). The "fundamentally hazardous character of the world is not seriously modified, much less eliminated," even though science has given us a measure of prediction and control.[10]

Pragmatism's affinity for the uncontrollable is evident in its very etymology, the Greek word *pragmata,* the plural of *pragma.* In some contexts, *pragmata* can suggest unsettled circumstances, of the sort that confront men in the *polis.* A "given but not static state of affairs," *pragmata's* implications "for a collectivity's past hopes, present plight, and future projects are as yet very much unresolved . . . Never wholly responsive to the impress of purposive design, these uncertain matters are always subject to unanticipated twists of fate, and so pregnant with the possibility of suffering and sadness."[11] Pragmatism's project is to recover *pragmata,* a necessary task given that classical philosophy enthroned Reason as supreme while devaluing ordinary experience as infected with contingency and thus beneath philosophical dignity. And the recovery is also necessary if the possibility of democratic politics is to be reinstated.

In its contempt for *pragmata,* rationalism is an anti-political project, argues the political theorist Timothy Kaufman-Osborn, for it seeks "to root politics in stable foundations by grounding its practice in something less corrigible and contingent than its own conduct," namely "reason's antecedently formulated truths" (25). For the pragmatist, politics is a mode of conduct that requires immersion in unsettled, shifting matters whose "meanings must always be reworked in light of the pressing needs and possibilities of the present" (315). The aesthetic, says Dewey, involves analogous unsettlement. Rather than subordinating experience to "something beyond itself" such as "systematic thought," the aesthetic is "experience directly had" in its "very movement" amid "the impact of harsh conditions," hence "freed from the forces that impede and confuse its development as experience" (*Art* 281, 274).

This understanding of politics, aesthetics, and pragmatism is suggestive regarding Du Bois's own tumultuous career of contesting received meanings and authorities and provides a (nonreductive) way of illuminating Du Bois's intransigent complexity. This quality continues to be noted but often unexamined in accounts of his career. Here is a representative statement: "Throughout his career Du Bois, America's greatest black radical scholar, could find no clear role for himself in the ranks of the Left" and "frustrated many potential allies with his complex positions" (Diggins 134). This describes what one might call the cost of making James's "strenuous life" a model of political practice; one is "without assurances or guarantees" in a world "still in process of making" (James *Writings* 940–941). So profound was Du Bois's investment in James's strenuous ideal that its heroic colors suffuse his 1944 retrospective narrative of his career. Embracing "chance" instead of "unchangeable scientific law," Du Bois declares: "I was continually the surgeon probing blindly, yet with what knowledge and skill I could muster, for unknown ill" ("Evolving" 57–58). This metaphor of crisis, of authority stripped of authority and flirting with chaos, sums up the impact of what he calls "Jamesian pragmatism" (58).

Pragmatism's lesson to Du Bois the social scientist was that "he could not stand apart and study *in vacuo*" (57). Abandoning the insulation of a spectator theory of knowledge (to borrow Dewey's phrase), Du Bois opened himself to a "certain tingling challenge of risk" (58). Du

Bois's decidedly Jamesian rhetoric aptly describes his life at the helm of
The Crisis for twenty-four years (1910–1934). There he "faced situations that called—shrieked—for action" if "social death" was to be
averted (57). Du Bois's remarkable, seldom-cited 1944 essay "My
Evolving Program for Negro Freedom," from which I have been quoting, charts the various "re-adaptations" he improvised over the course
of his career.[12]

The most dramatic revision was his pragmatist remaking of his sociology, for it set Du Bois "in the midst of action" and "continuous,
kaleidoscopic change of conditions." The hectic pace of the "hot reality
of real life" rendered his "previous purely scientific program" (his Atlanta University studies) old before it was even analyzed (56). Though
he had no time for the patient testing of scientific observation, neither
could Du Bois simply work "fast and furiously" by "intuition and emotion." Thus he seeks to be responsive to the raw unfolding of events
while simultaneously pursuing "ordered knowledge" of the race problem, which "research and tireless observation" would supply (57). Du
Bois is working in the grain of pragmatist science as James construed
it: his effort is to practice science as immersion in and reflection upon
gross experience, rather than science as preoccupied with technical ver-
ification and a specious objectivity.

Du Bois's self-portrait leaves out the more familiar Du Bois, the fastidious Hegelian idealist who in the opening pages of *The Souls of Black
Folk* invokes Hegel's model of World Spirit. How did he reconcile his
pragmatism with his Hegelianism? Not compelled to choose between
them, unlike many of his commentators, Du Bois let them interact and
correct each other's defects.[13] The question of Du Bois and Hegel is
part of a larger one involving pragmatism's tangled relation both to the
philosopher and to the uses to which he was put in nineteenth-century
America. William James was a steadfast critic of American Hegelianism,
which enjoyed a great vogue in the post–Civil War United States.
Hegel's vision of America as "the land of the future" where "the Burden of the World's History shall reveal itself" in effect invited an orgy
of exceptionalism (qtd. Zamir 124; see Zamir 122–133). American
Hegelians appropriated Hegel to legitimate American nationalism and
racism within an optimistic Christian teleology of manifest destiny. the
1880s an old Walt Whitman and a young John Dewey were among
those swept up in affirming the harmonious unity of a progressive,
rational State (Zamir 126).

Half a century later Dewey saluted Hegel for having permanently liberated him from the shackles of Cartesian dualisms. But Dewey noted that he had drifted away from the philosopher's "mechanical dialectical" form, a "schematism" of system that eventually came to seem "artificial to the last degree" ("From Absolutism" 8). William James also rejected Hegel's system, yet preserved what he, like Dewey, found vital in Hegel—his dialectical vision, his anti-dualist stress on concrete embodiment and on becoming. But unheeded by James the staunch individualist was the lesson of Hegel's dialectical logic for man and society. Two pragmatists of the next generation, Dewey and Du Bois, embraced Hegel's insistence on the primacy of mediation, of social bonds, of the contextual. Thus the Hegelian deposit in both men's thought inflected their pragmatism with a critical historicism.

Du Bois would concur with George Herbert Mead's pragmatist view that the trouble with Hegel's Absolute Idealism is its denial that "our life is an adventure." In the Absolute "all that is to take place has already taken place . . . There can be nothing novel in an Absolute" (Mead *Movements* 508). Du Bois's particular challenge became how to dispense with Hegel's synthetic system, which denied a place both for the "tingling challenge of risk" he valued and for the negative particularity of African American enslavement, while retaining Hegel's redemptive historicist teleology for black Americans (Zamir 126). In an influential discussion of "how Du Bois became a Hegelian," the historian Joel Williamson persuasively shows that Hegel's model of World Spirit presides over the opening pages of *The Souls of Black Folk,* where Du Bois extends the six world historical peoples that Hegel posits to include the Negro as "a sort of seventh son" with his own message for the world. Despite acknowledging that Du Bois was "eclectic," Williamson overstates Hegel's impact when he says that "Hegel gave Du Bois a philosophy and a purpose in life, both of which he very much needed" and also gave him a "formula" for psychic survival that justified a "separated black culture" (*Crucible* 402, 409). In sum, Williamson would have us believe that Du Bois seized Hegel's blueprint as Truth and the rest, as they say, is History.

Implied in Williamson's reading is that because Du Bois studied at the University of Berlin in the early nineties in the midst of a Hegelian revival, his earlier training in James's evolving pragmatism was erased when Hegel swept him off his feet. But when Du Bois encountered Hegel he had already assimilated James's critique of the philosopher, which was part of the way James worked toward pragmatism. "My quarrel" with Hegel, James said, "is entirely apropos of the problem of identity. I think all his other faults derivative from that" (qtd. Perry 1: 765). He conducts this quarrel in "On Some Hegelisms" (1882). James regrets that in Hegel's logic, contradiction, the identification of opposites, functions as a "universal solvent—or, rather, there is no longer any need of a solvent" since all things have been dissolved into one another. James finds Hegelism a virtual frenzy of "reconciliation" (reconciliation, quips James, "characterizes the 'maudlin' stage of alcoholic drunkenness"), an intoxicating emotion but one whose inevitable outcome is "indifferentism"—blindness to particularity and to "irreducible . . . real conflicts." Hegel's "all-devouring" system abstracts all individuality, leaving "no residuum," only identity (*Will* 205, 218, 221, 214).[14]

James's esteem for risk, particularity, and residuum informed Du Bois's own encounter with Hegel's closed system, which he felt compelled to revise not least because it failed to account for his own embodied residuum—mixed racial ancestry. Hegel accorded mulattoes no reality, for he regarded cultural hybridity as impossible. Given his own mixed blood and his training in philosophic pragmatism, Du Bois had ample reason to be sensitive to the repressions of fixed identity and separatist culture, and the need to defend the precarious residuum. Thus he injected "adventure" into Hegel's teleology by refusing synthesis or closure: "unreconciled strivings," he wrote in *The Souls of Black Folk,* animate African American psyches and history.

In short, Du Bois did not choose between pragmatism and Hegelianism but instead let them revise each other.[15] With its emphasis on mobility and turning, pragmatist method inclines the practitioner toward an adaptive eclecticism, and that mode seems to have been particularly congenial to the intellectually voracious Du Bois. To adapt and refashion became his reflexive response to the many theories and systems of thought to which he was exposed. Dewey's summary of his own similar disposition is resonant here: "I seem to be unstable, chameleon-like, yielding one after another to many diverse and even incompatible influences; struggling to assimilate something from each" ("From Absolutism" 9).

Du Bois combined intellectual lability and a combative disposition into a politics of risk and difficulty. Charged with being a source of "disorder" at the NAACP, Du Bois admitted without apology that "my temperament is a difficult one to endure" (*Correspondence* 1: 203). Difficulty also afforded him literary pleasure; I noted earlier his pride in the "penumbra of vagueness" in *The Souls*. Du Bois's refusal of transparency shaped both his literary and racial representations. And it informs his political practice, which disdains the transparency of Booker T. Washington's "singleness of vision and thorough oneness with his age" (*Souls* 393). The "Tuskegee Machine," as Du Bois dubbed Washington's vast network of patronage, mirrored the age's "triumphant commercialism" with its fetish of managerial efficiency and social control.

What does a political practice look like that evades transparency and efficiency? It risks seeming simply evasive or inept, accusations that have consistently dogged Du Bois. But such judgments ignore his pragmatist understanding of politics as an improvisatory mode of conduct responsive to the pressure of changing historical circumstances. He not only theorized his historicism but enacted it. Embarking on the "curious path which Negro America is travelling," Du Bois described it as running "up hill and down, through dark forests and sunny glades, but especially it turns and twists so frequently that one cannot see just where one is going" ("Dilemma" 180). This remark appears in "The Dilemma of the Negro" (1924), an essay which shows that Du Bois's difficulty seeing where he is headed is caused not by poor eyesight but by dwelling in "cruel paradox"—the discrepancy between the theory and practice of segregation. He argues that black Americans' abhorrence of segregation is "established policy" because Jim Crow enforces "subordination" and "lack of essential cultural contact." Yet, he adds, in practice blacks have offered only a half-hearted fight against school segregation, for they do not want "hateful white people teaching their children." What tempers their fight is the "potent fact that in a world of enemies one prefers to consort with one's friends in sheer self-defense." As the numbers of black people of culture and education increase, this tendency toward self-segregation will grow even among the "more aspiring Negroes" (180).

In this essay Du Bois recalls that when Cheyney College asked him to speak in support of its becoming a state-supported black school, his speech crystallized, while refusing to resolve, the paradox of segregation. Cheyney could not survive without state aid, he declared, and we cannot let Cheyney die, since "we need it." Yet, he added, "if you promote a great Negro institution, well supported . . . with teachers from the greatest universities in the world, this is Race Pride. But at the same time this is also Segregation." However, "if you seek to carry out the principles of democracy in America today you deliver your children to the mercies of white teachers who in many cases neglect or hate them." He implored his audience to remember that "the demands of democracy and the demands of group advancement cannot always be reconciled," and that "the race pride of Negroes is not an antidote to the race pride of white people; it is simply the other side of a hateful thing."[16] Affirming state support of Cheyney yet decrying the race pride of segregation, Du Bois seemed to send a mixed message. Testifying to this were the "intent faces" of his audience "staring up at" him with a "perplexity in which hostility and wonder were mingled." Du Bois recalls that "some accused me bitterly of advocating segregation. Others declared I was fighting segregation to the last ditch. Thus one sees in embryo signs of future cleavage within the Negro race as it faces this cruel paradox" (181).

Du Bois's stance at Cheyney and the response it provoked in his audience vividly reveal the risks that his political conduct courts. Some accused him of retreating to Bookerite accommodationism, a charge that had been made in 1917 when he supported United States entry into war. But the controversy of Du Bois's politics resulted not from his retreat but from his struggle to think in and through paradox. Rather than imposing goals and values grounded in reason's antecedently formulated truths—the foundationalist effort of rationalism—Du Bois's conduct is shaped by the contingencies of the historical experience within which he is embedded. And in 1923 that experience is riven by the clash of competing priorities and sympathies: black progress in this century has been largely separatist, so black schools must continue; integration is a risk, yet without it race pride congeals into hatred and a promise of democracy—the opportunity of interracial contact—withers. Much to the dismay of his audience, Du Bois's speech stages the clash instead of defusing or muffling it.

By enacting the "unreconciled strivings" of his double consciousness, Du Bois stirs the "hostility and wonder" of his perplexed audience. Yet his provocations express not perversity but historical responsibility: because the reality that confronts them is unsettled, he unsettles, keeping debate alive in his audience so that their perplexity might be clarified, if not dissolved. This dissonant perspective is not to be the endpoint but the tool of a more nuanced kind of political conduct, one supple enough to make distinctions and double moves rather than relying on a single "frontal attack." Within ten years Du Bois was urging both continued "agitation against race prejudice and a planned economy" of segregation (*Dusk* 777). Double consciousness would thus be crucial in meeting the range of Negro needs, needs which only began with "the question of securing existence, of labor and income." With Washington doubtless in mind, Du Bois warns that "Negroes must live and eat and strive, and still hold unfaltering commerce with the stars" (557).

Neither in the speech at Cheyney nor in "The Dilemma of the Negro" does Du Bois unequivocally state a position. He comes to Cheyney's defense but frames his support within the grim context of the irreconcilable demands of democracy and of group advancement. Segregation has seemed the fuel of black Americans' progress, but Du Bois sees danger "plainly looming"—a future "world war" fomented by race hatreds. Already segregation has nearly obliterated "the strongest spiritual tie" between the races in America—the venerable tradition (begun in Reconstruction) of interracial contacts fostered by black and white teachers "working together in the higher Negro schools" ("Dilemma" 182). Yet ten years later, in 1934, Du Bois will lose faith in the present possibility of integration and actively urge voluntary economic segregation as a means to earn a better living and to revive race pride. Meanwhile he reconceives integration as an ultimate, if not immediate, goal.

Refusing to dispense solutions, Du Bois's political conduct seems most concerned to register the "turns and twists" of the "curious path" on which black Americans find themselves. He had told his Cheyney audience: "Despite all theory and almost unconsciously we are groping on. We recognize one thing worse than segregation and that is ignorance" (*Crisis* 1: 361). Granting at the start that "one cannot see just where one is going," Du Bois risks "touching an old and bleeding sore in Negro thought," as he describes his turn from NAACP integrationism (*Dusk* 777). A surgeon blindly probing, Du Bois is willing to risk the pain of reopening wounds, ripping off scabs of habit grown indurate, of boundaries and identities grown calcified, all in an effort to reinstate the rawness of experience latent with possibility and potential.

In 1934 Du Bois interrogated the raison d'être of the NAACP—racial integration—and created a storm of controversy that would end only with his resignation. In his blunt view the net result of the quarter-century-long NAACP campaign against segregation had "been a little less than nothing," and he insisted that integration, the sacred goal that had founded the organization in 1910, must be modified and adapted in the light of what history had revealed (*Writings* 1241). To stand steadfast "on the 'principle' of no segregation" and wait until public opinion meets our position would be an exercise in futility. "I am talking about conditions in 1934 and not in 1910. I do not care what I said in 1910 or 1810 or in B.C. 700" (1240). Instead, Du Bois urged "self-segregation and self-association," not as a "final solution of the race problem" but as the opposite—a step toward ultimately erasing the color line. "This is the great end toward which humanity is tending," he granted, while adding: "it is just as clear, that not for a century and more probably not for ten centuries, will any such consummation be reached." Thus the present "practical problem" was "not a choice between segregation and no segregation" but "how shall we conduct ourselves" given "varying degrees of segregation" (1247–48). Voluntary collective economic segregation must be attempted both as a counter-move "against the compulsory segregation forced upon" blacks and as a way to build a foundation of self-support and self-respect beneath "the laboring masses" (774, 1245).

In urging segregation Du Bois was willing to expose his own vulnerability in order to unsettle from within the identity both of the NAACP and of segregation. The latter, he hoped, would be transformed from a traditional "badge of servitude" into a declaration of self-respect: "If you do not wish to associate with me, I am more than willing to associate with myself. Indeed, I deem it a privilege to work with and for Negroes" (1244). Du Bois likened his strategy to the serpentine movements of modern warfare in which spectacular frontal assaults are avoided in favor of combining forward marching with end runs and retreats. But, as he expected, the NAACP had little patience for Du Bois's indirections. "It was astonishing and disconcerting," notes Du Bois, "and yet for the philosopher perfectly natural, that this change of my emphasis was crassly and stupidly misinterpreted" (*Dusk* 778). The "philosopher," that is, the pragmatist Du Bois, finds fear of change and quest for certainty "perfectly natural" because he recognizes the difficulty of giving up the rationalist assumption that beliefs are possessed of finality rather than functioning as "tentative, hypothetical . . . guide[s] to action" (Dewey *Quest* 277).

His segregation plan was misread as a betrayal of his own lifelong fight for equality and as a capitulation to defeatism and/or black chauvinism. This last charge was hurled by a younger generation of black political intellectuals, including three at Howard University—Franklin Frazier, Ralph Bunche, and Abram Harris. They excoriated Du Bois as "provincial" for clinging to race as the primary political category instead of economics (though in fact his approach made the two indissoluble) and for failing to see that solutions would come from interracial alliances of black and white labor solidarity. Du Bois found in such faith a desperate optimism and a dangerous naivete. The NAACP reaction was disappointing but expected: "the bulk of my colleagues," Du Bois noted, "saw no essential change in the world. It was the same world with the problems to be attacked by the same methods as before the war . . . They recoiled from any consideration of the economic plight of the world or any change in the organization of industry" (*Dusk* 766).

In opposing the entrenched NAACP orthodoxy, Du Bois was moving left while they "stepped decidedly toward the right" (782). The breach was impossible to repair, Du Bois felt, unless he "made a complete surrender" of his convictions (775). But in nearing the loss of the *Crisis* editorship that had won him international fame, he had not become a convert to Marxism, even though he believed that "Karl Marx was one of the greatest men of modern times," and even though in his segregation strategy he concurred with Marx that "the way in which men earn their living" is the determining factor "in the development of civilization" (775). In the twenties he had declared that he "was not prepared to dogmatize with Marx or Lenin" or socialism, and he reiterates this in 1934: "I was not and am not a communist. I do not believe in the dogma of inevitable revolution in order to right economic wrong" (*Writings* 1187; *Dusk* 775).

In abjuring Marxism's necessitarianism, Du Bois willfully courts multiple paradoxes—challenging the NAACP while being part of the NAACP, advocating segregation to end segregation, risking humiliating blacks to instill pride in blacks. His logic of paradox risks his authority, and with risk comes exposure: Du Bois hears "the gale of laughter" produced by his proposal for self-supporting economic cooperatives in the tradition of Robert Owen and Charles Fourier. But he insists on the value of articulating the possibility, however laughable. "We have a motive" that Owen and Fourier never had: "We are fleeing not simply from poverty, but from insult and murder and social death . . . It will mean years of poverty and sacrifice," but success would mean "we have conquered a world . . . We become in truth, free" (1237–38). And being free means undoing hierarchies of domination and letting the anarchy of decentralization reemerge. His plan for consumers' cooperatives gave this anarchy political form. The usually cynical George Schuyler hailed Du Bois's idea as "anarchism in action" because no government, armies, or police would be necessary for its workings (qtd. Young 88). The NAACP refused to support either anarchy or segregation, and Du Bois resigned in 1934. Not for the first time, had he to bear the cost of daring to go astray. This marked the virtual end of his national political influence. He returned to the NAACP from 1944 to 1948 as head of special research, but by then Walter White, the mainstream liberal and a foe of Du Bois, had firm control of the organization.

Du Bois's pragmatist politics is strikingly akin to what Dewey in the thirties is delineating in theory. Both are devoted to the "flowering of human capacity" (Dewey) and recognize that "the tactics of those who live for the widest development of men must change accordingly" (*Dusk* 765). The old liberalism fatally lacked the ability to change because, says Dewey, it was shackled by "inherited absolutism." He offers a sustained critique of this liberalism in the name of a "renascent liberalism" "committed to the idea of historic relativity" (*Later* 11: 291–292). Dewey declares an "intrinsic" connection between "historic relativity" and experimental method; inscribed in both is the simple fact that "time signifies change." What experiment implies, "in contrast to every form of absolutism," is that ideas and theories "be taken as methods of action tested and continually revised by the consequences they produce in actual social conditions" (293). This precisely describes Du Bois's experimental attitude toward the sclerotic politics of the NAACP.

Thus it was profoundly appropriate that Dewey and Du Bois joined in an experiment in pragmatist politics. Together they helped form a socialist third party in 1929—the League of Independent Political Action, which lasted until 1933. Dewey was national chair, and Du Bois served as a vice-chair. In a 1933 essay on the League, Dewey is careful to insist that it is "not a party and has no ambition to become a party"; he defines its "function" as "looking toward the organization of the desired new alignment . . . it aims to act as a connecting link . . . a symbol for one type of approach to the problem" (*Later* 9: 67). And Dewey takes as praise the critique of the League program as "partial and tentative, experimental and not rigid": "We claim them as indications of our philosophy." On another occasion, asked to speak on the subject of "The Need For a New Political Party," Dewey immediately revised his topic and title to "Needed—A New Politics." He urged "the necessity for a new kind of politics, a new kind of moral conception in politics . . . some fundamental rethinking of our social and political relations" (*Later* 11: 274, 280–281).

Dewey's experiment in creating a politics that minimizes the props of identity was ridiculed and a label was promptly applied. The League was dismissed as "watered-down socialism." After all, a political party, even one that calls itself a league, is expected to take positions, to be (or appear to be) full of determinate content. As Du Bois did in 1934, Dewey courts scorn with his in-betweenness. But the deferral of identity is for a larger purpose—to disturb the assumption that Americans possess democracy as a foundational identity. Far from already achieved, democracy is a perpetual pursuit of an end that is a *"radical end"* because it *"has not been adequately realized in any country at any time"* (*Later* 11: 299; Dewey's italics).

In 1939, as fascism is on the march, Dewey draws the unsettling consequences of this claim. If democracy has yet to be adequately realized, we in the United States are fatally mistaken if we assume that democracy automatically maintains itself. Americans are tempted into dangerous mystification if they imagine democracy a stable entity engraved in a constitution and guaranteeing us immunity from the disease of totalitarianism. "Certainly racial prejudice against" Negroes, Jews, and Catholics, writes Dewey, is "no new thing in our life. Its presence among us is an intrinsic weakness and a handle for the accusation that we do not act differently from Nazi Germany" (*Freedom and Culture* 127–128).

Du Bois would in effect not only concur with Dewey's unsparing assessment but trumpet it as he was battered by cold war hysteria in the fifties. As a black American he had suffered viscerally all his life the gap between democratic ideals and realities. But in his old age the hypocrisies grew intolerable. With a bellicose anti-communism disguising its own imperialist designs, American triumphalism blared endlessly the supremacy of the American way of life while intimidating or crushing those who dared disagree. Indicted by the government on flimsy charges of foreign collusion, Du Bois was tried and acquitted, and largely left isolated, deserted alike by black and white liberals. In this context, praise of Stalin served as an instrument of Du Bois's contempt, a way to dramatize his disgust both with the suffocating smugness and hypocrisy of the vaunted American way and with his former allies who had caved in to its blandishments. In his admiration of Stalin, Du Bois pushes to the extreme the logic of his insistence on "being a problem."

But his relation to Stalin was more than an expression of defiance. Du Bois had been an enthusiast of the USSR since the Bolshevik Revolution in 1917 and had become committed to its socialist goals after his first visit in 1926. "The wonder is not that Du Bois joined the party in 1961," notes Arnold Rampersad, "but that he had not done so before" (262). Yet it would be misleading to say, as some have, that Du Bois idealized Stalin or that "the absolutes of Marxist-Leninist thought led him to repudiate the relativism of the pragmatic method" (Rampersad 264). While positing democratic socialism as his goal, Du Bois was not deluded into mistaking Stalinism for its *achievement*. He admired Stalin for building "the first successful socialistic state in the world" but had no illusions that Stalin had created a democracy. In 1957 Du Bois declared that the USSR was "not intended to be democratic; it could not have made democracy work by the popular vote of ignorant, superstitious, sick, and poverty-stricken peasants and wage slaves . . . The uplift of the Russian people was deliberately planned to start with a dictatorship and Stalin was the first and the successful dictator." But no one planned that "the dictatorship should last indefinitely . . . They expected increased participation of the mass of people in democratic control as Russia became more intelligent" (*Writings By* 4: 281). Stalin's death, in fact, had opened up the social order to greater "personal freedom."[17]

Du Bois's inveterate penchant for double moves always oriented his relation to Marxism, socialism, and communism. He was convinced of their ethical, moral, and political superiority to capitalism and promulgated this for decades. But at the same time none of them possessed "automatic power . . . to override and suppress race prejudice" (*Writings By* 3: 38). Thus Du Bois consistently qualified "the promise of socialism" by asking open questions designed to breed thoughtful deliberation: "how far can American Negroes forward this eventual end? What part can they expect to have in a socialistic state?" (38). He asked this in 1936, reiterating the skepticism he had expressed for years. Even in 1960, a year before joining the Party, Du Bois insists on the interrogative: "standing at the crossroads where we are emerging from serfdom into the twilight of freedom are we to become what Americans are or what human beings ought to be?" (*Writings By* 4: 316). In becoming a member of a depleted organization that even in its prime he had scorned, Du Bois announced his political impotence but not a surrender to party-line thinking. Rather, he protested the illusion that the "so-called American way of life" was coextensive with human freedom (316). Hence he explained his decision as an attempt to help restore democracy to America. Several months after joining, Du Bois enacted solidarity, neither with America nor Russia, but with Africa as he moved to Ghana to live his remaining two years in Nkrumah's independent state.

Du Bois's pragmatist politics of turning and groping confirms Dewey's cautionary remark quoted earlier that to sustain one's pragmatic faith in "creative making" commits "us to a supremely difficult task." Revisionary practice not only is the subject of *Dusk of Dawn* but is enacted in its narrative strategies. Du Bois's "Essay toward an Autobiography of a Race Concept," to cite the book's subtitle, intimately renders the growth of a pragmatist sensibility by making visceral encounters with *pragmata* central to its narrative development. From its opening image of Du Bois flying "round and round with the Zeitgeist," *Dusk of Dawn* is a book of turnings, particularly from the dogma of rationalism to what he described as the "scientific task of the twentieth century . . . to explore and measure the scope of chance and unreason in human action" (558). In short, Du Bois will move to pragmatism and to Freud. And also to Marx. For race prejudice, Du Bois will come to realize, is inseparable from its "income-bearing value" and is "the cause and not the result of theories of race inferiority" (649).

An emergent air of things unsettled begins with the title, *Dusk of Dawn*, an image which is meant to suggest "that subtle sense of coming day . . . even when mist and murk hang low." This image of liminality, of germinating possibility, becomes the apt emblem of the work's genesis. For "midway in its writing" the book suddenly "changed its object and pattern." His seventieth birthday had occasioned "unawaited remarks and comments," provoking a need to rethink his project. *Dusk of Dawn* had "threatened to become mere autobiography," a genre with "little lure" for Du Bois because of its subjectivist assumption that the importance of one's life resided in one's own personal influence on the world.[18] My life, Du Bois tells us, had its "only deep significance because it was part of a Problem . . . the central problem of the greatest of the world's democracies and so the Problem of the future world." "My living gains its importance," he says, "from the problems and not the problems from me" (716). Du Bois now offers the reader "what is meant to be not so much my autobiography as the autobiography of a concept of race, elucidated, magnified, and doubtless distorted in the thoughts and deeds which were mine" (551). But before long his pragmatist skepticism of the repressiveness of concepts will lead him to interrogate his subtitle.

The havoc of chance will be evident throughout, repeatedly derailing his and the epoch's late-Victorian trust that "it was a day of Progress with a capital P" (572). This derailment culminates the drama of Du Bois's early career, which began with laboring in the "ivory tower of race" scholarship. In thirteen years at Atlanta University he published 2,712 pages of research on American Negro problems (601). What startles him out of his "Ivory tower of statistics and investigation" is a "red ray which could not be ignored," a ray that appears "at the very time when my studies were most successful" (603). That uncanny, bloody portent announces the fate of Sam Hose, a poor Georgia Negro accused of murder in 1899. Du Bois hears the news while walking on Mitchell Street on his way to deliver a statement to the Atlanta *Constitution* pleading that Hose receive a fair trial. But Hose has already been lynched, his knuckles on exhibit at a Mitchell Street grocery. "I turned back to the university. I began to turn aside from my work . . . One could not be a calm, cool, and detached scientist while Negroes were lynched" (602–603).

This realization, expressed in the physical and figurative turns described above, shatters Du Bois's idealization of Reason and Truth as the pillars of a scientific sociology. A year later Du Bois writes "Sociology Hesitant," his unpublished critique of current sociological method as blind to the power of the contingent. After his unnerving encounter with the uncontainable, Du Bois's faith in the ideal of scientific detachment gradually fades, as does his earlier belief that "race prejudice was primarily a matter of ignorance" to be cured by massive injections of knowledge. By the 1930s Du Bois is ready to take "a still further step" and explore "the twilight zone" where the deeper springs of human motivation reside (760).

By making *Dusk of Dawn* "the autobiography of a concept of race," Du Bois maximizes flux, for the meaning of the "race concept" is in nearly constant upheaval as Du Bois encounters it from elementary school in Great Barrington to Fisk, Harvard, Berlin, and then in the first three decades of the twentieth century. In "The Concept of Race," the remarkable fifth chapter of *Dusk of Dawn,* Du Bois moves among biological, social, cultural, and historical explanations without settling upon one, as if to enact the one steady fact about the race concept— the "continuous change in the proofs and arguments advanced" (626). His late-nineteenth-century education had put him in the middle of tumult: no sooner had he "settled into scientific security . . . than the basis of race distinction was changed without explanation, without apology" (626). Du Bois imparts a vivid sense of this agitation in recounting how his effort to theorize his racial identity collided with changing facts and experiences (628).

Recall his decision "henceforward" to be a Negro as he entered the "closed racial group" at Fisk. This choice gave birth to race pride and a "theory of race separation" that he practiced at Harvard. But Du Bois's fine theory, alas, could not account for his own mulatto status. He remembers being ridiculed by colored friends for his "ultra 'race' loyalty" because he is embodied proof that "race lines were not fixed and fast" (628). "They pointed out that I was not a 'Negro,' but a mulatto, that I was not a Southerner but a Northerner, and my object was to be an American and not a Negro; that race distinctions must go. I agreed with this in part and as an ideal." Yet he resists the move to assimilation for fear that a mulatto elite would humiliate "too dark companions." In Europe his friendships with white people had subjected his separatist policy to additional doubts. Responsive to change as ever, Du Bois began to "waver": "I began to emphasize the cultural aspects of race." By 1911, when he attended the Universal Races Congress and had also absorbed the impact of Boas, he knew that "scientific definition of race" was impossible, as impossible as the attempt to "divide the world into races" (654).

Around 1920, having seen "science made the slave of caste and race hate," Du Bois began to dwell on what his turn-of-the-century race chauvinism had disdained as inadmissible—the fact of "intermingling" (630). He came to emphasize his mulatto status not least because it was precious proof of "intermixture" in a society and world seeking to legislate this out of existence. Not only had the U.S. Census deleted "mulatto" but scientific study of race-mixing in the United States was "almost non-existent," notes Du Bois. "We have tried almost by legal process to stop such study" because hybridity threatens "the economic foundation of the modern world"—which depends on "preservation of so-called racial distinctions" to ensure a permanent class of cheap labor (629). To reinstate what has been systematically erased, Du Bois recovers "interracial history" by presenting a detailed genealogy of his family in *Dusk of Dawn* (630).

In assessing the impact of his ceaseless agitation against the color line, Du Bois admits his helplessness to alter the immovable fact of "our continual unwillingness to break the intellectual bonds of group and racial exclusiveness," that "deep conviction of myriads of men that congenital differences among the main masses of human beings absolutely condition the individual destiny of every member of a group" (654, 656). Du Bois calls this unfreedom of segregation the "spiritual provincialism" into which he has been born, "and this fact has guided, embittered, illuminated and enshrouded my life" (656). The race

man's loyalty to his people, Du Bois admits, only reinforces group isolation and enacts a similar psychic attenuation: "He thinks of himself
not as an individual but as a group man" (651).

Du Bois's admissions do not simply pour out in confessional overflow. Never at a loss for invention, he subtly orchestrates his sense of
group enclosure, his rueful feeling of provincialism, and his cherishing
of an impudent "anarchy of the spirit." These cluster near one another
on three consecutive pages, but they pivot around and their meaning
is enlarged by the final paragraph of the book's central chapter, "The
Concept of Race." After the penultimate paragraph speaks of group
entrapment and its pernicious emotional effects, the concluding paragraph begins:

> This was the race concept which has dominated my life, and the history
> of which I have attempted to make the leading theme of this book. It had
> as I have tried to show all sorts of illogical trends and irreconcilable ten-
> dencies. Perhaps it is wrong to speak of it at all as 'a concept' rather than
> as a group of contradictory forces, facts, and tendencies. At any rate, I
> hope I have made its meaning to me clear. (651)

Here at the center of his autobiography, Du Bois turns against his
own subtitle for its factitious tidiness and dissolves "race concept" into
the "whirlpool of social entanglement and inner psychological paradox" which expresses his "life and action" (555). Given that concepts,
says William James, "cut out and fix, and exclude," Du Bois's turn
crystallizes what one might call the pragmatist aesthetic moment in the
Du Boisian text, the dispersal of the concept into indeterminacy and
"anarchy" (James *Writing* 746). Thus he eludes an epistemology of
segregation founded on the coercions of identity logic.

What instigates Du Bois's dispersal of meaning into "irreconcilable"
and "contradictory" elusiveness is the opposite—the bleak acknowledgment of "group imprisonment" (650). In the paragraph following
the conclusion of chapter five, that is, the opening of chapter six, Du
Bois faces the humiliation of caste. He displaces, if barely, the pain of
the encounter onto the elaborate metaphor of segregation which depicts "entombed souls" screaming behind "some thick sheet of invisible plate glass . . . in a vacuum unheard," who may "break through in
blood and disfigurement" (650). But it is Du Bois who is confessing
his psychic disfigurement and enacting its antidote. He locates the injury of segregation in the denial of "essential and common humanity,"
a denial inscribed in the racialization of thought and language. "All my

life I have had continually to haul my soul back and say, 'All white folk are not scoundrels nor murderers. They are, even as I am, painfully human' " (650). Then Du Bois recovers what is painfully human, unmarked by race: he speaks of the desire to live "without interference from others; to enjoy that anarchy of the spirit which is inevitably the goal of all consciousness" (652). The anarchy is all the more precious because, as his next two paragraphs show, black Americans are not Americans of the twentieth century but are forced to live as if in the medieval world, fixed in their stations, always "a thing apart."

In sum, at the center of *Dusk of Dawn* Du Bois stages between the lines a kind of allegory of his burden and redemption, the yoke of authenticity and the leap of invention. What his unwritten parable on the margins discloses is the aesthetic as inventive action—action that courts risk, incalculability, and anarchic possibility in a world of stifling segregation. Such action necessarily partakes of difficulty, in both literary and self-representation. For only difficulty can break the "spell" of stereotype and of hierarchy. These mechanisms of containment are disrupted "when the black man begins to dispute the white man's title to certain alleged bequests of the Fathers in wage and position, authority and training . . . when he insists on his human right to swagger and swear and waste,—then the spell is suddenly broken" (*Writings* 925). On one level, Du Bois's difficulty insisted on his human right to swagger and waste. As it was intended to do, such pugnacity nettled those around him.

"Surrounding you always, I may say frankly, I have found an atmosphere of antagonism," wrote an exasperated Joel E. Spingarn in 1914 (Du Bois *Correspondence* 1: 201). Spingarn was admonishing Du Bois, his respected friend and NAACP colleague, for relocating the *Crisis* offices from Vesey Street to the far tonier 70 Fifth Avenue, at double the monthly rent. Du Bois was not the ascetic he is often reputed to have been. One of the virtues of Lewis's biography is that it recovers Du Bois's swagger, his body and sexuality. Not only did he have extramarital affairs but, on numerous visits to Europe, he enjoyed the gracious luxury of haute-bourgeois salons, exhilarated at being temporarily free of " 'nigger'-hating America" (*Darkwater* 16).[19] Lewis writes of the "emotional lift" Du Bois received on his month-long European vacation in 1907. Being accepted "as an outstanding personality unstigmatized by color . . . went a long way toward drawing poison from the wounds he tried never to let show in America" (Lewis 371).

The practice of difficulty protected psychic wounds from being further abraded but also isolated him, not unlike racism itself. In wielding the weapon of personal distinction, he could not help replicating something of the brutality of the master class. Students "reflexively flinched when he approached," Lewis reports, frightened by how he "jauntily wielded his walking stick" about the Atlanta University campus. Du Bois was oblivious to the fact that the students had, when younger, been subjected to caning by white folks (Lewis 215). Du Bois himself seemed to intuit that he was imprisoned in distinction and in difficulty: "In my peculiar education and experiences it would be miraculous if I came through normal and unwarped," he acknowledged to Spingarn (*Correspondence* 1: 203). As compulsion, distinction trapped him in contempt and ceaseless productivity; as aesthetic sensibility, however, it released him from the capitalist reign of discipline and utility. He experienced "the leisure of true aristocracy—leisure for thought and courtesy" when he visited a village of the Veys in West Africa in 1924 (*Dusk* 647).[20]

Du Bois tropes distinction as taste, as style, as aesthetic receptivity, all of which flowered in him when he won a fellowship for graduate study in Berlin (1892–1894). Recalling that time, he wrote: "Europe modified profoundly my outlook on life and my thought and feeling toward it . . . something of the possible beauty and elegance of life permeated my soul" (587). And concurrent with his aesthetic awakening was "the opportunity . . . of looking at the world as a man and not simply from a narrow racial and provincial outlook" (*Autobiography* 159). To Du Bois, aesthetic bliss and the erasure of the color line would forever be fused. Europe and Africa, but not bustling America, afforded opportunity to enjoy sitting with Shakespeare and to experience daily life attuned to slower rhythms. "I had been before, above all, in a hurry," admits Du Bois in recalling his aesthetic initiation. "I wanted a world, hard, smooth, and swift, and had no time for rounded corners and ornament, for unhurried thought and slow contemplation. Now at times I sat still. I came to know Beethoven's symphonies and Wagner's Ring. I looked long at the colors of Rembrandt and Titian . . . Form, color, and words took new combinations and meanings" (*Writings* 587).

In the leisure granted by his 1892 fellowship, Du Bois surrendered to surfaces and appearances, feeling no obligation to leave the sensuous materiality of form and color in search of content or moral. In short, he developed the pure gaze of disinterestedness that, since Kant, has denoted the specifically aesthetic quality of contemplation. In *The Souls of Black Folk* he would describe this relaxed attention to objects of beauty as a way of seeking "freedom for expansion and self-development" in a "higher individualism which the centres of culture protect" (437). In Europe Du Bois learned firsthand the truth of Schiller's claim that imagination (viewer's and creator's) develops its "unrestrained capacities" only when want and necessity are satisfied. Otherwise, "imagination is bound with strong chains to the actual." In our time, Pierre Bourdieu finds the aesthetic disposition rooted in an "ethos of elective distance" from economic necessity (*Distinction* 54). Du Bois concurs: the creative impulse is freed only "when poverty approaches abolition; when men no longer fear starvation and unemployment" (*Writings* 1061). In such a world, "living begins," for the individual has the opportunity to develop and broaden "feelings and emotions through sound and color, line and form." For full expression, these emotions require "technical mastery of the media" (1060). This statement of 1938, continuous with what he learned in 1892, reaffirms his understanding of art as a medium whose formal properties and technique take precedence over external referents or subject matter.

A few months before Du Bois embarked to learn the pleasures of wasting time by sitting still in Europe, his philosophy tutor, Santayana, was pleading for a higher individualism in terms that would soon become Du Bois's. Santayana's answer to the question posed in his title, "What Is a Philistine?" published in the *Harvard Monthly* of May 1892, centers on the philistine's relation to time: the philistine mind "is in a hurry" and thus has the "habit of abbreviated thinking" manifested in his "asking the money value of everything." Price is an abbreviation, an "abstract term, invented to facilitate our operations." In reducing experience to abbreviation, the philistine "mental process is all algebra"; its dexterous use of symbols and "instruments of calculation" make "it forget the vision of the real world and the primitive source of all value in the senses and the affections" (Santayana 230–231). Hence the "indifference to the beauties of art," for "art appeals to the vividness of sensations" and the philistine "can never repose in sense, since every sensation is to him merely a sign and symbol" (232).

Du Bois's discovery of contemplation reverberates beyond the realm of self-culture to become an urgent part of his project to democratize access to the aesthetic as cultural capital. He seeks to instill cultural competence in black people, in particular the capacity to recognize a distinction between art and life. This is the basis of the aesthetic disposition which, says Bourdieu, "implies a break with the ordinary [in-strumental] attitude towards the world" (31). Not long after returning from Europe, Du Bois lectured on "The Art and Art Galleries of Europe" in rural Ohio, passing around penny illustrations of great works. Whenever you go to America's great urban centers, Du Bois implores his audience, "go to the art galleries, not rushing through pell-mell, but go sit down and look at a beautiful picture a half hour each week. It is an education, soul training which nothing can surpass" (*Against Racism* 36). In urging black people to enter the "kingdom of culture," Du Bois enacts his belief that the kingdom is not an elite's preserve but is open to anyone possessed of curiosity. His democratic cosmopolitanism is, to borrow Bourdieu's words, engaged in a "constant struggle for the universalization of the privileged conditions of existence which render the pursuit of the universal possible" ("Corporatism" 110).

The implicit logic of Du Bois's project strikingly echoes Schiller's argument that "our aesthetic disposition . . . is what gives rise to freedom"; hence "indifference towards reality and interest in appearance are a real enlargement of humanity and a decisive step towards culture" (125). The pleasure in appearances proves not only one's external freedom from necessity but also one's internal freedom, for the artist who imposes a form must possess "sufficient energy to repel the pressure of matter" embodied in the "reality of things." Drawing on his own experience in Europe, Du Bois likewise urges his audience to suspend the onrush of time, to bracket off life's ordinary urgencies. While we know that Du Bois read Schiller, there is no direct proof that he read the seminal *Aesthetic Education*. Yet one reason Du Bois would find it compelling is that Schiller addressed an age not unlike Du Bois's own, where "*utility* is the great idol" and "necessity is master and bends a degraded humanity beneath its tyrannous yoke" (Schiller 26). What results for "us moderns," says Schiller, is that "not merely individual persons but whole classes of human beings develop only a part of their capacities" (38).[21]

Du Bois's program of aesthetic education urged black people to visit American museums. Lest it seem that this be taken as patriotic boosterism, he adds that American collections "are but faint echoes of the great galleries of the world . . . Only in Europe can we study the art of the world." Du Bois followed his intoxicated Eurocentrism of 1896 with the mystical Afrocentrism of "The Conservation of the Races," a lecture given the next year. What connects them is a shared rejection, or at least limiting, of American identity. Our Americanism goes no farther, says Du Bois in the later address, than birth, citizenship, language, religion, and political ideals. Echoing Santayana, he declares that America is virtually barren of culture: "Little of beauty has America given the world . . . the human spirit in this new world has expressed itself in vigor and ingenuity rather than in beauty" (*Souls* 536). Intoning a rhetoric of romantic racialism, Du Bois warns that the destiny of the American Negro as the leader of "Pan-Negroism" is "not a servile imitation of Anglo-Saxon culture, but a stalwart originality which shall unswervingly follow Negro ideals" (820). Du Bois locates this originality in music, which he sees as the Negro's special gift to American culture. "There is no true American music but the wild sweet melodies of the Negro slave" (370).

After 1896 Du Bois's most sustained efforts to place aesthetic experience at the center of ordinary black life occur in his essay "Criteria of Negro Art" (1926), and then in his best novel, *Dark Princess* (1928). The latter work depicts one black American's effort to attain "the higher individualism." At one point, Matthew Towns seeks spiritual purification and so becomes a common laborer digging the Chicago subway. Yet the dreariness of his job sparks an ambition to rejoin what capitalism's division of labor has torn asunder—"thought and physical work," art and life, beauty and the quotidian. Soon Matthew realizes that all the "mud and filth and grayness" have left his "soul . . . starving for color and curve and form." Matthew chooses a Du Boisian antidote, spending an unhurried week at the Art Institute contemplating the masterpieces that capitalism enshrines: "I bathed myself in a new world of beauty." After his week at the museum, he emerges with wider vision, eager to resume work not as the automaton he had been but as "a more complete man—a unit of a real democracy" (279–280). His aesthetic education thus remedies what Schiller identified as the human being's reduction to a fragment under "collective mechanical life." When Matthew joins the union to try and make "higher individualism" available to his co-workers, however, he is quickly fired.

Like *Dark Princess*, "Criteria of Negro Art" argues that beauty can redeem the stunted human condition under capitalism and renew democratic possibility. The essay revives Du Bois's effort to democratize access to cultural capital. But his emphasis has shifted since the 1890s in two ways: from the discontinuity to the continuities of art and life; and from art as a unique racial gift expressing a people's essence to art's power to render racial identity irrelevant. Regarding the latter, he says: "Just as soon as true Art emerges; just as soon as the black artist appears," racial categories destabilize: "someone touches the race on the shoulder and says, 'He did that because he was an American, not because he was a Negro; he was born here; he was trained here; he is not a Negro—what is a Negro anyhow? He is just human' " (*Writings* 1002).

"Criteria of Negro Art" is best known for one of Du Bois's most quoted yet misunderstood statements: "Thus all art is propaganda and ever must be, despite the wailing of the purists" (1000). Readers at the time and since isolate this sentence as proof that Du Bois had nervously retreated from the modernism of the Harlem Renaissance toward a politicizing of art inspired by his enthusiastic visit to the Soviet Union in the autumn of 1926. But "Criteria of Negro Art" deserves a close reading to show how creative and intricate his position actually was.[22] Far from promulgating a vulgar Marxism, Du Bois conducts a pragmatist inquiry that prefigures Dewey's own project a few years later in *Art as Experience*. Du Bois unstiffens (James's word) congealed thinking and disarms defensive separations, while urging "wide judgment" and "catholicity of temper" (1001). From the opening, he insists on questioning a series of alleged oppositions: Truth and Beauty, propaganda and art, politics and culture, aesthetic experience and American blacks. Undergirding these dichotomies, Du Bois implies, are unexamined and confused cultural assumptions, a myopia that reflects the fact that both races are "hemmed in" in "all sorts of ways." Whites are constricted by the "racial pre-judgment" they demand of their artists, while blacks "are bound by all sorts of customs that have come down as second-hand soul clothes of white patrons" (1001).

His essay's most audacious move is an act of troping, as he revises, indeed defamiliarizes, "propaganda." Those who know Du Bois's essay only for its declaration that "all Art is propaganda" are likely to be puzzled by its opening pages, which describe the experience of beauty engendering moments of aesthetic bliss in the midst of daily life in philistine America. Du Bois had anticipated puzzlement. How can a civil rights organization, he imagines some thinking, "turn aside to talk about Art? After all, what have we who are slaves and black to do with Art?" (993). And he imagines others relieved that his talk will offer a pleasant respite from the struggle for equality. But both responses are wrong and for the same reason—they assume art to be inherently segregated from life. Anticipating by five years Dewey's effort to close "the chasm between ordinary and esthetic experience," Du Bois declares:

"The thing we are talking about tonight is part of the great fight we are carrying on and it represents . . . a pushing onward" (993).

Rather than immediately explaining how art and life are integrated, Du Bois continues the interrogative mode established at the opening. "What do we want? What is the thing we are after . . . Do we want simply to be Americans? . . . are we satisfied with its [America's] present goals and ideals?" (993). Deferring answers, Du Bois recalls the time he traveled to the Scottish border on a quiet Sunday, redolent of romance and remembered poetry. He "fell asleep full of enchantment" only to be rudely awakened at dawn by "loud and strident" pushing American tourists. "They struck a note not evil but wrong . . . their hearts had no conception of the beauty which pervaded this holy place" (994). Resuming his 1890s attack on philistine Americans, Du Bois sets up the boorish white tourist as a cautionary figure for blacks to define themselves against. Du Bois is confident that black marginality breeds skepticism of Philistine values: "Pushed aside as we have been in America, there has come to us not only a certain distaste for the tawdry and flamboyant but a vision of what the world could be if it were really a beautiful world." His essay's examples of the world's beauty suggest its variety and possibility: the cathedral at Cologne, a West African village at dusk, the Venus de Milo, a phrase of Southern music, but also "the glory of sunsets and the peace of quiet sleep" (995). "Yet," Du Bois adds, "today the mass of human beings are choked away from it, and their lives distorted and made ugly" (995).

Although his 1896 lecture on the art galleries of Europe urged blacks to visit museums, now Du Bois enlarges his notion of beauty beyond discrete artifacts, a view anticipating Dewey's regret that art is confined to museums. Art should be treated, says Dewey, neither as a pleasure of the idle moment nor as a means of snobbish display. Instead, art must become an "acknowledged power in human association." It is "a quality that permeates an experience" with "heightened vitality"; the effect on the psyche is to dissolve barriers of "limiting prejudices" and to expand sympathies (*Art* 334, 348, 326).

But the cultural goal of understanding art as power remains unrealized, says Dewey, thanks to the separation of the creation and enjoyment of "fine art" from "the normal processes of living." This divorce "is a pathetic, even a tragic, commentary on life as it is ordinarily lived. Only because that life is usually so stunted, aborted, slack, or heavy laden is the idea entertained" that art is nothing but the "beauty parlor of civilization" (27, 344). Art is trivialized by "compartmentalized psychology" which apprehends experience through a grid of dualisms—mind and body, beauty and use, art and life. Capitalism's "private control of the labor of other men for the sake of private gain" produces this psychology. And the oppositions that structure its epistemology originate "in fear of what life may bring forth. They [dualisms] are marks of contraction and withdrawal" reflecting the dominant economic and social arrangement (262, 22, 343). Only when "radical social alteration" (democratic socialism) relaxes economic pressure for private profit will Beauty have a chance to be restored to the experience of "the mass of men and women who do the useful work of the world." Until then, neither "art nor civilization is secure" (343–344). In seeking to renovate the conditions of democratic capitalism that splinter sensibility, Dewey's aesthetic politics make explicit what is implicit in both "Criteria of Negro Art" and *Dark Princess.*

Du Bois's answer to his essay's question "who shall let this world be beautiful"—"Negro Youth" who are stirring with a "new desire to create"—echoes Alain Locke's introduction to *The New Negro* anthology of the previous year (*Writings* 995). Locke, however, is one of the unnamed "wailing purists" Du Bois opposes in his oft-quoted statement about propaganda and art. In *The New Negro,* Locke had drawn a sharp generational divide—"Youth speaks and the voice of the New Negro is heard"—that announced a new departure (47). Gone is the "cautious moralism" and "guarded idealizations" of the elder generation (Du Bois's), along with their belief that "art must fight social battles and compensate social wrongs" (50). The "newer motive in being racial," writes Locke, "is to be so purely for the sake of art" (51). In reviewing *The New Negro,* Du Bois cautioned that Locke risked "decadence" by opposing Beauty and Propaganda too firmly (*Book Reviews* 79).

In "Criteria of Negro Art" Du Bois diverges from Locke's alleged diffidence about what Beauty has "to do with the world" (995). It is "the duty of black America," he declares, "to begin this great work of the creation of Beauty" (1000). Because he finds Locke's Platonic notion of Beauty inadequate to the task of this work, Du Bois turns from it and marries Beauty to Truth and Freedom, to "the facts of the world and the right actions of men" (995). This enacts the Jamesian pragmatist's turn "towards facts, towards action, and towards power." While acknowledging that "somewhere eternal and perfect Beauty sits above Truth," Du Bois insists that "here and now and in the world in which I work they are for me unseparated and inseparable" (995).

To this pragmatist and historicist construction of art as the practice that creates the "Beauty of Truth and Freedom" Du Bois gives the name "propaganda": "I stand in utter shamelessness and say that whatever art I have for writing has been used always for propaganda for gaining the right of black folk to love and enjoy. I do not care a damn for any art that is not used for propaganda" (1000). He radically defamiliarizes propaganda by giving it the function of restoring beauty to an impoverished American culture. His troping mimes art's power to confound classifications, to dissolve identity. He again salutes this power at the essay's end when "Art emerges" to prompt the question "what is a Negro anyhow?" "What is propaganda anyhow?" is an analogous question inscribed within the essay's interrogative rhetorical strategy.

In 1921 Du Bois had used the word in its familiar sense, admonishing those who "insist that our Art and Propaganda be one. This is wrong and in the end it is harmful" (*Crisis* 1: 301). Then he was concerned to honor the artist's freedom to depict black characters of moral complexity. His 1926 position inverts this earlier statement but not at art's expense. In stating that "all art is propaganda," Du Bois forces opposites to collide into each other, with the effect of setting both words into motion, releasing less conventional meanings. What results is a new distinction: propaganda freed from its usual degrading instrumentalism and, instead, "beautifully and painstakingly done," which is how he describes *The New Negro* (*Book Reviews* 79). This defamiliarized propaganda promotes the aesthetic unconfined to artifacts and become the practice of the art of living. Sponsored by the "higher individualism," this practice commences "the creation of Beauty" as an alternative to the philistinism that is coarsening American life.

The pragmatist logic of "Criteria of Negro Art," challenging and "unstiffening" dichotomized thought, unexamined assumptions, and premature conclusions, required a patient attentiveness that was little in evidence amid its readers' restless scramble for position-taking and polemicizing. That Du Bois's troping was ignored, and propaganda maintained its conventional meaning, testifies to the impatience he found afflicting both whites and blacks. On one side are white philistines, who "all tried to get everywhere first." On the other, young black writers, coddled by their muse of "eternal and perfect Beauty," are persuaded by admiring white readers that their art provides "the real solution" of the "Negro question." Du Bois imagines "both white and black" to be "whispering" " 'Keep quiet! Don't complain! Work! All will be well!' " (997). "Criteria of Negro Art" is intended as a wedge against premature closure: the NAACP "comes upon the field . . . to say that the Beauty of Truth and Freedom . . . is not in our hands yet." We must continue "agitation" along the color line. Thus Du Bois enacts in his essay's structure and strategies the aesthetic attitude of deferral, what Dewey calls the "resistances" to fluently mechanical action that the "heightened consciousness" of art produces (*Art* 261).

The received reading of "Criteria of Negro Art" as narrowly political suggests that it failed to communicate its pragmatist plea for wide judgment. Any explanation of this failure must consider that the essay was launched into a context of fiercely contested cultural politics, a climate that took a toll on the generosity of all the combatants and virtually ensured a misreading of Du Bois. His own capacity for wide judgment and catholic taste became a casualty of the times, and his bitter indictment of such books as *Home to Harlem* and *Nigger Heaven* sealed his reputation as genteel Victorian moralist. Confirming this image was Du Bois's warning that Locke risked decadence.

In defiance of Du Bois's warning, seven New Negroes gathered around Wallace Thurman in late 1926 to create *Fire!!*, a self-consciously scandalous new literary magazine dedicated to satisfying "the pagan thirst for beauty unadorned." The magazine's main source of energy was the desire to outrage the reigning authorities, especially Du Bois, who would allegedly reduce art to propaganda. Du Bois gave the magazine his blessing in *The Crisis* ("we bespeak for it wide support"). Though his welcome can be written off as merely strategic or perfunctory, Du Bois's gesture is also a clue that *Fire!!* and "Criteria of Negro Art" shared, in his view, a thirst for beauty. Two years later the thirst helped produce *Dark Princess*, which I will discuss in the next chapter. Wallace Thurman's attenuated grasp of Du Bois's position is made clear in *Infants of the Spring* (1932). In this roman à clef devoted to the literary and political ferment of the day, a young intellectual argues: "Dr. Du Bois has shown us the way. We must be militant fighters. We must not hide away in ivory towers and prate of beauty" (238).

A dozen years earlier Du Bois had been chastised for the opposite sin—of being all too eager to prate of beauty instead of struggling for rights. A. Philip Randolph, the major socialist intellectual to the left of Du Bois, claimed that the dandified Du Bois was a figure "whom no one in the streets could recognize as a radical" (qtd. Anderson *Randolph* 102). The opposite critiques of Thurman and Randolph share an unexamined premise (upheld by some Cultural Studies work in our own day) that Du Bois urgently refused—the antagonism between politics and aesthetics. "Criteria of Negro Art" turns the aesthetic into a militant part of a political, economic, and cultural movement. Harold Cruse is one of the few to recognize that Du Bois's essay was "the very first time" a major black intellectual had described Negro art "in its functional relationship to the civil rights movement" and thereby refused the "old European version of socialist programming wherein economics and politics took precedence over culture and art" (42–43). Pragmatism is the name I have used to describe Du Bois's "functional" approach to the aesthetic. His approach breeds skepticism of Locke's enthroning of Beauty as propaganda's opposite; Du Bois doubts that "there can be a search for disembodied beauty which is not really a passionate effort to do something tangible" (*Book Reviews* 79).

Du Bois's passionate effort to do something tangible with beauty recalls Oscar Wilde's "The Soul of Man under Socialism" (1891), which renewed Schiller's project for Du Bois's generation. Wilde urged a mood of "receptivity" in experiencing art, an openness that would serve as a model for a "true Individualism" all but crushed by the obsession with acquiring private property. Wilde's anti-bourgeois celebration of laziness and lying, but also his own "feminine" image and "inferior" Irishness, which allegedly could only mimic English culture, had led to his being caricatured as an uppity black dandy in cartoons in the American press in the 1880s.[23] Wilde's "to live is the rarest thing in the world. Most people exist, that is all" (262) is echoed in Du Bois's remark that "the man that spends his life earning a living, has never lived" (*Writings* 1060). What makes living possible, says Wilde, is the action of beauty, which dissolves "all the egotism" that drives the acquisitive spectator (280). Sounding a Wildean note, Du Bois warned his audience in his "Art Galleries of Europe" address, "how easily can a hideous combination of colors, or a tawdry picture make a man an aesthetic idiot for life" (*Against Racism* 34). Whether Du Bois found the balm of beauty in the art galleries of Europe or in a West African village "done in cream and pale purple," where "laziness; divine, eternal, languor is right and good and true," it was crucial to his vision of living a free life in an "aesthetic State" (*Writings* 646; Schiller, 140).

The Du Bois I have presented in this chapter is very much a man of the nineties, the decade of his intellectual maturity. Because he lived in the midst of the aesthetic movement as a student in *fin-de-siècle* Europe and was present at the creation of pragmatism, Du Bois knew each at first hand. This intimacy inoculated him against caricatures that portrayed the one as apolitical withdrawal and the other as loyal servant of the status quo. Instead, Du Bois's richly inward appropriation of pragmatism and the sense of beauty fashioned them into an aesthetic politics that helped animate his life's work. The bewilderment with which Du Bois would probably have greeted the current demand to choose between aesthetics and politics has much to teach our own *fin de siècle*.

5

Divine Anarchy: Du Bois and the Craving for Modernity

By the 1890s Du Bois recognized that black Americans were "yet struggling in the eddies of the fifteenth century," and that his mission was to help deliver them into a modern world where equality and liberty were American birthrights. One of his most audacious and least appreciated meditations on modernity is *Dark Princess,* the book he regarded as his personal favorite among all he wrote. Yet Du Bois suggests a certain ambivalence or defensiveness about his enterprise, for he subtitles *Dark Princess* a romance rather than a novel and ends it with an "Envoy" that thanks "the sprites" who have "helped him weave" his tale. Du Bois's deliberate archness here, which appears in other self-reflexive moments in his text, perhaps is meant to encourage readers to indulge his writing of a romance in a literary age of naturalism and realism. But Du Bois's indulgence involves other, more personal motives, for the book revives and prompts fantasies of release both inside and outside the text. This release is expressed in the acts of anarchy—sexual, political, aesthetic—that constitute the novel's consuming subject.

The pleasure Du Bois shares with William James in anarchy as a locus of creative energy is cognate with Emerson's notion of "abandonment," that influx of "new energy" whereby the intellect is "released from all service" (Emerson 459). Abandonment becomes the fulcrum by which the hero Matthew Towns achieves a cosmopolitan freedom. Twin acts of severance define his career—abandonment of medical school and, later, of Chicago politics. An adulterous love affair with a beautiful Indian Princess, Kautilya, will shatter Matthew's marriage and his budding political career while evoking outrage from the interracial coalition that had been backing Matthew's congressional bid. These acts untether him from responsibility and also permit his creator to express vicarious personal fantasies of liberation that originate in his frustrations with his "group imprisonment within a group." In short, the novel performs considerable psychic work, which may be one reason Du Bois was so fond of it. *Dark Princess,* which concludes with the birth of a royal male heir, re-presents and memorializes earlier experiences in Du Bois's life. The two most important are the death of his son in 1899 and his encounter with a stunning Indian princess at the 1911 Universal Races Congress in London.

But the novel has a particular resonance with the chaos and hysteria of the war years, a great historical moment of anarchy. At that time Du Bois was embroiled in perhaps the most bitterly controversial episode of his career—his quixotic alliance with Joel Spingarn, his close friend and NAACP colleague, to secure a captain's commission in the army. This effort, historians now conclude, required him to urge African Americans to rally behind the war. As Du Bois explained in retrospect, "so utterly crazy had the whole world become and I with it" ("Evolving" 59). The first portion of this chapter will trace his intimacy with Spingarn, the Jewish aristocrat and aesthetic theorist whom Du Bois called a "natural anarchist of the spirit" (*Dusk* 766). Spingarn's free spirit expressed his "craving for 'modernity' "—the need to be rid of the "older American moralism in thought and taste and action" and its "fetish . . . of dead forms" (Spingarn *Creative* 115). Spingarn and Du Bois created a bond of mutual fascination in which each encouraged the other's grandiosity in creative and destructive ways.

This friendship and *Dark Princess* together will provide a lens to view Du Bois's relation to modernity during the pivotal years from the First World War to the Harlem Renaissance, years when the visceral experience of risk and improvisation under crisis conditions grew most intense. His novel, written at the height of the Renaissance, depicts the colliding forces of modernity and modernism: the marketplace and oppositional individualism. *Dark Princess* strikingly complements another novel published the same year—Nella Larsen's *Quicksand,* with its portrait of the anarchic Helga Crane whom Du Bois so admires. Matthew Towns and Helga Crane redraw the boundaries of black American literary representation, boundaries which tended to confine libidinal energy to the activities of the criminal class or the demimonde and to limit portrayals of the black bourgeoisie to self-effacement and noble renunciation. Like Larsen, Du Bois challenges these strictures by injecting into black fiction modernist individualism, including the vagaries of inner life, in all its lavish excess or "gorgeousness," to borrow Larsen's word. Appropriately, one of Matthew's favorite works is *Hamlet,* the paradigm of Western inwardness.

In *Dusk of Dawn* Du Bois speaks of his "curiously seldom intimate contacts with fellow human beings across the color line." Only at "long intervals" did he emerge from his "colored world." And he notes that this remoteness "was born mainly of humiliating experience" (744). Yet *Dusk of Dawn* is dedicated to the memory of the recently deceased Joel Spingarn. The Du Bois–Spingarn friendship is rare and revealing precisely because to exist it had to cross the color line and "dwell above the Veil" (*Souls* 438). Interracial friendship, says Zora Neale Hurston, "makes a sorry mess of all the rules made and provided." One of the "strong attachments across the line" she mentions is Du Bois and Spingarn's: "the bitterest opponent of the white race that America has ever known, loved Joel Spingarn and was certainly loved in turn by him. The thing doesn't make sense. It just makes beauty" (921).

Many observers then and now would agree that the wartime alliance between Du Bois and Spingarn seemed to defy sense; indeed it courted disaster nearly every step of the way. Yet risk was, after all, a raison d'être of their collaboration. And the "beauty" it possesses derives from what might be termed the aesthetic activism that the two men share. If, as Spingarn says, "the virtue of all art is that it is always more or less mad," aesthetic activism risks madness by crossing the boundary separating art and life. The end of such activism is "to let one's self go." This freedom, says Spingarn, is "what art is always aiming at" and what "American art needs most of all" (*Creative* 96). With Spingarn's help, Du Bois lets go of some of the burden of being a race representative, relaxes the repressions of raced identity, while still seeking to move the struggle for civil rights forward.

The dedication of *Dusk of Dawn*—to Joel Spingarn, "scholar and knight"—contains an allusion worth pausing over. Spingarn was a distinguished scholar of Renaissance literature and criticism at Columbia until 1911. Then he became a knight, for he sailed into battle against the university's autocratic president Nicholas Murray Butler. Spingarn led a faculty protest on behalf of a professor whom the trustees had summarily fired without due process. Spingarn termed the firing whimsical, and when his criticism grew more caustic Butler warned him he was going too far. Spingarn persisted and Butler dismissed him. An outraged colleague, John Dewey, drafted a resolution on Spingarn's behalf, but it was defeated in a close vote. In the press, Spingarn scorned the "absolutely unmanly timidity" into which Columbia's faculty had been "cowed by Dr. Butler" (B. Joyce Ross 8). Controversy raged for months, but Spingarn was never reinstated.

Independently wealthy, Spingarn could afford to enact the knight-errantry of his "lonely warrior mood," as he termed his activist idealism. In a remark worthy of his recalcitrant individualism, he once declared his refusal to obey any man: "Why should I?" he asked rhetorically (qtd. Ross 15). Du Bois's sense of Spingarn as a valiant, if Quixotic, knight recurs in his brief portrait of his friend in *Dusk of Dawn*. "He was one of those vivid, enthusiastic but clear thinking idealists which from age to age the Jewish race has given the world. He had learned" of the NAACP "just after a crisis in his life"—evidently the Columbia dismissal—"and he joined us eagerly, ready for a new fight, a new thrill, and new allegiances" (741). Du Bois warms to Spingarn's spontaneous and generous activist idealism that finds social injustice intolerable. And his passion, bordering on impetuosity, is driven more by moral fierceness than by political convictions. Spingarn was an elitist who, says Du Bois, "was skeptical of democracy either in industry, politics or art . . . His interest was aroused in the Negro because of discrimination, and not in the interest of ideal methods of conducting the state . . . He wanted for me and my people freedom to live and act; but he did not believe that voting or revolution in industry was going to bring the millennium. He was afraid that I was turning [the time is the early 1930s] radical and dogmatic and even communistic" (766). In short, their friendship is founded not on a political common ground but on a temperamental affinity whose key element is willful anarchy.

Du Bois hails Spingarn as "the natural anarchist of the spirit," an appellation he would have bestowed on only one other white man, one similar in temper to Spingarn. But William James had already described himself as anarchistic.[1] This is virtually Du Bois's highest term of praise, his way of saying that Spingarn lives above the veil and knows no color line. Spingarn's cosmopolitanism argued for a deracializing of culture, a point revealed in an exchange he once had with the poet Vachel Lindsay about Du Bois's charge that Lindsay's poetry was primitivist exotica. Lindsay intended such poems as "The Congo," which celebrated blacks' "irrepressible high spirits," to "prophesy . . . a colored utopia." But Lindsay's Negritude, explained Spingarn, dismayed Du Bois because he wanted not a "separate and different" status but "to share in a common civilization in which all distinctions of race are blurred (or forgotten) by common aspirations" (qtd. Massa 167, 169).

Spingarn's career exhibits a quality of arrogant innocence bred of aristocratic insouciance. Du Bois noted this mixed innocence—"I sometimes listen to you quite speechless"—and found it winning: "I was both fascinated by his character and antagonized by some of his quick and positive judgments" (741). Spingarn was one of the many who said the same of Du Bois.[2] In short, the fascination was mutual, each likely viewing the other as an idealized mirror image. Our "basic faith in each other kept us going hand in hand," as Du Bois fondly recalled in *Dusk of Dawn*. And he added: "I do not think that any other white man ever touched me emotionally so closely" (741). We shall see that the ramifications of their psychic intimacy proved far reaching, as their friendship tapped the need in Du Bois's psyche for anarchic release.

Du Bois was especially struck by Spingarn's innocence when he would "urge easily co-operation and understanding" between those perpetual combatants—Du Bois and the NAACP board of directors. "You do not realize where the *real* rift in the lute comes"—the fact that "everything tends to this break along the color line," Du Bois informed Spingarn. "You do not realize this because there is no shadow of the thing in your soul. But you are not 'American' " (*Correspondence* 1: 206). This last remark is another of Du Bois's highest accolades. It is meant to suggest that Spingarn's Jewish idealism is immune to the American fixation on race. But Spingarn's admirable idealism is inseparable from his historical and political naivete. Thus in this same letter Du Bois is at pains to set the NAACP and his own role in historical context, so that "the pathos of an organization like ours" will become apparent to his friend. At least part of the "pathos" resides in Du Bois's audacious ambition to turn the NAACP into an instrument of his determination to move America beyond the color line. The organization was founded mainly by neo-abolitionists—wealthy, genteel white liberals moving with care and deliberation in fighting racism and seeking integration, and nervous about black aspirations of full "social equality"; Negroes were expected to behave with humility and gratitude (Lewis 477–478). Du Bois's ambition was of course to revise such expectations. His goal was indistinguishable in his mind from his effort to fashion the NAACP itself into an unprecedented experiment in "trusting black men with power" (*Correspondence* 1: 207).

A plea for trust is at the center of his extraordinary 1914 letter to

Spingarn from which I have been quoting. In proposing to "work out a plan in this organization for colored and white people to work together on the same level of authority and cooperation," Du Bois in effect is proposing to inject a salutary "anarchy of the spirit" into the NAACP. With anarchy comes risk and hazard: "of course there are imperfections, mistakes, shortcomings," admits Du Bois, whom Spingarn had charged with being the "chief . . . source of the disorder and lack of unity in our organization" (202). But from the point of view of Du Bois's pragmatist construction of authority, which is nourished by the "tingling challenge of risk," what is precious is "the right to make mistakes if the final result is big enough" (207). Du Bois's demand of the right of risk and error—"a full man's chance to complete a work without chains"—is unprecedented: until now "the colored man gets no such chance. He is seldom given authority or freedom." But the NAACP is also unprecedented, or at least is potentially so. Although by 1914 the NAACP had been in existence for four years, Du Bois describes himself as "working . . . to make the NAACP possible. Today it is *not* possible" (204).

What Du Bois means is that *his* NAACP, one that crosses the color line, one infused with a spirit of anarchy, remains to be created. "No organization like ours ever succeeded in America": either it became a paternalist group of white philanthropists lending a hand to the Negro, "or it became a group of colored folk freezing out their white coworkers by insolence and distrust" (206). This pattern is grounded in the assumption that power equals "authority over the other": thus if the "head is colored, the whites gradually leave" and vice versa. Du Bois's solution—to redistribute power so that blacks and whites will work together "on the same level of authority"—operates on a principle that resembles the anarchist belief that social progress is not the mere reversal of superiority. By creating "two branches of the same work" headed by whites and blacks "working in harmony," Du Bois hopes to end the internal strife built into conventional hierarchy. But he admits to Spingarn that the "connecting and unifying power between the two branches has not been found" (207). Perhaps, he avers, this power must reside in "one man"—Du Bois, most likely.

This last turn of the screw, which reinstates a single authority, suggests how fragile is Du Bois's pragmatist experiment in making authority horizontal, grounded in trust, risk, and chance. Du Bois's reorganization proposal was not formally adopted, and the turf battles to sort out the relation between Du Bois, *The Crisis,* and the NAACP seemed to become a way of life. But if "harmony" was never achieved, a more tumultuous, de facto version of what Du Bois sought was created. The perpetual struggles became the condition of sharing power across the color line. Du Bois's key ally was Spingarn, though he was careful not to be seen as the editor's constant champion. He usually sided with Du Bois, even when informing the Board that members resented "spending their hard-earned money in order merely to furnish Dr. Du Bois with a halo and a luxurious setting for the *Crisis*" (qtd. Lewis 496). Dr. Du Bois, Spingarn warned, "must not be coddled as a thing apart, a constant disproof of our hopes that white men and black men can work together" (qtd. 496).

But, on Du Bois's demanding terms, acceptance of his extravagances would be evidence that whites and blacks could work together across the color line. Dismantling the color bar would permit subjectivity to be less constrained and predictable and instead to be "painfully human." For then whites could no longer rely on what had seemed blacks' second nature—the array of preordained postures of abjection all designed to put whites at their ease. Gone, for instance, would be the pinched rectitude of humble black people grateful for the philanthropy of rich whites. Du Bois believed a "rupture of deference," as David Levering Lewis notes, was the "precondition" of black social equality (478). In this light, the permanent state of contention during Du Bois's near quarter-century of editorial tenure should be regarded as a measure of his success in renovating authority.

In Du Bois's retrospective words, he and Spingarn "fought each other continually in the councils of the Association, but always our admiration and basic faith in each other kept us going hand in hand" (*Dusk* 741). "It is difficult," Du Bois had said of the effort to persuade blacks and whites to cooperate. But difficulty was worth the effort, since, like anarchy, it was an emblem of value. They improvised a friendship unhampered by a conventional "code of morals or manners, the ready-made standards of any society, however great" (Spingarn *Creative* 141). This expresses Spingarn's impatience with "ready made standards" in an essay on "The American Critic" which is meant to admonish those who would submit poetry to a priori moral strictures.

An unmistakable, if unstated, connection exists between Spingarn's literary creed and his capacity for dwelling above the veil. Linking his aesthetic theory and cosmopolitanism was a fervent romantic individualism that proved both intoxicating and grandiose when made the basis of action. Spingarn's literary article of faith, one that prefigures the New Criticism (which was the title of his own 1910 aesthetic manifesto) was the integrity of aesthetic experience in the face of moralistic or utilitarian efforts to constrain the freedom of art. Because of its Puritan heritage, the United States is the "only civilised country where moral judgment takes precedence over aesthetic judgment." Thus the "first need of American criticism today is education in aesthetic thinking," for "taste is after all both the point of departure and the goal" in developing "a deeper sensibility" (*Creative* 131, 145).

Although Spingarn was born in 1875, his anti-Puritanism aligned him with the young intellectuals of the generation of 1910 in revolt against the genteel tradition—Bourne, Lippmann, Brooks, and Spingarn's good friend and neighbor Lewis Mumford. Indeed, Spingarn was a " 'cosmopolitan' cultural nationalist," in George Hutchinson's phrase, "years before his student Randolph Bourne enunciated his transnationalist thesis" (*Harlem* 376). In a 1922 look back at this group, Spingarn is pleased to note that he "foresaw and approved" the "craving for 'modernity' " that was born of the "spirit of revolt that has reigned in our literature for a dozen years . . . It was necessary to rid ourselves of the last remnant of the older American 'moralism' in thought and taste and action" (*Creative* 114–115).

In their wartime alliance Spingarn and Du Bois found new fields of action to satisfy their craving for the freedom of modernity. In 1917, amid protest from many in the NAACP and elsewhere, they had set aside their own integrationist principles and successfully campaigned for the creation of a segregated black officer training camp in Iowa. Six hundred trainees were soon enrolled. In defending his plan of "voluntary segregation," Du Bois said: "We face a condition, not a theory . . . it is either a case of a 'Jim-Crow' officers' training camp or no colored officers. Of the two things no colored officers would be the greater calamity" (*Darkwater* 234). Du Bois rationalized the segregation as the "high price of full citizenship in America" (Lewis 530). He, like many blacks, had to confront the ugly irony of having to plead for the right of black men to die for their country. While some black leaders believed the war represented an opportunity for blacks to bargain their loyalty and service to the state in return for civil rights concessions, Du Bois and Spingarn reasoned otherwise. Their guiding logic was that "blacks would earn fairer treatment . . . through selfless demonstrations of loyal citizenship in wartime . . . Full black participation in the war . . . would prompt an official commitment to upholding civil rights" (Mark Ellis 105–106).

The logic of Du Bois's position in 1917 had much in common with the technocratic version of pragmatism Bourne called "pragmatic realism," the creed that reigned at the *New Republic,* on whose editorial board Du Bois served. The board was composed of pro-war progressives led by Herbert Croly, John Dewey, and Walter Lippmann. They, like Du Bois (and Spingarn), began the war years trusting in the power of expertise to exert rational control over war aims and make them serve as an instrument of social reform. Although pragmatic realism was flattering to the many intellectuals and bureaucrats who professed it, its promise would fade in the glare of postwar carnage and democratic principles betrayed. By then "realism" would seem as naive and impotent as any other option. Randolph Bourne had predicted this in his stinging 1917 critiques of Deweyan pragmatism's instrumentalism and the mentality it had nurtured at the *New Republic.* Bourne declared what history would soon ratify: that war does not need patriotism, conviction, enthusiasm, or hope to sustain it. "Once maneuvered, it takes care of itself." "All that is really needed is the co-operation with government of the men who direct the large financial and industrial enterprises." Bourne's humiliating point to his fellow intellectuals was that "it makes not the least difference whether you or I want our activity to count in aid of the war" (Bourne 320).

The postwar Dewey would, in effect, revise his pragmatism in a Bournean direction.[3] And Du Bois would look back at the war years and describe his behavior as anything but imbued with realism. But in 1917 Dewey, Du Bois, and Spingarn were swept up in the grand optimism of Wilson's evangelical call to enlist in the war that would end war and commence an era of global democracy. Thus the stage was set for Spingarn's boldest plan.

Spingarn had secured a commission as a major in the Military Intelligence Branch (MIB), and his job was to shore up black loyalty for the war effort. He arranged a desk captaincy for Du Bois in June 1918. "He described in glowing terms the work they would do together to win the war for democracy in Europe and for civil rights in America" (Lewis 553). Typically, Spingarn's plans were short on detail and focus but long on ambition (Ellis 105). Yet a "shocked" Du Bois was sold. Without seeking advice from the NAACP board or even close friends, Du Bois agreed to seek the commission. But in making him the offer of captain, "Spingarn made a decision that would come deadly close to wrecking" Du Bois's career (Lewis 553). For in the July *Crisis* Du Bois published his notorious editorial "Close Ranks." Its most famous passage urged: "let us not hesitate. Let us, while this war lasts, forget our special grievances and close our ranks shoulder to shoulder with our white fellow citizens and the allied nations" (Du Bois *Reader* 697).

Although pleasing to the military, these words infuriated many African Americans. Du Bois was vilified by right, left, and center; they unanimously agreed that (in the words of an NAACP member) Du Bois "had reversed his whole life and is no more good to us" (qtd. Lewis 557). Monroe Trotter declared him "no longer a radical," but a "rank quitter in the fight for equal rights" (qtd. Ellis 113). Philip Randolph's *The Messenger* noted that although Du Bois wanted to help Wilson make the world safe for democracy, "we would rather make Georgia safe for the Negro" (qtd. Anderson *Randolph* 100–101). The phrase "forget our special grievances" became a flashpoint of anger. In asking blacks to forget their grievances over lynching, segregation, and disfranchisement, Du Bois seemed to betray his lifelong militancy for social justice and to capitulate to a Bookerite accommodationism. At a stormy NAACP meeting, Du Bois's request to hold the commission while editing *The Crisis* was rejected. And accusations were made that he had penned the "Close Ranks" editorial to buy himself the captaincy. Du Bois bitterly denied these charges.

But in fact they were well founded. The most thorough historical reconstruction of the episode, by Mark Ellis, concludes that Du Bois "distorted his real beliefs" (in social justice and patriotism as twin priorities) at Spingarn's request. In producing the meek sentiments of "Close Ranks," Du Bois's aim was to impress the military with his loyalty. Thus the editorial was timed "to coincide with his formal application for a commission" (Ellis 124). But the misadventure ended in late July 1918 when the application was suddenly rejected. Spingarn's recruitment plans had faltered not least because of a racist and anti-Semitic backlash at the Military Intelligence Branch, which was dominated by white Southerners. The controversy over "Close Ranks" and the army commission permanently damaged Du Bois's reputation and influence. But it also hurt the struggle for civil rights. Shattered was the precarious solidarity of the post–Booker T. Washington years. Now Garveyites, socialists, and other political factions used "Close Ranks" as a rallying point to rouse their loyalists and add new ones.

Before discussing the wartime alliance between Du Bois and Spingarn, it is worth pausing to consider, however briefly, the wider context in which Du Bois found himself. This can clarify what is easily lost sight of—the difficulty of Du Bois's position and its merits. His enemies conveniently ignored Du Bois's follow-up editorial to "Close Ranks" in August, in which he eloquently explained that his pro-war and pro–equal rights stance made no excuses for social injustice ("war does not excuse disfranchisement" or Jim Crow). Historians agree that Du Bois was far more realistic than the many who sought to use black loyalty as a bargaining tool in the deluded belief that such leverage really existed. In 1917–1918 Du Bois faced an especially perplexing version of a dilemma that many distinguished minds at this time grappled with—the question of how to balance conflicting values and loyalties. Even for a man who prized "double consciousness," the pressure of multiple allegiances—to Negro Americans, to America, to anti-imperialism, to patriotism, to equal rights, to nationalism, to Pan-Africanism—proved almost overwhelming. And especially in an atmosphere saturated in unprecedented, "deliberate and prolonged propaganda for war," as Du Bois noted years later. Like so many, he recalled having "partially succumbed" to Wilson's brilliant manipulation of national fear and hope. "I really believed that the first World War was a war to end war" (*Correspondence* 2: 272).

Randolph Bourne urged intellectuals to be "malcontents" rather than "realists" and to let their minds "roam widely and ceaselessly" by accepting suspense and deferral. But Du Bois did not have this luxury of detachment. He was, as he said in retrospect, "engulfed in a mad fight to make Negroes Americans" ("Evolving" 58). In "My Evolving Program for Negro Freedom," his retrospective essay of 1944, Du Bois gives a name to his vulnerable feeling of psychic and social upheaval. He admits to having felt "crazy." He summarizes the paradoxes and divisions that inevitably resulted from his impossible project of balancing opposed loyalties:

> I was fighting to let the Negroes fight; I, who for a generation had been a professional pacifist; I was fighting for a separate training camp for Negro officers; I, who was devoting a career to opposing race segregation; I was seeing the Germany which taught me the human brotherhood of white and black, pitted against America which for me was the essence of Jim Crow; and yet I was "rooting" for America; and I had to, even before my own conscience, so utterly crazy had the whole world become and I with it. (59)

Only at the end of 1918 when he visited France did he reach "a sort of mental balance." Unmentioned in this inventory of anomalies is the misadventure with Spingarn, which stands as a prime source and pure product of Du Bois's sense of the contagious craziness of the historical moment. Yet his alliance with Spingarn, I will argue, was not merely lamentable. It was also a creative effort at living above the veil, at making an interracial friendship work to ventilate his "provincial" role of race man.

In 1918, Du Bois and Spingarn were pilloried for arrogance, grandiosity, and opportunism. One black newspaper at the time denounced the pair as "genuflecting gentlemen . . . playing both ends of the game against the middle." Spingarn was blamed for his "mad meddling," and for being Du Bois's "evil genius" (qtd. Ellis 113). Lewis avoids the melodrama of this last description even as he renews the condemnation in light of Ellis's recent evidence that "Du Bois struck a deal, through Spingarn, with the War Department." The deal, says Lewis, "implied cold calculation and make-or-break audacity": Du Bois would use *The Crisis* to stir African American patriotism in return "for the heady opportunities he and Spingarn persuaded themselves their military commissions would yield. Personal vanity and civil rights aspirations were inextricably enmeshed" (555). Lewis describes Du Bois's quick response to Spingarn's offer as "an exercise in personal conceit." For Du Bois ignored the obvious "institutional constraints" that a captaincy would entangle him in, preferring to see the post solely as "another challenge to be turned to magnificent personal and group advantage" (554).

While these verdicts are just, they leave the significance of the alliance between Du Bois and Spingarn unexplored. In becoming "crazy," Du Bois tacitly admits how inadequate was the sense of control and "realism" he possessed at the start of the war years. With the world in an increasing state of chaos, Du Bois began revising his authority, opening it to an experimental venture in freedom. Whether by design or consequence, this experiment defied the complacent technocratic rationalism that Bourne had condemned. At the core of pragmatist "realism," argued Bourne, was a "philosophy of 'adaptation' or 'adjustment' " that had no capacity to create "new values": "If your ideal is to be adjustment to your situation, in radiant cooperation with reality, then your success is likely to be just that and no more. You never transcend anything. You grow, but your spirit never jumps out of your skin to go on wild adventures" (344). Scorning the "caution" and "regression" bred by adjustment, Bourne's Nietzschean/Jamesian individualism recommends "obstreperous vision."

On these terms, the partnership between Du Bois and Spingarn emerges as a volatile amalgam of opportunist "adaptation" to reality and transcendent vision that dared to pursue "wild adventures." Closing ranks with Spingarn, Du Bois worked on the inside of power, cutting deals, bending principles, to become what legal authority forbade—a black person free to be a "real and full American." This last phrase occurs in Du Bois's only comments about his wartime relation to Spingarn. "Of greatest influence on me undoubtedly was Spingarn's attitude toward the war. He was fired with consuming patriotism, he believed in America and feared Germany . . . It was due to his advice and influence that I became during the World War nearer to feeling myself a real and full American than ever before or since" (*Dusk* 741).

Of this last remark, Lewis comments: "real Americans are frequently past masters at making deals" (555). But this leaves out that "real and full Americans" are also uncoerced by the color line and are free to enjoy an "anarchy of the spirit." Such freedom meant, for Du Bois, cutting against institutional authority, be it the NAACP or the MIB. He played out his aborted military career by disregarding the protests of his own organization, which declared his integrity to be in question. Yet the MIB found his integrity too threatening. Although he attempted to act the role of loyalist, Du Bois could not erase his record of activism in a sudden burst of appeasement. The memorandum that led to the denial of his commission spoke of his "extreme views on the race problem," including his belief in blacks' "equality with the white race." Worse, his insistence "upon recognition of this alleged" equality sows "discontent among the colored population" (qtd. Ellis 114). A threat to both institutions, Du Bois enacts in the war years an assault on strategies of adjustment even as he preaches it in "Close Ranks."

This double move counts as another instance of the surrender to paradox and self-division that he acknowledged in his 1944 admission of having felt "crazy." Instead of struggling to resolve matters by imposing a streamlined consistency in "radiant cooperation with reality" (to borrow Bourne's phrase), Du Bois manages to offend nearly everyone. For his loyalty seems to reside solely with Spingarn. They collaborate on two projects, both undertaken in good faith and defensible on their own terms, yet each fraught with risk. In one, he and Spingarn pay the price of segregation to enable black men to attain military authority; in the other, Du Bois risks his integrity to gain a foothold inside the circle of power at MIB. In the ensuing fallout, especially from the bid for a captaincy, the surface unity of black politics is splintered and Du Bois becomes ethically tainted in the view of many.

But the tumult he creates is more than the result of vain overreaching. Rather, Du Bois's actions are those of "the surgeon probing blindly," and they insist on an historical truth that leaders and institutions preferred to remain hidden: that no one could serve the race as a fixed beacon of sanity above the mad fray, for all the possible paths to equality were hazardous gambles. He perceives that the array of options—to fight, not to fight, to bargain, to train in segregated camps, not to train at all, to close ranks—are little more than desperate stabs in the dark. By 1919, in the "Red Summer" of that year, the dark had become a nightmare of lynching and rioting. And Du Bois's fondest, guiding hope was dashed. Black soldiers returned from Europe not to an America full of gratitude and respect, as he had dreamed, but to a country frantic to put them back in their place.

In the war years Du Bois made it extremely difficult for black Americans to regard him as a reliable race man. Instead, "he was a one-hundred-percent American, all out for victory at whatever cost to civil rights," runs the usually admiring Henry Moon's representative assessment (15). But in that near forfeiture of trust, Du Bois achieved the freedom of risk. In refusing the insulation of a specious authority in a time of global crisis, he enacted a willful political ineptitude. And this was "not simply an error in his thought," to borrow a phrase that Nathan Huggins has used in explaining Du Bois's chronic "political ineffectiveness" (*Harlem* 34). Huggins explains Du Bois's "tortuous" permanent quandary as based on the clash between his "ultimate goal" of erasing the color line and making society color-blind, and the fact that to be politically effective "race-consciousness" must be exploited: "For the Negro to use politics to his ends, he had to do so as part of a Negro pressure group, not as a high minded independent" (35). Huggins's shrewd assessment pinpoints a central contradiction that we have seen Du Bois live (and that we will see Alain Locke enact in the next chapter). But the chaos of the war years and the alliance with Spingarn afford him release from the quandary by liberating him from the strictures of stalwart race champion. In effect, Du Bois and his friend form a private party of two. No wonder the black press dubbed Spingarn Du Bois's "evil genius." A recent historian says that "Du Bois was seduced by his own eminent philanthropist" (Ellis 124).

A decade later, in *Dark Princess,* Du Bois celebrates an analogous intimacy between Matthew Towns and Princess Kautilya. Their "absorption in each other" is conspicuous, arousing envy and, before long, a thunderous outcry. It echoes what Du Bois had heard in his own ears ten years before. "I am free!" shouts Matthew as he strides out with the Princess from what was to be the crowning moment of his political career—a dinner party his wife had arranged with Chicago's power elite. Onlookers chant a chorus of contempt: " 'These Negroes! . . . They are simply impossible!' " remarks one. Another says, "I wonder what the devil got hold of Towns, acting as though he was crazy?" Someone else says, "To think of a Negro acting that way . . . Won't we ever amount to anything? Won't we ever get any leaders?" (211–212). Matthew's political rival is left shocked before the spectacle of "human nature" acting "with such incalculable and utter disregard of all rules and wise saws."

Here Du Bois magnifies in fiction what in life he had done a decade earlier—exchanging the responsible for the incalculable, the predictable for the impossible. Matthew's sense of public disgrace is acute: "Now I am anathema to my people. I am the Sunday School example of one who sold his soul to the devil." And why? Simply for having chosen love, beauty, and ideals embodied in "the perfect friendship and communion of two human beings" (263). Matthew's idealism would probably have appealed to Spingarn. Like Matthew, who left medical school when its racist policies made his fury "burst its bounds," Spingarn abandoned his university career in the face of what he regarded as morally intolerable conditions. At Columbia the autocrat President Butler had, Spingarn wrote, "stifled all manly independence and individuality . . . All noble idealism, and all the graces of poetry and art, have been shrivelled by his brutal and triumphant power" ("A Question" 10).

Statements like these suggest that Du Bois models Matthew's florid romantic individualism not only on himself but on Spingarn as well. All three craved unfettered subjectivity free to express itself in "the graces of poetry and art." That such freedom is dangerously intoxicating has been noted since Plato: the *Phaedrus* speaks of the madness of poets—what is called "a divine release of the soul from custom and convention." Spingarn recalls this classical notion in "Creative Connoisseurship," a 1913 essay on modern art. The poet's madness "is nothing more or less than unhampered freedom of self-expression . . . To let oneself go—that is what art is always aiming at, and American art at this moment needs most of all" (*Creative* 95–96). Modernism had revived "this Dionysiac side of the Greek soul," and the revival had also brought potential for controversy since "those who are inhibited will always stand amazed by those who express themselves freely"

(96). The three "mad" men learned the truth of this at first hand, as each of their acts of letting go aroused public censure.

In his self-confessed craziness, Du Bois revealed his own version of the "divine release of the soul from custom and convention." In letting go, he seems to fuse psychically with Spingarn, the white man to whom he feels closest. A hint of blurred boundaries is evident as early as 1916 when Du Bois visited Spingarn's estate Troutbeck, near Amenia, New York for the first Amenia Conference on race. "I had no sooner seen the place than I knew it was mine. It was just a long southerly extension of my own Berkshire Hills . . . I saw its great trees. . .with a sense of utter friendship and intimate memory, though in truth I had never seen it before" (*Amenia* 210). What the psychic fusion produces in Du Bois is a feeling of having almost become a "real and full American" thanks to Spingarn's "advice and influence."

The poignancy of this statement derives from the impossibility of Du Bois's achieving this status he yearns for. And Spingarn was made to face the same impossibility during the war. Spingarn, a Jew whom a journalist once accused of being Negro, and Du Bois, who in Europe was routinely mistaken for a Jew: both remained irreducibly alien (Lewis 486, 141). But Du Bois's statement is also richly ironic. The man who almost Americanizes him is a Jew whom Du Bois had praised for not being American. And neither Spingarn's nor Du Bois's "consuming patriotism" makes him enough of a pure American to vanquish the suspicions of the MIB. Perhaps most ironic is that when Du Bois declares that he nearly felt himself "a real and full American" he is making less a statement of identity than of transition. As always with Du Bois, to be American was less a sufficient than an interim stage, one "to discard" for "something wider"—not only an "interracial culture, broader and more catholic than ours," but an international one that would include Europe and Africa ("Evolving" 58).

Given Du Bois's global perspective, it is apt that *Dark Princess* from the start is self-consciously embedded within the international matrix of high modernism. Kandinsky, Proust, Croce, vorticism, futurism, Picasso, Matisse are some of the names bandied about by the cognoscenti who gather for a Pan-Asian dinner party early in the novel. But even before this, Du Bois identifies Matthew with one of modernism's most glamorous icons: the expatriate aesthete abroad, in contemptuous rebellion from provincial America. "Exile" is the title of Part One. On the novel's first page, Matthew stands on the deck of a ship bound for Europe, replaying in his mind the moment when "his fury had burst its bounds" (4). Lost in thought, he barely registers the outside world he has exiled. Du Bois, in short, signals from the start that Matthew's exilic status entails a consuming inwardness, a particular privilege of modernist individualism. With his intriguing mix of skeptical detachment and inflamed emotions ("Matthew Towns was in a cold white fury" is the novel's first line) which heighten his receptivity to material surfaces, Matthew dominates the reader's experience of the book.

Reviewers in 1928 did not quite know what to make of *Dark Princess*. It presented a disconcerting blend of fervent Pan-African messianism, urban realism, and erotic intensity. This last dimension went generally unnoted by reviewers, who stayed on safer ground by emphasizing the novel as uplift propaganda. After all, Du Bois had embraced "propaganda" two years before, and, as a member of the older generation, was allegedly more Victorian than modern; had not his prudishness been outraged by *Home to Harlem* and *Nigger Heaven? Dark Princess* explodes these truisms and in return was greeted with small sales and abashed readers. Even sympathetic critics "seem to have regarded *Dark Princess* as a dirty old man's fantasy that should never have been published," says Claudia Tate in an apt summary of the critical reception ("Introduction" xxiv). Among reviewers only Alain Locke (understandably) had a clue about what Du Bois was up to: "the novel will be interesting and revealing reading to the white reader who has yet few ways of . . . seeing into the dilemmas of the intellectual Negro mind and heart" (qtd. Aptheker "Introduction" 28–29).

If we combine Locke's focus on the intimate portrait of the black intellectual and Tate's point about inadmissible sexual fantasy we can begin to grasp the audacity of *Dark Princess*. But we get a full sense of its daring only when we examine Wyndham Lewis's response. In *Paleface* (1929) Lewis made Du Bois's novel Exhibit A in his critique of the "intense anti-Paleface propaganda" promulgated by prominent white and black intellectuals of the twenties. The campaign had left educated white Americans with a "pronounced 'inferiority complex'" while providing "anybody and everybody who is not a *pur sang* White . . . a 'superiority complex'" (113, 117). "How useful this book is to sum up all this literature" notes Lewis (37). Wyndham Lewis's assessment is worth examining because to this day he remains the one critic attuned to the challenge of Du Bois's novel. So impressed was Lewis by the bold confidence of the characters that with half-seriousness he compared *Dark Princess* to *Uncle Tom's Cabin* as having the potential for fomenting in black people a "particular consciousness" of militant entitlement (41).

"The European culture of this gathering of dusky principals is in brief nothing short of staggering—they can mix Picasso with a 'tidbit of meat' and impale 'Futurism' on the way to a potato . . . For my own part I must confess that, in reading *Dark Princess*, I was somewhat abashed, myself, to remark that these Dark plotters were as familiar with 'Vorticism'—my invention—as with chopsticks. But I was flattered, too, of course" (34, 33). Thus wrote Lewis regarding the scene near the start of Du Bois's novel in which a black international elite revolutionary cell elegantly dines. The book's "fiery political purpose," (30) which begins with this dinner meeting, culminates in a prophecy (quoted by Lewis) that "in 1952, the Dark World goes free," and that whether in peace or in blood is up to the "Pale Masters" (*Dark Princess* 297). In fact, this prediction proved just five years off the mark, since Ghana, led by Du Bois's disciple Nkrumah, became the first post-colonial African nation in 1957.

Paleface is a satirical polemic that is a strange blend of white anxiety over the "rising tide of color" (in Lothrop Stoddard's famous phrase) and hope for an internationalism without a color line (67–68). Sounding like some contemporary critics of multiculturalism, Lewis laments the "racial turning of the tables" and "dogmatical mechanical reversals" of white to black (20). He lays blame for it on such romantic racial primitivists as D. H. Lawrence and Sherwood Anderson and, in particular, on the "exceedingly partisan and bellicose attitude" of H. L. Mencken and his friend Alfred Knopf (118, 29). Their collaborative venture *American Mercury*, with its stinging mockery of the provincialism and racism of WASP culture, and Knopf's publishing program, called "The Negro in Borzoi Books," together put in print most of the leading black literary intellectuals of the twenties. Mencken and Knopf's "constant featuring of Negro subjects" (to promote the "colored phantasies of Borzoi big guns" as Lewis's refrain puts it) had "certainly been instrumental . . . in improving the Negro's position a great deal in the North," but at the cost of a "mere reversal of a superiority—a change in its *colour*, nothing more—rather than its total abolition" (21, 41).

Especially egregious in encouraging this reversal, says Lewis, is *Dark Princess*, even though published by Harcourt:

What it seems to imply is that the White World is "finished" . . . and that it is the "Coloured Races," or the Non-European, who have done it or are doing it, and are to be the beneficiaries of a reversal of political power. That is why the tactless assaults of the Borzoi big-guns have to be checked and are certain in the end to cause a disturbance and make it worth somebody's while to take up the cause of the "Paleface." That championship is a title that is going begging, but for the moment only. (85)

Two years later, in *Hitler* (1931), Lewis would welcome a promising new champion of the beleaguered paleface, one who seemed determined to restore white pride and put an end to the flirtation with primitivist exoticism by decadent intellectuals busy "sentimentalizing with regard to the Non-White world" (qtd. Jameson *Fables* 181).

In Lewis's fevered logic Knopf, Mencken, Du Bois, et al. encourage the counter-response of Hitlerism, whose message, innocuous enough in 1930, is, says Lewis, "How about giving your White Consciousness a try for a little—it is really not so dull as you may suppose!" (181). What remains unclear is how Lewis squares his interest in Hitler (of whom he is neither "critic" "nor yet as advocate" he warns at the start) with his regret in *Paleface* of "mechanical reversals" and his favoring of a universalism founded on color's "total abolition."

Lewis granted *Dark Princess* the compliment of recognizing its audacity. But this compliment goes far beyond Du Bois to salute implicitly modern black intellectuals (or at least the many cultivated by Mencken and Knopf) as powerful agents of revolutionary consciousness. Not only are black intellectuals fierce exponents of modernist iconoclasm, both artistically and politically, but the impact of their representations has potentially alarming global repercussions. At this point Lewis conveniently assuaged his worry by confidently claiming: "The Negro is much too happy-go-lucky to approach these matters [of attaining a "superiority complex"] with the same earnestness as his mentors . . . above all, he [the average Negro] wishes to identify himself with his Paleface neighbors as far as possible . . . He has much more in common with Babbitt than with the Colored Intellectual" (41–42). Lewis sympathizes with the frustrations of "the Colored Intellectual[s]"—"I am sure anyone would have the same experience who attempted to go to the help of the Paleface"—while paying the tribute of taking them seriously enough to fear them.

The cosmopolitanism of *Dark Princess* seems to unnerve Lewis, who finds "staggering" the multinational dinner party scene where erudite anti-imperialist Indians, Chinese, Japanese, an Egyptian, and an African

American elegantly dine. "They talked art in French, literature in Italian, politics in German, and everything in clear English" (*Dark Princess* 19). Lewis's defensiveness manifests itself in his misreading of the novel's cosmopolitanism, which he reduces to "mechanical reverses" of color superiority. In fact, as we shall see, *Dark Princess* is far closer to what Lewis professes to admire in his less threatened moments—the "spirit of internationalism" that has abolished color (Lewis 68).

Matthew Towns, an American black who has recently sailed to Europe after abruptly abandoning a brilliant career as a medical student, by luck finds himself at the dinner party in Berlin. His presence is conspicuous, for American and African blacks have not been invited. Representatives of "much of the Darker World" doubt their abilities. Matthew hears familiar phrases—"Superior races, the right to rule, born to command—inferior breeds . . . the rabble"—attached to new referents. "How humorous it was to Matthew to see all tables turned; the rabble now was the white workers of Europe; the inferior races were the ruling whites of Europe and America. The superior races were yellow and brown" (19, 24). Challenging this programmatic doctrine that only the darker peoples of China, India, Japan, and Egypt possess "natural inborn superiority," Towns unsettles the smug aristocrats with a moving rendition of "Go Down, Moses" ("that came out of the black rabble of America," he scornfully informs his auditors). His performance prefaces his main point: the "one thing of real value" America is teaching the world is that culture is not private property, not "the hereditary monopoly of a few," but available to a majority of mankind if they are only given opportunity (26). Matthew's universalism refuses any part in an organization that has erected "a color line within a color line, a prejudice within prejudice, and he and his again the sacrifice" (22).

Matthew's democratic intervention proves fruitful; one of his listeners—Princess Kautilya of Bwodpur—will later say she began to fall in love with him when he sang the slave song. And the next Pan-African conference not only makes room at the table for black America and black Africa, but is guided by Matthew's perspective: we recognized, Kautilya tells him, "democracy as a method of discovering real aristocracy" (225). The Princess will later explain: "only Talent served from the great Reservoir of All Men of All Races, of All Classes, of All Ages, of Both Sexes—this is real Aristocracy, real Democracy—the only path to that great and final Freedom . . . Divine Anarchy" (285). This is the political vision that will be realizable once "the Dark World goes free." Akin to the "kingdom of culture" above the veil of the color line,

"Divine Anarchy" predicts a globally democratized Talented Tenth housed in a nearly utopian space of freedom. Here the "unclassified residuum" of "wild facts, with no stall or pigeon-hole" (James's phrase) would circulate rather than be unduly subjected to invidious distinctions and disciplinary control.[4] In glimpsing the definitive dissolving of aristocracy and democracy into each other, "Divine Anarchy" commemorates Du Bois's long effort (shared by Alain Locke) to fashion cosmopolitanism into an instrument of democracy.[5]

The political and sexual anarchy of *Dark Princess* is faithful to anarchy's political premise, which derives from the word's literal meaning—without a ruler. And the novel acutely intuits the intimate affinity between anarchy and cosmopolitanism. This link is evident in the original Greek Stoic ideal of a "cosmopolitan utopia" as a primal erotic and political anarchy that defies the borders that guarantee identity and instead makes "a clean sweep of laws, differences, and prohibitions of established society" (Kristeva *Strangers* 60). Two possibilities, Julia Kristeva notes, are available to a life without constraints or limits: "either absolute cynicism based on individual pleasure, or the elitism of lucid self-controlled beings . . . In other words, cosmopolitanism will be either libertarian or totalitarian—or else it will not be" (61). But Du Bois's "Divine Anarchy," at least in its political if not its sexual register, offers a democratic alternative.

In his abhorrence of Marxism and democracy, Wyndham Lewis ignores Du Bois's vision of "Divine Anarchy" though it not only accords with the "universal state" Lewis professes to admire but also avoids precisely the binary reversals of superiority that Lewis decries. Indeed, anarchism specifically disdains such symmetrical inversions. Its root assumption is not absence of government but absence of domination. The Russian anarchist Prince Kropotkin, who, like Du Bois, attended the 1911 Universal Races Congress, conceived anarchism as the "only criticism of society which is not a technique for the seizure and transfer of power by one group against another, which is what all such doctrines amount to—the substitution of one authority for another. What is particular about anarchism is not its criticism of society but the creative way of life it offers that makes all programmatic doctrine impossible." Thus says Barnett Newman, the abstract expressionist painter and anarchist, introducing Kropotkin's memoirs (Newman 45).

But something else bothers Lewis about *Dark Princess*, he admits. He quotes Matthew's initial reaction to the sight of the Princess: "First and above all came that sense of color: into this world of pale yellowish and pinkish parchment, that absence or negation of color, came, suddenly a glow of golden brown skin" (*Dark Princess* 8). Lewis comments that "in language of this sort in fact our poor [White] World is always described in a most disrespectful and wounding manner" (30). And after noting that Matthew soon punches out a boorish paleface who is bothering the Princess, Lewis mutters, "Exit the White World" (31). But in its refusal of mere reversals *Dark Princess* proposes also to Exit the Colored World, so devoted is Du Bois to depicting the anarchy of a sexual passion that, at least for a time, obliterates everything outside itself.

In short, the abstract and idealized utopia of "Divine Anarchy" coexists with, indeed is overshadowed by, the novel's depiction of a more earthly "divine anarchy"—the union of Matthew and Kautilya. Their affair possesses a hermetic intensity first signaled in the mood cast by the Berlin café where they initially meet: "its cool dark shade, its sense of withdrawal from the world" suffuse Matthew (14). Having been groomed as a "Race Man" (as was Bles, the passive hero of Du Bois's first novel, *Quest of the Silver Fleece,* and prefiguring Ellison's narrator) by Sara, his brilliant, coldly ambitious black bourgeois wife, Matthew now resigns from the cynical world of political power games. He brings his lover to his "attic nest," where they build their own utopian space exempt from all interference. In post-coital reverie, "Kautilya listened dreamily," as "the world floated away . . . There was a sense of warmth and luxury about her. Silk touched and smoothed her skin. Her tired body rested on soft rugs that yielded beneath her and lay gently in every curve and crevice of her body . . . In silence she lay in strange peace and happiness—not trying to think" (217).

The magnified, eroticized attention to the Princess's body that is conspicuous here pervades the novel, imparting a fetishistic intensity that disrupts the realist surface while distracting both the reader and Matthew himself from what is ostensibly the novel's more serious business—the world of politics, present in both a convoluted plot of urban political infighting and a messianic plot of global racial redemption. The political narratives of *Dark Princess* are continually challenged, if not entirely sabotaged, by the subjectivism of Du Bois's modernist technique of a central consciousness. Much of the narrative is filtered through Matthew, whose liberation from politics coincides not only with his passion for the Princess but with his aesthetic initiation. Matthew, in sum, discovers his sensibility and learns to cultivate it, a project that Du Bois regards not as merely personal but as of considerable social importance, as we will see.

The psychic energies circulating in Du Bois's romance derive their intensity from the force of the repressions that give them birth. Du Bois implies that in sacrificing his identity to the group, the race figure is provincial in the way a medieval serf is provincial: both have their being defined outside themselves, by place of birth, by province, locked within a closed, hierarchical community. The American race champion must bear the additional pain of "screaming in a vacuum unheard" by the white "passing throng" who walk outside, blithely enjoying the blessings of modernity. And it is not only the race advocate but all black Americans who suffer a disorienting sense of being out of synch. This disequilibrium is a product of the "double life" that "every American Negro must live, as a Negro and as an American, as swept on by the current of the nineteenth century while yet struggling in the eddies of the fifteenth century" (*Souls* 502).[6]

In sum, the white racist and his enemy the race champion, the former deliberately, the latter inadvertently, have stranded blacks in a premodern social structure, thus cheating them of their American birthright of individualism, that "novel expression, to which a novel idea has given birth," in Tocqueville's famous phrase. Du Bois describes the content of this novel idea as freedom "to be one's self without interference from others," but he is at pains to point out that such freedom is historically specific. It is only in "highly civilized times and places that the conception arises of an individual freedom and development," and it is the right of a "privileged minority" protected by the enslavement of others. A "man born in the European sixteenth century," Du Bois says, was "not fully a man," for he was confined, mentally and physically, as if by divine decree, to a social class that "made and limited his world." "Much as I knew of this class structure of the world," Du Bois comments, "I should never have realized it vividly and fully if I had not been born into its modern counterpart, racial segregation" (*Dusk* 653).[7]

Typical Southern black communities discourage individuality "out of self-defense," notes Ralph Ellison. They construct pre-individual groups in order to create an "elaborate but limited defense mechanism" whose logic is that "for the Negro there is relative safety as long as the impulse toward individuality is suppressed." Thus the black child is trained "away from curiosity and adventure" and from reaching out "toward Western culture when it stirred within him" (*Shadow* 91–92). In "such a society the development of individuality depends upon a series of accidents" (89). To minimize the risk of such accidents was, in a sense, the mission of Booker T. Washington's disciplinary uplift.[8]

Although he seeks to awaken people to the pleasure of enjoying the sensuous materiality of artworks, Du Bois does not encourage material acquisitiveness. Indeed, he dubs the "desire to be rich" a feature of "the old theory of individualism," a liberalism that is conformist and politically naive (*Dusk* 766). Instead, Du Bois's democratic socialism, we will recall, aims at a "higher individualism" that "seeks a freedom for expansion and self-development" and affirms that "living is not for earning, earning is for living" (*Souls* 437). This complements William James's famous contempt for the "Bitch-Goddess Success" and his support for an "ideal of free individuality through a spontaneous social life, which is the ideal of Socialist and Anarchist alike," as Randolph Bourne said of James (qtd. Clayton 72). In describing the good life as one that gives "rein to the creative impulse," Du Bois conceives this life as secular and inward, centered on cultivating sensibility. Sensibility is the decisively modern domain, says Nietzsche, for it originates in the purely human, finite realm of the sensible, in contrast to the "truth-world" of the transparently "intelligible" presided over by the divine (Ferry 21).

"The project of consecrating to the study of sensibility an autonomous science" was named aesthetics in 1750. Thus, notes Luc Ferry, aesthetics "presupposes the withdrawal of the divine perspective" and legitimates a resolute subjectivism that "represents a decisive rupture with the classical point of view" (20). As Ferry has recently observed, "aesthetics is the field par excellence in which the problems brought about by the subjectivization of the world characteristic of modern times can be observed in a chemically pure state" (27, 3). Inseparable from the rise of sensibility and aesthetics is the birth of taste—"the very essence of subjectivity"—which places the beautiful "in a relation to human subjectivity so intimate that it may even be defined by the pleasure it provides, by the sensations or sentiments it provokes in us" (19). As a sensible object, the beautiful object is thus unintelligible and "ipso facto becomes irrational." And taste is "understood as the subjective correlative of the irrationality of the beautiful object" (21–22). By seeking to inculcate in the masses a taste for beauty and aesthetic discrimination, Du Bois decisively links black Americans to what is "the surest sign of the onset of modern times" (18).

In his inwardness Matthew Towns is preoccupied with a beautiful object—the Princess—and the spell she casts is a direct threat to his will to fulfill political responsibility. This conflict culminates on board a speeding train where Matthew is working as a Pullman porter and as a secret agent for a black American radical group. At this point he has returned from Berlin, lovesick for the Princess, doubtful he will ever see her again. In a mood of nihilistic anger Matthew has arranged with a Garveyesque revolutionary to blow up the train he is working aboard to avenge the brutal lynching of a beloved fellow porter. When he reads the "poster" he and his conspirators have printed to explain to the authorities their suicidal undertaking, Matthew's inveterate self-distancing asserts itself: "It was rodomontade. It was melodrama," he realizes. Perennially the appraising observer, he tries to wash his doubts away in a flood of grand rhetoric: "He was going out in triumph . . . The world would know that black men dared to die . . . All the enslaved, all the raped, all the lynched, all the 'jim-crowed' marched in ranks behind him . . . He was going to fight and die for vengeance and freedom" (85–86).

As he furiously attends to the "dozen pairs" of shoes that demand his polishing, his inner exultation and guilt ("he thought of the porters, riding to death") make him increasingly hysterical. But suddenly "then his heart stopped. Then it was that he noticed the white slippers . . . he knew they had moved . . . He saw but the toes, but he knew those slippers—the smooth and shining, high-heeled white kid, embroidered with pearls. Above were silken ankles, and then . . . he heard the thin light swish of silk on silk and knew she was standing there before him— the Princess" (89). Her identity deferred until her clothes have announced her, the Princess, radiant in her sartorial nimbus, awakens Matthew to the reality of his deadly mission: "My God! He was carrying the Princess to death! . . . Where was the impulse, the reasoning . . . that seemed to point to a train wreck as the solution of the color problems of the world? Was he mad?" (90). Matthew's self-reproach recognizes the absurd disparity between his goals and his actions, a disparity replicated in the scene's juxtaposition of his lofty rhetoric of political heroism and what dissolves it—those smooth, shining white slippers. Set inside Matthew's fetishistic consciousness, this scene reveals the novel's nearly operatic display of the inflammable passions unleashed by political and sexual delirium.

Matthew's "withdrawal from the world" prompted by erotic absorption is checked by a counter-impulse—his growing involvement in the culture and commerce of artistic modernism. Unsure at the beginning of the novel "whether Picasso was a man, a city, or a vegetable," Towns undergoes an aesthetic education that leaves him increasingly indifferent to pursuing a promising political career as a tool of the Chicago political machine, which has made him a state legislator and is soon to deliver him a congressional seat (20). Of course, his love for Princess Kautilya ultimately triggers his resignation, but his visceral need for art is nearly an equal intoxicant. Matthew's bedazzled week at the Art Institute culminates a steady movement toward incorporating aesthetic experience in his daily life. Contemplation will soon be joined by consumption as Matthew intuitively refuses the puritanical aesthetic idealism of bourgeois gentility.

Before tossing away his career, he prepares a "retreat," a private "attic nest," as a way to escape his wife, the canny political operator Sara Andrews. Her hardness, her lust for status and disgust with "all sympathy, all yielding, all softness," starve Matthew's aesthetic sensibility and spur his purchase of silken Chinese and Turkish rugs and copies of paintings by Picasso and Matisse to hang on the walls: "he was half-consciously trying to counteract the ugliness of the congressional campaign" (193). But in furnishing a well-appointed bourgeois interior, Matthew is not seeking moral redemption. He simply wants the relief of aesthetic bliss afforded by his chosen commodities. "It was not moral revolt. It was esthetic disquiet," Du Bois notes of Matthew's earlier moment of disgust with the "political game he was playing" (147). Matthew's expensive (Du Bois tells us how much he pays for his purchases) interior decorating, and his cherished rugs and prints and museums, all exist within the same marketplace where his career in machine politics thrives. Enabling both the career and the refuge is the market's democratic premise—that everything is for sale.

Matthew reaches this conclusion in an earlier scene, as he strolls among the crowds on New York's Broadway with a minister friend. The latter is alarmed at the "painted" women he sees and asks Matthew if they are "for sale." "Yes, most of them are for sale—although not quite in the way you mean. And the men too." The puzzled minister asks him to explain. "In a great modern city like New York," declares Matthew, "men and women sell their bodies, souls, and thoughts for luxury and beauty and the joy of life . . . They are content to do things and let things be done" (63). As they sit in a theater watching a show, Matthew notes how few black people are present. Poverty prevents them, yet without the global toil of cheap black labor "you and I could not enjoy this," he notes. Again, his point is not to seize the moral high ground but instead to recognize the enabling conditions of bourgeois privilege. Minister and Matthew acknowledge "that all luxury is built on a foundation of poverty," and that (in the minister's words) "we are consenting too" to this fact: "we're in the mess" (64).

This acceptance of the primacy of the market as the condition of modernity informs Matthew's adoration of the Princess; he is indifferent to transporting her to or associating her with a haven of unspoiled natural beauty. Instead, from his first glance at her, Kautilya is an unearthly icon who stirs "wildly beautiful phantasy" in the aroused Matthew (8). Her "jeweled flesh"—"a king's ransom lay between the naked beauty of her breasts; blood rubies weighed down her ears"—complements her "regal air" of "self-possession," making her a glamorous human commodity, as if out of the pages of *The Great Gatsby,* published three years before (19, 307, 8, 19).

At moments she seems a direct descendant of another fictive princess—Henry James's Christina Light, the Princess Casamassima. Captive to their own lives of privilege, both women are eager to plunge below the placid surface of their pampered daily routine to reach "real life," which for each resides in radical politics. Both make a descent into the lower classes ("I put aside my silken garments and cut my hair," notes the dark princess) and exult when they find "life, real life," as Kautilya describes her union organizing on the Lower East Side of New York. What had "begun as a game and source of experience to me suddenly became real life," she says about having been "beaten and jailed for picketing" (224). Such is the "education of a Queen" (223). Her freedom to try on and discard various roles on the lower rungs of the social ladder (she is a servant, waitress, and factory worker before reaching New York) and to reemerge in silken garments after soaking up enough "real life" testifies to the dizzying pace of American modernity's romance of mobility. Matthew's own fluid movements exploit the same conditions of urban possibility.

By refraining from making Matthew morally superior to these conditions, Du Bois avoids the anti-modernity characteristic of much high modernism. Yet his refusal of the aesthetic idealism that underwrites modernism's oppositional stance tends to be ignored by the received wisdom which appoints Du Bois the role of genteel moralist. His disgusted reaction to Claude McKay (he said he felt like taking a bath after reading *Home to Harlem*) and to Carl Van Vechten are usually cited as evidence of his Victorian taste. Yet Du Bois's dismissal of McKay's novel "remains something of a mystery, for his own novel *Dark Princess*—published the same year—was even more irreverent with respect to bourgeois morality," as Wilson Moses has been virtually alone in observing (*Black Messiahs* 121). The early Harlem scenes in Du Bois's novel depict Matthew escorting his black minister friend, a tourist from Atlanta, to a cabaret for a midnight supper. Although the clergyman, predictably, is made uneasy, Matthew happily ends up spending the night with a prostitute he meets in the club. In later years, he more than once fondly recalls her "abandon" and the charms of her "young, live body" when he is saddled with passionless and "respectable" Sara (66, 153, 192).

Defining one current in *Dark Princess*, then, is an image of modernity as a morally neutral marketplace where all is permitted and possible, including refuge from it in aesthetic or erotic release. It is tempting to locate the other current—the messianic plot forecasting the world's "ultimate emancipation"—as opposing this vision of modernity. But in her shrewdest political insight, the Princess defines "working within" modernity's "centers of power" to be the unique "advantage" of American blacks when they are compared to those "kept outside"—the dark races of the rest of the world. In Africa, Asia, and even Europe, "the closed circle of power is narrow and straitly entrenched; the stranger can scarce get foothold." But "your people," Kautilya tells Matthew, "are working within. They are standing here in this technical triumph of human power and can use it as a fulcrum" to "uplift" the darker races (285–286). Even though they remain tyrannized by segregation, educated American blacks potentially partake of the advantages of technological mastery offered by the democratic marketplace of American modernity. To be outside modernity is to be in oblivion.[9]

The most important political work in *Dark Princess* derives from where one would least expect it—in the book's intimate portrayal of Matthew's free-floating subjectivity. Readers encounter him in a range of moods—desiring, passive, furious, egotistical, ironic, self-pitying, idealistic, adoring. In representing Matthew's self-preoccupation in all its "kaleidoscopic change" (to borrow Du Bois's phrase about his pragmatist sociology), Du Bois claims for himself and his character a (white) modern bourgeois privilege: the cultivation of aesthetic sensibility. Matthew, in short, is a black American Hamlet. Often he is an embittered, opaque spectator of his own life. And his reading of *Hamlet* ignites immediate identification: "he and I suffered . . . an all too easily comprehended hesitation at life" (270). Late in the novel, having reunited with Kautilya, he rapturously rereads the play as part of his "purification" so that he "may rise out of selfishness and hesitation and unbelief" and "accept the spiritual purity of love" (270). Exemplar of Western individualism, Hamlet specifically embodies subjectivity stubbornly resistant to utilitarian rationalism's imperatives of efficiency. "Since Hamlet, hesitation has been a sign of thinking and humanity for modern thinkers," note Horkheimer and Adorno in 1944; now "the person who has doubts is already outlawed as a deserter" (*Dialectic* 205). Thus reaffirming Hamlet in the modern world can be a political act rather than a refuge in inwardness. In Du Bois's case, appropriating Hamlet as the model of black subjectivity in *Dark Princess* constitutes a triple resistance—against the congealing of inner life under the demands of segregation and of racial "group imprisonment," and against what Matthew calls the "white Leviathan," the "vast, remorseless machine" of modernity's disciplinary control (7).

To understand the subjectivism of Du Bois's representation as political nearly inverts one of the most influential critiques of modernism. Georg Lukács would find the lavish attention that Du Bois pays to interior life a symptom of modernism's decadent "ontologism," which depicts modern man as essentially lonely and asocial, wallowing in a morass of subjectivity, in flight from historical reality. Although he would have saluted the communalism of Matthew and Kautilya's political vision, Lukács would probably have judged Du Bois's representation of Matthew a perverse collapse into the solipsism and ahistoricism of monadic individualism. And the portrayal of Matthew is seemingly unredeemed by any effort to shape his subjectivity into historical typicality representative of larger social forces. The classical and critical realists (Balzac, Mann) whom Lukács favors made the individual character at once particular and general. Modernism, in his view, tears asunder realist wholeness, as subject is split from object, a fragmentation that commences with Flaubert and Baudelaire and is exacerbated by impressionism and symbolism.

In his classic rebuttal to Lukács, Adorno notes that "Lukács of all people ought to know that in an individualistic society loneliness is socially mediated and so possesses a significant historical content" rather than testifying to an ontological condition ("Reconciliation" 158). The subjectivism of modern art that makes Lukács so indignant, says Adorno, is at once truth and appearance. "It is truth, because in the universal atomistic state of the world, alienation rules over men." However, it is appearance inasmuch as, "objectively, the social totality has precedence over the individual, a totality which is created and reproduces itself . . . through the contradictions of society." Modern literature "shatter[s] this appearance of subjectivity by setting the individual in his frailty into context" (160–161).

The penultimate scene of *Dark Princess* affirms the historically conditioned nature of Matthew's subjectivity by setting it within the contradictory social totality. Du Bois, in short, is closer to Adorno's notion of "totality in and through contradiction" than he is to Lukács's redemptive wholeness. Thus Du Bois suggests a wholeness but an "antagonistic" (Adorno's word) one by staging the apotheosis of Matthew's subjectivism within its surrounding frame of the objective reality of Jim Crow America. This occurs when Matthew is the lone passenger on a seven-hour plane flight from Chicago to Virginia to reunite with the Princess and meet his newborn son. Analogous to those moments when the narrative freezes as Matthew's fetishistic gaze magnifies surfaces, the scene of Matthew aloft in the air dilates with an exultation that halts the plot's momentum. At first the vastness that surrounds him makes him feel dwarfed—"a tossing, disembodied spirit. . . . He was alone in the center of the universe" (304). But he relaxes into a kind of Emersonian trance of omnipotence: in the air Matthew "was triumphant over Pain and Death . . . He was the God-man, the Everlasting Power, the eternal and undying Soul. He was above everything—Life, Death, Hate, Love. He spurned the pettiness of earth beneath his feet" (305). But his transcendent self aloft must come down to earth and be "plagued" by the ugly pettiness of racial realities. Landing in Virginia, he suffers, figuratively, a deathly erasure. As the pilot is cheered and thronged by white admirers who whisk him off to a "steaming bath and breakfast," "Matthew climbed wearily down and stood dizzy, dirty, and deaf," ignored by all. He is lucky to find something to eat after walking three miles, bathing in a brook, and boarding a Jim Crow train.

The shock of transition from omnipotence to invisibility that Matthew suffers juxtaposes two jarring moments of the American social totality: the romance of American individualism and the prison of anonymity erected by white supremacy. From the novel's start, fury at racism has been a catalyst of his inward turn. And in the penultimate scene fury and inwardness are so entwined that Matthew is still reeling when he boards the train. His emotions are in chaos: "He could not think. He could not reason. He just sat and saw and felt in a tangled jumble of thoughts and words, feelings and desires, dreams and fears . . . He sat seeing nothing and yet acutely conscious of every sound, every movement, every quiver of light" (306). Anticipating his arrival home but bruised by the social indifference that isolates him, "he wanted to cry and sing, walk and rage, scream and dance."

After his inwardly turbulent plane and train ride, Matthew stays at the margins of events in the novel's final pages, as if relieved to surrender his interiority and fuse into the collective identity of his new family. "With strangled throat and streaming eyes" he reunites with the Princess (and of course "he kissed the sandals on her feet") and their infant, is married to Kautilya, and watches as their son is baptized by the Townses' ancient black preacher (307). Then the book concludes as three Brahmins who have journeyed from the Bwodpur court emerge to anoint the infant "Messenger and Messiah to all the Darker Worlds!" (311). Thus the romance of messianic redemption has the last word in *Dark Princess*. One might read the final reunion as suggestive of a utopian synthesis that in good Hegelian fashion sublates—cancels and preserves—the contradictions that Matthew had confronted most intensely in the bruising passage from plane to earth. The Pan-African movement offers its spirit of collective struggle as a release from such tensions. Will Matthew the inveterate skeptic be able to reside in synthesis, or will his anarchistic sensibility seek more idiosyncratic expression? This is one of the questions *Dark Princess* leaves open.

The birth that punctuates *Dark Princess* reverberates within and without the novel. It echoes the initial scene of Matthew's humiliation which drives him from medical school. The Dean forbids him obstetrics training—"Do you think white women patients are going to have a nigger doctor delivering their babies?"—and Matthew stalks out enraged (4). The birth that concludes the novel in effect overthrows the ban on birthing imposed by white racism at the start. The final glimpse of Matthew as proud father "swaying the babe up and down," the blessed infant already with a "silken turban" round its head, redeems in fiction the most painful personal episode in Du Bois's life—the death of his infant son. In "Of the Passing of the First Born," Du Bois had identified with his son, even fused with him, as he imagined that in the "poise" of the boy's "curl-crowned head" was "all that wild pride of being" that he, the father, still kept in his own heart (*Souls* 510). But what, Du Bois muses, "shall a Negro want with pride amid the studied humiliations" inflicted by white supremacy? Before banishing his thoughts as "idle words," Du Bois wonders if his son was perhaps fortunate to depart "before the world had dubbed" his "ambition insolence" and taught him "to cringe and bow."

In his grief Du Bois understands his son's death as only a more literal version of the psychic death inflicted upon all in America whose skin color condemns them to "grow choked and deformed within the Veil" (510). There is also a hint that black people of unrepentant pride and ambition (including himself and potentially his son) draw punishment upon themselves from a society terrified of blacks who are unwilling to know their place. Du Bois's life of course will testify to his refusal to be intimidated, to "cringe and bow," as he redeems his son's life in his own, as if he takes up his son's foreshortened life and makes it his own. *Dark Princess* ends with the son reborn as a royal savior, hence free to harbor all the "wild pride" he likes. Thus by staging this rebirth Du Bois permits himself to renew and perfect the bond of identification, indeed the psychic fusion, that he had known with his own infant.

"Self-indulgent phantasy" is how one of Kautilya's advisers describes her infatuation with Matthew, and the phrase applies to the novel as well (299). But the fantasy I have suggested—that Du Bois's novel memorializes and idealizes his powerful identification with his blessed son—turns out to have more than a tenuous link to actuality. For a confidence that he is one of the blessed is prominent in Du Bois's own self-representations. And it is an image entwined with his intimacy with Spingarn, a Jew and thus one of the "chosen." I will conclude this chapter with a look at how Du Bois's "wild pride of being" chosen sought maximum exposure and challenge.

In the memoir "The Shadow of Years" Du Bois declares himself one of the "Lord's anointed." He begins the essay by recalling the Berkshire Hills of his birth, the hills he felt he had returned to when he visited Spingarn's Troutbeck. One reason he feels chosen, he notes at the essay's end, is that the year before he had "looked death in the face." "But it was not my time." In January 1917 Du Bois underwent a successful second kidney stone operation. In attendance was Joel Spingarn's personal physician, "as much for my own peace of mind as for yours," Spingarn had told Du Bois (qtd. Lewis 524). To help ease the financial stress of his six-week recovery, Du Bois accepted a loan from Spingarn, one of a number over the years.

"The Shadow of Years" is entwined with Spingarn from the start. It was first published in February 1918 in *The Crisis* as the text of Du

Bois's after-dinner speech for his fiftieth-birthday celebration, a testimonial banquet that Spingarn organized. Two years later Du Bois reprinted it as the opening chapter of *Darkwater*. Du Bois's self-representation in "The Shadow of Years" makes vivid the extent to which Spingarn had become a model of aristocratic ease that fused seamlessly with Du Bois's own considerable sense of distinction. But not only the content but the timing of the memoir's original publication and republication make it revelatory and politically charged. By first issuing the essay in the midst of his wartime controversies—between the officers' camp and the bid for the captaincy—Du Bois had devised yet another way to undermine his own authority as self-sacrificing race man. To turn from "group identity" to self-mythologizing may be to exchange one trap for another. But for Du Bois "The Shadow of Years" functioned as a cathartic escape from the stasis of exemplarity.[10]

Like most of Du Bois's various autobiographical self-representations, the essay tends to flaunt his sense of distinction and indifference to being "what Americans call a 'good fellow' " (*Autobiography* 283). Characteristic is the moment in *Dusk of Dawn* when Du Bois proudly tells of the "impudent" letter he wrote ex-President Hayes, then head of the Slater Fund for black education, for being in "bad faith" about the endowment's commitment. After having "deluged" President Hayes with letters on his behalf, Du Bois won a fellowship: "I remember rushing down to New York and talking with President Hayes in the old Astor House and then going out walking on air. I saw an especially delectable shirt in a shop window. I went in and asked about it. It cost three dollars, which was about four times as much as I had ever paid for a shirt in my life; but I bought it" (*Dusk* 586). This note of insouciant triumph is amplified in "The Shadow of Years."

Du Bois's insouciance is invariably mixed with contempt, as the famous opening pages of *The Souls of Black Folk* make evident. They disclose that the spur to distinction is rooted in hatred of the smug arrogance of "the religion of whiteness." Later in the book Du Bois speaks of "the temptation of Hate," with its "cold and shuddering arms," as a specter continuing to shadow the childhood of black Americans. At best, the specter grows fainter and "less sinister" but never fades away; it diffuses itself and lingers "thick at the edges" (513–514). This diffusion permeates "The Shadow of Years." Here is reprised the "fiercely sunny" strife of his childhood when difference in skin color created "distinctions" that "exalted" rather than burdened him (*Dusk* 627). Arnold Rampersad attributes the magisterial tenor of the essay to Du Bois's self-conscious construction of a prophetic role; casting himself as one of the chosen, an instrument of a divine will, he confesses feeling "drawn up into higher spaces and made part of a higher mission," at times pitying his "pale companions, who were not of the Lord's anointed" (*Darkwater* 12).

Yet for all his transcendence Du Bois is careful to delineate the social and class boundaries of his world even as he tramples over them to achieve a unique status. Although he was living in genteel poverty, Du Bois's self-exaltation left him indifferent to the "lure" of wealth but also made him the "natural companion" of the rich, with whom he shared contempt of the poor Irish and Germans who "slaved in the mills." Reflecting back on this, he exclaims: "Of such is the kingdom of snobs!" (10). The key to this kingdom was winning acceptance to Harvard (after taking a degree at Fisk), which catapulted him over all the competition. "Harvard was a mighty conjure-word in that hill town," and even "the mill owners' sons had aimed lower" (13). Although his exaltation was inseparable from "tireless effort," effort is precisely what "The Shadow of Years" erases. Instead, its keynote is ease. Bourdieu calls ease "the most visible assertion of freedom from constraints which dominate ordinary people," the perfect "coincidence of 'is' and 'ought' " and the "self-affirming power it contains" (*Distinction*, 255–256).

Dubbing his first twenty-eight years the "Age of Miracles," Du Bois says, "I seemed to ride in conquering might . . . I *willed* to do! It was done. I wished! The wish came true . . . I willed and lo! I was walking beneath the elms of Harvard,—the name of allurement" (14–15). Flaunting the magical thinking of infantile narcissism, Du Bois locates the source of his sublime confidence in his mother's worship: "She did not try to make me perfect. To her I was already perfect" (11). Even when he reflects that his omnipotence may be nothing but "sheer Luck," he banishes any self-doubt simply by going "doggedly to work" (17). "The Shadow of Years" is the most stylized rendering of the mythopoeic cadences and flights of epic rhetoric that Du Bois tends to employ in his memoirs. And Du Bois candidly admits that his turgidity results from seeing "not too clearly, but through the thickening veil of wish and afterthought" (13). This tacit confession suggests that perhaps a conscious design controls his mythmaking. His self-celebration as the chosen one functions in part to align him with Spingarn precisely at a time when political astuteness might have counseled circumspect sobriety rather than a trumpeting of distinction.

Because the controversies of 1917–1918 had damaged Du Bois's prestige with the NAACP constituency, one would have expected a chastened Du Bois to emerge in the aftermath. Thus 1920 should have been a time for trimming, not unfurling, his sails. These assumptions would be correct if Du Bois had valued a Bookerite "singleness of vision." But such modesty was tantamount to slavery. Du Bois sought liberation in being a problem, and his memoir was one means to this end. Thus instead of letting "The Shadow of Years" recede into the background as an excusably self-congratulatory after-dinner speech for a single occasion, Du Bois reprinted it twice. When it appeared in 1920 as the opening chapter of *Darkwater,* Du Bois in effect handed ammunition to the rising Marcus Garvey, who that same year attacked him for elitism and not being "100 per cent Negro" (qtd. Vincent 93). And the next year Garvey contemptuously lumped Du Bois with such notorious decadents and "hypersensitive critics" as Walter Pater and George Santayana (Garvey 98). Whereas Du Bois and the NAACP appeal to the "Beau Brummel, Lord Chesterfield, kid gloved, silk-stocking" professionals of the "Talented Tenth," says Garvey, he (Garvey) appeals to "the hard working man who earns his living by the sweat of his brow" (98). Sweat is precisely what the cult of distinction disdains. A horror of the natural and an air of icy detachment, an "unshakable determination not to be moved," says Baudelaire, all distinguish the dandy, the emblematic marginal man of urban modernity who loves "*distinction* above all things" (Baudelaire 29, 27).[11]

Du Bois had always attracted controversy by enacting his belief that those of distinction must dress the part. His style blended European sophistication with more than a hint of dandyism that his critics were adroit at lampooning. To William Ferris, once a Du Bois idolator but by then a Garveyite, Du Bois was "too dainty and fastidious . . . to lead the masses of his race" (Ferris "Darkwater" 343). This is from his skeptical review of *Darkwater.* Ferris found "The Shadow of Years" particularly grating. Indeed, Ferris was so provoked that he declared that one reason *Darkwater* would alienate "the black masses" was that Du Bois looked "down upon their infirmities from the heights of his own greatness" (347). Ferris singles out the "kingdom of snobs" passage as one of a number expressive of a "patronising manner." At the start of his review, Ferris remarks that when he read the bookjacket claim that "Even more than the late Booker Washington, Mr. Du Bois is now the chief spokesman of the two hundred million men and women of African blood," he was tempted to place a question mark after it. But Ferris feels no need to resist the temptation after reading "The Shadow of Years" and recalling the outrage that the "Close Ranks" editorial provoked (343). Du Bois had succeeded in goading readers to question his status as chief spokesman.

In short, at the opening of the postwar decade "The Shadow of Years" is yet another self-inflicted blow to Du Bois's stature as the race's foremost representative. His turn against his own authority is an act of freedom, indeed an act of aesthetic "madness," but also has a political meaning. His turning seeks to revise dominant and destructive styles of black leadership—the demagogic and charismatic. The former is typified by Booker T. Washington's Tuskegee Machine, which was funded by white philanthropy and used, said Du Bois, to suppress "the Negro intelligentsia" and hammer "it into conformity" (*Dusk* 608). Marcus Garvey's cult of personality combined charisma and demagoguery. In preaching the "success mentality" to make the Negro come "into his own as a standardized race," Garvey, like Washington, inculcated undeviating obedience in his followers. Du Bois never hid his contempt for charisma: "My leadership was a leadership solely of ideas. I never was, nor ever will be, personally popular. This was not simply because of my idiosyncrasies but because I despise the essential demagoguery of personal leadership; of that hypnotic ascendancy over men" which demands "personal loyalty and admiration" over all else (*Dusk* 775).

A "charismatic model of political authority," notes Adolph Reed, is "fundamentally antidemocratic" and tends toward the authoritarian because its "antiformalism leaves acclimation as the sole principle of popular validation" (*Jackson* 34–35). Bequeathed to blacks by white elites, this "organic leadership style" has dominated black politics for a century, forcing "black aspirants for leadership to base their claims on grounds of racial authenticity" rather than on the democratic procedures of electoral representation (32). Relying on the dubious premise that leadership is founded on "unmediated representation of a uniform racial totality," black charismatic style assumes a "complete identity of racial interests," and dissent bears the "stigma of race treason" (35).

Distrusting the organic and anti-formal, esteeming the difficult and denaturalized, Du Bois valued the dissent that anti-charismatic leadership encourages. He not only resisted pressures to conform but admired that resistance in others, even when it took the form of attacking him. Rarely holding grudges against his opponents, he would even come to the support of harsh critics like A. Philip Randolph and

E. Franklin Frazier, and he enjoyed the scathing satirical portrait that George Schuyler drew of him in *Black No More* (*Book Reviews* 153– 154). Thus he enacted his effort "to give the other fellow his due even when I disliked him personally and disagreed with him logically" (*Autobiography* 284). Such flexibility is indicative of the premium Du Bois put on exchange and dissonance as weapons against dogma.

Yet his disdain for charisma co-exists with his self-image as a prophet, one of the "Lord's anointed," "drawn up into higher spaces and made part of a mightier mission" (*Darkwater* 12). As early as his twenty-fifth birthday he gives voice to his sense of mission. He muses in his diary (published in part nearly seventy years later in his *Autobiography*): "is it egotism—is it assurance—or is it the silent call of the world spirit that makes me feel that I am royal and that beneath my sceptre a world of kings shall bow" (*Against Racism* 28). Such statements give evidence, says Joel Williamson, that Du Bois suffered (and enjoyed) a "Messiah complex" (*Crucible* 410).

The prophet is the ideal type of charismatic authority, according to Max Weber. Weber's seminal theory of charisma derives from the history of religion and takes as its paradigm the prophet unassimilable to the institution of the church. By its very nature, notes Weber, charisma is "not an 'institutional' and permanent structure, but rather, where its 'pure' type is at work, it is the very opposite of the institutionally permanent" (Weber 248). Antithetical to the bureaucratic and the regulated, charisma is founded on "inner determination and inner restraint" that "must stand outside the ties of this world, outside of routine occupations, as well as outside the routine obligations of family life" (246, 248). Du Bois is frequently linked to this elected distance: an early biographer emphasizes that "he was often called a 'stranger' in his race" and that "his influence was lessened by the fact that he never consciously worked at creating disciples" (Rudwick 307, 320). Du Bois's NAACP colleague James Weldon Johnson concurs with this last point, noting that even Du Bois's admirers found him "cold, stiff, supercilious," a disposition that has "limited his scope of leadership to less than what it might have been . . . The great influence Du Bois has exercised has been due to the concentrated force of his ideas, with next to no reinforcement from that wide appeal of personal magnetism" (*Along* 204).

Suspicious of charisma, yet invested in a prophetic mission, Du Bois conjoins contraries to reinvent the race champion as dandy-prophet. Du Bois obviously diverges from Weber's ideal type of charismatic, who is inherently anti-institutional. And he modifies the antisocial bias of the dandy while remaining in touch with what the dandy, according to Baudelaire, establishes—a "new kind of aristocracy" based on "divine gifts" rather than money or genealogy (Baudelaire 28). The dandy's historical origin is in "periods of transition," in the space between a fading aristocracy and a democracy poised to level distinction (28). Analogous is Du Bois's transitional invention—the "Talented Tenth," a strategy to propagate democracy by first creating a vanguard party. Not only did Du Bois mix and revise intentions, roles, tactics, and authority, as was his pragmatist habit, but his relation to institutions was similarly unstable, especially, as we have seen, to the one he helped found.

At the NAACP Du Bois served as an unelected race leader and a self-styled prophet. And to this extent he is of course complicit with the anti-democratic bias of black political representation. At the same time, his multiple strategies of denaturalization—the "Talented Tenth," the cult of distinction, aesthetic education, the flaunting of mulatto status, the ritual of choice to dramatize race as chosen rather than a biological given, and the construction of representation as troping rather than transparency—all work to turn race leadership from the eliciting of conformity and loyalty to the provocation to think and debate. And to experience beauty in daily life. The capacity for aesthetic experience insinuates new possibilities beyond the utilitarian routine of enforced labor and habit and the debasement of thinking by the rule of stereotype.

To feel and act upon aesthetic impulse in private and in public was to pursue a path of freedom from the medieval caste system called Jim Crow. Du Bois trod this path throughout his career, in 1917–1920 doing so with nearly reckless abandon and creative improvisation. In those vertiginous years Du Bois courted risk and suffered injury because he insisted on living within the tumult of modernity. Thus he entered territory hitherto assumed off-limits to blacks (the Military Intelligence Bureau) and charted new territory (a black officers' training camp) while embracing what was traditionally forbidden—a "real and full American" patriotism. In these experiments, undertaken in alliance with a Jewish aristocrat intellectual, Du Bois imbued his struggle for modernity with an exhilarating "anarchy of the spirit."

6

Motley Mixtures:
Locke, Ellison, Hurston

The interracial nexus comprising three generations of Harvard pragmatists—William James, his student Du Bois, and his admirer Alain Locke—embodied a collective quarter-century of advocacy of philosophical and cultural miscegenation that helped trigger the creative ferment of the 1920s in "mongrel Manhattan."[1] But the revolt against cultural and racial purism was soon to wane. And Locke, a professor of philosophy at Howard, a self-described "cultural cosmopolitan" and "philosophical mid-wife" to the Harlem Renaissance, would in subsequent decades devote a number of valuable essays to pondering what had gone wrong and what might have been (*Philosophy* 16). In 1950 he confessed to being both "proud and ashamed" of having signed the " 'New Negro's' birth certificate" (232). The Harlem Renaissance, he believed, "failed to accomplish all that it could," for it was hampered by race chauvinism's "false conception of culture" (232). Although haunted by a sense of missed opportunity, Locke continued to find James's work a fruitful way to rethink the relation of color and culture. Locke's retrospective reflections, from which he constructed his theory of cosmopolitanism, constitute an untapped legacy for contemporary efforts to move beyond identity thinking.

Locke believed, as did Dewey, that James had hinted at a "vital connection between pluralism and democracy" that it was incumbent upon his successors to elaborate (Locke *Philosophy* 53). A statement of 1942 summarizes his allegiance to James's legacy: "When William James inaugurated his all-out campaign against intellectual absolutism, though radical empiricism and pragmatism were his shield and buckler, his trusty right-arm sword, we should remember, was pluralism . . . Today, in our present culture crisis, it is both timely to recall this, and important . . . to ponder over it" (*Philosophy* 53). Although Locke is conventionally labeled a cultural pluralist (and at times refers to himself as one), his philosophy, as this statement implies, makes him more precisely a Jamesian or pragmatist pluralist. Part of the burden of this chapter is to show the force of this distinction.

In a late summary of his life, Locke described himself as born in "the key of paradox." He was, for instance, adamantly anti-imperialist, universalist, and internationalist but was "forced by a sense of simple justice to approve" of "militant counter-nationalisms" in Turkey, Palestine, India, and elsewhere (*Philosophy* 16). And his cosmopolitanism did not prevent him from being "an advocate of cultural racialism," if only as a "defense counter-move for the American Negro" (16). His penchant for tactical counter-moves recalls Du Bois and suggests the capaciousness their shared pragmatism encouraged. Locke's commitment to the "paradox" of multiple options informs all his cultural practice, particularly his important, if unfulfilled, efforts in the twenties to fashion a democratic cosmopolitanism. It would somehow balance "the fullest sharing of American culture and institutions" with a nonchauvinistic notion of "race consciousness" and with James's skepticism of identity as a foundational category ("New Negro" 12).

Locke intended to enlarge black Americans' traditional and narrow options of either assimilation or nationalism. But a number of factors combined to hamper his liberatory project: historical circumstances bluntly discouraged any loosening of racial classification, and Locke's position as "New Negro" publicist required, he later acknowledged, that he turn race into a "commodity" (*Philosophy* 232). This unavoidable chauvinism also reflected unresolved contradictions in his own thinking about the status of race.

Later admirers of Locke's ideals also swam against prevailing currents. Ralph Ellison and Albert Murray pondered a pragmatist pluralism that, borrowing Murray's words, thrives on "complexity and confusion" and is allergic to whatever "has any presumptions of purity."[2] Such impurity was anathema to sixties black political and cultural nationalists and to many multiculturalists in the eighties and nineties. Intervening in the early debates in the 1970s about what, in the next decade, would be called multiculturalism, Ralph Ellison celebrated American culture as an "appropriation game" (*Territory* 28). This expressed a Lockean stance that had to wait until the nineties to acquire new currency in our post-identity moment. Two decades before an audience was prepared to grasp it, Ellison renewed Locke's cosmopolitan critique of "vested ownership" in culture. Ellison's "The Little Man at Chehaw Station," like Pauline Hopkins's *Of One Blood*, is an ingenious intellectual history that weaves together various strands. To this crucial late-seventies essay we now turn.

Lambasted by the Black Arts movement of the sixties as apolitical, canonized for decades by white liberals and neoconservatives as an icon of blandly affirmative Emersonian individualism, Ralph Ellison has suffered both caricatures. Now he is being rehabilitated by postmodernism: Isaac Julien, the black British avant-garde filmmaker, has invited him in from the cold. In the self-consciously postmodern venue *Black Popular Culture* (1992) Julien acknowledges Ellison as an important predecessor and borrows a phrase from *Invisible Man* for his essay's title. In "Black Is, Black Ain't: Notes on De-Essentializing Black Identities," Julien urges skepticism toward the stubbornly persistent assumption of a "unitary blackness" and enlists Ellison as an ally (271). What Julien admires in Ellison is his understanding of black identity as "open-ended . . . a fluid continuum . . . made and remade" (255). Julien grasps that the effort he shares with Ellison to make blackness more malleable derives from a critique of identity. This critique tends to be overlooked in Ellison criticism, which either absorbs it into a thematics of existentialist despair (the anguish of invisibility) or assumes that identity is the prize for which his novel's narrator quests.

Isaac Julien's response to Ellison makes vivid that the novelist's skepticism of identity has postmodern affinities. But Ellison's stance is part of a pragmatist lineage which aims not merely to make identity more fluid but to abolish its status as a grounding term. Like Du Bois and Locke, Ellison rejects both the transparency posited in being representative and the security this perspective affords. Instead, says Ellison, "we are representative not only of one but of several overlapping and constantly shifting social categories" as we negotiate a democratic cultural and social order that is a "whirlpool" of motion (*Territory* 19). Although Julien makes no reference to this passage, his regret at a "resurgence" of "binaristic thinking that makes people feel safe in their separate groups" and his plea for a "wider frame of reference" in "talking about blackness" (271) summarize Ellison's own concerns in "The Little Man at Chehaw Station," from which the above passage is taken.[3]

This essay, a critique of cultural pluralism or what would now be called multiculturalism, gave little comfort to Ellison's enemies. A favorite whipping boy of black nationalists, Ellison was accused of spending most of his time "in flight from his own people" and of having wandered "away from home" (qtd. Cruse 507–508). He "permanently retreated to the elitism of heroic individualism," in the judgment of a recent critic (Watts 119).[4] As a revival of ethnic and racial consciousness was under way by the late seventies, Ellison defends the melting pot in "The Little Man at Chehaw Station" while condemning "the newly fashionable code word 'ethnicity' " with its "blood magic and blood thinking" (*Territory* 21).

But the essay is hardly a nostalgic yearning for "one hundred per cent Americanism." Rather, Ellison, the allegedly apolitical elitist, intervenes to unsettle radically both terms of the melting-pot-versus-cultural-pluralism debate. And what makes his perspective radical is what makes it political: he recovers implicitly the root sense of politics as civic participation in a public world, one emancipated from the private realm of the *ethnos* where social organization by natural descent reigns. Ellison sees the move from *ethnos* to *politkos* as imperative if we are ever to actualize in the present the nation's "revolutionary" democratic ideals of equality. Only if we are willing to grapple with *pragmata* (unsettled circumstances) and forsake the security of an already grounded identity, usually one that has "emerged out of our parents' past," can we become political beings capable of "antagonistic cooperation" within America's democratic chaos (19, 26).

Ellison's essay is a seminal statement of Jamesian pluralism, which is to say that it interrogates rather than enshrines identity logic.[5] This interrogative line of thought links James, Du Bois, and Locke but also touches Zora Neale Hurston, whom Locke knew at Howard, and Ellison and Albert Murray, both of whom paid tribute to Locke in 1973. All of them are particularly alert to the threat to freedom found in what James calls "vicious intellectualism" and Dewey the "fallacy of definition"—the use of concepts to erect rigid classifications. As Albert Murray says, "even the most precise concepts are only nets that cannot hold very much flesh-and-blood experience" (*South* 59). And "transitional and connecting links" tend to slip through these nets (Dewey *Art* 216–217).

The effort to preserve such links will shape the responses of pragmatist writers to what, by the twenties, was a national preoccupation: the question of what constitutes American identity. According to the received wisdom, pragmatism's answer is cultural pluralism, promulgated in 1915 by Horace Kallen. Defying nativist demands for assimilation, cultural pluralism honors the multi-ethnic reality of the United States by celebrating the immigrant who preserves his origins to become a hyphenated American.

But cultural pluralism, including Randolph Bourne's, was silent about black Americans, ignoring that they had, in Du Bois's words, "actively . . . woven" themselves "in the very warp and woof of this nation" (*Souls* 545). Not only was Kallen blind (or indifferent) to such hybridity, his pluralism was actually unpragmatist in its affirmation of the primacy of identity/difference. The divergence between pragmatism and Kallen's pluralist championing of immutable ethnic difference occurred as soon as his "Democracy versus the Melting Pot" appeared in *The Nation* in February 1915. Shortly after, in a letter to Kallen, Dewey said he disliked the "implication of segregation" in Kallen's conception of a pluralist democracy as an orchestra of discrete identities (qtd. Westbrook 214). The hyphen must connect, not separate, Dewey warned in 1916. The American is "himself a hyphenated character. This does not mean that he is part American and that some foreign ingredient is then added. It means that . . . he is international and interracial in his makeup" (qtd. Kallen 131).[6]

In a similar cosmopolitan spirit, Du Bois, just prior to World War I, sought, he said, to build an "Internation" founded on an "interracial culture, broader and more catholic than" any currently existing here ("Evolving" 58). But the war derailed his dream of establishing a "human unity." In 1933 he lamented that the ideal of the "Inter-nation, of Humanity, and the disappearance of 'race' from our vocabulary" had yet to become a reality (*Writings* 1022–23). "The Little Man at Chehaw Station" in effect recovers this dream and imagines what a nonracialized understanding of American culture would mean. Ellison turns race into culture, that is, into practices and commitments shaped by historical and political constraints but untethered to origin and ownership.

As a music student at Tuskegee in the mid-thirties, Ellison met the little man by way of the classical pianist Hazel Harrison. After Ellison gives a lackluster trumpet performance, Harrison tells him: "You must *always* play your best, even if it's only the waiting room at Chehaw Station [a "lonely whistlestop"] because in this country there'll always be a little man hidden behind the stove . . . and he'll know the *music,* and the *tradition,* and the standards of *musicianship*" (4). Without formal education or institutional address, the little man's "unaccountable knowingness" personifies a "cultivated democratic sensibility" which confounds all class hierarchies (9, 15). The very presence of Hazel Harrison—a student of Busoni's and a friend of Prokofiev's, one of whose signed manuscripts is atop her piano—in a basement studio at Booker T. Washington's Tuskegee instances a bizarre improbability worthy of the "little man." To "conventional minds" Harrison and the protagonist of her anecdote are eruptions of "irrational" cultural "chaos" (30).

Not simply the cry of its occasion (a dissent from black nationalism), Ellison's essay is an exemplary act of retrieval, recovering what Kallen's cultural pluralism erased—the "motley mixtures" (Ellison's phrase) alive in the pragmatist pluralism of James, Du Bois, Locke, and Dewey. At a 1973 Harvard symposium honoring Locke, Ellison and Murray used the occasion deliberately to reclaim Locke's legacy. Concurring with his friend Murray's remark that "the last thing" Locke wanted "was to be locked in an ethnic province," Ellison declares that Locke sensed above all that modern American culture was "the experience of human beings living in a world of turbulent transition" and that it led him "to deal with Afro-American folklore and music from a background that included his studies with James and Royce" ("Alain Locke" 18, 21).[7] In linking Locke, James, and "turbulent transition," Ellison deftly, if elliptically, summarizes the pragmatist legacy that he redeems in "The Little Man at Chehaw Station."

In sum, "The Little Man at Chehaw Station" opens a window on this tradition which, in appropriately Jamesian fashion, each member refashions. This lineage aims to restore the connectives eliminated by the deadening effects of segregation, both racial and philosophical. It does so by reinstating, in Dewey's phrase, "what is left over . . . excluded by definition from full reality," what goes astray by eluding or disrupting the reign of system (*Experience and Nature* 48). Pragmatist pluralism is, to borrow Hurston's words, "disturbing to the pigeonhole way of life," for it disinters what various forms of absolutism—identity claims grounded in biology, ethnicity, foundational philosophy, nationalism, or white supremacy—seek to keep buried: tangled and muddy overlap, "motley mixtures" (Hurston 581).

In his 1904 essay "A World of Pure Experience" James gives a glimpse of experience liberated from imposed classifications. He calls his radical empiricism a "mosaic philosophy," but his mosaic is quite different from multiculturalism's mosaic of pluralistic harmony. Indeed, James invokes the image promptly to deconstruct it: "In actual mosaics the pieces are held together by their bedding, for which bedding the Substances, transcendental Egos, or Absolutes of other philosophies may be taken to stand. In radical empiricism there is no bedding; it is as if the pieces clung together by their edges, the transitions experienced between them forming their cement" (*Writings* 1180). In this pluralistic universe without "bedding," the self is not already in place but is an "affair of relations" produced in the transitions experienced. "Life is in the transitions as much as in terms connected" and experience grows by its edges, with one moment "proliferating into the next by transitions" (1180–81).

James's radical empiricism (like Dewey's *Experience and Nature,* as we shall see) can be read as a philosophical allegory of what a world beyond the veil of the color line would be like to live in, a world not shackled to identity logic and not deformed by what every foundationalist philosophy requires—a principle of a "single, final, and unalterable authority" (Dewey *Political Writings* 46). That it was read as allegory is apparent. Consider, for instance, the opening lines of Locke's "The New Negro": "in the last decade something beyond the watch and guard of statistics has happened in the life of the American Negro and the three Norns who have traditionally presided over the Negro problem have a changeling in their laps. The sociologist, the Philanthropist, the Race-Leader are not unaware of the New Negro, but they are at a loss to account for him. He simply cannot be swathed in their formulae" ("New Negro" 3). Locke has constructed a figure embodying James's "unclassified residuum." The philosopher would have cherished the existence of this elusive changeling defiant of categories, including separatism, who affirms his Africanity as part of America's pluralist democracy.

In his figure of the "little man" behind the stove at Chehaw Station, Ellison salutes Locke's Jamesian changeling and devises one of his own. The importance of Ellison's little man is not immediately obvious, given that he partakes of the "anonymous and lowly" and exudes a "tricky democratic anonymity which makes locating him an unending challenge" (9, 11). What gradually becomes apparent is that his anonymity and elusiveness are consequences of a rare ability—to experience our "fractured" culture as "an intricate whole" rather than as a collection of racial or ethnic enclaves (9). To resist this atomized provincialism is to achieve a "democratic anonymity"—an individualism unanchored to identity and become a "free-floating sensibility" that understands culture as founded on learning ("appropriation") rather than the passivity of inheritance (9). This powerful anonymity brings Ellisonian invisibility out of the basement and into the light of day.

The "little man" becomes a metaphor for the dissonant, incalculable possibilities bred by democratic turbulence, that "whirlpool of odds and ends," to quote a bit of Ellison's strikingly Jamesian imagery that suffuses his evocations of American "wholeness" (20). James's anarchic mosaic of edges and transitions that rupture identity and purity becomes in Ellison our "complex and pluralistic wholeness" always in cacaphonic motion (16). This also tallies with Locke's dynamic sense of democratic cultural unity as "fluid and functional" rather than "fixed and irrevocable"; its "vital norms," says Locke, are "equivalence and reciprocity rather than identity" (*Philosophy* 101). The little man, in turn, seems to emerge from invisible man's epiphany (after the death of Tod Clifton) about those unaccountable "men of transition" who wander "outside of historical time," like "birds of passage who were too obscure for learned classification . . . of natures too ambiguous for the most ambiguous words" (*Invisible Man* 439–440). These straying remnants, invisible man realizes, mock Brotherhood's pretensions to control history as one would a force in a laboratory experiment.

Ellison's essay in effect binds together William James and Alain Locke, rewriting cultural pluralism under their aegis. What results is not Kallen's opposition of cultural pluralism versus the melting pot but instead a synthesis which Ellison dubs a "pluralistic melting pot" (38). To appreciate this synthesis requires deferring pursuit of "The Little Man" until we look at the threads Ellison weaves to remake his pragmatist pluralist heritage, a weaving that expresses his "American compulsion to improvise upon the given" (24).

A crucial thread is the debate that presided over the birth of cultural pluralism, which became better known many decades later as multiculturalism. Kallen, a devoted Jamesian, coined the phrase cultural pluralism in 1915, but actually began to formulate it as early as 1905 in response to then-dominant nativist demands for "one hundred percent Americanism," a purity that immigrants could achieve by joining the "melting pot." Kallen, a German-born Jew at Harvard, developed his anti-assimilationist views in 1905 when he encountered the brilliant black undergraduate Alain Locke.

According to Kallen's remembrance Locke was "very sensitive, very easily hurt" and insisted that "I am a human being" and that "his color ought not to make any difference . . . We are all alike Americans." But

Kallen, certain that Locke was mistaken, told him: "It *had* to make a difference and it *had* to be accepted and respected and enjoyed for what it was" (qtd. Sollors "Critique" 269). Two years later Kallen met Locke again in England, where Locke was the first black Rhodes scholar at Oxford and Kallen was on a fellowship. They continued their earlier conversation, with Locke again asking "what difference does the difference [of race] make?" "In arguing out those questions" the phrase " 'cultural pluralism,' the right to be different," was born (269).

Adamant that Locke must organize his life around race, Kallen converted "the right to be different" into a command, thus imprinting on pluralism an element of coercion that has remained indelible in its contemporary incarnation as multiculturalism. The note of bullying paternalism in Kallen's attitude toward Locke makes vivid how a "dictatorship of virtue" brought cultural pluralism into being.[8]

A symptom of Kallen's rigid pluralism is his well-known belief that men "cannot change their grandfathers" for "what is inalienable in the life of mankind is its . . . psycho-social inheritance" (*Culture* 220). And this "ancestral endowment" is impervious to class mobility. "He remains still the Slav, the Jew," Kallen notes of those who emerge "from the proletariat into the middle class" (97). A corrosive contradiction vitiates cultural pluralism—Kallen shares a belief in "the eternal power of descent, birth, *natio,* and race" (in Werner Sollors's words) with his racist, nativist opponents (Sollors 260).

A philosophy that refused to make a fetish of difference would seem to speak directly to Locke in his debate with Kallen. Thus William James's lectures at Oxford were exceptionally timely and suggestive. Locke and Kallen heard James renounce identity thinking (the belief that "the essences of things are known whenever we know their definitions") and speak of experience as nothing but "overlap" (*Writings* 728, 761). Yet, to judge by their later work, the two evidently came away with very different understandings of James's "radical empiricism," the name he gave his pluralism. What Kallen retained was a minor point—a depiction of the pluralistic world as a "federal republic," which Kallen interpreted to mean separate ethnic nationalities coexisting harmoniously in an "orchestration of mankind."

Locke, in contrast, grasped Jamesian pluralism as an indictment of philosophical thought that is grounded in the logic of difference/identity. Such thinking not only breeds separatism but is destructive of democratic equality. The goal of James's critique was to turn Philosophy into philosophy, for the history of the former was deformed by invidious segregation, by repressions and prejudices inflicted by Cartesian idealism. Idealism enthrones epistemology—the "spectator theory of knowledge," in Dewey's famous phrase—at the center of Philosophy, whose premise is "the divine right of concepts to rule our mind absolutely" (763, 756).

James exposes the paradox that what "gives us our chief superiority to the brutes, our power, namely, of translating the crude flux of our merely feeling-experience into a conceptual order" depends on excluding and segregating (*Writings* 727). To conceptualize is to "exclude everything but what we have fixed. A concept means *a that-and-no-other*" (746). Concepts can become "recipes for denying to the universe the character of contingency," to borrow Dewey's words (*Experience* 42). In culminating James's effort to overthrow idealism's identity logic, *A Pluralistic Universe* (his book of Oxford lectures) liberates what Philosophy had excluded and repressed—a world of "all shades and no boundaries" where "each part hangs together with its very next neighbors in inextricable interfusion" (761, 778).

In 1925 James's philosophical allegory of equality proved particularly fertile. Published that year was *The New Negro*, with Locke's introductory essay and Dewey's *Experience and Nature*. Resistance to segregation animated both texts. In his essay Locke called it "delusion" to believe that the "trend of Negro advance is wholly separatist, and that the effect of its operation will be to encyst the Negro as a benign foreign body in the body politic. This cannot be—even if it were desirable." It cannot be because blacks are Americans who were already here when the Pilgrims landed; as Du Bois pointed out in 1903, America is already miscegenated. Whereas the fiction of separatism functioned, says Locke, as an "opiate" to soothe "American nerves . . . unstrung with race hysteria," one place needing no such fix, suffering no such hysteria, was Manhattan in the 1920s ("New Negro" 12).

The same year the Columbia University professor John Dewey, a New Yorker since 1904, exploded the philosophical basis of separatism. Renewing for the twenties James's radical empiricism and pluralism, *Experience and Nature* redescribes philosophy as a "critique of prejudices."[9] Particularly in his impassioned opening chapters, Dewey targets the prejudices embedded in the "classificatory device[s]" used by the classic and "genteel tradition" to elevate "unity" and "permanence" to supreme Being. This elevation occurs at the cost of relegating

"unreconciled diversity," "the recalcitrant particular . . . the ambi-
guousness and ambivalence of reality," to a "metaphysically inferior"
order of existence (*Experience* 41–42).

Critiquing prejudices, recovering mixture, dissolving segregation, redeeming what is classified as inferior: Dewey's stance in 1925 amounts
to a war on Philosophy's Jim Crow regime, a war that complements
his political practice and thinking. *Experience and Nature* evokes philosophically Dewey's activism on behalf of democratic equality, for he
describes the texture of a world at last unchained from the "metaphysics
of feudalism." Upheld by prevailing philosophies and even emancipatory social theories, this metaphysics is grounded on "a notion that
inherently some realities are superior to others" and that the world is
defined by a "fixed order of species, grades or degrees" (*Political Writings* 45–46). In contrast, democratic equality flourishes in a world still
in the making, says Dewey, echoing the familiar words of James.

One reason Locke found James's revolt against segregation compelling was that at Oxford Locke viscerally experienced the exclusions and
categories underwritten by identity logic: he encountered the racism of
Southern Rhodes scholars who were "committed to challenging his
right to be there" (Stewart 418). As his biographer, Jeffrey Stewart,
notes, Locke lived as an Oxford aesthete and dandy against a "backdrop
of constant and serious attempts to exclude him from social affairs that
included Americans" (418). Amid the hostility, an oasis of hospitality
was the aptly named "Oxford Cosmopolitan Club" made up of students from South Africa, Egypt, India, Russia, and Norway (419). This
group soon became Locke's intimate circle. It was in this context of
experiencing both the pain of racism and the antidote of cosmopolitanism that Locke heard James's lectures. Small wonder James's celebration of impurity and condemnation of exclusion spoke to him in
ways that Kallen did not hear. Locke would always find inimical the
separatism and purism of Kallen's pluralism: we "must abandon the
idea of cultural purism," he wrote years later; the "Afro- or Negro-
American [is] a hybrid product" who is becoming "progressively even
more composite and hybridized" as he interacts with "common cultural life" (*Philosophy* 213).

Locke came to these convictions firsthand: not only the racism of
Americans but also the condescension of the British spurred him to
spend his three years at Oxford traveling every chance he found to the
more racially tolerant Paris, Berlin, and London. They were also more
sexually tolerant. In these cities Locke "could enjoy a relatively open

gay lifestyle," another dimension of his hybridity (Stewart 427). Locke's community of friends at the "Cosmopolitan Club" began to raise his racial and political consciousness, making him come to grips with the cultural legacy of his Africanity and with the outrages of imperialism. With their help and the ideas of James, the leading American anti-imperialist, Locke began devising a cosmopolitanism structured by a dialectic of universal and particular, American and "New Negro," nationalism and internationalism. In 1911, the year he returned to the United States, Locke was on his way to becoming an Africanist and an antirace race man.

This was a remarkable transformation. The twenty-two-year-old Locke had arrived at Oxford determined to resist the dictates of Jim Crow: "I am not a race problem. I am Alain LeRoy Locke . . . I'm not going to England as a Negro" (qtd. 412). His dreams were not to serve the race but to have a professional career as a "journalist, perhaps as an art critic, perhaps even as a British civil servant" (424). We have seen how his adamant individualism was transformed. But for all the exhilaration of his newly awakened sense of race responsibility, and the career it would provide, "a feeling of sadness and even resignation seems to have accompanied the decision to become a race leader" (427). As Stewart observes, the sexual and intellectual freedom of an expatriate life was not easy to surrender.

Cosmopolitanism became the crucial mediating term enabling Locke's move from expatriate aesthete to race man. As a source of freedom, cosmopolitanism mitigated the sacrifice in two ways. First, as we saw with Du Bois, becoming a cosmopolitan race man foregrounded the act of choice. If he arrived at Oxford refusing to accept the coercions of racial identity, declining to become synonymous with the "race problem," he left an incipient race man. But this change was not capitulation to racist ascriptions. Rather, Locke left with his right of refusal still intact. This freedom is what Locke's cosmopolitanism affords. As he says in his 1914 summary of his years at Oxford: "one had every facility for becoming really cosmopolitan" which for him meant having "the very rare opportunity to choose deliberately to be what I was born, but what the tyranny of circumstances prevents many of my folk from ever viewing as the privilege and opportunity of being an Afro-American" (qtd. Stewart 428). The paradoxical formulation "to choose deliberately to be what I was born" recalls Du Bois's "henceforward I was a Negro" (*Autobiography* 108). On a literal level the choice Du Bois implies and Locke affirms is illusory (neither man can, or imagines he can, choose to be white or deny he is black). But both statements forgo the literal, for their concern is to dramatize or ritualize the effort to denaturalize racial identity, replacing biology with will, identity with action.

Cosmopolitanism would mitigate, for Locke, the sacrifice of becoming a race man in another way: his racial role would not entail renouncing the urbane pleasures of European culture. His "Cosmopolitan Club" colleagues were living proof that this was possible. They made vivid to him that culture is "composite," derived from the ceaseless, reciprocal "exchange and transplanting of cultures" (*Philosophy* 233, 206). To recognize that, "for all its claims of distinctiveness," civilization is a "vast amalgam of cultures," is to approach, said Locke, a "solution reconciling nationalism with internationalism, racialism with universalism." But, he added, with rueful knowledge, this is "not an easy solution,—for it means the abandonment of the use of the idea of race as a political instrument," a use which confines culture to "proprietary interests" (203).

Locke knew the difficulty of the solution because his propagandist role for *The New Negro* inevitably involved using race as a "political instrument." He made the "counter-move" of cultivating "race pride" as a way to strengthen "race-co-operation" (16). These double moves were required to promote, in his words, a "unique social experiment"—the "forced attempt" by the "New Negro" "to build his Americanism on race values" ("New Negro" 12). Writing in 1950, Locke regretted that twenty-five years earlier race had become a "market-place commodity" once the Renaissance "took on public momentum and offered that irresistible American lure of a vogue of success, a ready means of quick recognition" (*Philosophy* 232). And this occurred despite Locke's contempt for "racial chauvinism," a contempt reflected in his anthology's premise that "the substance of Negro life was emphasized, not its complexion" (232). *The New Negro,* Locke reminded readers, included five white contributors, enacting the intention of the renaissance leadership to make the movement "democratically open to all who might be interested" (232). Locke's larger point is that "if a 'New Negro' is not born and reborn every half-generation or so, something is radically wrong" (231–232). For it means that "the Negro" has been arrested yet again in stereotype and remains "more of a formula than a human being" ("New Negro" 3).

The political production of formula and stereotype flourished in the 1920s, as the melting-pot ideal of assimilation and the Jim Crow enforcement of identity and difference dominated. Though different models of social control, both erased all official recognition of the fact of racial or ethnic mingling. After 1920 the mulatto category was dropped from the U.S. Census as the one-drop rule tightened its binary grip. Neither Kallen's pluralism nor Locke's cosmopolitanism was anything but a minority position with appeal mainly to fellow intellectuals. Not until the 1970s did Kallen's pseudo-Jamesian pluralism achieve popularity when it was reborn as multiculturalism.

Locke's cultivation of paradox has always kept him out of focus. Contemporary critics tend to simplify by casting him either as a race man or as an apolitical aesthete.[10] In his own day, his role as purveyor of what he later called "defensive, promotive propaganda for the Negro" tended to overshadow his ardent democratic vision of limitless cultural interchange (*Philosophy* 234). Far better known, for instance, than his critique of cultural purism is his urging of a "renewed race-spirit that consciously and proudly sets itself apart," as he writes at the conclusion of his foreword to *The New Negro* (xxvii). Locke had an impact in Harlem Renaissance circles, but the younger generation (including Hurston, Hughes, and Thurman), to which he had aligned the "New Negro," tended to resent his (and Du Bois's) stress on racial propaganda. In the fierce generational politics of the Harlem Renaissance, Locke found himself, much against his will, being yoked with an older group of race men.[11]

One of Locke's enduring legacies is as a trenchant theorist and practitioner of what is now known as strategic essentialism. For Locke, this was not a glib panacea; unlike many contemporary advocates, he recognized the high risk of failure built into it. The struggle for ethnic cultural recognition, he acutely realized, inevitably produces a chain reaction of rival race chauvinisms. What Locke called the nervous, compensatory assertions of "minority jingo" produce "counter-jingo." It is an evil but not "the root of the evil." The root is the original offense of "majority jingo," better known as white supremacy. According to Locke, "minority jingo is the defensive reaction, sadly inevitable as an antidote, and even science has learned to fight poison with poison. However, for cure or compensation, it must be the right poison and in the right amount . . . minority jingo is good when it succeeds in offsetting either the effects or the habits of majority jingo and bad when it re-infects the minority with the majority disease" ("Jingo" 308). Judging both jingo and counter-jingo "dangerous," Locke took on the nearly impossible project of finding the precise dosage of "compensatory racialism" that would avoid separatism (312). Perhaps his most important lesson for contemporary cultural politics is the sober assessment of how great is the chance of reinfection.

At least three factors converged to stall Locke's precariously balanced effort: historical impediments combined with Locke's "counter-jingo" obligations of uplift, as well as his own unresolved attitude toward race. In one sense, as a race man and pragmatist, Locke was in a dilemma similar to Du Bois's and both prefigure a contemporary difficulty: how to reconcile a philosophy that refuses the primacy of identity with the politics of racial group advocacy. One of Du Bois's tactics, as we have seen, was to construct a pragmatist matrix that set politics and art in fruitful interchange as modes of conduct able to improvise new practices in response to changing facts. Though unsuccessful in persuading the NAACP to perform this suppleness, Du Bois sought to close the gap between (philosophy) theory and (politics) practice. In contrast, Locke had none of Du Bois's bold political activism, and confined his politics to cultural politics. As well, Locke enunciated his theory of cosmopolitanism *post facto*, after the Harlem Renaissance, his principal site of engagement, had largely run its course. Nevertheless, for both Du Bois and Locke the "kingdom of culture"—deracialized and non-exclusionary—was the "end of . . . striving."

Neither man, however, surrendered race; yet each had a different relation to it. Unlike Locke's, Du Bois's sense of his Africanity was insistent and passionate, however romanticized and inflated, a matter of profound emotional identification. "My African racial feeling," he said in *Dusk of Dawn,* was a "large determinant of my life and character. I felt myself African by 'race' and by that token was African." At the 1924 inauguration of Liberia's president, where Du Bois presided as the United States Envoy, he spoke of the pride "Negro Americans . . . have in their race and lineage . . . in the potency and promise of Negro blood" (*Dusk* 638, 645). Du Bois's visceral identification with Africanity has a very different temperature from Locke's coolly pragmatic, excavational relation to Africa. He views it not in personal terms but as an overlooked aesthetic tradition worth mining, a heritage that could serve as a vehicle for race pride. Yet blood rhetoric seeps in. He asks of Afro-Americans: "If the [African] forefathers could so adroitly master these mediums [of sculpture, painting, and the decorative arts], why not we?" ("Legacy" 256). The hint of biologism in "forefathers" is made explicit a few lines later. Europeans appropriate African sculpture, says Locke, as an expression of the "exotic curiosity" of those who "inherit by tradition only." In contrast, Afro-Americans inherit as "blood descendants, bound to it [African art] by a sense of direct cultural kinship" (256).

The persistence of race as "blood" in Locke's cosmopolitanism is vividly disclosed in his *Race Contacts and Interracial Relations,* his remarkable lectures of 1916, first published in 1992. This persistence is especially striking given that these lectures take dead aim at the mystifications of race: whereas race advertises itself as "biological," "intrinsic," and "inherent," in fact race is a social and political practice of domination that Locke calls "imperialism" (12, 23, 24). Yet Locke's project is not to repudiate race but rather to "redeem" and "revise" it, as if he believes that to expose the status of race as "fiction" and as a "political instrument" somehow will neutralize its destructive power of invidious distinction (85). In short, his adroit deconstructions contain an element of naivete. His lectures read as the work of a gifted but overly zealous disciple of Nietzsche, James, and Boas.[12]

Races, says Locke, are "ethnic fictions" lacking both "purity of blood and purity of type. They are the product of countless interminglings" and "infinite crossings" and "maintain in name only" a "fetish of biological purity" (11). This fetish of innate purity functions as a badge of superiority, which, for Locke, actually "refers only to the political fortunes of a group and not to any intrinsic or inherent qualities" of race (22). Hence historically weaker, dominated groups are misrepresented as biologically "inferior people" (23). Locke's politicizing of race may empty it of biologism but not of use. Rather than abandon race, Locke maintains it: "we must . . . admit that it is of advantage to a group when it can consider itself an ethnic unit" (12). He calls the advantage "race pride."

In ways similar, we shall see below, to Jean Toomer's vision of an "American race," Locke refuses to retire the word "race" while seeking to detoxify it of biologism and chauvinism. "To redeem, to rescue, or to revise" the "thought and practice of race should be the aim of race theorists" (85). This amounts to turning race into culture: "if you have the same manners and customs and have allegiance to the same social system you belong to the same race . . . even though ethnically you may not" (79). This culturalist model would seem to dispense with the idea of race altogether. But it turns out that Locke's main effort is to develop "a higher type of race consciousness," one where "race type blends into the civilization type" and "culture-citizenship" becomes the "goal of race progress and race adjustment" (100, 99). To achieve "culture-citizenship" requires a simultaneous process of social assimilation and "group contribution to what becomes a joint civilization" (99). Hence he calls for a provisional racialism, a "counter-theory" of "race pride"—"secondary race consciousness within a group"—in the midst of continuing "social assimilation" (96).

These elegant theoretical formulations of 1916 would be put into practice nine years later with *The New Negro*. But its "forced attempt to build . . . Americanism on race values" would inherit the theory's unresolved contradictions (*New Negro* 12). Their source is in Locke's elastic invocation of race as variously social, cultural, and civilizational, but also biological—expressing a "sense of kind . . . of kith and kin" (11). He mainly tends to turn race into culture—shared "manners and customs" ("when you are an American in all your beliefs, mores and social customs, for example, you are of the same race") (79). At other times he invokes "race pride" as the salutary stimulus needed by an "alien group" for "more rapid assimilation" (96). "Pride in itself is race pride" (97). But why use the word "race" if this group pride is grounded on nothing but shared customs and beliefs? Finally, it seems that Locke fails to heed the implications of his own recognition that race maintains "in name only this fetish of biological purity" (11). If the "name only" is poisonous, it would seem futile to try to redeem or rescue race practice rather than abandon it. Boas, for one, was moving in the direction of abandonment.

So was Locke by 1930. Perhaps disenchanted by the commodity status of race in the twenties, he found it harder to "argue for raciality as a desirable thing" and, he said, was "close to a rejection of race as something useful in human life and desirable to perpetuate" (203). By 1950, four years before his death, he urged integration—as "collaboration and fraternization"—as a "new frontier" (234). "Let us ask boldly and bravely, what then are the justifications of separate Negro churches, of separate Negro fraternities, schools, colleges?" And he applauded Franklin Frazier's remark that "the best future goal" of Howard University "might well be to lose its racial identity and become simply a great university" (234).

Locke's admirers Ellison and Murray try to minimize talk of "race." Its deadly reductionism anchors behavior to descent (identity). But cultural and artistic skill, notes Ellison, "come as a result of personal conquest, of the individual's applying himself" (*Territory* 31). At the 1973 Locke symposium at Harvard, Murray declared that one of racism's "most vicious and most destructive aspects . . . is the very fact that it is designed to make black people think of themselves in terms of race" ("Alain Locke" 27). By no "ethnological definition or measurements," says Murray, are "U.S. Negroes" a race. Rather they "make up a very distinct sociopolitical group with discernable cultural features peculiar to itself" (*Omni* 124). Ellison, for instance, often speaks of "we Negroes" as a distinct group who "inherited a group style." But we are, he says, "bound less by blood than by our cultural and political circumstances" (*Collected* 746, 750). Hence the "group style" was not genetically transmitted but, says Ellison, was "taught to me by Negroes, or copied by me from those among whom I lived most intimately" (751).

If black Americans possess "cultural features peculiar" to themselves, these features are also available to anyone inclined to and capable of appropriating and applying them. For they are grounded not in race or origin but rather in performance. Says Murray: "anytime you're talking about conduct, you're talking about culture," anytime you talk, for instance, about music, "about rhythm and timbre," "that's culture . . . you're talking about all those actions" ("Alain Locke" 27). For Murray, cultural conduct is above all a "process of stylization; and what it stylizes is experience . . . It is a way of sizing up the world, and so, ultimately, and beyond all else, a mode and medium of survival" (*Omni* 54–55). In accord with Kenneth Burke's notion of art as "equipment for living" and Hurston's emphasis on "the will to adorn," Murray says style is what makes one human: "all human effort beyond the lowest level of the struggle for animal subsistence is motivated by the need to live in style" (55).

Growing up on the outskirts of Mobile, Alabama, in the twenties, Murray regarded the (white) cowboy actor Tom Mix as a supreme exemplar of style and would laugh at the absurd spectacle of "white boys trying to act like Tom Mix": "How could Pritchard, Alabama peckerwoods ever know what Tom Mix was all about?" (*South* 13). Murray's question raises others: Is he suggesting that compelling style is the sole property of black people? But what about Tom Mix? Or has Tom Mix in effect blackened himself by dint of his stylishness? Murray provokes such questions while eluding them because they depend on a premise he denies—that American culture is coded by a binary color scheme. For Murray American culture is mulatto, indeed is so "interwoven" that (borrowing with approval C. Vann Woodward's words) all Americans, including Negroes, "are part-Negro, but only part."

Negroes "are not white people disguised beneath dark skins and Caucasians are not black people beneath white skins" (*South* 19). Tom *Mix* indeed. But if Murray's goal is to replace race with culture, his investment in the mulatto seems to reinstate a racial category. We should read Murray's use of "mulatto" as at least partly metaphorical, a word meant to frustrate invidious binary (black/white) racial distinction. In short, mulatto functions as an antirace race category.

Dismissive of the rhetoric of authenticity, Murray finds futile the effort of "revealing what it is really like to be black." Nonetheless black writers continually make the effort and white publishers encourage it, as if "complexion, street address, and police record" are enough to ensure success (*Omni* 98). But "being black is not enough to make anybody an authority on U.S. Negroes, anymore than being white has ever qualified anybody as an expert on the ways of U.S. white people. It simply does not follow that being white enables a Southern sheriff, for instance, even a fairly literate one, to explain . . . the atonality of Charles Ives, the imagery of Wallace Stevens, abstract expressionism" (97). This reveals Murray's anti-proprietary approach that dissolves the correlation of color and culture.

"We have so narrowly been involved with race, as against culture," says Ellison in 1973, "that we have reduced ourselves to an extent that the most unreconstructed white South was unable to do" ("Alain Locke" 27). Ellison goes on to summarize the position he would elaborate five years later in "The Little Man at Chehaw Station": "I would not counsel giving up the struggle against racism, you have to do that to stay alive. But the complexity, the American-ness, along with the African-ness of the Americans is a mystery and is a far greater challenge" (27).

In "The Little Man at Chehaw Station" the word "race" has a negligible presence, for it constitutes the "blood thinking" that Ellison seeks to banish and replace with "the mystery of American identity," a phrase he repeats several times (*Territory* 25). Like Locke's effort to replace "identity" with "equivalence" and "difference" with "unity in difference," Ellison's formulation seeks an alternative to the exclusionary dichotomies of racial thinking (qtd. Akam 260). By arranging "mystery" and "identity" on either side of "American," Ellison makes "American" the mediating term of a nexus, all three of whose elements are reciprocally entwined, complicating one another, demanding to be grasped at once rather than separately. Thus to understand the complexity of Americanness, Ellison implies, requires revising American individualism's bias toward atomism. Enforcing monadic separatism, atomism blinds one to the mythical "little man" of the essay's title. For he incarnates the incalculable American whirlpool of overlap and overflow.

Around Hazel Harrison's "riddle" of the little man and her own eloquent exemplification of it, Ellison builds an essay that pays homage to her teaching. He turns the little man into the spark for a virtuoso improvisation upon his major theme: "the challenge of arriving at an adequate definition of American cultural identity" (21). Part of Ellison's "joke" is that the thrust of his essay makes this last quotation virtually oxymoronic: "adequate definition" and "American cultural identity" are antagonistic and hence the "challenge" resists solution. The endless act of arriving awaits.[13]

The little man, emblem of the random and disruptive, reminds us that American identity is not a preordained given to discover and to know, but instead eludes adequate definition and offers the experience of uneasy bewilderment. Indeed, for Ellison, when it comes to defining America, skepticism of adequacy is the only adequacy. In contrast, to surrender to definition, to identity, is "to impose unity upon an experience that changes too rapidly for linguistic or political exactitude" (29). Adequacy, then, must be reconfigured as something other than exactitude, indeed as what frustrates exactitude. This frustration is called art: "it is in the very *spirit* of art to be defiant of categories" (32).

And as a "source of confusion, a threat to social order," the little man is an emblem of the aesthetic. And he is also a political instrument. For Ellison savors the little man's unaccountable status as a "goad" toward "a perfection of our revolutionary ideals" of equality (7–8). To achieve the ideal of equality and to achieve art require forsaking the comforts of the already given, the timeless realm of the *ethnos* run by habit and custom, for the risks of improvisatory, that is, political, conduct in the "turbulence of the present" public life (25). Like Du Bois and Dewey, Ellison conceives democracy and art not simply as doctrine or knowledge or contemplation, but as strenuous ways of being in the world.[14]

Requiring an agility to engage the challenges of *pragmata,* the American democratic way of being is difficult to sustain. "It offers no easily recognizable points of rest, no facile certainties as to who, what or where (culturally or historically) we are," and hence it tempts us to "symbolic acts of disaffiliation" (20). In symbolically severing oneself from the whole of American culture, one is granted the "psychic security" of homogeneity usually found in elected group identity or "inherited divisions" that organize people into ethnic or racial or religious provinces (19). In short, "we cling desperately to our own familiar fragment of the democratic rock" and call that fragment our identity (16). Against the threat of impurity inherent in democracy's tendency toward dispersal, group identity functions as a defensive response, Ellison implies, a symptom of phobic anxiety whose source is "the psychic uncertainty" endemic to an "open society" biased toward the future and potential rather than tradition.

Ellison detects another symptom of anxiety about impurity and uncertainty in cultural pluralism's categorical rejection of the melting pot as the enemy of ethnic identity. "The melting pot concept was never so simplistic or abstract as current arguments would have it." Nor was it a "con-game contrived by the powerful" (25, 27). Ellison calls it a "conceit" or "metaphor" for a "cultural integration" that involved a liberating "melting of hierarchal barriers" (27, 25). This melting enabled the improvised and "eclectic mixing" called American culture, a mixing that included "even the slaves." They "were grudgingly recognized as seminal sources of American art" and "their music, poetic imagery, and choreography" given "a prominent place in our national iconography" (26). Here Ellison inserts what both cultural pluralism and the original melting pot of white ethnicities suppressed—the crucial presence of African American culture in forming an American culture that is a "continuing process of antagonistic cooperation" (26). In the "clear, pluralistic, melting-pot light of American cultural possibility," Ellison restores the "complex actuality" of pragmatist pluralism (38, 29).

To hide from that light, to deny the melting pot, is to retreat from the "goal of cultural integration" and instead to express "the current form of an abiding American self-distrust"—ethnic chauvinism (25). Much to his chagrin, Ellison discovered his own insufficient trust in cultural possibility. His recounting of this moment of discovery concludes "The Little Man." Three years after his exchange with Hazel Harrison, and having nearly forgotten it, Ellison was in New York when, out of the blue, he found himself face to face with the little man, or, more precisely, four such men. Listening through a basement door, he hears the voices of four "formally uneducated" black workers speaking angrily about a topic of which, by all logic of class, race, and culture, they "should have been oblivious." They are "locked in verbal combat over which of two celebrated Metropolitan Opera divas was the superior soprano!" (34). It turns out that for years these men have been

Met extras; "give us some costumes," one of them tells a shocked Ellison, "and we make about the finest damn bunch of Egyptians you ever seen" (37).

Feeling as "though a bizarre practical joke had been staged," Ellison hears this revelation "with Hazel Harrison's voice echoing in" his ears. It mocks what Ellison calls his "pride in my knowledge of my own people" (37, 33). But Ellison now discovers that his proudly proprietary knowledge of what he presumed were his "own people" in fact was the seductive, chauvinistic pseudo-knowledge of stereotypes, what he calls "social concepts that cast less illumination than an inert lump of coal" (38). Taken in by the tidiness of generalizations, Ellison has had to unlearn them in order to have his "appreciation of the arcane ways of American cultural possibility . . . vastly extended" (37). Never again will he forget that democracy, like art, "is an assault upon logic," that is, the logic of identity (30).

Thus chastened, Ellison in 1978 is wary of what counts as adequate definition. This extends to skepticism of the familiar anchorage implied by the phrase "American identity." He reveals it to be an anxious invention, a makeshift enclave of homogeneity, a merciful point of "rest" to keep democratic chaos at bay (20). Like all Jamesian pragmatists, Ellison seeks to reinstate what identity represses—the banished residuum, the unaccountable little man. The residuum vanishes when we "identify with the parts" rather than with the "complex and pluralistic wholeness" (16). This wholeness is "greater" than its parts, and that "difference, that new and problematic quality—call it our 'Americanness'—creates out of its incongruity an uneasiness within us" (16).

This identity claim—"call it our 'Americanness' "—is made in passing and seems to unravel as it is written, hedged with anxious quotation marks and placed within a hurried pair of dashes. And these marks aptly convey the inferential status of " 'Americanness,' " which is diacritical rather than substantive, engendered as the incongruous "difference" between part and whole. This diacritical difference breeds "uneasiness" because it is not grounded in a stable hierarchy ordered by blood but instead reflects a fluid "collectivity" of styles and traditions that together constitute the "whole." And "in relationship to the cultural whole, we are, all of us, white or black, native-born or immigrant— members of minority groups," equally dispossessed, equally entitled residua (16).

"Call it our 'Americanness' ": Ellison invokes the term tentatively, gingerly, to suggest that it is burdened with an impossible task: to arrest "fluid pluralistic turbulence" in a single word. But " 'Americanness' " is especially susceptible to misuse, for it is a "futuristic concept" that has conventionally been used to delimit what is illimitable: "the 'Americanness' of American culture has been a matter of Adamic wordplay—of trying, in the interest of a futuristic dream, to impose unity upon an experience that changes too rapidly for linguistic or political exactitude" (26, 29). " 'Americanness' " defies exactitude because its identity is not preordained (something to which one measures up) but rather is the very process of playing "the appropriation game." Like Crummell's cosmopolitan thievery, "the appropriation game" has created culture throughout history. In America the game is unceasing, and generates a volatility that encourages the "precious" freedom to improvise a self from diverse elements. And the act of making an "improvised form, the willful juxtaposition of modes," reveals an "essential 'Americanness' " (24). At this point, it seems reasonable to infer that cosmopolitan and American are synonymous.

As if seeking to prevent, or at least defer, either term from freezing into a foundational or national essence, Ellison turns "essential 'Americanness' " into another oxymoron by grounding it in practice not identity. Consider the context in which it appears: recalling the sight of a dashiki-clad blue-eyed mulatto in English riding boots and breeches and with a homburg on his "Afro-coiffed head," Ellison comments that "whatever the identity he presumed to project" he was "exercising an American freedom . . . in his freewheeling assault upon traditional forms" (22, 24). In other words, the Americanness of this "American joker" is found not in a prior affirmation of essence, a fact of descent, but instead is *derived* from his act of assemblage. Exaggerating to glaring visibility what American or any cosmopolitans habitually do, the "joker" achieves identity through his improvised pastiche.

By insisting on the primacy of the performative as the unstable ground of identity, Ellison in effect flirts with a Jamesian dilemma. For when we conceptualize the performative we arrest it; concepts "cut out and fix, and exclude." But this dilemma resolves itself when we recall that James warns not against concepts as such but against their "misuse," which occurs in "forgetting" that "concepts are only man-made extracts from the temporal flux" and not to be treated as "changeless, true, divine" (James *Writings* 746, 728). Belief in "blood magic and blood thinking" instances this forgetting. To celebrate "ancestral blood" as the ground of identity breeds self-mystification—the diminishment of one's sense of common humanity by absorption in a group mentality. Marooned in the *ethnos,* one is also insulated from the demands for political and cultural improvisation inherent in a social order of "cacaphonic motion," a "vortex of discordant ways of living" (20). A monolithic identity forged in "blood thinking" not only prefers the static but simultaneously requires to sustain itself the production of difference as degraded, dangerous otherness. This stigmatizing often leads, says Ellison, to "brutal racial assaults" upon "sacrificial victims" to fortify the boundary of self and other (21). Meanwhile the "mystery of American cultural identity" is ignored (25).

Jean Toomer had discovered this neglect in the mid-twenties. After living among a variety of classes and nationalities, he remarked that "very few United States citizens were aware of being Americans," that is, members of a "new race" that transcended racial or ethnic identity. He concluded that "they were aware of, and put value upon, their hearsay descents, their groupistic affiliations." "Consciousness of being colored had become fixed," and "divisions, separatisms, and antagonisms" ruled (*Wayward* 121–122). Such race identification invites the divide-and-conquer strategy practiced by administrative elites. They depend on efficient classification and herein is the concept's precise utility: when "we name and class" something, says James, "we say for the first time what it is, and all these whats are abstract names or concepts. Each concept means a particular *kind* of thing . . . Once classed, a thing can be treated by the law of its class, and the advantages are endless" (728).

Ellison, Toomer, and James are describing some of the effects of the dogmatism of identity logic. When applied to culture, this logic insists that "it is only once we know who we are that we will be able to tell what we should do; it is only when we know which race we are that we can tell which culture is ours" (Michaels 15). By the twenties, the primacy of identity—"the difference of oneself from others"—unites seeming enemies. "Difference Not Inferiority" is a Klan slogan of the twenties, and "the right to be different" is Kallen's creed of pluralist tolerance (65). Because nativist and cultural pluralist both spurn universal for local criteria, both invoke "the identity of the group as the grounds for the justification of the group's practices." Severed from whatever one actually does and believes, culture "now becomes something that can be lost or stolen, reclaimed or repudiated" (14, 16).

But this orgy of ownership hardly characterizes the whole of American modernist thinking about race and culture. At least one alternative tradition has provided a sustained counterpoint of critique directed at cultural pluralism. Starting with Du Bois's "kingdom of culture" (1903), including Dewey's dissent from Kallen (1915–1916) and Locke's rejection of "cultural purism" and theorizing of cosmopolitanism in the twenties and thirties, this lineage creatively appropriates an antiseparatist Jamesian pluralism whose byword is "reciprocity rather than identity" (Locke *Philosophy* 101). Ellison and Murray drew on this rich counter-tradition, and they, in turn, have influenced contemporary skepticism of racial/ethnic absolutism.

This chapter will conclude with a look at two other writers in this tradition. The freedom of Hurston and Toomer from conventional obligations of racial uplift set them in the direction that Locke theorized—a democratic realm of post-identity, the "always moving" "frontiers of culture" where, in the absence of "special proprietary rights," "all we should be sanely concerned about is freer participation and fuller collaboration" (233). This realm imagined by Locke was nothing less than utopian, as visionary as the erasure of Jim Crow adumbrated by Hurston and Toomer.

Answering the title question of his 1942 essay—"Who and What is 'Negro'?"—Alain Locke wrote: "there is, in brief, no '*The Negro*' " (210). That same year, in *Dust Tracks on a Road,* Zora Neale Hurston concluded chapter twelve of her autobiography by noting that "there is no *The Negro* here" (733). The two writers refuse a group label for similar reasons. Locke points to such factors as "internal splits," "divergent loyalties," and "class structure." Says Hurston: "our lives are so diversified, internal attitudes so varied, appearances and capabilities so different, that there is no possible classification so catholic that it will cover us all" (733). Without saying so, both Locke and Hurston were chafing at the "still all-too-prevalent formula psychology" inscribed in the laws of Jim Crow (Locke *Philosophy* 211). Its laws, said Hurston in 1945, have a "psychological" purpose—to promote in the minds of blacks, by daily "physical evidence" of exclusion, a sense of doomed fatalism in a world where whites, seemingly, are "First by Birth, eternal and irrevocable" (948).[15] Hurston urged immediate repeal of all Jim Crow laws.

Yet she was a famous critic of the Supreme Court's 1954 *Brown v. Board of Education* decision that ended the legality of segregation. But her dissent on *Brown* is within the logic of her stance on Jim Crow. The core of her position (as distinct from some of her rabid anti-Communist accusations attached to it) was that the integration that black and white liberals had legislated was actually an insulting assimilationism that implicitly said the best way to educate blacks was to whiten them. This integration (or Hurston's construction of it) was, to borrow her phrase, "not a human right," but "a concession from the throne" of white power and perpetuated its supremacy under cover of ending it (948). In short, the Court's "cure" was worse than the disease. Under *Brown* the debilitating polarities of privilege and inferiority would remain secure. Hurston preferred to dissolve Jim Crow by the root, by "underskin injection" that would eradicate racial classification.[16]

In her adamancy in 1945 about repealing Jim Crow Hurston sought to call democracy's bluff by demanding that it at last become a reality and not merely a ballyhooed ideal tantalizingly out of reach for the "dark world" at home and abroad: "All this talk and praise-giving has got me in the notion to try some of the stuff . . . I don't know for myself, but I have been told that it is really wonderful" (945). Conspicuous in this piece, "Crazy about Democracy," and in her two other major late essays, "The 'Pet' Negro System" (1943) and "What White Publishers Won't Print" (1950), is Hurston's propensity to expose what she called "the wide gaps between ideals and practices" (793). In "The 'Pet' Negro System" she observes that in theory the color line is strictly upheld, but in practice it is crossed by interracial friendship: "this friendship business makes a sorry mess of all the rules made and provided" (920–921). The fact that friendship makes race count "for nothing at all" is a "tribute," says Hurston, "to human nature. It will be bound by nothing" (921).

Her pragmatist esteem for the unbounded and residual includes alertness to what threatens them: the power of foundational discourse—in this case white supremacy—to employ concepts and classifications to create an illusory seamlessness. *"The Negro"* instances this factitious transparency. Her effort, in effect, to denaturalize this phrase and reveal it as ideology constitutes one way Hurston assaults the master classification system of Jim Crow. Thus *Dust Tracks* makes good on what Hurston had told Nick Aaron Ford in 1936: "I have ceased to think in terms of race; I think only in terms of individuals" (qtd. Ford 8). Subsequent world events strengthened her conviction. With the Aryan supremacy of Nazi propaganda in mind, Hurston in 1942 noted that "what the world is crying and dying for at this moment is less race consciousness" (784).

Hurston's skepticism of preordained classification had been nurtured by her long (if combative) association with Locke, which began at Howard University in the early twenties. And it was nurtured too by Franz Boas, her beloved "Papa Franz," who encouraged her work in anthropology after she studied with him during her years (1925–1927) at Barnard. Given Boas's deep influence on Locke's 1916 *Race Contacts and Interracial Relations,* Hurston was exposed to a particularly intense infusion of antifoundational thought. The intellectual intersection between Boasian anthropology and Jamesian pragmatism and radical empiricism occurs in the figure of Wilhelm Dilthey. The German philosopher of culture and hermeneutics influenced Boas's insistence on contextualist, historicist understanding.[17] Dilthey and William James enjoyed a mutual admiration; indeed, there are "remarkable resonances" in the "ideas they developed from 1890 to 1910" (Kloppenberg 29). Both topple Philosophy from its idealist and rationalist foundations, lowering its gaze to the individual's immediate lived experience. In other words, Dilthey and James participate in the late nineteenth century's radical reorientation of Philosophy's traditional mission as the quest for acontextual, purely logical certainty.[18] Because the individual's understanding is inseparable from experience, says Dilthey, "it contains something irrational because life is irrational" (qtd. Kloppenberg 105).

This was part of the background from which Boas emerged to encounter in his early work "the general problem of classification." He contested the positivist habit of subsuming diverse phenomena under such classifying devices as "prior definition" and "idealized type" (Stocking "Basic" 3). Opposing what he called "premature classification," Boas declared that "the object of our study is the individual, not abstractions from the individual under observation" (qtd. Stocking 3). And for Boas the "most important cases were always those which provided exceptions to some rule or law" (15). George Stocking locates Boas's Diltheyan legacy in the way he conceives anthropology not as the scientist's search for covering laws to encompass a range of phenomena but as the historian's attempt at "understanding of phenomena" for their own sake. Boas argued in 1887, notes Stocking, that the " 'mere existence' of each individual fact or event entitled it 'to a full share of our attention; and the knowledge of its existence and evolution in space and time fully satisfies the student, without regard to the laws which it corroborates or which may be deduced from it' " (qtd. Stocking *Race* 154). Boas was said to be "so obsessed with particulars" that he "could not see general outlines or forms" (qtd. 212).

If one may call anything in Hurston's chaotic final fifteen years a pattern, the reorientation from race to individual, emphatic in *Dust Tracks* (especially in the unpublished chapter "Seeing the World as It Is") sets a pattern worth taking seriously. For it brings Hurston into focus as an antirace race figure who, like Jean Toomer, insists on contesting group identity. Yet Hurston's and Toomer's insistence has been easy to lose sight of, given that it is entwined with the oblivion that swallowed each of their careers. While their difficulties are attributable to the obvious personal causes, including waning creative powers, poor health, and, in Hurston's case, woeful finances, the obscurity that engulfed them (despite the fact that they were busily writing) was also the culture's verdict. And what Hurston and Toomer did or did not do to incite this verdict has cultural significance.

Their offense, in brief, was to refuse to enter "The American Museum of Unnatural History," that storehouse of stereotypes and clichés that Hurston imagined at the dead center of white Anglo-Saxon American culture. The American Museum is built on the WASP's proprietary assumption, evident from slave times, that "our culture" can, at best, be aped "on the outside" by black people. But "turn him [the black man] loose, and he will revert at once to the jungle" (951). Hurston then pinpoints what the WASP sense of cultural ownership depends on: the refusal to believe that people of any color or ethnicity are capable of "the ingestion and digestion of western culture." Hurston's terms suggest that culture is sustenance for those who partake and is available to anyone with the curiosity to taste it. Yet a curtain of "public indifference" keeps this fact inadmissible and its consequences invisible. "Hence the lack of literature about the higher emotions and love life of upper-class Negroes and the minorities in general" (951).

The Museum of Unnatural History is a monument to white indifference to and repression of black complexity. Its cornerstone is the "folk belief" that "all non-Anglo-Saxons are uncomplicated stereotypes. Everybody knows all about them . . . They are made of bent wires without any insides at all" (951–952). Hurston has a vexed relation to stereotypes (having been accused of producing them), as we shall see. But by 1950, when she wrote of the American Museum, she had left behind black folklore to explore other subjects. "Race pride is a luxury I cannot afford," she noted in 1942; "it is a sapping vice." And she adds: "Why should I be proud to be a Negro? Why should anybody be proud to be white?" (783).

Hurston's rejection of group identity by the forties is based in part on a sense that collectivities inevitably traffic in stereotypes as the very basis of relating to and remaining distinct from other groups. Groups as such are imaginary entities, Fredric Jameson notes, for they are always fantasized or abstracted from "discrete individual contacts and experiences which can never be generalized in anything but abusive fashion" ("On" 273). The "inevitability of the stereotypical" remains, regardless of how sanitized or positive the collective abstractions. In this light, says Jameson, Utopia could "only mean . . . a world in which only individuals confronted one another, in the absence of groups; or a group isolated from the rest of the world in such a way that the matter of the external stereotype (or 'ethnic identity') never arose in the first place" (274). Hurston's novels of the thirties, particularly *Their Eyes Were Watching God,* could be said to invest in the latter form of Utopia, her career in the forties and fifties in the former. But animating both of her utopian investments is a consistent effort to defeat the identitarian force of stereotype.

Although Hurston renounced it, race consciousness kept being urged upon her. In her later career Hurston battled what she called "intellectual Jim Crow"—liberals' "condescension in fixing us in a type and a place" (qtd. Hemenway 299). She is describing the enforced racialism of the white educated lay public that is comfortable reading about two kinds of Negroes—"only the fractional 'exceptional' and the 'quaint.' " The "average, struggling, non-morbid Negro is the best-kept secret in America" (955, 954). Black Americans of "opulence and education . . . are as real as the sharecroppers" (918). Given the narrow class compass of Hurston's fiction, her pleas are striking. She urges wider representation not simply to remedy an aesthetic lapse but to defuse racism. The fact that whites are not shown that black Americans "are just like everybody else" breeds "that feeling of difference which inspires fear" (952, 954). "To know how the average behaves and lives" is "to grasp the penetration of western civilization in a minority" (954). Like Locke, Hurston shrewdly perceives how a proprietary relation to culture either obstructs or is blind to this penetration, a blindness which foments "aggression" (Locke), for it requires and produces an alien, polluted Other.

Hurston resolves to short-circuit the destructive dynamic of identity/difference that undergirds Jim Crow. Beginning with *Dust Tracks,* she refuses, like Toomer, to play by the racial rules of the game. Choosing not to enter the American Museum of Unnatural History, she, inevitably, inhabited the unclassified residuum. From the margin she generated a remarkable variety of projects which she left in various states of incompletion. In 1945 she wrote two-thirds of *Mrs. Doctor*, a novel she described as about the "upper strata of Negro life." But she stopped after her publisher "Lippincott (timid soul) decided that the American public was not ready for it yet" (qtd. Hemenway 303). In 1948 she published to small acclaim *Seraph on the Suwanee*, her last novel and her first with white characters. She told her editor, reports Robert Hemenway, "that she was proud of the book because it demonstrated her ability to write about both races" (308). Eatonville's folklore now issued from the mouths of a white Florida family (315).

Her next projects were works about heroic Jewish history. "Just Like Us" was her proposed title for a "history and philosophy of the Hebrews," and it was designed, she said, "to alter the slovenly and inimical attitude towards the modern Jew" (343). In the 1950s Hurston completed and failed to publish another novel with a white hero. She described another manuscript—about Madame C. J. Walker, the millionaire black hairdressing entrepreneur—as the first "truly indigenous Negro novel" written "from the inside. Imagine that no white audience is present to hear what is said" (338). But after 1948 no audience of any color would hear from Hurston, save in short, agitated bursts in magazines. In the last dozen years of her life, she published no books.

While hardly the only black intellectuals to boycott the American Museum (the novels of Larsen, Fauset, and Du Bois, for instance, lodge this protest), Hurston and Toomer are notable for the extremity and self-consciousness of their refusal. Each, in a sense, narrated the oblivion they both chose and had forced upon them as they deliberately moved beyond the limits of what white publishers and other guardians of cultural order would permit. Hurston's disregard of racial labels should be understood as in part a self-erasure designed to frustrate the literary marketplace's machinery of classification. "Seeing the World as It Is" (the remarkable chapter of *Dust Tracks* that her publisher successfully discouraged her from including) and "What White Publishers Won't Print" are profound efforts to imagine an alternative, that is, a nonproprietary, cosmopolitan understanding of race and identity. Alone and impoverished in the Florida back country, Hurston lived this utopian understanding, investing it with the "irresponsibility" that so many who knew her found compelling (Hurst 23).

In this light some of the bizarre aspects of her last dozen years configure new meanings. Her indifference to material possessions and to money; her determination (from 1945 to 1948) to travel to Honduras (which she did) to discover a mysterious Mayan city (which she did not); her capacity for relaxation ("Zora floated on Biscayne Bay and sunned on the beach for the next five months, waiting for the Honduras expedition to begin"); her newfound range, in class, race, and ethnicity, of literary projects; her psychological identification with Jews, evident in, among other things, her plan to write a play about the fall of Jerusalem in A.D. 70, a "whale of a story," she called it, "the struggle of a handful of Jews against the mightiest army on earth, that they might be free to live their own lives in their own way"—together, these suggest her freedom from obligation and embrace of anarchy (Hemenway 324, qtd. 343). In "Seeing the World as It Is" Hurston had adumbrated her desire to achieve a mode of unconstrained being, an individualism unharnessed to race or to fixed identity: "I do not wish to close the frontiers of life upon my own self. I do not wish to deny myself the expansion of seeking into individual capabilities and depths by living in a space whose boundaries are race and nation" (786). In an improbable but powerful way, Hurston's last years ask what, since the Greek Stoics, "cosmopolitan utopia" has always asked: "is it possible to live without constraints—without limits, without borders—other than individual demands"? (Kristeva *Strangers* 60).

An epiphany triggered her breakthrough: "Light came to me when I realized that I did not have to consider any racial group as a whole. God made them duck by duck and that was the only way I could see them. I learned that skin was no measure of what was inside people. So none of the Race clichés meant anything anymore" (731). Yet Hurston had been accused of perpetuating those clichés by, among others, Alain Locke and Richard Wright in their respective reviews of *Their Eyes Were Watching God*.[19] Locke complained of the effect of "oversimplification" due to the abundance of "pseudo-primitives" who people the novel, while Wright accused Hurston of reviving "the minstrel technique" that delights the 'white folks' " (qtd. Gates and Appiah 17–18). Though the cogency of these remarks is dubious, they infuriated Hurston, as did other critiques. While hardly one to back down from criticism, Hurston after 1942 did change artistic direction. The implication is not that she was intimidated into changing or that she sought the approbation of her critics. Rather, an intensely racialized critical climate spurred her move toward the universalism limned above and adumbrated in *Dust Tracks*, a move to a world where "there is no *The Negro* here."[20]

Hurston was proud that she had never turned any of her books into "a lecture on the race problem," which would have made them "sociology" rather than art (qtd. Ford 8). Her resistance to race responsibility had consistently nettled black critics. *Dust Tracks* only produced more nettles, even without its cosmic chapter that sees "the world as it is" free of the imposition of category. "Miss Hurston," said Arna Bontemps, "deals very simply with the most serious aspects of Negro life in America—she ignores them" (qtd. Hemenway 289). Her biographer calls her autobiography a "discomfiting book" because of her "deliberate refusal—after documenting the shared life of Eatonville [her all-black hometown]—to interpret her later career in any context other than that of individual achievement" (Hemenway 283).[21]

Hemenway provides a sensible explanation of the downward arc of Hurston's career after *Dust Tracks:* she turned her back on "the resources that had previously sustained and inspired her art." He adds: "she had dropped the folk material that was the substance of her art, and she paid a heavy price" (315, 327–328). That she paid is not in dispute; less clear is why she was willing to incur the cost. What investment or gamble was she making? I have described that gamble as the abandonment of conventional props of coherence, the result of her fashioning a homemade cosmopolitanism. For by renouncing "terms of race" and, indeed, all "organized creeds" as "collections of words around a wish," she was putting herself beyond reach of the various "intellectual Jim Crow" regimes that would discipline her (764). After all, how does one control someone who describes "the stuff" of her "being" as "matter, ever changing, ever moving, but never lost; so what need of denominations and creeds to deny myself the comfort of all my fellow men?" (764). In exposing classifications as mere "collections of words," Hurston, like William James, obstructs their propensity to freeze into the factitious reality of Race.

Hurston's determined bid for freedom from "the Race Problem" began with her first novel, *Jonah's Gourd Vine,* and, as we have seen, was reaffirmed and given new direction in the forties and fifties (713). Toomer sought the same freedom, and pursued it in life, if not in art, almost as soon as his masterpiece, *Cane,* was published in 1923. In 1932 he wrote that after *Cane* "I became interested in a way of life which took me far away not only from the race question but from literature . . . And not only what I was called did not matter, but even many of the things which formerly I had deeply valued did not matter. My new values were in another world, and into this world I had placed myself completely"

(*Reader* 102). For the rest of his life the only art he was interested in creating was meditations on his new life of cosmic consciousness. By the early twenties Toomer was convinced that he was "one of the first conscious members" of a "new race," a "united human race" he came to call the "American Race" (*Wayward* 121). The ambiguous relation between human and American race, universal and particular, would be a puzzling part of Toomer's discourse. When Toomer realized how few U.S. citizens were aware of belonging to the "American race," he was struck at how "thorough [a] job had been done in the matter of racial conditioning." Who was Toomer to try and intervene? Neither reformer nor propagandist, he decided it was not his business: "I had best let it alone. Which is just what I did" (122).

Toomer's vision of post-identity had to wait until the 1990s to be taken seriously. What Toomer envisioned, the political writer Michael Lind prescribes: "Americans should think of themselves as belonging to only one race—the human—and to only one nationality—the American" (296). In *The Next American Nation* (1995) Lind says Toomer's proto-liberal nationalist vision can help "address the enduring legacy of centuries of white supremacy: racial separation by class" (301). Lind calls his nationalism "liberal" to distinguish it from the Progressive, coercive, unhyphenated nationalism of Theodore Roosevelt, and from pseudo-universalist or " 'organic' crypto-racist nationalism" (275).

In recovering Jean Toomer Lind ignores the ambiguity that Toomer tended to create between his Gurdjieff-inflected universalism ("my race is the human race") and his particularism (Americanism). He refused identification as white or black, but in rejecting racial purism Toomer remained within a discourse of race. As George Hutchinson has noted, "rather than erasing all racial 'traces of difference,' Toomer envisioned a *new* difference as fundamental—as, indeed, the only (and the inevitable) route out of America's continuing racial nightmare" ("Toomer" 244).[22] Toomer's new American race was one of mixed people of "racial blendings." He told James Weldon Johnson, "my poems are not Negro poems, nor are they Anglo-Saxon or white or English poems." Rather, they "spring" from a "new race . . . we may call it the American race" (*Reader* 106). Significantly, Lind's admiration for Toomer does not include maintaining "American race." Lind speaks of a "trans-American" nationality, republic, community, or identity, while regretting the hyper "race-consciousness" promulgated by "multiculturalism" and the racial labeling mandated by the U.S. Census. Lind wants "nationality" to replace not only race but ethnicity as well (Lind 274).

At rare moments Toomer resolved the ambiguity between his universalism and Americanism. In an undated piece entitled "The Americans" he brings together his dematerialized cosmic Gurdjieff perspective and his American vision. "What I really mean by the American race is the human race," he declares, and what makes the American group unique is not blood but "consciousness" (*Reader* 110). Above all, it is a consciousness skeptical of names: "After having for years been hypnotized by labels and suggestions to believe we were less than human, merely Caucasian, or Mongolian, or Negroid, merely African, Russian, Italian, American . . . after having been identified with these surfaces, we are emerging from these limitations, we are waking up . . . we are realizing our basic human stock . . . our fundamental and universal humanity." He then adds: "Those who have or who are approaching this . . . realization—these are the ones I mean when I say Americans. These Americans are not of America only; they are of the earth. And . . . they of course exist in other national groups. These are the [natural?] conscious internationalists" (*Reader* 110).

Here the essay ends. America, by this point, seems to emerge less as a new race or an old one and more as a metaphor for a new mode of being that is born by breaking the hypnotic spell of identity logic and by dissolving what the spell has created: surfaces which have been classified and segregated into blood and race and nation. America is post-identity: "we are nonidentifying from surfaces and from the preferences and prejudices associated with them" (110). No longer do "matters of genesis"—deciding who is authentically American—"overshadow matters of Being" (96). For America incarnates "possibilities far in excess of any yet realized" (99). (James Baldwin, as we shall see, holds comparable views of America's utopian potential). Yet these possibilities, says Toomer, depend on eluding "one or the other of two extremes" that traditionally have limited the Negro: "either he denies Negro entirely (as much as he can) and seeks approximation to an Anglo-Saxon (white) ideal, or . . . he overemphasizes what is Negro. Both of these attitudes have their source in a feeling of (a desire not to feel) inferiority" (qtd. Kerman and Eldridge 96–97).

In the final, rhapsodic pages of *Black Skin, White Masks,* Fanon, like Toomer, Hurston, and William James, moves beyond identity logic. Refusing the "supremacy game" of invidious racial classification and stripping himself of particularity, Fanon dismisses "matters of genesis" to face humanity at large: "In the world through which I travel, I am endlessly creating myself. I am a part of Being to the degree that I go beyond it . . . Superiority? Inferiority? . . . At the conclusion of this study, I want the world to recognize, with me, the open door of every consciousness" (229, 231–232). But Toomer diverges from the Nietzschean Fanon and the pragmatist Du Bois over "the problem of action" (Fanon) and of material embodiment. Toomer negates both. "The important thing is consciousness," says Toomer: "In America we have a new body. And having recognized this let us forget it . . . Let us be born above the body" (*Reader* 110). The purity of his idealism and his paradoxical commitment to a raceless race of Americans left few beyond his circle of fellow visionaries to enter into and grasp his thinking. Like "cosmic Zora" who belongs "to no race nor time," Toomer was content to float, a self-described "exile" dispersed into random pieces. "I am broken glass, shifting, now here, now there, to a new design," he once described himself. "And because I am in this city, physically soft and quiet, I am glass fragments blown by a low wind over asphalt pavements" (*Reader* 277, 281).

Hurston too invoked the image of glass fragments, in response to the question that forms the title of her 1928 essay "How It Feels to Be Colored Me":

> I feel like a brown bag of miscellany propped against a wall. Against a wall in company with other bags, white, red, and yellow. Pour out the contents, and there is discovered a jumble of small things priceless and worthless . . . In your hand is the brown bag. On the ground before you is the jumble it held—so much like the jumble in the bags, could they be emptied, that all might be dumped in a single heap and the bags refilled without altering the content of any greatly. A bit of colored glass more or less would not matter. (829)

This is an image of a self beyond the worry of propriety or the proprietary, the authentic or the discrete. Her jumbled self forecasts the modality of being that Hurston would embody as she entered the oblivion and cosmopolitanism of her last decade and a half. If the stereotypes that line the walls of the American Museum of Unnatural History are "without insides at all," Hurston's "bag of miscellany" is virtually all "insides," possessed of a precarious, because contingent, uniqueness. Yet "in company with other bags," hers is also "just like everybody else": its individualism does not fixate upon identity and thereby breed the violence of "insurmountable difference" (952). The nonproprietary individualism that Toomer took to its highest and hermetic cosmic exfoliation, Hurston here sets before us as an icon of a plausible, earthly post-identity. And her bag of miscellaneous jumble is an apt icon of pragmatist pluralism itself, with its esteem of "inextricable interfusion" (James) "motley mixtures" (Ellison) and "limitless interchangeableness" (Locke).

7

The Agon *Black Intellectual:* Baldwin and Baraka

In his remarkable eulogy at the funeral of James Baldwin in 1987, Amiri Baraka finds it "supremely ironic" that "for all his aestheticism and ultra sophistication," the "rare lyricism of his song, the sweeping aesthetic obsession with feeling," Baldwin was *"at the same time!"* a leader for civil rights who "demand[ed] that we get in the world completely." His voice, "as much as Dr. King's or Malcolm X's, helped shepherd and guide us toward black liberation" (*Reader* 453–454). What is surprising about these words is their source: they come from a writer often regarded (with some, if not complete justification) as Baldwin's antithesis. Besides being rhetorically stirring, as the occasion demanded, Baraka's eulogy hints that he has reconsidered his belief that aesthetic inwardness and political activism are irreconcilable. His rethinking was perhaps encouraged by the friendship between Baraka and Baldwin that had developed by the 1980s.[1] After noting Baldwin's love of "beauty—art," Baraka declares: "Jimmy was a 'civil rights leader' too." He addresses this remark to "thinkers of outmoded social outrage." The phrase seems self-directed, as if Baraka is chiding himself, acknowledging that he, not Baldwin, has become "outmoded." If "social outrage" has grown stale, what remains vital to appreciate and what Baraka salutes in 1987 is the stunning simultaneity of Baldwin's aesthetic and activist commitments.

What follows concerns Baldwin's challenge to the opposition between art and politics invoked by leftists and liberals alike, a challenge that orients his cultural critique. His realignment of the aesthetic and political derives from his acute sense of the primacy of entanglement, the fact that every "each" we perceive contains an other. Discreteness and autonomy are convenient fictions. But the American social order and its legitimating discourses consistently misrepresent (by segregation) the reality of entanglement—racial, sexual, perceptual—or fail to represent it at all. Baldwin's project amounts to the effort to remedy this failure by finding new language adequate to what he calls America's "bottomless confusion," the "motley mixtures" Ellison insisted upon (*Price* 241). Perhaps the primal entanglement that frames Baldwin's enterprise is between art and life. As Robert Penn Warren once observed: "What Baldwin has most powerfully created is a self. That is his rare and difficult work of art" (Warren 297). Yet the creation called James Baldwin is not a testament to the labor of merely inward self-culture. Rather, notes Warren, his interior life and the "exterior fate of the country [are], for dramatic purposes, merged" (281). This merging generates his "magisterial authenticity" of "utterance" (296). But the rhetorical effect of authenticity and the ideology of authenticity are two different matters, and Baldwin, as we shall see, critiqued the latter as he created the former.

After examining Baldwin's intricate stance, I will return to Baraka, whose early career, the *New York Times* said in 1971, made him the "obvious heir apparent to James Baldwin's crown." But "Jones took a sharp and unexpected turn from the gilded pathway . . . One of the most promising young black writers fell into critical decline" (qtd. Riley 89). What the orthodoxy views as decline, Baraka understands as a journey from white to black, from intellectual to activist, from playing at white bohemian to plunging into collective struggle in "the homeland to help raise the race" (*Autobiography* 202). His autobiographical novel, *The System of Dante's Hell,* offers an allegory of this journey. But trusting the tale, not the teller, I will argue that Baraka's intentions and his text are at odds, and that their conflict generates a more complicated story than a return to roots.

What he praises in 1987 as Baldwin's "supremely ironic" balancing act of art and politics would have struck Baraka a quarter-century before as not simply contemptible but baffling. For Baldwin's stance eludes the terms of Baraka's "color code of class distinction." He defines this phrase in his *Autobiography* (1984). For Baraka, "growing up was a maze of light and darkness," as the book's opening sentence attests. But before too long he had exited the maze, in part thanks to "B-B-Y-W," his shorthand for the "basic colors"—black, brown, yellow, and white—that he discerned on the streets of Newark (42). Baraka's "color code" describes a descending scale of diminishing reality (315). Black is "the real and the solid and the strong and the beautiful," while brown ("my family and me") is only "half-real and half-lodged in dream and show." Yellow and white have lost even that foothold on the real; they are absorbed in bourgeois careerism, adrift in fantasies of acquisition. The code, Baraka declares, "taught me early what America was" (315).

In 1963 the code identified Baldwin as white. For, in the eyes of the leading Black Arts militant, Baldwin had forsaken activism to wallow in "sensitivity," cultivating "the sanctity of his feelings," his blackness merely "gay, exotic plumage" (*Home* 117–118). And as a sensitive white man Baldwin was, ipso facto, a "faggot," Baraka's shorthand term of abuse that refers less to sexual preference than to the weakness and "softness" of the middle-class white male.[2] "Most American white men are trained to be fags" by the very privileges that make them " 'masters' of the world," in the famous words of "Sexual Reference: Black Male" (*Home* 216). They lead lives insulated from "the real," from the "pain" of physical labor, and, instead, "devote their energies to the nonphysical," to "luxury," becoming "effeminate and per-verted" (216, 220). Baraka's mockery of the sensitive, soft white man has a specific reference: the "estrangement, alienation . . . syndrome" of "Euro-American intellectuals." This class imagines itself "separate from the rest of the culture" and free to lament society's philistine materialism while staying above the vulgarity of politics (218–219). "And the most extreme form of alienation acknowledged within white society is homosexuality" (219). The homosexual, then, in Baraka's view, is the acme of elitist withdrawal from political responsibility.

Not surprisingly, the anti-intellectual fury of Baraka and other Black Arts poets suggested more than a little anxiety about how to justify the fact of their own poetic careers and to explain what those careers im-plied about their own masculinity.[3] As I will discuss in the second part of this chapter, Baraka's construction of the intellectual as a category that violates black manhood resonates with Booker T. Washington's ridicule of the black intellectual as a dandified fop. But if, for both men, *black intellectual* is an oxymoron, Baraka is fascinated by this tension, immersing himself in its contradictions in *The System of Dante's Hell* and in an early play, *The Toilet*. As his autobiography reveals, his fasci-nation, predictably, derived from an initial enchantment. In the early fifties, while in the air force, Baraka discovered the vocation of intel-lectual. Its indifference to race and contempt for conformist careerism seemed to offer liberation from the color and class snobbery of the black and white bourgeoisie. As he works through his ambivalences, his texts are drawn into dialogue with Claude McKay, the writer whom Baraka esteems as his major predecessor in making art out of the agon *black intellectual.*

By 1987 Baraka was able to come to grips with what his "color code of class distinction" could not encompass in 1963: the fact that a homosexual black aesthete not only managed to be politically engaged and influential but possessed an authority that spanned classes and colors and nations. Baldwin's status as an international literary lion who still mattered in the ghetto was made vivid to Baraka when he took Baldwin to Newark's Scudder Homes project, "toilet bowl of the world." There "one young brother his hat turned half way around said, 'I just read *Just Above My Head,* Mr. Baldwin. It's great! How you doing?' " (*Reader* 455). Using a universalist rhetoric ordinarily inimical to his nationalism, Baraka calls Baldwin's ease in straddling seeming contraries—the local and the cosmopolitan, the political and the aesthetic—characteristic of the "great artists of all times. Those who understand it is beauty And Truth we seek, and that indeed one cannot exist without and as an extension of the other" (454). This recalls Du Bois in 1926, when, in "Criteria of Negro Art," he asks what has "Beauty to do with the world . . . with the facts of the world and the right actions of men?" (*Writings* 995). Although Du Bois grants that both activists and artists would answer "Nothing" (as in effect did Baraka in 1963), he insists that "here and now and in the world in which I work" Beauty and Truth "are for me unseparated and inseparable."

Whether intentional or not, Baraka's echoing of Du Bois is apt, for it situates Baldwin where he belongs, within the miscegenated lineage of pragmatist pluralism. Its premise is that in the United States "the mulatto is mainstream," to borrow Albert Murray's famous phrase.[4] Baldwin weighs the consequences—especially the denials and repressions—of what most white Americans in the 1950s and 1960s were loath to confront: that the defining fact of the American continent was the "interracial drama acted out on" it, a drama that "created a new black man" and a "new white man too." And "no road whatever will lead" white Americans "back to the simplicity" of a European village or take black Americans back to Africa (*Price* 89). Together, white and black were left alone with America, in Perry Miller's phrase, bound together in deracination. Created by history as an "entirely unprecedented people" (rather than multiply precedented, as cultural pluralism might put it), America severs roots. Estranged from forebears and from the past, it is uniquely situated "to prove the uselessness and the obsolescence of the concept of color. But it has not dared to accept this opportunity" (99, 374). Instead, we persist in thinking of ourselves as a "white nation," Baldwin said in *The Fire Next Time* (1963); we cling to mythic, monstrous "innocence" and condemn the country to "sterility and decay" (374, 89).[5]

Baldwin images America here and elsewhere as a kind of sacred ideal, virtually a magic solution to racism. In his thinking national identity seems to replace racial identity. Ordinarily such a substitution would solve little, for nationalism would then assume the essentialist functions usually borne by race. But for Baldwin national identity is "unprecedented" in that it represents a deracialized ideal that renders color irrelevant. In other words, for Baldwin the category of America (as a still-to-be-realized ideal) is, finally, less nationalist than cosmopolitan or, more precisely, offers the promise of an end to racial essentialism in a cosmopolitan nationalism. Baldwin's ideas link him to Du Bois (recall Du Bois's goal of an "Internation" founded on "human unity") and Locke. And also Ellison. For Baldwin's affirmation of America as an ideal recalls invisible man, near the end of his broodings, affirming "the principle on which the country was built and not the men" because, even though "we had been brutalized and sacrificed" in the name of that plan, "the principle was greater than the men" (574).

A prophet of post-ethnicity, Baldwin regarded black and white as "obsolete terms" that must be dispensed with so that ultimately society could become "joyously color blind" (qtd. Troupe 148). While this goal remains unrealized, the individual black child, stressed Baldwin, must be taught "that he doesn't have to be bound" by the color line; he must learn that American history, like the world itself, is "more various, more beautiful, and more terrible than anything anyone has ever said about it"—"and that it belongs to him." Reiterating this Du Boisian injunction, Baldwin urges black Americans to "claim it all— including Shakespeare" (*Price* 332; Standley and Pratt 252).

Baldwin did not always embrace this sense of free access. At least at the start of his career, he felt outside Western culture because he regarded it as white. Baldwin speaks of being a "kind of bastard of the West" at the start of his first collection, *Notes of a Native Son* (1955). This status estranges him not only from "Shakespeare, Bach, Rembrandt," and Chartres, but from the Empire State Building: "These were not my creations, they did not contain my history . . . I was an interloper; this was not my heritage" (*Notes* 6–7). He reiterates these sentiments in "Stranger in the Village," the collection's concluding essay. First published in 1953, the essay narrates Baldwin's unease as the one (and first) black man living in a remote Swiss mountain village. In a famous passage he describes illiterate Swiss peasants as "related, in a way that I am not, to Dante, Shakespeare, Michelangelo . . . Go back a few centuries and they are in their full glory—but I am in Africa, watching the conquerors arrive" (*Price* 83).

This passage has puzzled readers and prompted the question of why Baldwin, whose career stands as its refutation, would embrace a pillar of racist ideology—that culture has a color.[6] As Stanley Crouch remarks, "such simplifications are akin to the kind of reasoning that manipulated illiterate rednecks into violent attempts at keeping 'their' universities clean of Negro interlopers. Or convinced black nationalists . . . that they were the descendants of 'kings and queens' brought to America in slave ships" (Crouch 232). Baldwin's error is to assume cultures are innate, as if genetically transmitted by blood, instead of acquired through individual will and prolonged education, formal or otherwise. "Not all native-born citizens necessarily possess the culture of their country," Tzvetan Todorov remarks; "one can be French by origin and still not participate in the cultural community" (387).

Yet Todorov's point is Baldwin's too, one he makes implicitly at the end of "Stranger in the Village." Native-born Americans do not participate in the American cultural community if they are blind to the "interracial drama" that created the American continent. Instead of participating, they remain "in a state of innocence" (*Price* 89). The essay's final sentence—"this world is white no longer, and it will never be white again"—puts "innocence" on notice that its days are numbered. Thus it turns out that the essay's lament of cultural dispossession is part of a larger dynamic. In short, if *Notes of a Native Son* begins with the author's confession of bastardy, by the end he has worked his way through estrangement to a confident sense of legitimacy. And he grounds this legitimacy in American citizenship. "Stranger in the Village" concludes with the black American no longer an "interloper" in the West. He is a "citizen, an American; as American as the Americans who despise him" (88). Rather than erased or revealed as delusional, bastardy has been set in dialectical relation with American; each term modifies and complicates the other. Yet for all its artfulness, the dialectic of stranger and citizen played out in *Notes* is muted, inferential, overshadowed by what Baldwin makes most conspicuous—the moment of bastardy. This left Baldwin vulnerable to justified accusations of racial essentialism.

"Stranger in the Village" narrates a passage from destitution to inclusion that proved decisive. Baldwin's rhetoric of dispossession had largely faded by the early sixties. "He was struck anew to discover how far he had come since he had unhappily walked in the streets of that village in the Swiss Alps . . . Now he saw that in all time all people had exchanged and appropriated cultures, and in doing so reshaped them."[7] He summarized this new understanding in a 1984 preface to *Notes of a Native Son*. Baldwin provides a more supple sense of the relation of race to culture by distinguishing between his "inheritance"—"specifically limited and limiting"—and his "birthright"—"vast, connecting me to all that lives" (xii). Their relation is entangled: "one cannot claim the birthright without accepting the inheritance." Using these terms, he recalls his original challenge as a writer: he had to try to "describe that particular condition" which was his inheritance and, simultaneously, "with that very same description," he had to claim his birthright. Evidently, Baldwin in 1984 hopes that this dialectic of particular and universal will be the lens through which a new generation of readers will encounter *Notes of a Native Son*.

Baldwin's dialectical cosmopolitanism, like Du Bois's, avoids the polarizing logic of an ideology of authenticity. This condemns the colonized to pursuing mirror-image opposites, phantoms of pure whiteness and pure blackness. Fanon warned of this futility. But Baraka also has a surprising relevance here. For near the end of his 1984 *Autobiography* he alludes to Fanon when he explains what he now calls "the special foolishness of white-hating black nationalism." "Breaking out of the jail of white possession, even while reinventing the same shit in black face," was still playing "a supremacy game." Had he better understood Fanon, notes Baraka, he might have profited from Fanon's lesson that "pathological intellectuals will rush headlong, unknowing, into love of their oppressors" and then when they discover the "trap, how they have been used, they rush again headlong, or heartlong now, into Africa of their mind" (322–323).

Baraka's self-reflection here might be the seed of his revaluation of Baldwin in 1987. In recognizing that the ideology of authenticity encourages the "supremacy game," Baraka gains sufficient distance from his "spectrum of color understanding" not only to call his own style of "social outrage" "outmoded," but to find room in his vocabulary for universalist terms.

Baldwin was suspicious of partisans of racial authenticity, for they drape themselves in purity. And purity is always a danger, since "by definition [it] is unassailable" (*Price* 297). The immaculate cloister of white supremacy into which most Americans enclose themselves is a retreat into a provincialism founded on "monumental aversion to experience" and enslavement to the "tyranny of the mirror" (96, 374). Baldwin's effort to undermine this condition of suffocating narcissism necessarily commits him to the task faced by all pragmatist pluralists— turning identity from an accomplished fact that excludes and forecloses to a continuing practice of skepticism: "To ask questions of the universe, and then learn to live with those questions, is the way" one "achieves" one's "identity" (326). To equate identity with the interrogative turns out, however, to have affinity with a national identity— American. For "no one in the world seems to know exactly what it [America] describes" (171).

Given the preoccupation of Baldwin's essays with identity (the word is far and away his favorite, notes a critic) one can gain the impression that, in the manner of pop existentialists or American ego psychologists, Baldwin extols identity as the panacea for psychic and social alienation.[8] But this suggests identity as pride of possession and is precisely Baldwin's target. For Baldwin, identity is closer to being possessed than to being in possession. To an interviewer he described himself as a locus of "strangers called Jimmy Baldwin," comprising children, men, and women. "There are lots of people here" (Standley and Pratt 79). His acceptance of strangers within is consonant with the image he used to describe his own life—"a journey toward something I do not understand, which in the going toward, makes me better" (*Price* 234). Underwriting this submission to groping exploration is a premise he articulated in a 1984 interview: "Everything is in question, according to me. One has to forge a new language to deal with it" (Standley and Pratt 231).

Baldwin's linguistic skepticism enacts his commitment to the hazards of living the interrogative. This stance intimately aligns him with his literary hero Henry James, the prime mediator of pragmatist skepticism to Baldwin.[9] Upon his repatriation to the United States in 1904, where he walked the streets of urban America, James was struck that America's

"too-defiant scale of numerosity" and its "hotch-potch of racial ingre-
dients" made conclusions—definitive, categorical judgments—about
what defines the "American character" difficult. The country is an "*illegible word . . . belonging to no known language*." And James takes
pleasure in this open question, as he avails himself of the "liberty of
waiting to see" (*American Scene* 121–122). The living of questions,
not the answering of them, becomes the imperative of the self-described
"restless analyst" of *The American Scene* who ventures into the ethnic
"whirlpool" of New York. Although Baldwin is said to have read *The
American Scene* only late in life, from the start of his career he shared
the book's fascination with "the discovery of what it means to be an
American." This is the title of Baldwin's essay which begins: " 'It is a
complex fate to be an American,' Henry James observed." After this
homage, James departs the essay, but his skepticism of conclusions lingers. "The very word America," notes Baldwin, "remains a new, almost
completely undefined and extremely controversial proper noun" (*Price*
171). This conveys precisely the spirit of skeptical inquiry that animates
The American Scene.

James finds that a "fatal futility" shadows the effort to assume or
define an authentic, a priori American identity. He articulates that futility in the form of a question precipitated by his 1904 visit to Ellis
Island, the site of immigrant entry to New York: "Which is the American . . . which is not the alien," he asks himself, in a "country peopled
from the first . . . by migrations at once extremely recent, perfectly
traceable and urgently required" (124). The question poses an unsettling challenge—"where does one put a finger on the dividing line"
between alien and native? And by blurring the boundaries of coherence,
this challenge haunts him as the "reminder not to be dodged," the
reminder of how precarious is his own—or anyone's—claim to a genuine American identity (85, 124).[10]

On his travels across the country, what dismays Henry James, as it
will James Baldwin, is the absence of any humbling sense of the precarious and, instead, the serene triumph of American identity in all its
homogeneous innocence. James describes "the country at large . . . as
the hugest thinkable organism for successful 'assimilation' " (124). For
the plague upon the American scene is a static "sterility of aspect"
caused by the absence of a "due proportion of other presences, other
figures and characters . . . representatives of other interests, exemplars
of other possibilities" (427). Nowhere is this more evident than in the
South. On his visit there James witnesses the pathetic spectacle of a

people unwilling to renounce the "luxury" of purity—the "Confederate dream" of white supremacy for "which hundreds of thousands of men had ever laid down their lives" (371). Forty years after the collapse of the Confederacy James still detects "the incurable after-taste of the original vanity and fatuity" of the "Slave-scheme" (373–374). The "Confederate dream" maintained itself by "active and ardent propaganda," a "general and a permanent quarantine" that kept "the light of experience" and the "reality of things" at bay. Thus the South shut itself into an "eternal 'false position,'" a perverse provincialism made up of a "hundred mistakes and make-believes, suppressions and prevarications" (376).

The target of the suppressions and prevarications enabling the "Confederate dream" was of course the humanity of black Americans. James finds that the Jim Crow South remains as "imprisoned" as ever in denial of the "thumping legacy of the intimate presence of the Negro" (375). And he does not flinch from confessing his own denial of black Americans. Recalling his sight, a few days before, in the Washington train station, of "an African type or two"—a "group of tatterdemalion darkies lounged and sunned themselves"—James admits having had his own "ease of contemplation" threatened. For in Washington James is forcefully reminded that, though plantation days are long gone, to see free blacks in public is to see "the Southern black as we knew him not . . . [A]nd to see him there, ragged and rudimentary, yet all portentous and 'in possession of his rights as a man' was to be not a little discomposed, was to be in fact very much admonished" (375).

In admonishing himself for having failed until now to recognize "the Southern black" as fellow citizen (though at best a segregated, despised citizen in 1904 Jim Crow America), James replays in a minor key the revelation of Ellis Island. There he came to grips with the fact that he shared the "sanctity of his American consciousness . . . with the inconceivable alien" (85). The affirmed claim of the black man is another "reminder not to be dodged." But the "afflicted South" is resolutely blind, condemned to its "eternal 'false position,'" enslaved, that is, to the ironclad separatism of Jim Crow. It draws a curtain over the fact of intimacy between black and white, the fact that "the negro had always been, and could absolutely not fail to be, intensely 'on the nerves' of the South" (376). Figuratively, "on the nerves" tells us that blacks are an irritant; but read literally the phrase imparts James's sharper point by injecting the Negro inside, making him disconcertingly present within the body, life, and mind of the white Southerner.[11] James will "tread" on "tiptoe" around this scandalous truth, but does not shy from uttering the "immitigable fact" of how much the Negro "must loom, how he must count, in a community [the South] in which . . . there were comparatively so few other things" (375).

The South is a "social order founded on delusions and exclusions," and its barrenness is an ominous portent of what the national norm might become (391). America's prime delusion, says James, is to believe that one has the *choice* of excluding or affirming the claim of the alien, a delusion exposed by James's crucial questions: "which is the American . . . which is *not* the alien . . . where does one put a finger on the dividing line . . . and identify any particular phase of the conversion?" What James suggests is that affirming the alien is, ultimately, not a freely considered option or a concession to an Other but a recognition of what has already occurred: "We, not they, must make the surrender and accept the orientation" (86).

James's pointed skepticism about dividing lines, his understanding of them as instruments of repression masquerading as natural boundaries designating an alleged " 'American' identity," aligns *The American Scene* with a book William James had sent to Henry in 1903, a "decidedly moving book by a mulatto ex-student of mine" (William James qtd. in Kenneth Warren 112). Addressing white America near the end of *The Souls of Black Folk,* Du Bois asks: "Your country? How came it yours? Before the Pilgrims landed we were here. Here we have brought our three gifts and mingled them with yours . . . Actively we have woven ourselves with the very warp and woof of this nation—we fought their battles, shared their sorrow, mingled our blood with theirs" (545). Du Bois's pinpoint pressure on the possessive pronoun "your" begins to loosen white America's stranglehold on an American history it would prefer to keep buried. He alerts white America that it does not have the choice to reject black America; their bloods are already mingled. Henry James and Du Bois both portray American identity as never anything but miscegenated.[12]

Hence there is a Du Boisian and Jamesian (Henry and William) resonance in Baldwin's own abiding belief that "whether I like it or not, or whether you like it or not, we are bound together. We are part of each other" (*Price* 234). As with Ellison, Baldwin's insistence on overlap rather than discreteness drives his impassioned indictment of American identity as insufficiently motley, that is, insufficiently American. In rejecting the monadic, Baldwin protected himself against playing the "supremacy game" (though on occasion he succumbed to glorifying blacks as noble savages) or applying a "color code of class distinction." Such efforts to organize experience impose a specious clarity and certitude that Baldwin finds at odds with the aesthetic. As Baraka exclaimed in his eulogy, Baldwin had found a way to fuse the aesthetic and the political. The question is how he accomplished this.

The aesthetic moment, for Baldwin, is one wherein "you see differently." He credits the painter Beauford Delaney, a key early mentor, with this teaching. "I remember standing on a street corner with Beauford . . . and he pointed down and said, 'Look.' I looked and all I saw was water. And he said, 'Look again,' which I did, and I saw oil on the water and the city reflected in the puddle. It was a great revelation to me. I can't explain it. He taught me how to see" (Standley and Pratt 235). Baldwin's act of seeing is an epiphany of nonidentity, where the crust of discrete definition dissolves into the fact of simultaneity and connection: the banal puddle of water is not itself alone but contains something else, which turns it into a reflecting mirror. Aesthetic vision is not without cost; it risks the imprecision of astigmatism. But to relax discrimination can be a means of understanding what ordinary sight overlooks—how objects nest within objects, are inside of, part of, each other. The color fixation of Jim Crow vision, in stark contrast, produces a stunted flatness that erases everything but skin pigment and the train of stereotypes it evokes. While working in a defense plant in New Jersey in the forties, Baldwin discovered this firsthand: "I learned in New Jersey that to be a Negro meant, precisely, that one was never looked at but was simply at the mercy of the reflexes the color of one's skin caused in other people" (*Price* 132).

To "see differently" becomes an imperative, at once artistic and political, that Baldwin rhetorically seeks to instill in his readers. His homosexuality intensified his differential vision, making him acutely sensitive to the artifice of bounded identity: "all of the American categories of male and female, straight or not, black or white were shattered, thank heaven, very early in my life" (681). Baldwin inscribes his wariness of identity in his famous title *Nobody Knows My Name*. Rather than referring to his own bastard status or an existential anguish, Baldwin's namelessness announces his Americanness. Unlike the French or English or Chinese, who are "born into a framework" of identity, "the one thing that all Americans have in common is that they have no other identity apart from the identity which is being achieved on this continent" (234).

But faced with the historical imperative of achieving identity, and the psychological imperative to risk unsettlement, white Americans have instead embraced the "failure of identity" in the form of an ahistorical, defensive, claustral "innocence" (qtd. Troupe 155). This failure consists not of an insufficiency or an absence but rather of a congealing of identity, expressed in a deluded confidence of possession, a presumption that identity has already been achieved and is no longer an open question: that America, for example, is a white heterosexual Christian nation where black people know their place.

It is within the logic of this critique that one should understand Baldwin's distrust of the mirror opposite of pure white identity, the mantra "I'm black and I'm proud" which, by 1972, had a gleaming new label, "Afro-American." This last phrase, Baldwin declares in that year, "is but a wedding . . . of two confusions, an arbitrary linking of two undefined and currently undefinable proper nouns. I mean that, in the case of Africa, Africa is still chained to Europe, and exploited by Europe, and Europe and America are chained together; and as long as this is so, it is hard to speak of Africa except as a cradle and a potential" (*Price* 551). If white identity erases history by freezing it, thus suppressing "the interracial drama" of miscegenation, "Afro-American" affirms identity at the price of an analogous concealment—the web of imperial relations of dominance. In both cases, black and white, the unequivocal affirmation of identity purchases the sterile stasis of arrested vision. Identity is affirmed at the expense of the aesthetic (in Baldwin's sense), that way of seeing "differently" premised on the fact that whether we like it or not we are bound together and are part of each other (234).

Acceptance of the inadmissible fact of intermixture is one way to start achieving something different from innocence, something that admits difference but is beyond obedience to the "obscenity of color." He calls this acceptance of impurity "love" by the final pages of *The Fire Next Time*. Baldwin uses love "not merely in the personal sense but as a state of being, or a state of grace" characterized by "daring and growth" (375). The grace granted by love disrupts white America's habit of vigilance in "guarding and keeping" its "system of reality," and forces it to risk acceptance of the alien: the white man must "consent, in effect, to become black himself." This will release him from color phobia—a symptom of "the Negro's tyrannical power over him"—and inspire him to leave white America and become part of America (370, 375).

Baldwin's emphasis on "love" in *The Fire Next Time* implicitly entwines race and sexuality, a double discourse that his novels graphically articulate. By the end of his life, Baldwin makes explicit in nonfiction what, at least since *Another Country*, he had dramatized in his novels—that the kind of "love" most conducive to color blindness is bisexual and homosexual.[13] But in the final paragraph of his collected essays he sublates this particularity into a universal. He urges recognition that "we are all androgynous because each of us, helplessly and forever, contains the other—male in female, female in male, white in black and black in white. We are a part of each other." However "inconvenient and even unfair" we find this fact, "none of us can do anything about it" (690). The primal sense that "nobody knows my name" turns out to be at once Baldwin's, America's, and universal.

Androgyny is Baldwin's final name for the permeable self of nonidentity that he discovered in his streetcorner epiphany of aesthetic vision and in his imperative of "love." More important than what we call this dispersal of identity are the uses Baldwin found for it. For he turned androgyny into a practice. What this amounted to, at a particularly telling moment, was a strategic equivocation, not unlike those turn-of-the-century instances examined in Chapter 3, which variously pose Du Bois's question of how it feels to be a problem. I refer to the moment in *The Fire Next Time* when Baldwin replies to Elijah Muhammad's demand for identity at their dinner in Chicago.

Baldwin has been summoned for possible recruitment into the movement after praising Malcolm X in public. When Baldwin tells the Muslim leader that he left the church twenty years before, Elijah asks him: "And what are you now?" " 'I? Now? Nothing.' This was not enough. 'I'm a writer. I like doing things alone.' " He goes on to tell Elijah that he has many white friends and is not against interracial marriage. "Love is more important than color," he tells himself. By now a "stifling feeling" has overtaken Baldwin, a sense that the Muslims assume he "belonged to them": "where else, after all, could I go?" (363). The overbearing tension is not unfamiliar to Baldwin; he feels as if he is back in his "father's house." To readers of "Notes of a Native Son" the exchange with Elijah specifically echoes the one "real question" that Baldwin's father ever asks him: " 'You'd rather write than preach, wouldn't you' . . . I answered, 'Yes' " (142). Another remark also resonates, from earlier in *The Fire Next Time:* "Goodbye, Mr. James Baldwin. We'll soon be addressing you as Mr. James X" (358). Someone had uttered this to Baldwin as he emerged from a joint television appearance with Malcolm X, where he had agreed with much of the Muslim diagnosis, if not its conclusions.

Like the Muslim "X," Baldwin's "Nothing" to Elijah Muhammad is an act of repudiation and renaming that—in the minimalism of its response—mocks the disciplinary force of identity. The Muslims' "X" both symbolizes the unknowable African name and replaces the white slavemaster's, while also serving as the provisional mark until God returns to give a Holy Name. In short, "X" figures identity as a process of change even as it claims, in its mysterious cipher-like quality, a kind of essential identity. But Baldwin's "X," his "Nothing," is more elusive because unclearly affiliated; he equates it with being a "writer" and one who "likes doing things alone." Baldwin's response doesn't signify an embrace of group solidarity based on lost origin, or race, or imminent, ordained revelations of the sacred. Instead of affiliating, his "nothing" forecloses, echoing (as he implies) the oedipal moment of severance from father, family, and church. In the exchange with Elijah Muhammad, Baldwin negates external connections to preserve autonomy. In effect, he names himself as an intellectual. Which is to say his "nothing" expresses how it feels to be a problem, that is, a figure of deferral and equivocation displaced from origins. Baldwin recovers the deracination that marks the modern intellectual.

To become an intellectual required, Baldwin later recalled, a "particular rupture . . . exceedingly brutal" that occurred when he "left the pulpit, the church, and home." This was a "deliberate repudiation of everything and everyone that had given me an identity until that moment" (455). Baldwin used the word *intellectual* less often than his preferred synonym "maverick." I was a "maverick," he explained in 1984, "in the sense that I depended on neither the white world nor the black world. That was the only way I could have played it . . . I had to say, 'A curse on both your houses' " (Standley and Pratt 230).

The Fire Next Time enacts this delicate maverick balance, for in it he carefully moves between positions, refusing to "pacify the liberal conscience" by condemning Malcolm X and embracing Martin Luther King (*Price* 358). Baldwin finds Malcolm's love for blacks compelling and is sympathetic to Muslim militancy. But, in his view, the "two nations" separatism of the Muslims replicates the Jim Crowism preached by the white Southern political establishment (376). Yet if separatism is defective, so is the liberal panacea of integration. Baldwin scorns its complacent racist assumption that white people possess "some intrinsic value that black people need, or want" (374). It is "the

Negro, of course, who is presumed to have to become equal" to "white standards." But Baldwin, like Du Bois, "would not bleach his soul in a flood of white Americanism" (Du Bois *Souls* 365). Echoing Du Bois, he says: "I am one of the first Americans to arrive on these shores" (376). Integration must be reconstructed on a basis of mutuality and miscegenation. Above all, we must achieve "the transcendence of the realities of color, of nations, and of altars" (*Price* 375, 368). Without this transcendence, we imperil the effort to "end the racial nightmare, and achieve our country" (379).

Baldwin's concern to achieve America crystallized in Europe. He savored the irony that only expatriation from 1948 to 1957 proved to his "astonished" self that he was "as American as any Texas GI." Europe released him from the "illusion" that he hated America (172). His expatriatism (periodic by the mid-fifties) became the way Baldwin himself enacted "transcendence," as he ventured beyond the veil of color. "The fact that I went to Europe so early is probably what saved me" (Standley and Pratt 230). It made possible his investment in a maverick cosmopolitanism as a mode of being that encouraged choice and invention rather than fidelity and authenticity.[14] In Europe he creatively deferred the demand of identity, as if "I? Now? Nothing"—his later response to Elijah Muhammad—had already become his watchword. In Europe Baldwin was released from compulsory heterosexual American masculinity and free to embody its negations—intellectual and homosexual. In "The Discovery of What It Means to Be an American" (1959) he mocks the "paralytically infantile" 1950s "American ideal of masculinity" fixated on flexing one's muscles to prove that one "is just a 'regular guy' " (*Price* 678, 173). In addition to the yoke of heterosexuality and anti-intellectualism, Baldwin left America because the "fury of the color problem" was forcing him to be "*merely* a Negro; or, even, merely a Negro writer." Rather than accept this color line, Baldwin "wanted to find out in what way the *specialness* " of his experience could connect to, instead of divide him from, other people (171).

Articulating his "specialness" required creating a new relation to the very instruments of his entrapment, the stereotypes that reduce one to "*merely* a Negro." In America he had been locked in a defensive battle with the frozen imagery of "natural," authentic blackness: "I had never listened to Bessie Smith in America (in the same way that, for years, I would not touch watermelon)" (172). In a 1961 interview he speaks of running in shame from blues, jazz, the church—"all of these stereotypes that the country inflicts on Negroes" (Standley and Pratt 4). But in Europe he faced his shame by reclaiming what he had rejected in America. Stalled in Paris on his first novel, *Go Tell It on the Mountain*, he left "armed with two Bessie Smith records and a typewriter" to settle in the Swiss Alps, an "absolutely alabaster landscape" (*Price* 172). "In that icy wilderness, as far removed from Harlem as anything you can imagine," Baldwin played the records every day and in three months composed his first novel. Bessie Smith's cadence and beat and tone made it possible for him, "technically as a writer, to re-create Negro speech." And the music enabled another act of recovery: of Baldwin's childhood speech rhythms, lost when he buried his blackness to adopt "white people's image" of him (Standley and Pratt 4). "In Europe she helped to reconcile me to being a 'nigger' " (*Price* 172).

The story Baldwin tells of Bessie Smith allowing him to "dig back" to his disowned blackness is, on one level, a standard roots saga, as the prodigal wanderer learns that "even the most incorrigible maverick had to be born somewhere . . . nothing will efface his origins" (175). But Baldwin also turns upside down the familiar tale of recovered roots. His tool of subversion is perspective by incongruity (to borrow Kenneth Burke's phrase). This strategy of dissonance is consistent with what sent him to Europe in the first place—escaping the prison of stereotypes. If listening to Bessie Smith in Harlem freezes her energy in cliché, placing her amid Switzerland's white blankness releases her genius. And she became a technical resource for Baldwin's craft. Finally, then, it is her artistry, not her color, that Switzerland releases for a fledgling novelist. Switzerland, that is, functions to defamiliarize and decontextualize what racist America has congealed into static images of racial authenticity. Baldwin performs a similarly disruptive act. He sets the recovery-of-roots tale inside the story of the birth of a novelist, not "merely a Negro writer." This makes bedfellows of Bessie Smith and Henry James. For she was not the only one offering assistance. James's center-of-consciousness method also proved crucial for helping to solve difficulties of narrative form in *Go Tell It on the Mountain* (Standley and Pratt 238).

As he recovers his Harlem speech and crafts a bildungsroman of Jamesian texture, Bessie Smith and Henry James join Baldwin in the desolation of Switzerland. But others also hover in the Alpine wilderness. His novel's autobiographical hero is inspired by the "lewd, brutal swagger" of (an unnamed) Bette Davis in *Of Human Bondage:* John

Grimes "wanted to be like her, only more powerful, more thorough, and more cruel" (39). Many years later Baldwin would celebrate his youthful love of Bette Davis and confess why he found her compelling: she was a movie star, she was white, and "she was ugly" (560). "And when she moved, she moved just like a nigger." Best of all, she, like Baldwin himself, had pop-eyes (*Price* 560). This "astounded" and delighted Baldwin, whose father had repeatedly called him ugly: Bette Davis helped him discover, he recalled, that "my infirmity might not be my doom." Baldwin was at the movies in the first place only because a young white school teacher had taken him in hand. Orilla "Bill" Miller took Baldwin to movies, museums, theater: "she escort[ed] me into the world." Above all, Bill Miller made it impossible for Baldwin to hate white people. The fact of her "difference" from other whites, Baldwin says, "had to have a profound and bewildering effect on my mind" (559). Inassimilable to the parade of menacing white folk that occupied his imagination and life, Bill Miller, like Bette Davis, remakes whiteness and blurs identity: "She, too, anyway, was treated like a nigger, especially by the cops, and she had no love for landlords."

The lessons of this heterogeneous gallery of tutelary figures (one could add the black painter Beauford Delaney, who gave Baldwin a home in Greenwich Village and a way out of Harlem) helped Baldwin out of the conundrum of color he faced before expatriating: "Obviously I wasn't white . . . but I didn't quite know anymore what being *black* meant." For he was becoming an intellectual after having been brought up in a world where such an aspiration was "not so much wicked" as "insane" (Standley and Pratt 5, 202). Baldwin felt he had to "re-create" himself "according to no image which yet exists in America" (6). Hence the imperative "to make oneself up as one went along" and his elaborate choreography of snow, Switzerland, Bessie Smith, et al. (*Price* 298). This is Baldwin finding a blank page upon which to improvise an oxymoronic self—*black intellectual*. Like Adrienne Kennedy constructing selfhood as collage (in which Bette Davis again is prominent, as we shall see), Baldwin performs an act of flagrant artifice, as he blends black and white, Europe and America, high and popular culture, into an assemblage designed to catalyze his artistic birth. The "specialness" that emerges—the creation called James Baldwin—embodies what he calls "enormous incoherence" and Henry James calls a "hotch-potch" (*Price* 243). Which is to say he is utterly American. Guided by "no image which yet exists in America," Baldwin's "specialness" does not divide him from others, as he feared, but connects with what his country's history has created—"an entirely unprecedented people" (*Price* 99).

We have seen that Baldwin's staging of his birth as a novelist required an initial flight from authenticity and then a leap of invention. Remaining in America, Baldwin realized, subjected one to the "fury of the color problem," not only its violence but its inertia. "The white man is sealed in his whiteness. The black man in his blackness." Fanon might as well be describing Jim Crow. Actually, he is depicting its psychic equivalent—the condition of "dual narcissism" that structures the "black-white relation." "Each [is] sealed into his own peculiarity," a separation that inevitably produces a "vicious circle" of manichean color consciousness (*Black Skin* 9–10, 44–45).

Fanon offers a sample: "I am white . . . I possess beauty and virtue, which have never been black . . . I am black; I am the incarnation of a complete fusion with the world, an intuitive understanding of the earth . . . and no white man, no matter how intelligent he may be, can ever understand Louis Armstrong and the music of the Congo" (45). While appearing to affirm race pride, these dueling fantasies of color actually create for the colonized an "infernal circle" of self-contempt. For the terms used to define black identity already concede its relegation to the realm of the uncivilized, of amoral instinct (116). This unwitting concession reflects unconscious distrust "of what is black in me," a distrust born of the "unreflected imposition of a culture"—its myths, prejudices, folklore. This imposition makes whiteness the internalized measure of what it means to be human (191). As we know, the Fanon of *Black Skin, White Masks* has "only one solution"—to reject white and black as "equally unacceptable" and to opt for the "universal" (197). In the aftermath of an end to color consciousness, "the Negro is not. Any more than the white man" (231). Or as Baldwin put it in an oftrepeated remark: "you're only white as long as you think I'm black" (qtd. Leeming 281). He insisted on placing the ultimate locus of value in whatever proves the "uselessness and the obsolescence of the concept of color" (*Price* 373).

Without the leap of invention, what prevails is "the supremacy game" (to recall Baraka's rueful phrase assessing his own sixties nationalism): various forms of tribalism, white and black. Black nationalism or Negritude fits as comfortably into this "game" as do the varieties of white supremacy. For all of them, the static, manichean color code reigns, as if coextensive with reality. In such contexts, to be black with intellectual aspirations is to be "forever in combat with" one's "own image," as Fanon described the dilemma of the colonized educated black (*Black Skin* 194). The color line preordains psychic combat, for the grid of color deems as racially discrete—(white) mind and (black) body—what *black intellectual* mixes. Thus the reduction of the black intellectual to an oxymoronic status.

So naturalized was this reduction in the world of color caste that it informed the assumptions not only of canny accommodationists like Booker T. Washington but of more politically progressive figures. In 1920 the socialist Bernard Shaw could remark without self-consciousness to Claude McKay: "It must be tragic for a sensitive Negro to be a poet. Why didn't you choose pugilism instead of poetry for a profession?" McKay answered: "poetry had picked me as a medium instead of my picking poetry as a profession." But the irrelevance of his response was brought home to him when reviews appeared in 1920 of his first book of poems. In most of them, McKay recalled in his autobiography *A Long Way from Home,* "there was a flippant note . . . at the idea of a Negro writing poetry. After reading them I could understand better why Bernard Shaw had asked me why I did not go in for pugilism instead" (*Long* 61, 88).

In two linked novels—*Home to Harlem* (1928) and *Banjo* (1929)—McKay, a Jamaican expatriate and self-styled "troubadour wanderer," in effect broods upon Shaw's question as he attempts to explore what fascinated and tormented him—the psychic tensions of being black and intellectual. His mouthpiece in both novels is Ray, a melancholy, meditative, expatriate Haitian, sidekick of two lusty black vagabonds—Jake in Harlem and Banjo in Marseilles. In both novels Ray's bitterness is bound up with a more or less permanent writer's block. A quandary gnaws at him: he loves the free-spirited, raw exuberance of life with his pals in the "Ditch" of Marseilles—"from these boys he could learn how to live." Yet "he could not scrap his intellectual life and be entirely like them. He did not want or feel any urge to 'go back' that way" (*Banjo* 322). He wants "to hold on to his intellectual acquirements without losing his instinctive gifts. The black gifts of laughter and melody and simple sensuous feelings" (322–323).

But at the end of *Banjo* Ray remains chained to the same limited choices. He opts for instinct and hoboing with Banjo, who embodies the irrepressible vitality of the "black race" (324). Banjo is surprised by Ray's decision: "Youse a book fellah," he tells Ray on the novel's last page, "and you' mind might tell you to do one thing and them books persweahs you to do another" (326). But Ray really has little choice; after all, anything beats being taken for one of the "mixed-bloods"—the "educated Negroes"—that "lost crowd" of the deracinated. The only hope of salvation for them, says Ray, is "to find yourself in the roots of your own people" (201).

McKay's scorn of the black bourgeoisie and celebration of working-class "natural gusto" as the "soul of his race" helped make *Banjo*, in the thirties, beloved of the French Negritude poets (321–322). Ignored was the novel's less affirmative strand, its grim assessment of the psychic cost on Ray of living by a "color code of class distinction" (Baraka). Amid its high spirits and pride in black soul, *Banjo* is also a portrait of a black intellectual left stillborn, thwarted by an iron polarity—instinct versus intellect—that offered no artistic fulfillment, only the prospect of regression. In his final scene in *Home to Harlem*, Ray has written his own epitaph. Just before he departs the novel, he laments the burden of his "little education." He wonders, he says, "sometimes if I could get rid of it and go and lose myself in some savage culture in the jungles of Africa. I am a misfit" (*Home* 274). So was McKay, who, unlike Ray, made his misfit status the condition of his creativity. McKay urged "group pride" and racial solidarity while being criticized for his perennial wandering, what Alain Locke called his "chronic and perverse truancy" (Locke *Critical Temper* 64).[15] He was forever wary, says Harold Cruse, "of wholehearted commitment to anything but his own art" (48).

McKay's contradictions are present in his autobiography; there he grapples with the conundrum of color that so preoccupies Ray. As if he has internalized Shaw's opposition between poet and pugilist, McKay essentializes color even as he decries "the suffocating ghetto of color consciousness" (*Long* 150). "The problem of color," he says in *A Long Way from Home*, "was my main psychological problem . . . Color-consciousness was the fundamental of my restlessness" (245). His white friends sympathize but mistakenly think he wants "merely to exchange" his "black problem for their white problem." They fail to grasp "the instinctive and animal and purely physical pride of a black person resolute in being himself and yet living a simple civilized life like themselves. Because their education in their white world had trained them to see a person of color either as an inferior or as an exotic" (245).

The equanimity of this passage is striking. For it is relatively rare that McKay affirms pride in blackness *within* rather than against "civilized life." More typically he depicts blackness as Western civilization's "great, unappeasable ghost": "how like a specter you haunt the pale devils!" (145). This, admittedly, is said in anger after his color denies him a front-row seat when he attends a play as drama critic for *The Liberator*. As he sits alone in the balcony, "quivering in every fiber," his thoughts turn to vengeful pride in the power of "Blackface" to shock and disturb white people: "make them uncomfortable; make them unhappy!" he exults. By the end of this interior monologue, McKay is dreaming of the jungle and the chance to be "a real original Negro in spite of all the crackers. Many a white wretch, baffled and lost in his civilized jungles, is envious of the toiling, easy-living Negro" (146).

It is tempting to explain the shift from the equanimity of the first passage to the romantic primitivism of this one as the product of Mc-Kay's justified fury. But the scenario of black vitalism as the envied, repressed "other" of Western rationalism summarizes the critique Ray reiterates time and again over the course of two novels. The problem with this perspective is that in criticizing whites for containing people of color within the categories of exotic and inferior, McKay repeats the same containment. This amounts to McKay's "infernal circle" (Fanon), one that he bequeaths to his surrogate Ray.

In brashly rejecting "intellect," the bookish, contemplative Ray reveals more bluster than conviction, one symptom of his general confusion. For all his celebration of "the soul of his race" and their "legendary vitality," when it comes to his own writing he disdains racial uplift and erases the color line. In a passage that Du Bois singled out for praise, Ray explains that his stories span the color spectrum—"black and brown and white"—because "if I am a real story-teller, I won't worry about the differences in complexion of those who listen and those who don't . . . a good story . . . is like good ore that you might find in any soil" (*Banjo* 115). Yet this universalism doesn't prompt him to interrogate his own fixation on color or his belief that civilization is inherently "the white man's civilization" (164). He requires these convictions as articles of faith to undergird his understanding of racism as rooted in white envy of the "happy irresponsibility of the Negro in the face of civilization" (313). To those who have put away childish things, the spectacle of blacks taking spontaneous pleasure in life baffles and torments, like a "red rag" that challenges "the mighty-bellowing, all-trampling civilized bull" (314).

In itself there is some merit in this explanation (a version of which is shared by the Frankfurt School's interpretation of anti-Semitism as cultural envy of "the thought of happiness without power" or anxiety; Horkheimer and Adorno 172).[16] The problem is the use to which it is put. It becomes not only an excuse for Ray's lethargy but also a club to beat those blacks who will not play their assigned role as oasis of the natural. Predictably, "educated Negroes" are held up for particular ridicule, for allegedly being "ashamed of their race's intuitive love of color, wrapping themselves up in respectable gray." Ray's path is clear: "No being ashamed for Ray. Rather than lose his soul, let intellect go to hell and live instinct!" (164–165). As the novel proceeds, Ray locks himself into his tidy binary allegory, which requires elaborate rationalizations to shore up the flimsiness of his categories. For instance, in a lucid moment he admits that to be "irresponsibly happy" is impossible for those, like him, with an "observant and contemplative mind." But, he claims, "a black man, even though educated, was in closer biological kinship to the swell of primitive earth life. And maybe this apparent failing under the organization of the modern world was the real strength that preserved him" (323).

The suspicion that Ray serves up this crude biologism to excuse his own "failing" is confirmed when in the next paragraph he recalls with sympathetic insight (instead of his customary mockery) the "educated Negroes he had often met in large cities of Europe." Just like the Martinican intellectuals Fanon discusses, who quote Montesquieu or Claudel in the doomed hope of erasing their color, these black urban intellectuals toted "heavy literature . . . to protect themselves from being hailed everywhere as minstrel niggers, coons, funny monkeys for the European audience—because the general idea of the black man is that he is a public performer" (323). In moments like this Ray emerges from his self-protective allegory to recognize that the despised "educated Negro" is not a synonym for race betrayal. Instead, he realizes that in venturing out to face the pressures that shape and deform their daily life, some black intellectuals attempt strategies of resistance *within* the world rather than retreating. "Find a place in it" the narrator says to Ray, as if imploring him to enter "civilized society" (324). But "Ray had found that to be educated, black and his instinctive self was something of a big job to put over" (323).

Too big a job, it turns out. Ray's internal struggle ends in a failure to find any alternative to the rigid color code he relies on to flatten the world and its options, a code that makes *black intellectual* shorthand for a painful ordeal of self-division. Having "wanted to live his life free of the demoralizing effect of being pitied and patronized" (275), Ray exits *Banjo* as he did *Home to Harlem*—an aimless "misfit," patronized as a "book fellah." The dead end in which Ray strands himself is the story in *Home to Harlem* and in *Banjo* that tends to get lost in discussions of McKay's Negritude, realism, and primitivism.[17] But McKay's subtlest achievement is his disquieting portrait of a black intellectual entangled in a web of confusion, defensiveness, and insight. Ultimately, Ray is not simply McKay's mouthpiece or surrogate but a cautionary figure of self-critique. To better observe his own knotted psyche, McKay separates himself to gain detachment and to watch his protagonist slowly suffocate amid the hectic rhythms and tumultuous vitality of the life around him. That Ray cannot confront his own futility, let alone find an antidote, becomes a measure of his terminal inertia. McKay builds this stasis into his novel. Hardly venturing from "the Ditch" of Marseille, *Banjo*'s lack of narrative momentum lives up to its subtitle— a "story without a plot." Whatever emotional power *Banjo* possesses is in its fidelity to the malaise of its self-divided hero.[18]

Home to Harlem and *Banjo* represent the black intellectual as "forever in combat" with his own image. This Fanonian theme, as we shall see, is partly what draws Baraka to McKay.[19] In his short story "New-Sense," Baraka implies that Ray suffers from "diseased intellectualism." This means "wanting to understand what's going on, rather than just getting in it moving. Like Jake and Ray in my man's book. Jake moved straight and hard and survived with a fox in Chicago" (*Tales* 96). Baraka salutes McKay and Jake for being "straight ahead people, who think when that's what's called for, who don't when they don't have to. Not the Hamlet burden, which is white bullshit, to always be weighing and measuring and analyzing, and reflecting" (96). Ray, Baraka implies, is a prototype of the intellectual as hypersensitive narcissist. Addicted to "constant dreaming," Ray's final line in *Home to Harlem* is a lament to Jake: "why are we living?" (*Home* 274). This is vintage Ray, crippled by the "Hamlet burden" (*Tales* 96). As McKay describes him, he was "too easily moved for the world he lived in . . . He drank in more of life than he could distill into active animal living. Maybe that was why he felt he had to write" (*Home* 222, 265).

For Baraka, as for McKay, this imbalance is instantiated in *black intellectual*. This identity is not only a betrayal of class solidarity with the working man's genuine blackness, but a condition of psychic torpor characterized by degrading passivity, paralyzed contemplation, and a "pale" complexion. Baraka's label of "faggot" for the (white or black) intellectual makes this effete effeminacy explicit. And Baraka's Ray embodies it; "New-Sense" depicts him "sailing around the stupid seas . . . he masturbated among pirates . . . dying from his education." Baraka reads Ray's internal combat as symptomatic of his homoerotic attachment to Jake and Banjo. McKay provides ample evidence for this, from Ray's desertion of his Harlem girlfriend ("he hated Agatha and, for escape, wrapped himself darkly in self-love") to the "French-kiss" he shares with Jake upon their reunion in *Banjo*, to his final decision to leave another girlfriend for the "joy" of life on the road with Banjo. The latter warns Ray, in the novel's last lines, "Don't get soft ovah any one wimmens, pardner. Tha's your big weakness . . . Come on, pardner. Wese got enough between us" (*Home* 264; *Banjo* 292, 326).

The most telling line in Baraka's engagement with McKay in "New-Sense" is not mockery but identification. In passing, the narrator of the tale notes that "Ray, [is] a name I'd already saved for myself" (96). This seems to nod to *The Toilet* (1964).[20] In Baraka's short play a character named Ray, a black high school gang leader and intellectual (praised by the principal as a credit to his race and "smart-as-a-whip") fights, in the high school bathroom, a white classmate, Karolis, who once made homosexual advances to him. Unlike "New-Sense," where Ray is scorned as embodying everything contemptible, *The Toilet* offers no such convenient scapegoat. Instead an open question is at its center, the question Karolis asks his would-be lover: "Are you Ray or Foots?" the latter being Ray's gang name (59).

What generates the play's tension is Ray's inability to answer the question, for his relation to Karolis is equivocal. What has gone on between them is swathed in mystery. Ray makes no denials when Karolis speaks of the love note he once sent him ("saying you were beautiful") and reminds Ray that "right here in this filthy toilet" "you said your name was Ray . . . You said Ray. You put your hand on me and said Ray!" (59–60). Ray's silence to Karolis's demand ("Did I call you Ray in that letter . . . or Foots?") infuriates Karolis. When he almost chokes Ray to death, Foots's gang pulls them apart and stomps Karolis. But his last words answer his earlier question: "No, no, his name is Ray, not Foots. You stupid bastards. I love somebody you don't even know" (60). Beaten to unconsciousness, Karolis is slumped in a heap alone on stage. Then Ray returns. The stage direction notes that he "looks quickly over his shoulder, then runs and kneels before the body, weeping and cradling the head in his arms" (62). This is the play's end.

Baraka had disowned this final tableau by the late seventies, calling it "tacked on" as a gesture of "rapprochement" and "friendship" to his white bohemian circle of the early sixties. "The manuscript stops at the end of the fight" (Reilly 130–131). Perhaps this urge to disown the final image expresses anxiety about a softening not only toward whiteness but toward its (for Baraka) virtual synonym—homosexuality. Yet the anxiety is beside the point, just as the tableau is, finally, redundant given what has already occurred: Ray's silence in the face of Karolis's recital of their intimacy and the latter's triumphant realization— "His name is Ray . . . I love somebody you don't even know." In short, the play's closing tableau underlines what already has been disclosed: a triple "rapprochement"—with whiteness and homosexuality, and the intellectual.

The Toilet presents a reconfigured Ray, no longer an impotent Hamlet (as in "New-Sense" and in McKay's novels) and instead someone we don't even know—gangleader, male lover, intellectual. Lest one conclude that contraries have been reconciled, the remade Ray is at best only inferential, existing nowhere but in the space between Karolis's insinuations and Ray's silence. Yet the "rapprochement" offered in *The Toilet,* however tentative, does expose Baraka's ambivalence toward the objects of his loathing, even his secret affinities. "Ray, a name I'd already saved for myself" distills the ambivalences that work to disrupt or at least complicate the bellicose masculinism that reigns in *Home.* Like *The Toilet, The System of Dante's Hell* is, as we shall see, at odds with its own intentions, as it too discloses the presence of "someone you don't even know"—the narrator—a black intellectual whom the author of *Home* would excoriate.

Baraka's indictment of the black intellectual as the slave of white "faggot" models exempts black intellectuals who are involved in black music and working-class folk traditions. The white model's cult of alienation defines the literary intellectual, who is alleged to have sapped black writing in America of vitality. The mediocrity of black literary production, according to Baraka, is due to its being "a social preoccupation rather than an aesthetic one" and a "rather daring way of status seeking" (*Home* 108). Black authorship amounts to little more than the desperate effort of bourgeois Negroes to whiten themselves by acquiring a specious sophistication and refinement conveyed by the mantle of white middle-class culture. Baraka finds this apolitical condition rampant in the group he most despises, the mulatto bourgeoisie. This class, addicted to the "artificial," has produced the "Negro intellectual," that hapless, compromised figure beloved by white liberals

(14). It was not Baraka but Eldridge Cleaver who provided the most notorious formulation on the subject. Cleaver equates the black intellectual (he has Baldwin in mind) with a "bootlicking Uncle Tom" who inevitably "becomes a white man in a black body" (101). In Baraka's view, either the writer dilutes black culture by abandoning "local (i.e., place or group) emotional attachments," thus becoming "yellow" or "white," or else he honors those attachments by living them as an organic intellectual (*Home* 108).

Baraka's harsh dualisms structure his social and cultural vision. And whatever ambivalences emerge, as in *The Toilet,* have escaped the fortifications of his militant color essentialism. While ambiguity may be highly prized, indeed fetishized, by new criticism as the hallmark of high-modernist irony and paradox, Baraka's color code outlaws it. He also abhors the literary artifact as a bourgeois commodity, preferring a process-oriented, functionalist poetics he calls "art-ing" (see Sollors *Populist Modernism* 77–81). Thus his Beat aesthetic clearly has pragmatist affinities, including esteem for improvisation and spontaneity. But, by the mid-sixties, Baraka's performative poetics became the instrument of his color code and any unclassified remnants were eliminated. The basic arc of his career testifies to this elimination. Baraka represents his career not as Baldwin does his—as a modernist voyage into the unknown and illegible—but as a Dantean journey from waywardness to redemption, white to black.

After setting up the Black Arts theater and school in Harlem, Baraka in 1965 returned to Newark, the city of his birth, where he still resides. He memorialized this event in the title he gave his collected essays: *Home* (1966). Its preface promises that "by the time this book appears, I will be even blacker." What had interrupted this darkening was a prolonged "go" at being white, first as a student at Howard University, where "they teach you how to pretend to be white." Then, after the air force, with a white wife, he was a Greenwich Village Beat bohemian: "having been taught that art was 'what white men did,' I almost became one" (qtd. Reilly 9, *Home* 10). But he realized he had naively entered a "bubble of fantasy"; the freedom of bohemia was little more than another version of "the elitist alienation" of high modernism (*Autobiography* 316).

Ever since Baraka's move out of the Village in 1965, observers have noted that guilt seems to have spurred his resolve to grow blacker and blacker. In his autobiography he confirms that "I *was* guilty for having lived downtown for so long with a white wife" (210). Up in Harlem he was dogged by his white past, and his rivals at the Black Arts project exploited this weakness to undermine his leadership. Another vulnerability and source of guilt is Baraka's own lack of racial purity (he describes his genealogy as mostly brown, with some yellow and a bit of white). Given his dislike of mixed-bloods, this occasions no Du Boisian pride (43). Rejecting white, embracing black: these are the exclusionary moves mandated by his zero-sum "supremacy game." The absolutism Baraka invested in both colors testifies to his need for expiation and to the futility of finding it. This circularity was Fanon's warning, one that Baraka later acknowledged he had failed to heed.

In returning home to Newark, Baraka began redeeming his status as one of the "heretics," the name he gave to those who roam hell's deepest part in the final section of his autobiographical novel *The System of Dante's Hell* (1965). The heretics, Baraka explains in the chart he supplies outlining his Dantean system, have committed "heresy, against one's own sources, running in terror, from one's deepest responses and insights." The particular heretic who descends is the protagonist/narrator. Now an air force gunner, he has fled his "own sources" and is consigned to "the Bottom, where the colored live" outside Shreveport, Louisiana. There he attempts to purge his guilt, which has accrued not only from living and writing white but also from "treachery to kindred"—helping to gang rape a black woman (107). This "imitation white boy" from New Jersey discovers grace "in the arms of some sentry of Africa," Peaches the whore. Meeting her blackens him into blissful anonymity: "I was nobody now . . . Nobody. Another secret nigger. No one the white world wanted or would look at" (*Dante* 130). Peaches has made him a real black man not by love but by violence— by slapping the white sissy intellectual out of him ("fuck me, you lousy fag," she taunts him in one of her milder moods) (140).

Yet he abandons her, and when he returns it is to hide out from the police, who he fears want him for being AWOL. Although now contented with Peaches and domesticity ("a real world. of flesh, of smells, of soft black harmonies and color"), he nevertheless leaves her again to "find sweet grace alone" (148, 150). More mundanely, he needs to escape the Bottom and return to his army unit. The scenario of redemption and solidarity is destabilized further by the novel's conclusion. The narrator/ soldier ("Mr. Half-white muthafucka") receives a beating at the hands of three black men who scorn him as a "slick city nigger." While there is a cathartic quality to the scene, the book's final line—"I woke up 2 days later, with white men, screaming for God to help me"—is equivocal about his deliverance from whiteness to blackness. As is the narrator's penultimate act: he hallucinates that he sits "reading from a book aloud" to whores dancing on tables (152).[21]

The slaps that Peaches delivers mime those Baraka administers to himself by writing a novel that intends to redeem his straying from blackness. But, as I have suggested, that straying is, finally, uncontainable. Black solidarity threatens to unravel by the end. This loss of control plagues Baraka's effort to make *The System of Dante's Hell* what he had hoped—his "breakaway book" that would definitively announce his return to blackness (qtd. Reilly 156). But a risk of subverting one's own intentions inheres in the homeopathic logic which governs Baraka's project—to write a modernist text as his way of taking leave of modernism.

With its idealist aesthetics and its commitment to sovereign subjectivity, modernism, says Baraka, fetishizes the "sensitive" observer. He equates this with self-indulgence, with the "Hamlet burden." Yet Baraka saturates *The System of Dante's Hell* in the sensitive. Until the final chapter of "fast-narrative" in the "Bottom" episode, the novel exfoliates in lyrical, if obscure detail, free "association complexes" from the mind of a bookish, detached observer ("if anyone ever lived in a closet, it was me") through whose mind pass shards of memory which eventually will cohere into narrative episodes (153, 50). Brooding, he hangs from the window or porch of his home: "Nothing to interest me but myself" (153, 50, 15). A mood of masturbatory self-absorption dominates: "On a porch that summer, in night, in my body's skin . . . Dead in a chair in Newark . . . My feet, my eyes, my hands hung in the warm air. Foppish lovely lips. Allen wrote years later. A weeping wraith" (29). In a late image that exemplifies the presiding sensibility, he recalls: "Thomas, Joyce, Eliot, Pound, all gone by & I thot agony at how beautiful I was. And sat sad many times in latrines fingering my joint" (119).

Baraka cloisters himself and his reader inside this central consciousness as a way, he hopes, to expunge the "Ray" in himself—his morbidly self-absorbed inwardness—and becomes a "Jake" down in the "Bottom" with Peaches. In other words, to purge himself of modernism, he must first craft a modernist text. And this unavoidable double bind exposes Baraka's enterprise to the risk of ambivalence. To be done once and for all with what he loathes—white, intellectual, faggot, modernism—he must first become that object of contempt. This constitutes

Baraka's "infernal circle," which ensures that he remain in combat with his own image. Whereas an iron defense system incorporated in the "color code of class distinction" insulates and sterilizes *Home, The System of Dante's Hell,* like *The Toilet,* attains aesthetic density and richness. This is derived from Baraka's unprotected stance of immanence: he is immersed within this vicious circle rather than seeking transcendence. And this immanence opens him to ambivalence, "forbidden" identifications. The status of homosexuality, in particular, is reconfigured in ways that would not be predicted given Baraka's contempt. His own narrator's homoerotic sensibility and homosexual behavior undermine Baraka's blanket hostility. Just as *The Toilet* revealed, through Karolis, that "Ray" was "a name I'd already saved for myself," *The System of Dante's Hell* also saves "Ray" for itself even as it is supposed to eliminate him and celebrate Jake's homecoming.

The novel's most graphic representation of internal combat is the allegorical playlet within the novel entitled "The Eighth Ditch." Ditch nods to the locale of *Banjo,* and the two protagonists reprise Ray and Jake: a sensitive middle-class black and an "underprivileged Negro youth." The two are Boy Scouts and share a tent. The ghetto youth dubs the other a "sheep," code for "careerist Negro."[22] The sheep lies on his stomach throughout the episode, absorbed in reading a book, a posture that confirms his attitude of contempt and condescension. The narrator of the playlet calls "The Eighth Ditch" a "foetus drama." For, it turns out, the ghetto youth embodies the sheep's future—his awakened black consciousness—and is visiting the bourgeois scout to tell him he is not yet fully born: "You sit right now on the surface of your life. I have, at least, all the black arts. The smell of deepest loneliness. I know things that will split your face" (*Dante* 84, 83).

The visitor ends up sodomizing the bourgeois scout ("I want you to remember me"), who mutters "I guess I'll get pregnant" (87). The sheep is right; the visitor has impregnated him with his future, and tells him: "you, my man, are still in a wilderness. Ignorant and weak. You can be taken. It's 1947 and there are at least 13 years before anything falls right for you" (84). In "The Eighth Ditch," homosexuality, as in *Home,* is linked (in the "sheep") to the despised passivity of elitist detachment. But, less predictably, it is also a mode of power, of consciousness-raising that initiates one into genuine blackness. It will also become at times in the novel a locus of tenderness and regard. In short, homosexuality moves from the fixity of abjection to suggest multiple possibilities.

The sheep's absorbed reading facilitates his being raped, an association between the literary and homosexual that the novel makes throughout. "In Chicago I kept making the queer scene," says the narrator, and when one pickup asks him his name, he replies: "I said my name was Stephen Dedalus. And I read Proust and mathematics and loved Eliot for his tears . . . One more guy and it was over. On the train, I wrote all this down . . . The journal says 'Am I like that?' " (57–58). The question remains open in "The Bottom." At Peaches's house his memory drifts back to "Chicago. The fags & winter" and his "hunting for warmth" (138). This fond memory of having "been loved" is directly juxtaposed against Peaches's casual brutality, her cursing, punching, and slapping that express her demand: "Get hard" (139). As she tries to arouse him, she asks: "You don't like women, huh? No wonder you so pretty . . . ol bigeye faggot . . . They let fairies" into the Air Force these days? Crying, he thinks of saying to her: "Please, you don't know me. Not what's in my head. I'm beautiful. Stephen Dedalus . . . Feel my face, how tender. My eyes. My soul is white, pure white, and soars. Is the God himself. This world and all others" (140).

"Stephen Dedalus" links this reverie to his earlier homosexual encounter and reminds him of another: a "black man under the el took me home in the cold." The next morning the narrator "crawled out of bed" and left, feeling "Loved. Afraid" (140). But in the immediate now, Peaches is upon him; weeping and humiliated, he finally performs and then slips away: "I wanted to get out. To see my parents, or be silent for the rest of my life" (141). The suicidal despair this suggests soon materializes in a voice that whispers to him; it is a man "kneeling in the dark, at the end of the world" begging for sex. Then the man starts to howl, "like some hurt ugly thing dying alone" (142). After passing this secret sharer, the narrator encounters a dying black soldier who "just moaned and moaned losing his life on the ground." Looking at the man, the narrator says: I "saw myself" (144). When he leaves Peaches for the last time, he seems to have returned to his "Ray"-like inwardness; he wonders about "what had happened. Who I was and what I thought my life should be. What people called 'experience' " (150). And then the three black men beat him.

Thus the tightly woven redemptive allegory that structures *The System of Dante's Hell* grows frayed upon close inspection. The "fast-narrative" of the "Bottom" chapter turns out to be as elusive as the "association complexes." In sum, what the novel offers, and immerses us in, is not the clarity of the color code but the opacity and untidiness of "what people called 'experience.' " In this uncertain light, the climactic moment of transition from white to black bears reexamination. Dancing with Peaches, "the light white talking jig, died in the arms of some sentry of Africa . . . I was nobody now, mama. Nobody. Another secret nigger. No one the white world wanted or would look at" (130). This affirmation of "nobody" has been described as an Ellisonian epiphany of invisibility as a mode of freedom, of "seething fluidity" and possibility. But the liberating freedom from identity in the white world that the narrator is alleged to feel as he "bathe[s] himself in blackness" may be a reading that honors Baraka's redemptive intentions but ignores their subversions in the text (see Benston *Baraka* 22; Benston "Ellison, Baraka" 336).

The struggle between intention and subversion generates a space of ambivalence that the novel, given its commitment (beginning with its title) to "system" and control, seeks to outlaw. Yet we have seen that the space of ambivalence, comprising all that is to be purged in the act of writing (whiteness, modernism, homosexuality) ends up infiltrating the system. This infiltration remains marginal, eating away at the edges of the allegory of redemption. And it must remain marginal, for the allegory prevails on condition that ambivalence not be granted recognition. The affirmation of "nobody" enforces this nonrecognition. Within its announcement of a return to mother Africa is another yearning—for the comforting protection of an oblivion that would terminate peremptorily a literary project that is losing, if not out of, control. "It was a trip toward a white-out I couldn't even understand . . . the fasteners to black life unloosed" and "you free-float."

This is how Baraka has described the anxiety that gripped him as he was "trying to become an intellectual" in the fifties (*Autobiography* 120). His novel's immanence revives his fear of becoming unloosed, of having his blackness whited out. To die into anonymous blackness would arrest the free-float, would end the threat of ambivalence. But the narrator does not die; the epiphany of "Nobody" is not definitive; the novel and the unloosening continue. In short, Baraka's "Nobody" seeks to resolve what, against his will, remains unresolved—the agon *black intellectual*.

By the mid-sixties the internal ambivalences animating *The System of Dante's Hell* would give way to the strict color code of *Home* and of the Black Arts project. In this context arose an inevitable question: On what basis is the pursuit of an elite activity—the making of art—justified? Baraka's answer implicitly invoked the familiar Leninist notion of a cadre of vanguard intellectuals: "They, the people, are the bodies . . . and it is *the heads* that are needed"—the "conscious Black Man" must "prepare the people" (*Home* 250). But these "heads" would not be the skeptical nonconformists valued by his earlier Beat aesthetic, with its esteem for artistic freedom. The "heads" of Baraka's "Black Aesthetic" movement conceive art as articulating the "correct image of the world" and as an instrument of revolutionary consciousness-raising (251). Its three watchwords are Collective, Functional, and Committing, and the art it produces, says Baraka, is "supposed to be as essential as a grocery store" (qtd. Sollors 189; see 186–187). For all its instrumentalism, Baraka's aesthetic still placed its political faith in the power of art and of intellectuals, an investment that Black Power radicals like Stokely Carmichael would find suspect, which is to say, bourgeois.

The question of how to negotiate the gap between the elite and the mass has long been a source of debate. It began with Marx's failure, says Alvin Gouldner, to "systematically confront the question" of "*who* speaks Marxism, *who* originates it, *who* calls upon the proletariat to perform its historical mission."[23] In the sixties, third world revolutionary intellectuals such as Fanon and Amilcar Cabral pondered how colonized intellectuals might resist internalizing the colonizer's imperialist perspective and help articulate revolutionary consciousness. Cabral called this resistance a necessary "reconversion" that was possible for a minority of intellectuals willing not only to speak *for* the masses in solidarity but to live *with* them on a daily basis. This daily intermixing would be mutually liberating, and provide the grounds for the intellectual to educate mass consciousness responsibly.

Such later African writers as the Kenyan Ngũgĩ wa Thiong'o reaffirmed this stance. Ngũgĩ accused two famous Nigerian writers, Wole Soyinka and Chinua Achebe, of the arrogance of class (national bourgeoisie) privilege in their construction of the intellectual as spokesman or representative for the people. Instead, Ngũgĩ stresses the need for intellectuals to "unclass" themselves and to speak not only on "behalf of" but "in terms of" the people.[24] More recently, Gayatri Spivak has sought to mitigate the same problem Ngũgĩ addresses—the inherent elitism of a "politics of representation" which presumes to speak on behalf of the subaltern. Where Ngũgĩ speaks of unclassing, Spivak urges unlearning. She argues that the feminist postcolonial intellectual must "learn to speak to (rather than listen to or speak for) the historically muted subject of the subaltern woman." And in the process the intellectual "*systematically* 'unlearns' female privilege" (Spivak 291).

Unlearning and unclassing are strategies of redemptive asceticism. And they are in the service, paradoxically, of strengthening (by chastening) the intellectual's role. Some militants push asceticism past its limits, neatly disposing of the dilemma of the intellectual's relation to the people by liquidating the intellectual. Stokely Carmichael said in 1966: "We have to say, 'Don't play jive and start writing poems after Malcolm is shot.' We have to move from the point where the man left off and stop writing poems" (qtd. Harper "Nationalism" 253). This erasure of *black intellectual* as a meaningful category expresses what one critic has called "the dominant sense of the suspect nature and relative ineffectuality of artistic and intellectual endeavours in the Black Power movement" (Harper 254). In such a context to speak of black intellectuals being in combat with their own image seems irrelevant; the internal combat is over, collective struggle erases the intellectual. There is a novel that takes as its subject the very process of erasure, and the residue it leaves.

"How to be a writer at a time like this, in the midst of the world's most painful truths, a communicator doomed to silence?" (230). This question is posed by the central consciousness of *Why Are We So Blest?* (1972), a remarkable, disturbing novel by Ayi Kwei Armah of Ghana set in the late sixties in the United States and Africa. Though the Black Power movement is a sympathetic presence in the novel, the source of the "painful truths" that ignite Armah's sense of futility is not black oppression in America. Rather, it is America's oppression of African blacks, specifically the murder of Patrice Lumumba in 1961 by the CIA. This event crystallized Armah's belief, in his words, that Western imperialism wanted only "parasitic, dictatorial regimes" and would not abide having "potentially creative Africans in power" (Armah "One Writer's Education" 47–49). Confirming this pattern were analogous imperialist efforts to promote dictators in China, Cuba, and Vietnam.

Why Are We So Blest? merits some discussion here because it complements and culminates the project Baraka set himself in *The System of Dante's Hell:* the violent repudiation of *black intellectual* as intolerably inauthentic. Inseparable from this rejection is the paradoxical strategy Armah shares with Baraka: he seeks to write himself out of high modernism by using its very techniques. Armah's radical skepticism of the value of art is expressed in an intricately crafted experiment in fragmented point of view. A controlling narrative voice (Solo) "creates" what we read, that is, he sets before us episodes of his own life as they intersect with and comment upon the excerpts he makes from the posthumous journals of a now deceased young Harvard-educated African intellectual (Modin) and his American lover, who survives.

The (intended) telos of Baraka's novel—the declaration "Nobody"—could be said to orient Armah's as well. But its meanings are quite different. Where Baraka's "Nobody" is meant to announce a moment of black solidarity, Armah's is an emblem of negation; in particular it designates his protagonist's ineluctable passage toward suicidal destruction. If, as Baraka's career attests, *black intellectual* is a dilemma from which one can escape, for Armah the status of the educated or Westernized African is nonnegotiable, a virtual suicide note. In ten years (1968–1978) Armah published five novels and in the ensuing two decades has published none. On one level this silence affirms the status of writing in the novel as an activity bereft of use or meaning. *Why Are We So Blest?* poses a question that its author finds difficult, if not impossible, to resolve: How can one write in a world where "to be an African now, and a mere artist" is "to choose to be a parasite feeding on spilt entrails" (232)?

From the novel's first sentence, the presiding consciousness, a disenchanted, deracinated Algerian translator named Solo, lives a nearly posthumous existence: "Even before my death I have become a ghost, wandering about the face of the earth" (11). But even this minimal subsistence is a scandal amid the "wreckage" that imperialism has made of Africa: "In this wreckage there is no creative art outside the destruction of the destroyers. In my people's world, revolution would be the only art, revolutionaries the only creators. All else is part of Africa's destruction" (231). Not surprisingly, Solo's creative efforts are continually stymied. Whenever he sits down and tries to write he feels behind him "presences disapproving" of his "unborn thoughts, harsh voices raised in contradiction of my unwritten words," for all around him "the revolution in its making demands . . . so much of everything" (12).

Yet what Solo's oppressive sense of futility fails to account for is the novel we are reading, which he has assembled and "authored." Somehow, in the crevices of the wreckage, in the "little speck of fugitive water sent up into the air by huge waves," there is a glint of possibility, "much as an isolated drop might in itself capture the light of the sun in a rainbow that . . . still in its shrunken round self contains an image of the larger beauty" (12). The status of these lyrical moments is double: Solo casts them in the past tense as what he "had hoped" to find, but in the act of consigning them to oblivion he has already invoked them, an erasure that leaves a residue. This double move—of invocation and erasure—is the formal device that expresses the ambivalence that marks Solo's self-divisions and confusions. More important, this ambivalence is the source of his aesthetic sensibility. Its texture is suggested when he reads Carson McCullers's *Ballad of a Sad Café*, the rhythms of the words absorbing him into its "story of the ambiguity of love, of its closeness to hate" (28). Unnerved by his own capacity for imaginative surrender to complexity, he asks himself later, "what would I not give to attain the healing simplicity of hatreds unmixed with love?" (231). He envies the "protective world of the revolutionary militant, untouched by doubts concerning purpose and personal justification" (61).

Refusing healing simplicity, Solo instead exists unprotected, open to and identifying with what he abhors, a stance which makes possible his "authorship" of the novel. Love also enables it. He has an unconfessed, unrequited, but intense love of Modin, the doomed, brilliant African scholarship student at Harvard who crosses paths with Solo in North Africa. Solo develops a friendship with Modin but fails to separate him from his American girlfriend, whom Solo loathes.[25] Left Modin's notebooks, Solo finds that they have "broken [his] paralysis," allowing him to enter into dialogue with them, as he becomes absorbed in "speculating, arranging and rearranging . . . to catch all possible meaning." Thus, as if against his will, he turns parasitism (he calls his rearranging mere useless exercise) into a condition of creativity (231).

Early in the novel, Solo despairs at being stranded between living and dying: "I wish I could have gone completely dead with the first loss of hope. To go on, capable of being moved and yet to have lost all sense of destination, to have no desired place" is "torture" (54). But this nomadism also suggests his status as an intellectual, that is, one who lives without "healing simplicity" or fixed "destination." Solo is severed from origin, "wandering about the face of the earth," and his first words suggest the primal dislocation that engenders the intellectual. He images this deracination when he calls himself "spume, a little speck of fugitive water . . . split from the parent water and flung upward into the sky" (11). What produces this spume are the huge waves "crashing against hard obstacles." Analogously, Solo's creative energies derive from what his thoughts obsessively crash against in hatred and desire—the imperialist West, the privilege of the intellectual, the possibility of love and of meaning.[26]

If the condition of being "an African now, and a mere artist" is to be a parasite on Europe, becoming an "authentic African" is an impossible project (221–222). And African intellectuals should be intensely aware of the authentic as a postlapsarian mirage. For these intellectuals are hybrid, born of "the potent poison of European penetration." Modin theorizes why no antidote has been found for the poison: those "who get into a position to find out the composition of the European poison absorb so much of it" themselves, that they "become completely incapable of creating a real, workable *maji* [antidote]. We are addicted to the poison that kills us" (222). In this journal reflection, Modin implicitly confesses his own particular addiction, his love for a self-absorbed white Radcliffe student who will be implicated in his death.

Modin writes this entry just as he is becoming convinced that his academic work at Harvard is "just a game . . . nothing real. Knowledge should be lived. So why continue" (221). How would it be possible, he ponders in his diary, "for an elite trainee in the imperial system . . . to reject the calling marked out for him and turn himself into an authentic African" (222)? Modin seems to convince himself, against reason, that a quest for authenticity will be the genuine *maji*, a way to vanquish his humiliating conviction that he is nothing more than a modern-day "slave trader" betraying his people for the profit of an elite white education and a "soft, padded" place in the ruling African bourgeoisie (235). Modin not only indicts the educated African as inherently a tool of imperialism, a "privileged servant of white empire." Intellectual labor itself becomes, for him, intrinsically a betrayal, an "unwillingness to connect organically with the African people" (221).

Modin's manichean logic flattens all to melodrama, a response which bespeaks the blind shame and rage he feels at himself and his opportunities. And this desperation makes his mixture of anti-intellectual romanticism and rigid essentialism toxic. "I find a positive direction impossible to choose," he confesses, because he has been taught only negative ones (223). Implicitly he realizes that his desire to be an "authentic African" is a "negative" direction, tantamount to a death wish, for to achieve the authentic would involve participating in "war against the invader." War, Modin declares, "should be the educational process for creating new anti-European, anti-imperial, anti-elitist values" (222). Scorning as compromise the option to "stay within elite structures to disseminate anti-elite awareness," he leaves Harvard intending to join a liberation movement in North Africa. After meeting with skepticism and manipulation from the professional revolutionaries, who are suspicious that an intellectual actually wants to engage in combat ("the battlefield is not a place for intellectuals," one tells him), Modin spiritually disintegrates and then is murdered—castrated—in the Sahara. Death brings him what he has sought for—the mark of authenticity.

The bleak impasse to which Armah leads his protagonists in *Why Are We So Blest* creatively reworks his own experience of the crisis inscribed in *black intellectual*. Armah is writing within the bitter aftermath of African independence. Seventeen years old when Nkrumah's Ghana was born in 1957, Armah left Ghana in 1959 and entered Harvard in 1960, the year sixteen other African nations achieved independence. Like many African intellectuals, Armah had been inspired by Nkrumah's initial success and also by Fanon's stirring optimism that a Marxist revolution was under way in Africa. But decolonization proved a nearly traumatic mockery of hope when it became clear how little had been changed by the removal of a colonial presence. Independence seemed to amount to an exchange of a colonial capitalist white elite for an African neocolonial one controlled by overseas capital.[27] The African bourgeois elite aspired to Western-style, consumer-driven hedonism, while the masses remained as powerless as ever.

Yet to Armah in Cambridge, Massachusetts, this process, which unfolded over a period of years, was not yet visible. Fanon's vision of radical social transformation in Africa still seemed compelling. The more immediate shock was the CIA-orchestrated murder of Lumumba, an ally of Nkrumah's and a "creative," progressive voice for African unity. This event changed Armah's relation to the United States and to Africa. As he recounted in a 1985 memoir, he shifted his course of study: he stopped studying literature and began to write fiction and also embarked on interdisciplinary work in sociology, economics, and politics to deepen his understanding of what was happening in Africa ("One Writer's Education" 47–49). He later intuited the link between his new interests as an awakening to the importance of creativity. He was most drawn to "persons and groups that had worked to create new, better social realities in place of those they had found at birth." This "more difficult and necessary type" of creativity, though essentially anonymous, was the kind to which he now pledged to devote his life.

In 1963, without gaining his degree, he left Harvard for a "7,000 mile trip over four continents." But he was only to find that "the way to a really creative existence was in fact closed to me." For what he had witnessed was the neocolonial order—"an old world masquerading as new"—subsisting as an "incurably parasitic" set of "ruling arrangements." Nine months after he left Harvard, he recalls, he "found [himself] with only one exit." It led back to Cambridge, the world he had abandoned and had come to loathe. A "nervous breakdown" ensued. He eventually recovered, took degrees at Harvard and Columbia, and then returned to Ghana.

During his convalescence one question summed up his quandary: "how to work up some semblance of motivation for living in a world dying for change, but which I couldn't help to change. I knew I could write, but the question that immobolised me then remains to this day: of what creative use are skillfully arranged words when the really creative work—changing Africa's social realities for the better—remains inaccessible?" When he decided on a writing career, he did so not because he imagined it an alternative to parasitism but rather because he saw it as "only the least parasitic option open to me." Armah remarks that as a writer he was "in the position of a spore which, having finally accepted its destiny as a fungus, still wonders if it might produce penicillin." This metaphor suggests that Armah, like Solo and unlike Modin, finds a way to sustain a faith in art within a reality of parasitism and impurity. His novel enacts this strategy by dramatizing the making of art as the residue born from the agon of the black intellectual locked in combat with his own manichean fatalism. From fungus comes penicillin; however minimal or abject, the black intellectual survives *malgré lui.*

Setting out to throw his anger "into the world's face," Ellison's invisible man realizes, after six hundred pages, that in "the very act of trying to put it all down . . . some of the anger and some of the bitterness" have been "negated." So instead of fury, "I approach it through division," he remarks, "I denounce and I defend." This becomes the way he "get[s] some of it down" on paper. "I denounce because though implicated and partially responsible, I have been hurt to the point of abysmal pain, hurt to the point of invisibility. And I defend because in spite of all I find that I love. In order to get some of it down I *have* to love" (579–580). Ellison's declaration of "division" as the fuel of his artistic making is nearly as canonical as what helped inspire it—Du Bois's description of "unreconciled strivings" and "double consciousness." Baldwin clearly stands within this lineage of fertile, catalytic ambivalence.

We have seen that Baraka and Armah also set out enraged and to enrage, only to have these passions dissipate (or at least grow more complicated) in "the very act of trying to put it all down." Yet what makes the status of ambivalence in Baraka and Armah post-Ellisonian is that it is neither declared, embraced, nor celebrated but only inferred, as if pried out against their will, in the midst of furious onslaught. But "division" subsists in their texts, even if elusive as "spume," a stubborn aesthetic wedge preventing the closure of cherished certitudes and color schemes. And at rare moments ambivalence is surmounted in expressions of human solidarity. Consider the final tableau of *The Toilet*. Consider Baraka in 1984: "Finally, I am an internationalist and it is clear to me now that all people have contributed to the wealth of common world culture" (*Autobiography* 120). Consider Solo's words, early on, in a passage easy to forget amid the fury that will occupy most of the novel: "The thing I hoped to hold was love, the attraction of one person to his opposite, the power that brings the white to the black and leads them all to open to each other areas of themselves which they have long kept hidden from everybody else" (12). This passage explains better than any other what enabled Armah to remain somehow loyal to art.

8

Cosmopolitan Collage:
Samuel Delany and Adrienne Kennedy

amuel Delany (b. 1942) and Adrienne Kennedy (b. 1931), whose respective careers in fiction and theater began in the early 1960s, are both distinguished experimental, avant-garde writers. Their work is attracting a growing critical literature; indeed, with their presence in the *Norton Anthology of African American Literature* (1996) they can now both be officially regarded as canonical. More controversial is whether they are "actually black *enough*," as Delany has described the challenge posed by skeptical white critics "who've chosen to question my blackness" (*Silent* 50–51). In response, Delany offers a counter-challenge:

> Look, I *am* black. Therefore what I do is part of the definition, the reality, the evidence of blackness. It's *your* job to interpret it. I mean, if you're interested in the behavior of redheads, and you look at three and think you see one pattern, then you look at a fourth and see something that, for some reason, strikes you as different, you don't then decide that this last person, despite the color of his hair, isn't really red-headed. (51)

In short, do not let the category (the "pattern") become proscriptive.

Kennedy's work embodies a similar warning against peremptory definition. The genesis of her remarkable memoir *People Who Led to My Plays* (1987) makes this clear. She wrote it in response to those who would domesticate her obdurate strangeness. In Kennedy's surreal dramatic universe, for instance, a young black woman in love with movies who is writing a play as her family attempts to cope with tragedy lets Hollywood stars like Marlon Brando and Bette Davis take the leading roles in her life and speak for her. Inevitably provoking bewilderment in her viewers and readers, Kennedy often faced requests for explanation. "Who influenced you to write in such a nonlinear way?" was a typical query, as Kennedy notes in her preface (*People* 3). In response she wrote an autobiography, but a nonlinear one, a wittily perverse rejoinder that frustrates the implicit demand for (linear) identity. A black intellectual yet again devises a brilliantly inventive equivocation to answer a version of the primordial question: "How does it feel to be a problem?"[1]

To return to the earlier question about being "black *enough*": if the literal reference is skin tone (both writers are light-skinned), its deeper source derives from the fact that Delany and Kennedy not only refuse the conventions and epistemology of realism and naturalism but deliberately seek to frustrate and interrogate expectations about what *black intellectual* means. Each grapples with the conundrum of color, culture, and class. Through an innovative use of collage and fragmentation, Delany's recent autobiographical writings and Kennedy's plays and memoir represent the subjectivity of intellectually precocious, intensely bookish progeny of the black upper middle class. What I will call an antiproprietary selfhood emerges from their texts, a self rendered as open and revisable, a palimpsest or braid of overlapping familial and cultural affiliations, practices, identifications, and disavowals.

For Kennedy, collage or fragmentation becomes a defense against and a counter-response to the sealed objecthood of stereotype, a logic that she shares with Fanon in *Black Skin, White Masks*. As if explicitly to affirm that affinity Kennedy quotes from Fanon in her play *She Talks to Beethoven* (1989). We shall see that his words cast a retrospective light on the evolution of her career. Collage, for Delany, arises from his sense of experience and identity as "leafy and layered" fragments that cohere provisionally into a "sweeping tapestry," sedimented with and impinging upon other fragments, a decentered ontology he images in his master-trope of suspension as a theme and technique (*Longer Views* 150, 158). In disorienting the social and psychic production of linear meaning, Delany makes imperative new ways of being and seeing. This challenge informs his memoir *The Motion of Light in Water* (1988), his collected self-reflections *Silent Interviews* (1994), and his short novel *Atlantis: Model 1924* (1995). One way he disturbs conventional ways of sense making is to displace race (which he calls a "biological fantasy") with class and, to a lesser extent, with sexuality (*Silent* 8).[2] In *Atlantis* he at times disrupts sentences and plot, suspending their forward movement by breaking them off into double columns of unrelated narrative in a quest to render materially the experience of simultaneity.

Delany's fracturing of unitary identity testifies implicitly to the relevance of double consciousness to postmodern sensibility. But if the Du Boisian legacy of dispersed selfhood endures in new inflections, what does not endure in Delany and Kennedy is the anxious obligation of race work to represent and uplift. That anxiety created for earlier generations an art and affect of ambivalence and division which reflected a struggle for artistic freedom amid racist constraint. With Delany and (especially) Kennedy that constraint and struggle remain. But they also relish fluidity and dispersal as the forms and themes of creative invention untethered to mimetic fidelity. Collage, as we shall see, is a genre that refuses to "embody a kind or class" or "to illustrate a principle"; instead it incarnates the incommensurable and thus militates against the demand to be representative. Liberated from responsibility to representation, both political and aesthetic, Delany and Kennedy bring the tensions animating the antirace race lineage to formal and psychic resolution.

Delany and Kennedy could be said to offer black intellectuals manumission of the burden of representation in a way analogous to Charles Johnson granting the slave narrative "manumission of first-person viewpoint" in his novel *Oxherding Tale* (1982). In his self-reflexive remaking of the genre Johnson liberates first-person, the one "invariant feature" of slave narrative, by exposing it as philosophically incoherent. The Self, this "perceiving Subject," not only is "anonymous, as Hume points out in his Treatise" but, "as all Kantians claim . . . is a product of experience and cannot precede it," in short, is a "palimpsest, interwoven with everything—literally everything—that can be thought or felt" (153). This explodes the fiction of the detached observer as first-person subject. In actuality, "the Subject of the Slave Narrative, like all Subjects, is forever *outside* itself in others . . . parasitic" (153). In all three writers the revelation of self as collage promotes a salutary distrust of the naturalized conventions—racial, narrative, ontological—that produce intelligibility by inflicting the segregation of discrete boundaries. Such conventions encourage what a character in Johnson's novel calls "thinking [in] *essences* . . . Giving nouns the value of existence." But "people endure. Not names. There are no 'Negroes.' Or 'women' " (146).[3]

As a signal breakthrough in the history of modernist visual and literary art, collage is an innovation freighted with technical, cultural, and ideological significance. Unsettling the boundaries of art and life, collage instills what Picasso called "strangeness" to contest the sanctions of tradition and hierarchy. Collage challenges organic aesthetics of unity, linearity, harmony, and closure. Until Romare Bearden began creating collages in the 1960s, works that Albert Murray has called "the visual equivalent to blues composition" because of their emphasis on "impromptu invention," African Americans had not usually figured in discussions of collage (*Blue Devils* 117).[4] Yet consider the paired epigraphs that Du Bois selected for each chapter of *The Souls of Black Folk*. At the head of each chapter, save the last, Du Bois juxtaposes two kinds of epigraphs and typographies—musical bars of the Slave Songs and lines of (mostly) English poetry. They can usefully be read as proto-collages that remake conventional relations of color and culture and thus anticipate the contemporary collages central to this chapter. Du Bois devised them in 1903, less than a decade before collage appeared in the cubism of Picasso, Braque, and Gris.

The musical notes Du Bois selected for his epigraphs are unidentified, but the poetry is by, among others, Elizabeth Barrett Browning, Byron, Edward Fitzgerald, Whittier, Swinburne, and Tennyson. The final chapter, "The Sorrow Songs," retains the musical bars but replaces the verse passages with lines of a "Negro Song." Du Bois then opens the chapter by explaining why each chapter includes bars of music: "They that walked in darkness sang songs in the olden days—Sorrow Songs . . . And so before each thought that I have written in this book I have set a phrase, a haunting echo of these weird old songs in which the soul of the black slave spoke to men" (536).[5] Rather than mere historical curiosities, the slave songs, says Du Bois, are the "most beautiful expression of human experience" this nation has created. Their anguish is mixed with hope that "sometime, somewhere, men will judge men by their souls and not by their skins" (544). In devoting his last chapter to explicating them, Du Bois is publicizing this hope and this unique art form that "still remains as the singular spiritual heritage of the nation" (537).

In bringing forth, if only in the silence of print, the musical notes of anonymous, communal expression—"the rhythmic cry of the slave"— Du Bois implicitly enters the sorrow songs into the world "kingdom of culture." But he does more. His paired epigraphs at the head of his chapters represent the "kingdom" itself in miniature as a utopian realm above the Veil where sorrow songs and Swinburne dwell together "uncolored." In setting together in the same space selected fragments not simply from different genres but virtually from different worlds (or at the least from radically segregated traditions, audiences, and cultures), Du Bois rends the Veil to construct proto-collages. "Coiled in a kind of anarchic symbiosis," in Eric Sundquist's suggestive phrase (468), these quotations generate a play of possibility that partakes of the democratic, indeed anarchistic force of collage. Picasso would tap this energy less than a decade later.

Not by accident was Picasso's commitment to innovation nurtured in the Barcelona of the 1890s and then in Paris; both artistic milieus were saturated in anarchist ideals of pacifism and internationalism.[6] Dismissing patriotism, organized religion, and private property, these ideals encouraged unbounded appropriation and hybridity. Inspiring Picasso's collages, for instance, were beads, shells, and fabric from Africa. For the eclectic Du Bois, Africa also proved aesthetically liberating; by mixing a "tropical African" style into his English "training and surroundings" he was able to cast off "restraint" (*Book Reviews* 9). Picasso found a strikingly "democratic way" to fulfill "the project of subverting the high art of oil painting": he clipped legible newspaper quotations, often reports of political events, and pasted them to his still life images to create his collages of 1912–1913 (Leighten 145). Picasso himself described his collage experiments as the effort to show "that different textures can enter into a composition to become the reality in the paintings that competes with the reality in nature." He sought "strangeness," he said, "because we were quite aware that our world was becoming very strange and not exactly reassuring" (qtd. Hoffman 7).

Du Bois was similarly invested, as we have seen, in employing defamiliarizing devices of estrangement in *The Souls of Black Folk*. He wove a "penumbra of vagueness" and filled his text with "abrupt transitions of style, tone and viewpoint," an abruptness nowhere more emphatic than in his bluntly incongruous double epigraphs (*Book Reviews* 9). Together their discrepant textures establish an aesthetic space of anarchic democracy that competes with a Jim Crow reality ordained as nature. The alternative realm projected by Du Bois's collages topples hierarchy and revokes class and race privilege by erasing the color line that insulates the sanctity of high (white European) culture. Du Bois, in short, exploits the bias in collage toward a liberating parataxis, a mode of presentation that accords each element the same weight by banishing preordained or systematic orders or categories.

Du Bois's collages of quotation should be regarded as part of the epoch of cosmopolitan modernism, with its international scope and anarchistic iconoclasm. Du Boisian modernism conceives the "divine anarchy" of the "kingdom of culture" as projecting a "world [that] is not to be construed as a fixed order of species, grades or degrees. It means that every existence deserving the name of existence has something unique and irreplaceable about it, that it does not exist to illustrate a principle, to realize a universal or to embody a kind or class" (Dewey *Political Writings* 46). Thus John Dewey evokes the "mathematics of the incommensurable" that takes the measure of both a democratic social order and the kingdom of culture.

Du Bois's brilliant intuition of collage as an assault on vested proprietary rights to culture provides a germane (and overlooked) antecedent, if not quite a black tradition, for approaching Delany and Kennedy. Du Bois remains compelling once one accepts the obvious—that his fervent democratic idealism altogether lacks the deadpan tonalities of contemporary irony of which Delany and Kennedy are connoisseurs.[7] But there is little irony in Kennedy's belief in a kingdom of culture; indeed, the building of her own kingdom is the principal activity in *People Who Led to My Plays*. An entry in her memoir nicely figures this project: in the 1950s she buys a "beautiful map of France" to trace the separate travels of three people whom she admires: Emma Bovary, James Baldwin (whose *Notes of a Native Son* she carries in her purse), and Marcel Proust. "My map was painted in vivid colors on papyruslike paper. I treasured it" (*People* 91).

The demand to be representative, says Delany, is as futile as "asking a farmer with a haystack to pick out the most representative straw. You just can't do it. Any straw picked out is going to be provisionally representative at best" (*Silent* 197). In place of the specious stability offered by the representative, Delany renders experience as a "progression of sensation-saturated fragments . . . fragments whose constitutive aspects always include other objects, other subjects, other sediments" (198). Thus when asked to discuss how, when young, he developed an awareness of language, Delany does not choose the ideal-typical or the exemplary, but instead evokes the paratactic "range of idiolects anyone growing up in a great American city hears and reads in any number of situations."

Language flowed over the kitchen table with his mother and aunts, to school lunchrooms where friends whispered urgent stories, to the "obscene, easy chuckling tales" at the corner shoeshine parlor, to the "bilingual jokes" of the Hispanic boys to whom he taught remedial English. Language flowed in reading novels by Dickens, Himes, and Austen, and in hearing his father's declaiming of Dunbar, Weldon Johnson, and Twain (197). Unmasterable, multiple, overflowing any structure designed to contain it, language, like experience, is in promiscuous flux—all shades and no boundaries. Belonging to everyone and no one, language mocks efforts to arrest it in claims of ownership. The aesthetic, says Delany, is another name for this elusiveness, this excess that defeats system, purposiveness, and identity (9).

Given his respect for the anarchic and uncontainable, Delany, like Kennedy, grants neither "identity" nor "race" the status of a master, transparent signifier, the telos or Truth of discourse. Since the early seventies Delany has been a devoted student of antifoundationalist thought ("Foucault, Derrida, and Barthes claim our attention because . . . they are astonishing *writers*") and a skeptic of identity politics. Group identity, he observes, disciplines and confines one even as it may grant political efficacy. Delany distrusts "Gay Identity," regarding it as a policing device when it is anything more than a "provisional or strategic reality" (*Silent* 249; *Longer Views* 142). He adds: "For me, Gay Identity . . . is an object of the context, not of the self—which means that, like the rest of the context, it requires analysis, understanding, interrogation, even sympathy, but never an easy and uncritical acceptance" (*Longer* 143). Of race, Delany says: a "complex of lies, contradictions, and obfuscations is fundamental to the very notion of race and has been used to oppress and exploit a group of people who occupy a certain historical position, who have arrived at the present along a certain historical trajectory" (*Silent* 224). When he does use "race" he is careful to ask "if that is the proper term for what I take to be in all of its manifestations a system of political repression grounded on a biological fantasy" (8).

In Kennedy's work the complex status of race as both biological and cultural fantasy is conspicuous. One way she suggests this complexity is her shifting use of quotation marks. In her memoir Kennedy occasionally puts the word *Negro* in quotes. Of Lena Horne she remarks: "In the MGM movies as a 'Negro' woman, she was magical, romantic, a person of hypnotic glamour." This first use of quotes suggests "Negro" as a (media) construct, but a paragraph earlier Kennedy describes seeing Lena Horne on stage: "a Negro woman, a beautiful, vital spectacle" (*People* 61). Here Negro implies race pride. When Kennedy learns that most of the white people in her parents' hometown in Georgia came from England, she "realized dimly that this meant some of our ancestors too had come from England, since, like most 'Negro' families in the town, we had white relations as well as 'Negro.' I became very interested in 'England' " (*People* 22). Here the quotation marks ironically inflect "Negro" to expose the fiction of race, a fiction duplicated by those whom she calls "*'White people'*: they tried to hold you back" (14). [8]

People Who Led to My Plays is a collection of titled short entries of several sentences (the longest are a few paragraphs) often juxtaposed to related photographs that together narrate Kennedy's life up to the eve of her first play's New York production. Instead of anchoring the flow of words and images to the usual narrative cruxes of Significance, nodes of epiphanic revelation and psychological depth, Kennedy evokes a dreamily associative, wayward rhythm. This establishes for the reader an intimacy with her idiosyncratic voice. But this intimacy also distances because it is nearly always mediated through objects—the welter of personal keepsakes and cultural paraphernalia that Kennedy treasures. The materiality of memory has rarely been made so vivid.

In spinning out her threads of associative memory, Kennedy often produces witty, if disconcerting, juxtapositions. Filling two pages, for instance, are five entries: "*Miss Bell:* A fourth-grade teacher. She told my mother I would have a 'nervous breakdown' if I didn't stop trying to be the best in everything in class." This is followed by "*Ginger Rogers and Fred Astaire* (after seeing their movies): Gracefulness must be sought. It's possible the sublime could exist in your daily life," then a picture of Rogers and Astaire dancing, then "*My Mother:* Her china cabinets and hatboxes. There is beauty in order," adjacent to which is a picture (presumably) of her mother's china cabinet. The next entry is "*An article (1930s) about my father:* . . . describing the intensity and fruitfulness of his social work," and then "*Hitler:* He was the person who caused a tower to be built in the school playground across the street from our house . . . This tower was a watchtower in case an attack from the Germans or Japanese occurred." In the middle of the entry (which continues onto the next page), at the bottom of the page, opposite Astaire and Rogers, is a newspaper photo of Hitler parading with Nazis.

Kennedy's rigorous parataxis shrugs off conventional obligations of sense making, leaving it to her readers to stitch together her words and images into some narrative coherence or depth. Thus one might say of the above collage that it clusters around the theme of making or imposing order. But there is a certain futility about this observation, which testifies to Kennedy's larger aim—to expose as factitious the imposing of coherence or identity in the first place. In short, *People Who Led to My Plays* "makes the possibility of its meaning its most meaningful issue," as Kimberly Benston has noted (Benston "Locating" 116). Although without a central consciousness to impose meaning within the text, the memoir makes its scrapbook form an (anti-)principle of structure, one that foregrounds the "appropriation game," to borrow Ellison's phrase, as a model of composing a life and a self. But, more precisely, we *infer* a life and a self, since, as in any stranger's scrapbook, detail and specificity combine with muteness and opacity to disorient any effort at certainty.

A lifelong collector of postcards, figurines, and photographs of family, movie stars, writers, and historical figures, Kennedy came to realize when she began to write how inextricable was her creativity from her "collection": "I was in dialogue with the photographs, prints, postcards of people. They were my alter egos" (*People* 96). Her blurring of boundaries reflects the omnivorous identifications of childhood—"how real the unreal is" she remarks after watching her young son "in his cowboy suit . . . or sitting in his Indian tent" (82). Having learned to read at age three, Kennedy has always, she says, "made very little distinction between fictional people and real people, dead people and living people . . . The point is, if I'm reading a book about Beethoven in July, Beethoven is definitely more real to me than members of my family at that moment" (Diamond "Interview" 145). She has never lost touch with the fluidity of appropriation that marks the mimetic world of childhood.

In her voracious childhood reading, Hollywood films and glamour emerged to become her prime reference points: "My mother looked to me to be a combination of Lena Horne and Ingrid Bergman" (50). In a public interview Kennedy once declared, "As long as I can remember I've wanted to be Bette Davis. I still want to be Bette Davis," an identification she explored in her 1976 play *A Movie Star Has to Star in Black and White* (qtd. Diamond "Mimesis" 131). The passions of her fantasy life saturate Kennedy's dreamlike plays. They begin, she notes, as a "growth of images" that resists the censoring intellect to express her "inner psychological confusion and questions stemming from childhood" ("Adrienne Kennedy" 1157).

In the sixties, recalls her director Michael Kahn, Kennedy was "severely ostracized. Her plays were considered neurotic and not supportive of the black community," not offering a "positive image of blackness" (Kahn 192). Kennedy herself remembers being attacked as "an irrelevant black writer . . . I was criticized because there were heroines in my plays who were mixed up, confused" ("Adrienne Kennedy" 1160). The witty understatement of this last remark is vivid once one encounters on the page or the stage the best-known Kennedy heroines. The "Negro-Sarah" in her debut work, *Funnyhouse of a Negro* (1964), comprises "herselves": Queen Victoria Regina, Duchess of Hapsburg, Jesus, and Patrice Lumumba. And the main figure of her next play, *The Owl Answers* (1965), is "She who is Clara Passmore who is the Virgin Mary who is the Bastard who is the Owl." A production note reads: "The characters change slowly back and forth into and out of themselves, leaving some garment from their previous selves upon them always to remind us of the nature of She who is Clara Passmore's . . . world." The scene is "a New York subway is the Tower of London is a Harlem hotel room is St. Peter's. The scene is shaped like a subway car" (*One Act* 25–26).

The play opens with Clara, described as a "plain, pallid Negro Woman" with the "soft voice" of a Savannah schoolteacher, seated in the subway as four people enter—Shakespeare, William the Conqueror, Chaucer, and Ann Boleyn—dressed in their appropriate period costumes. This group, called "They," recites its lines not individually but collectively. As guards in the Tower of London, "They" have the play's first word: "Bastard," uttered accusingly to Clara. "You are not his ancestor. Keep her locked there, guard." Shakespeare slams the Tower Gate shut. Clara protests: "We came this morning. We were visiting the place of our ancestors, my father and I. We had a lovely morning . . . my father leaning on my arm, speaking of you, William the Conqueror." But They interrupt: "If you are his ancestor why are you a Negro? . . . Keep her locked there" (27–28). Before long Ann Boleyn, who has turned into "Bastard's Black Mother, who cooked for somebody," tells Clara of their kinship: "Clara, you were conceived by your Goddam Father who was the Richest White Man in the Town and somebody that cooked for him" (30). The intrepid Clara, as we shall see, is not to be denied her heritage or her freedom and ends up finding God, who comes to her as an owl.

Edward Albee's production workshop, which staged Kennedy's *Funnyhouse of a Negro* in 1964, produced a more famous play that same year—LeRoi Jones's *Dutchman*. It bears comparison with *The Owl An-*

swers, for both works tap the political unconscious to release uncensored material. *Dutchman,* like *The Owl Answers,* occurs on a subway and forsakes the constraints of realism ("In the flying under-belly of the city . . . Underground. The subway heaped in modern myth" sets *Dutchman's* scene) to stage a nightmarish clash between rival white and black claims to cultural legacies. The metamorphoses and miscegenation that characterize "the nature" of the world of *The Owl Answers* rupture any possibility of maintaining discrete, stable boundaries, cultural or psychic.

In *Dutchman,* in contrast, a battle over cultural ownership at least in part sparks the war between Clay, a black middle-class intellectual, and Lula, a homicidal white woman whom he encounters on the subway. When Clay tells Lula, "in college I thought I was Baudelaire," she immediately counters, "I bet you never once thought you were a black nigger," and taunts him as "the black Baudelaire." Lula wants Clay to know his place, and calls him an "escaped nigger" who has "crawled through the wire and made tracks to my side." Before long Lula has aroused Clay's black nationalist consciousness: "you don't know any-thing," he tells her, "Not the pure heart, the pumping black heart. You don't ever know that. And I sit here, in this buttoned up suit, to keep from cutting all your throats" (*Baraka Reader* 86, 93, 97). By insisting that culture is a white preserve, the predatory Lula makes it impossible for Clay simply to be the Baudelaire he enjoyed being in college. And her sexual conquest of black men incites Clay's counter-claim that jazz is the property of white-hating blacks. By the end Lula stabs Clay, and the play concludes as she readies herself for her next victim.[9]

A ferocious verbal energy drives both *Dutchman* and *The Owl Answers,* as each unleashes the violence latent in claims that culture has a color. In *Dutchman* the rage that erupts between Clay and Lula ulti-mately amounts to their shared demand that white and black know and keep their places and protect their cultural property: each character is "in full narcissistic cry, each sealed into his [and her] own peculiarity," to borrow Fanon's words (*Black Skin* 45). In *The Owl Answers,* the distinguished foursome "They" embody this proprietary view. But it is continually undermined by the play's frenzied transmogrifications. The phantasmagoria of Kennedy's play formally enacts the impossibility of absolute ownership, of taking unequivocal title to culture or identity—an impossibility distilled into the recurring invocation of "bastard."

To read *The Owl Answers* (1965) against her memoir of 1987 (as Kennedy implicitly invites us to do) allows us to see how entwined are the biological and cultural fantasies that animate her imagination of race. To know that Kennedy's discovery of English ancestry aroused her interest in England gives a biographical literalness to Clara's defiant claim: "I who am the ancestor of Shakespeare, Chaucer and William the Conqueror, I went to London . . . They all said who ever heard of anybody going to London but I went. I stayed in my cabin the whole crossing, solitary. I was the only Negro there" (*One* 36). But the literal has small purchase in Kennedy's dramatic world. There the claims of blood and the claims of culture become virtually indistinguishable.

This blurring could hardly be otherwise for a writer who depicts her primal moment of identity formation in the following entry: "*Adrienne Ames* (my mother and my name): My mother often told the story of how when she was pregnant she went to a movie and saw Adrienne Ames and decided to name me for her" (*People* 10). And she juxtaposes to this entry a picture of her namesake, the (white) actress. Here, early in her memoir, Kennedy fashions a double genealogy: the seven words of the entry's title suggest two mothers, a cultural one and a biological one, who together produced Adrienne Kennedy. As if echoing in parodic homage Frederick Douglass's own act of self-naming (from a Walter Scott novel), she topples biology (blood, nature) from priority in any hierarchy and makes it coexist on the same plane with culture. In revealing her double maternity, Kennedy also shows, in the figure of her (biological) mother, the self's startling receptivity to and permeability by mass-produced icons of beauty.

We soon learn that movies not only presided over Adrienne Kennedy's birth but mediated and nurtured the intersubjectivity she achieved with her mother: "She shared her secret thoughts and tears over the movies she took me to see so that I learned early that there was a secret locked inside movies and songs that caused 'adults' to cry, to become quiet, to reminisce" (12). Her understanding of interiority was deepened in eighth grade after she read the English Romantic poets. Learning that in expressing sorrow and beauty the Romantics were also often social misfits and outsiders, Kennedy remarks that such were the "thoughts a thirteen-year-old 'Negro' girl responded to." Not long after, she comes to identify Wordsworth and his nostalgia for boyhood with her father's melancholy attachment to the past (42, 57).

Neither Kennedy's Anglophilia nor her bewitchment by movies is the figure in the carpet that holds the "truth" of her identity. Rather, selfhood is a theater of impulse, mimetic and otherwise, of ceaselessly shifting appropriations, identifications, and fantasies, collectively named "the people who led to my plays." This sedimented self's lability, its helpless plasticity under the impress of heterogeneous cultural commodities, inspires her autobiography's collage form. The scrapbook miscellany pays formal tribute to Kennedy's mimetic fluidity by saluting a comically various group of mentors, all experts in transformation. They include the Wolf Man (Lon Chaney: "he held a power over me. Metamorphosis . . . would become a theme that would dominate my writing"); Emerson ("From his essay 'Circles': 'there are no fixtures in nature' ") and the elusive Kim Novak in *Vertigo* ("watching [her] change identities was enthralling") (17, 109).

Of the many "contradictory voices" she hears, Kennedy says: "I didn't know it at the time, but all of these people mingling in my life, my thoughts and my imagination were leading to a strengthening of my writing" (86, 110). The act of writing, which she began in her childhood diaries, and eventually the pursuit of a life of writing, inject a saving measure of coherence into her diffuse, amorphous self. But if writing provides coherence it also violates race and gender norms. "Ever since I was twelve I have secretly dreamed of being a writer. Everyone says its unrealistic for a Negro to want to write," says Kennedy speaking of herself through a character (*One* 99). Describing anxieties she felt during the 1950s, she wonders: "was I even capable of being an author? I wanted a 'destiny.' " But "careers connected with great destiny all seemed to be for men" (*People* 94).

Not only writing but particular writers increasingly aroused her adoration and ambition. She yearns both for a literary career and for what she calls at one point (musing about three of her heroes, Brando, Elia Kazan, and Tennessee Williams) "an artistic brotherhood." "Would I ever be part" of one "like this? Ever?" (95). Asked by an interviewer if she had ever been part of a sisterhood, Kennedy responded no, "I don't feel that . . . I identify with writers—dead writers, living writers, men and women. That's given me a tremendous sense of security" (Diamond "Interview" 150).

A category neither gendered nor raced, "writers" are part of Kennedy's "kingdom of culture," which is, like Du Bois's, deracialized, beyond the veil. And, like Du Bois, Kennedy confronts within the veil the racist realities of American life. She describes herself as a "black writer who is an Off-Broadway playwright" and says that "race and the history of race, and the part race plays in world politics, is . . . very real to me" (151, 153).[10] That reality is especially acute in her most recent play, *Sleep Deprivation Chamber* (1995), about the actual arrest of her son on trumped-up charges of assaulting a police officer and resisting arrest (charges later disproven in her son's civil suit).

Kennedy's memoir concludes with her own version of that signal trope of black authenticity—a return to roots. She sails to Ghana in 1960. Nkrumah's achievement of independence made it a heady time, and this exhilarating visit sparks a breakthrough in her writing: "it was there I started the lines of two plays, *Funnyhouse of a Negro* and *The Owl Answers,* and the lines had a new power, a fierce new cadence" (*People* 119). And she publishes her first work—a short story in *Black Orpheus,* a West African literary magazine. "Are you a writer?" people now asked. " 'Yes,' I said. 'Yes' " (121). When she makes a skirt out of blue cloth with Nkrumah's face printed on it—"it had become a kind of national cloth"—she feels she has "sealed [her] ancestry as West African" (122). Kennedy's affirmation of race and writing has special meaning because it helps mitigate the trauma of racism she suffered in the early fifties in the dorm life of Ohio State and then in the English department, where, evidently, she was barred from majoring because of her race. Culture was a kingdom marked "whites only." The psychic death this rejection inflicted on her is the subject of her play *The Ohio State Murders* (1992).

Africa brings to fruition seeds of aesthetic impulses that were planted years earlier. For instance, *Guernica* led Kennedy to place her characters in a "dream domain." Now, in West Africa, she notes: "A few years before, Picasso's work had inspired me to exaggerate the physical appearances of my characters, but not until I bought a great African mask from a vendor on the streets of Accra, of a woman with a bird flying through her forehead, did I totally break from realistic-looking characters" (*People* 100, 121). What she first discovered as a child at the movies, watching *The Seventh Veil*—that the heroine, Ann Todd, "wore 'veils' to mask her hidden thoughts, feelings, and personae"—becomes an artistic resource once she is "surrounded by African masks" in Ghana (49).

For Kennedy affirming blood ties is simultaneous with affirming cultural ties. Hence it is not surprising that her return to roots fulfills a "dream of transformation" that Bette Davis first made vivid to her fifteen years earlier. Reflecting on the "avid dream of transformation" in *Now, Voyager,* Kennedy muses: "I still also daydreamed of myself as this character. She was plain. She was troubled . . . then one day she took a trip on an ocean liner and total fulfillment came to her . . . One day I'm going to take a trip on an ocean liner, I thought" (91). Her dream comes true when she and her husband take a "miraculous voyage aboard the *Queen Mary*" to Europe and West Africa. As she boards the ship, she vows that, "like the character in *Now, Voyager,* when I returned from the journey I would be transformed" (115).

The multiple reverberations of the ancestral voyage create a certain dissonance in "Myself," the final entry in *People Who Led to My Plays.* A reproduction of the postcard of the grand ocean liner that took her back to the United States is at the top of a text that tells us Kennedy returned with a completed play in her suitcase, one that would be performed a few months later in New York. "After years of writing . . . I would be on the pages of *Vogue* and in Leonard Lyons' column" (125). In this fairytale-like enactment of the American dream and of the "up from slavery" topos of triumph over adversity, Kennedy splices together artistic and racial redemption with the attainment of gossip-column celebrity status. This unsettling mix deprives the reader of any unproblematic identification with her.

And yet to call Kennedy's self-portrayal here ironic or dissonant is imprecise if it implies a lapse from some ideal harmony or organic unity. The dissonance Kennedy *does* create derives from her insistence on heterogeneity as the counter to stereotype's strict enforcement of homogeneity. As an antidote to this "crushing objecthood" (Fanon), Kennedy's paratactic style foregrounds respect for the unaccountable, the unique, that which arises from the capacity, to borrow Fanon's words, to introduce "invention into existence." That Kennedy's journey to Africa expanded her race and literary consciousness while at the same time fulfilling her effort, in her words, at "compulsively trying to make myself a twin of Bette Davis in *Now, Voyager,*" is a concatenation unchartable by system, recalcitrant to category: "how real the unreal is" can be now be affirmed by its inverse: how unreal the real is (116, 82).

To escape being sealed in the inert abstraction of objecthood, Kennedy enacts, in her own way, Fanon's leap of invention. And perhaps this is one reason that Fanon is a haunting presence in Kennedy's later cycle *The Alexander Plays.* In effect, she adopts him as a guiding spirit, for he is in sync with her own psychic and artistic working through of the conundrum of color and culture. The central figure of the cycle, Suzanne Alexander, a black American playwright who has lived in West Africa for some years, is married to David Alexander, once a colleague of Fanon's in Blida and now "a writer, political activist, and biographer of Frantz Fanon" (*Alexander* 28). David is described as "extraordinarily handsome . . . he looks like Frantz Fanon" (28). In *She Talks to*

Beethoven (1989) David is missing and feared dead. A radio report announces: "now that Fanon may be dying of cancer, Alexander has become highly vocal in keeping Fanon's words alive" (11).

One of the selections David reads is the famous opening of chapter five of *Black Skin, White Masks.* "The Fact of Blackness" begins " 'Dirty nigger!' Or simply, 'Look, a Negro!' "[11] These words rob Fanon of subjectivity, turning him into an "object among other objects" and dashing his "one great hope"—"to be of the world." Sealed in "crushing objecthood," Fanon is "indignant" and demands an explanation: "Nothing happened. I burst apart. Now the fragments have been put together again by another self" (*Black Skin* 109). This logic of willful explosion informs the end of the same chapter, when Fanon expresses outrage at how Sartre has assimilated blackness to a "minor term" in his dialectic. "The Negro is a toy in the white man's hands," Fanon notes. "So in order to shatter the hellish cycle, he explodes." Then he can rebuild with his own hands. In the chapter's final paragraph, just before lines that Kennedy has David Alexander quote, Fanon writes that he "refuses to accept" the "amputation" of being resigned to one's color. "I feel in myself a soul as immense as the world . . . my chest has the power to expand without limit" (140).

Why does Kennedy (through her surrogate Suzanne Alexander) marry Fanon's colleague, biographer, and virtual double? Why is she so keen on keeping Fanon's words alive? Because his understanding of stereotype as violent objectification and his counter-response of self-fragmentation that dismantles the object tally with her own. What is more, Fanon's logic and words help explain her artistic development, her struggle to "be of the world," to feel "as immense as the world" and "without limit." Kennedy's first produced play, *Funnyhouse of a Negro,* represents a shattered psyche but one helpless to remake or rebuild itself. For the heroine is adrift in a world of grotesquely exaggerated stock types who end up (literally and figuratively) hounding and suffocating her. *Funnyhouse,* though, served the crucial function of being purgative, a nightmare overflow of rage in metaphoric accord with Fanon's remark, also quoted by David Alexander, that "at the level of individuals violence is a cleansing force, it frees a man from despair and inaction" (*Alexander* 19). After the catharsis of *Funnyhouse,* Kennedy, akin to Fanon, devised ways, as we shall see, to remake the self and avoid being sealed in "crushing objecthood" or amputated by one's color.

Appropriately, *She Talks to Beethoven,* the play in which Fanon's presence is first manifested, abolishes barriers—racial, ethnic, or temporal—to celebrate the communion between creators. Suzanne Alexander, whose "continued deep love for European artists such as Sibelius, Chopin, and Beethoven" is well known, is writing a play about Beethoven, and while her husband is missing she converses with the deaf composer (7). Beethoven's solicitude sustains her during her ordeal. By the end, David is safe and returns home. The play's final exchange is between husband and wife:

> *Suzanne:* David. You sent Beethoven until you returned. Didn't you?
> *David's Voice:* (Not unlike Beethoven's.) I knew he would console you while I was absent. (23)

One might reasonably assume that the play Kennedy brought back in her suitcase, a play born out of a newly discovered "strength in being a black person and a connection to West Africa," would affirm blackness. But instead *Funnyhouse of a Negro* (1964) has been described as a "Lament for Being Black" (Scanlan 105). Yet this is only partially just. It is also a lament for being white. To be trapped in a world obsessed with color, black and white, is to exist as if in a funnyhouse, in a continual state of torment wherein oblivion seems a blessing. This is the unfortunate place where Kennedy's heroine "Negro-Sarah" finds herself. She first appears on stage with a bloody mass of pulp where her face should be, with a noose around her neck, and carrying her kinky hair, apparently awaiting an imminent execution that by the end she performs with her own hands. In the closing tableau she is hanging by the noose, a suicide. Residents of the Funnyhouse include Sarah's dream selves parading around in various stages of decay: a faceless man with an African mask, Jesus as a hunchbacked dwarf, and a woman (Sarah's mother) carrying a bald head back and forth across the stage. And accompanying this procession is incessant knocking on doors announcing that Sarah's father has returned: "he keeps returning forever" (*One* 21). Amid this desolate landscape the only fertility is found in Kennedy's lyrical monologues, their beauty of language embedded in hypnotic repetitions.

A tale of color as fate defines the family romance that preoccupies Sarah's life and her monologues. Color distinctions doomed her parents' marriage; her light-skinned mother quickly grew estranged from her dark father ("she didn't want him to save the black race" and "she spoke of herself trapped in blackness"), but one night he raped her ("raped by a wild black beast") and Sarah was born of that union (5, 14–15). Soon after, the mother went mad and began losing her hair ("She is in the asylum. In the asylum bald") (11). Her father tried suicide, failed, and is now seeking Sarah's forgiveness "for being black" but also is stalking her, a pursuit dramatized throughout by his relentless knocking (18). Sarah's suicide cheats her father of success.

Her color-coded fixations are evident from the start:

> We hear KNOCKING: It is my father. He is arriving again for the night. He comes through the jungle to find me. He never tires of his journey . . . How dare he enter the castle, he who is darkest of them all, the darkest one? My mother looked like a white woman, hair as straight as any white woman's. And at least I am yellow, but he is black, the blackest one of them all. I hoped he was dead. Yet he still comes through the jungle to find me. (3)

Many, and more vicious, variations are played upon these chords, all of which announce the doom of color. This fate has left Sarah permanently "in between" her dark father and her light mother.

Instead of a plot, *Funnyhouse* amounts to the menacing pursuit of one stereotype by another: Sarah "the tragic mulatta" (in this version a self-hating black bourgeois intellectual fixated on whiteness) is stalked by the "father" she disowns—the Race Man whose mother had urged him "to be Jesus" and to "Save the race, return to Africa, find revelation in the black" (14, 18).[12] But along with the rhetorical mannerisms of cliché Kennedy mixes in imagery that is opaque to analysis and possessed of the poetic precision of some schizophrenics. The Race Man's rhetoric is messianic—"heal the race, heal the misery, take us off the cross"—and regressive: he pleads with Sarah to "help him find Genesis, search for Genesis in the midst of golden savannas, nim and white frankopenny trees and white stallions roaming under a blue sky, help him search for the white doves, he wanted the black man to make a pure statement, he wanted the black man to rise from colonialism" (14–15). But preoccupied with her mother's fate, Sarah is indifferent to his entreaties: "I clung to my mother. Long after she went to the asylum I wove long dreams of her beauty, her straight hair and fair skin and grey eyes, so identical to mine" (14).

Funnyhouse bears mad witness to the derangements inflicted by the suffocating sterility of a color-coded world. Eerily nonexistent in the play is the "kingdom of culture" that *People Who Led to My Plays* so carefully constructs. Instead, we find ourselves within a carnival fun-nyhouse that seems a macabre version of Hurston's American Museum of Unnatural History. The Du Boisian ideal of a deracialized realm above the veil has been replaced by its antithesis—the national monu-ment to stereotypes sealed in the isolation of invidious racial distinction. To read *Funnyhouse of a Negro* after *People Who Led to My Plays* makes it virtually impossible to see either text separately. Together they weave a web, not of connections but of discordancies. Indeed, the play seems violently to annul the memoir.

Given that Sarah, its heroine, is "torn enough by the question of race to kill herself," says Kennedy, one is tempted to regard the play as the raw, uncensored truth of the unconscious and the autobiography as the daylight work of repression (*Deadly* viii). But this of course ignores that both texts are carefully composed performances. Rather than adjudi-cating which work is most real, we do better to grasp their relation chronologically: *Funnyhouse* dramatizes the psychic work that Kennedy needed to perform in order to avoid being paralyzed at the deathly impasse reached by Negro-Sarah. If Sarah is a kind of alter ego of her creator, she is also a grotesquely exaggerated one, as befits an occupant of a funnyhouse. As we shall see, Sarah dies that her creator survive.

Kennedy was almost trapped in her own impasse during rehearsals of *Funnyhouse* at Edward Albee's workshop. Her anxiety was great, for it was the first work that she had not "softened" and "censored." In-stead, she had permitted "the material" of her unconscious to come out "and not be frightened about it" ("Adrienne Kennedy" 1157). Yet she wavered about putting such revelations on stage. At one point she excised the text's ubiquitous use of the word "nigger" and told Albee: "I'm worried about what I said about my parents even though it was fictionalized. I don't want it performed" (qtd. 1160). But at his urging she restored her cuts and the play was produced as she had first written it.

Funnyhouse dramatizes a world bereft of any source or means to tran-scend race. But despite its suicidal terminus, *Funnyhouse* is also an act of purgation if one puts it in the context of Kennedy's career. For the play sets the stage, so to speak, for its companion piece a year later. In *The Owl Answers* (1965) Clara Passmore achieves transcendence by defying the cultural and racist interdictions of "They" (Shakespeare et al.). Ignoring their cries of Bastard, "you are not God's ancestor," Clara, in a trance, kneels to say, "I call God and the Owl answers. It haunts my Tower [the Tower of London where They have imprisoned her] calling, . . . it comes, feathered, great hollow-eyed with yellow skin and yellow eyes, the flying bastard." From her tower she calls to the Owl and to God: "I am only yearning for our kingdom, God" (40, 43).[13] The plucky, defiant Clara withstands any number of humiliations, including verbal assault and attempted rape, but will not be denied her God (in whatever form) and her human desire for a kingdom beyond this world.

"Negro-Sarah," in contrast, says "I know no places . . . I find there are no places but my funnyhouse . . . I try to create a space for myselves in cities . . . but it becomes a lie" (7). Sarah has only one refuge, her funnyhouse, which is her narrow room in a New York apartment. It is a shrine to whiteness, dominated by a huge plaster statue of Queen Victoria, Sarah's "idol" and one of "herselves." But Victoria, like the Duchess of Hapsburg (another of "herselves"), is mulatto, and her "unmistakably Negro kinky hair" is falling out in clumps (6). "Victoria's chamber," as Sarah calls her room, is papered with "old photographs of castles and monarchs of England." Victoria, Sarah tells us, "always wants me to tell her of whiteness. She wants me to tell her of a royal world where everything and everyone is white and there are no unfortunate black ones. For as we of royal blood know, black is evil and has been from the beginning" (5). In the final tableau that reveals the swaying body of Sarah hanging dead, "the plaster statue of Queen Victoria" is described as an icon of "astonishing repulsive whiteness, suggested by dusty volumes of old books and old yellowed walls" (22). Rather than offering an ideal or a refuge, Victorian gentility strangles in its own clichés and becomes synonymous with death and decay.

Faceless Sarah is forever out of place, "in between."[14] And her only positive desire is for whiteness. But this is not merely racial self-loathing. By pushing to its limit the cliché of the mulatto bourgeoisie in flight from blackness, Kennedy reveals that Sarah's desire for whiteness is, above all, a desire for oblivion that would free her of any color and indeed of any sentience. "I long to become even a more pallid Negro than I am now; pallid like Negroes on the covers of American Negro magazines; soulless, educated and irreligious. I want to possess no moral value, particularly value as to my being. I want not to be. I ask nothing except anonymity. I am an English major . . . I write poetry filling white page after white page with imitations of Edith Sitwell" (5–6). Here Kennedy turns her satiric rendering of black and white Anglophiliac gentility into an anguished quest for a terminal bleaching that effaces all.[15]

Sarah's suicide is the only present-tense action in a play compulsively absorbed in the past. Her death fulfills a craving for exit while also leaving a residue of possibility. What survives in the wake of its fury is Kennedy's artistic life, purchased at the cost of the death of her heroine, her monstrous double. By creating an asphyxiating world imploding under the weight of bloated, hideous icons of whiteness and blackness, Kennedy confronts and exorcises all that would force her to accept the "amputation" of invidious color distinction.[16] *Funnyhouse of a Negro* is an act of space-clearing reminiscent of James Baldwin's removal to the blank whiteness of Switzerland as a way to begin erasing the stereotypes that blocked his efforts to become an intellectual rather than "merely a Negro writer." As we have seen, Baldwin staged his artistic birth in response to the imperative "to make oneself up as one went along." The demand to improvise was inevitable after an upbringing in a ghetto world where aspirations to be an intellectual were "not so much wicked" as "insane." Though solidly middle class, Kennedy faced similar demands to invent and proved equal to the necessity of a violent cleansing.

James Baldwin makes a brief but telling appearance near the end of Delany's *The Motion of Light in Water*. At the urging of an Aunt who knows the older writer, the twenty-three-year-old Delany phones Baldwin. "As I dialed, I felt nervous and expectant. I'd been as impressed by Baldwin's essays as I had by any nonfiction I'd ever read." But the conversation is awkward and brief, little more than " 'I just wanted to say hello to you. It was nice to talk to you. Good-bye.' 'Good bye.' " Where, Delany wonders, "might the conversation have gone if I hadn't been leaving the next day, and I had been able to press him actually into meeting?"[17] Delany never does meet Baldwin. But their "non-conversation," as Delany terms it, is a resonant moment because it makes visible the disconnection that is the most striking link between them. As one reads Delany's memoir of the Harlem childhood of a brilliantly precocious black bisexual writer in a tense household headed by a hostile father and a protective mother, it is difficult not to be continually reminded of Baldwin. And it is just as difficult not to be struck by the vast difference within superficial similarities. To inspect some of the implicit tension between Delany and Baldwin (crystallized in the phone call) makes vivid the shaping force of social class.

Delany is a third-generation member of a distinguished Harlem family (part of which is chronicled in the 1993 bestseller *Having Our*

Say, by his centenarian aunts Sarah and Elizabeth Delany). His upper-middle-class childhood in a three-story private house (in which his father's funeral home occupied the first floor) included prestigious schools (Dalton and Bronx Science), summer camps (among them the Vassar Summer Institute for Gifted Children), and music and art lessons. Thanks to his cultured mother, also Harlem born and a subscriber to that bible of Jewish old left muckraking, *I.F. Stone's Weekly,* he received ample opportunity and encouragement. By six he was attending the New York Philharmonic's Young People's Concerts and in high school he was composing violin concertos. "My mother was always concerned," he recalls, "that my sister and I have the broadest possible cultural exposure" (202). This lesson was not lost on her son, who announces at the start of his memoir that among its inspirations are Frederick Douglass's slave narrative and *Roland Barthes* by Roland Barthes. Later we shall see how these both shape his text.

The class privilege that facilitated Delany's immersion in culture enabled him to avoid Baldwin's sense of being a "kind of bastard of the West," a status that Baldwin surmounted. But Delany also avoided what Baldwin's feeling of illegitimacy left him vulnerable to—confinement to writing about "the Negro problem." In 1955, as he introduced his first collection, Baldwin confessed the anxiety and frustration of the colonized: "the price a Negro pays for becoming articulate is to find himself, at length, with nothing to be articulate about. ('You taught me language,' says Caliban to Prospero, 'and my profit on't is I know how to curse')." He goes on to defend his subject matter: "I have not written about being a Negro at such length because I expect that to be my only subject, but only because it was the gate I had to unlock before I could hope to write about anything else" (*Notes* 6, 8).

On one level (race), Baldwin's act of unlocking emancipated Delany's generation from having to repeat his pioneering effort. But on another (class), Delany was largely exempt from Baldwin's subaltern anxieties of legitimacy. Delany's class consciousness bred a confident ease of access to Western culture. Two other factors exempted him from Baldwin's ordeal: his color (he describes himself as "light-skinned enough so that four out of five people who met me . . . assumed I was white") (*Motion* 52), and his literary ambitions. Delany's were virtually the opposite of Baldwin's. Whereas Baldwin sought and quickly achieved the status of cosmopolitan New York public intellectual, an ambition that required his expatriation, Delany stayed in New York and channeled his precocious intellectual prowess into establishing a career in a genre that offered neither mainstream fame nor influence but enough quick money to maintain his East Village bohemian life. By the early sixties paperback science fiction had emerged as a new niche in New York publishing, and by the age of twenty Delany was well positioned in the market.

But not only publishing was opening. Delany had the good luck to opt for New York bohemia at a ripe historical moment, just prior to its late-sixties mass routinization. Cheap rents, unfettered sexual opportunity, and a burgeoning avant-garde in music, theater, and literature made Greenwich Village an intoxicating experiment in leveling the boundaries between life and art. By the beginning of the sixties the stern elitist formalism of modernism was giving way to "happenings": "an idea was abroad . . . that art must somehow get up off the printed page, must come down from the gallery wall" (111).

To sum up the pivotal difference that constitutes the Delany/Baldwin connection: whereas for Baldwin in the ghetto *black intellectual* was an oxymoron that he first had to disown and then to reinvent on his own terms, Delany appropriated "intellectual" as an unproblematic, deracialized description of his immersion in cultural life. Ironically, but inevitably, Delany understands himself as an intellectual by turning against the class privileges that made possible his pursuits in the first place. In recalling his unhappy adolescent participation in "the Jack and Jill of America" network of middle-class black social clubs, Delany finds them "beneath contempt for intellectuals" (39). The petted child of the bourgeoisie rejects its social rituals by exercising the privilege of the modernist individualism that he has been carefully fed since boyhood. The scenario is so familiar in the lives of intellectuals that one almost misses how intensely and persuasively Delany here and throughout focuses on class rather than race, enacting his belief that "anything 'positive' in the system associated with 'race' can be translated into terms of class" (*Silent* 8).[18]

In the urban ferment in which he chose to conduct his life as an intellectual, the marginal status of Delany's chosen genre of writing fit easily. He felt unconstrained by the generic demands of science fiction because it involved little compromise of his high modernist literary taste. Indeed, sci-fi was an arena decidedly more plastic than the market offered by commercial fiction of the early sixties, with its bias toward bourgeois domestic subjects. Thus his novels included a "good deal of non-linear storytelling": "I would try for science-fictional effects comparable to those that, in my other reading, had so struck me . . . I knew that I wanted my books to convey the same air of abstract topicality as Auden's longer poems" (*Motion* 104).

Delany internalized the New York of the first half of the sixties as an active collaborator in his anarchic imaginative and erotic life. The activities of walking, talking, writing, and cruising for sex are entwined, and all of them occur incessantly and almost insatiably, be it on streets, subways, or bridges. This torrent of unceasing motion, traversing Central Park, the Brooklyn Bridge, the St. Marks Baths, among other places, neither possesses nor seeks any point of secure rest. The form of Delany's memoir affirms this autotelic trajectory: though the text is broken into numbered sections, the numbering is full of gaps that serve to undercut the appearance of numerical precision. Implicitly admitting this, Delany calls his book "these most arbitrary fragments" (300). Other conventional props of coherence and boundary are in evidence but, again, in parodic form. The bare frame of a bourgeois narrative is visible—a young couple, marriage, domesticity—but the actuality is anything but conventional.

The eighteen-year-old Delany shares a loving but fragile open marriage and a cramped, ratty apartment with the nineteen-year-old poet Marilyn Hacker, whom he met when they were both prodigies at the Bronx High School of Science. "Who were we, this Jew from the Bronx, this black from Harlem?" (9). Although Delany immediately mocks this "bipartite interrogation" of his own query, the question will linger, to be answered only implicitly. The East Village apartment he shares with Hacker is hardly a haven amid urban chaos, but simply more of it. Rats prowl the sink, dogs dirty the halls, friends seeking to crash often drop in, as, occasionally, do lovers who sometimes end up in bed with both of them. Delany's frankly declared homosexuality (which outweighs his bisexuality) means that, as often as not, he will be out and about, partaking of abundant "varieties of human pleasure" that 1950s New York offered the male "homosexual," to use the period word Delany prefers (175).[19]

Delany possesses a Du Boisian (and Ellisonian) capacity for thriving in a vortex of turbulent incongruities. He describes his journey from home in Harlem to school at Dalton, just off Park Avenue, as "in social terms a journey of near ballistic violence," though in personal terms it is painless (10). Bisexuality itself becomes another source of incongruity. For instance, the night before he is to travel with Hacker to Detroit to obtain a marriage license (age-of-consent and miscegenation laws made it possible for them to be legally wed in only two states) he is "in bed with an older, sensitive man. Between bouts of sex, we talked of some of my reservations" about the impending marriage. "I never regretted" having married, his companion tells him—"it's been quite wonderful for me" (3).

Instead of shaping the episode for comic or poignant or absurd effect, Delany plays it utterly deadpan. He holds the scene's multiple transgressions in suspension. Here and throughout, his characteristic tone is captured in what he says about the ride from Harlem to Dalton: the journey was "carried out each day in more or less indifferent silence." This tonality I will later describe as instancing "the Neutral" (borrowing Roland Barthes's word), one of whose forms is "suspension of judgment" (Barthes 132). The Neutral minimizes the tendency to moralize and psychologize and sets Meaning in an inferential rather than dominative register.

Suspension not only describes Delany's tone but structures his subjectivity, which takes its shape from the Brooklyn Bridge. Sexually and racially equivocal, he incarnates, in his words, a "pivotal suspension . . . a kind of center, formed of a play of ambiguities, from which I might move in any direction" (*Motion* 52). His supple stance dispenses with a depth model of the psyche, and instead Delany derives identity from his practices. Or, as he puts it, in declaring himself bisexual he was "upholding . . . the behaviorist approach to psychology ('You are what you do')" (156). This has the effect of depsychologizing subjectivity, as does the therapy program he enters when he suffers a nervous breakdown in his mid-twenties. His treatment is "firmly oriented toward the present, rather than toward the historical retrieval of psychic minutiae" of the Freudian approach (201).

On his own Delany begins "hunting through" his past. He makes the predictable discoveries (or recoveries): moments of childhood terror, rage, helplessness. And when he glances briefly at his family's distinguished social status among the Harlem elite he confronts his angry relationship to his violent, remote father, who early on suspected his son's sexuality. But this brief descent into memory is tucked away as a discrete episode in the book's final third, long after Delany's New York life has been set before us without comment. Thus the explanatory power of his psychological or "depth" narrative is minimized. The therapy program "cures" Delany without normalizing him. Instead of his being disciplined into heterosexuality, his phobias are eliminated and he is enabled to resume both his "pivotal suspension" and his up-and-down urban ramblings.[20]

It is tempting to read Delany's minimizing of psychology in his memoir as a defensive maneuver of resistance. But this interpretive temptation, which implicitly seeks to penetrate his defense and identify the "real" Delany, reflects a bias toward "depth" and misses the force of Delany's neutrality, which disdains such efforts at mastery. Barthes uses the Neutral in *Barthes,* the book Delany salutes as a predecessor. Given Barthes's famous contempt for Meaning and the Name as instruments of domination, he has an inevitable affinity with Delany. A term analogous to William James's "unclassified residuum," the Neutral connotes a defiance of "the binary prison" that produces the perfect polar symmetry and legibility of "a pure paradigm . . . without a leak, without a flaw, without any overflow toward the margins" (Barthes 133). Figures of the Neutral, says Barthes, include "delectable insignificance . . . suspension of judgment . . . the principle of delicacy—drifting— pleasure in its ecstatic aspect: whatever avoids or thwarts or ridicules ostentation, mastery, intimidation" (132).[21] In short, Barthes conceives the Neutral as suspension inflected with some of the drifting pleasures of flânerie, a mix that recalls Helga Crane's "suspensive conflict" as well as Delany's economy. The Neutral is suffused with what Barthes calls the "thrill of meaning," that is, a meaning that "does not permit itself to be 'caught'; it remains fluid," resisting "the definitive form of a sign grimly weighted by its signified" (97–98).

One reason Delany's meanings remain fluid is that they are unconstrained by the grimly weighted signifieds of black autobiography. Frederick Douglass's narrative is paradigmatic of the genre, where suffering is redeemed by violent self-assertion that culminates in accepting the mantle of Race Man and his burden of representation. Delany, to recall, initially announces Douglass's text as a precursor, but then (characteristically) suspends his presence, letting Douglass cast a shadow by virtue of remaining a silent witness. He is a ghostly presence here, as are tropes of anguish, self-hatred, victimization, redemption, and uplift, themes that would not be unexpected in a memoir of a black bisexual in fifties America. Douglass and the tropes of tragedy preside silently as the stock of background expectations that inevitably condition acts of reading and writing. And meaning is produced by the "subversion of expectations," as Delany discovered in Allan Kaprow's breakthrough performance piece of 1960 (115).

In Delany's book the generic expectations of black autobiography are subtly raised then left unfulfilled, suspended like the "near ballistic violence" hovering above the "more or less indifferent silence" in which Delany undertakes his Harlem/Dalton circuit. This standoff can be read as a figure for how Delany subverts the "general locatability of 'what happens' " throughout his memoir. Such elusiveness was a lesson of Kaprow's "Happenings in Six Parts," an epochal event in enlarging modernist sensibility. Expecting "Dionysian plenitude"—a "totalized whole" "rich in meanings . . . full of resonances"—he instead experienced "Apollonian" "sparsity," "absence, isolation" (114–115). *The Motion of Light in Water* creates in the reader a similar disorientation by its various modes of thematic and tonal suspension, which are embedded in a larger incongruity: the text's Apollonian indirection is a narrative medium that cuts against the grain of the Dionysian events it reports.

In 1995 Delany published a kind of companion to his memoir, an untypically compact and chiseled novel, *Atlantis: Model 1924*. At once family chronicle and literary history, it continues to meditate upon and ingeniously extend the figure of suspension so conspicuous in *The Motion of Light in Water*. *Atlantis* celebrates the remarkable post–World War I migration of the Delany family's second generation (ten brothers and sisters) from North Carolina to 1920s Harlem. The novel embeds this migration within the matrix of urban aesthetic modernism. Events are filtered through one particular central consciousness—the author's father, also named Sam—the youngest sibling, who in 1924 is a sixteen-year-old venturing to New York to join the family. Delany renders the urban, the aesthetic, and the modern as a visceral experience that culminates in Sam's "disorienting" walk across the Brooklyn Bridge. He is "suspended more than a hundred feet in mid-air above glass-green water" while "relishing the feel of this miraculous suspension above the brilliant river" (66–67).

The shock of suspension is pivotal: it grants Sam what he has craved from the start—the vertiginous thrill of urban immensity in overview. And crossing the bridge brings the young Delany into conversation with Hart Crane, the presiding laureate of Brooklyn Bridge and of modernism, who immediately immerses Sam in his own creative maelstrom of projections and references—Jean Toomer, Samuel Greenberg, the Roeblings, and New York as a modern, unsinkable Atlantis. Poet of the world's longest suspension bridge, Crane is also the modernist master of rhetorical suspension who defers "the semantic, referential instrumentality of language all but completely," as Delany has noted in his essay on the poet (*Longer* 210). In his lengthy exchange with

Sam, Crane articulates an aesthetic of the ineffable, the uncontainable, and the "borrowed" that the novel as a whole will celebrate as a cosmopolitan insouciance regarding ownership and origin. This relaxing of boundary is analogous to the way modernist poets, including Hart Crane, produce meaning, according to Delany—by provisionally suspending the disciplinary tribunal of "intention, consciousness, and reason" (*Longer* 193). They sit in judgment of the performance "after the fact."[22]

The special achievement of *Atlantis: Model 1924* is that Delany weaves modernism and its makers into a tapestry each of whose sides we touch: the historical moment—the intellectual ferment of "mongrel Manhattan"—and its underside, the quotidian texture of familial, daily, lived reality. Delany intimately renders the way public and private experience impinge on each other. As well, he makes an imaginative and precise intervention into modernist and African American literary history, a move evident from the start as Delany invokes traditional African American narrative tropes—"up from slavery" and the journey north—only to give them new turns.

The patriarch of the Delany clan, Henry Beard Delany, born into slavery on a Georgia plantation in 1858, is in many ways an anti-type of Booker T. Washington. Though he shares the Wizard's boundless energy, Delany concentrates on accumulating and investing intellectual and cultural capital—in his children and in the college he heads. "This prodigy of black learning, this learned black prodigy, this prodigious black learner" was a catalyst in the development of St. Augustine College in North Carolina and was later its chancellor (22). A linguist and theologian, Delany was at home in Aramaic, Arabic, Hebrew, Greek, and Latin, and eventually was elected Bishop of the (interracial) Archdiocese of North and South Carolina, the first black bishop in the United States. His wife, daughter of a free black woman and a prosperous white landowner, was educated at the college and later became dean of women. The Delanys settled their family on the campus of St. Augustine. "Growing up in that atmosphere," noted one of their daughters, "among three hundred or so college students, reading and writing and thinking was as natural for us as sleeping and eating" (Sarah Delany 62).

In the surrounding town of Raleigh racial violence was rife, and though the Delany daughter would later remark, "you'd think they'd have gone after the uppity darkies at Saint Aug's who were getting an education," racists seemed to regard the campus and the seminary (part of the college) as off-limits (109). Delany Sr. was determined that his children's privileged childhood prepare them for professional school and for the modern urban world. All were expected to leave home. "You owe it to your nation, your race, and yourself to go," his daughter recalls her father saying (112). A "voyager on the ocean of theology and ancient languages," Delany fused race responsibility and worldliness into a hybrid one might call rooted cosmopolitanism. And he instilled this dual legacy in his progeny. Of course, they had to make the necessary modifications. In *Atlantis: Model 1924* the daughter who hopes to follow her father's "linguistic explorations" as a scholar soon goes off instead to dental school at Columbia "with the realization there was little enough a black man could do with Greek and Aramaic . . . (the suffrage bishopric was after all an anomaly). Still less, a black woman" (22). She translates Seneca in her free time.

Encouraging the younger generation to sever ties to the rural South and to relocate intact in New York, Delany Sr. embodies for his children both the propulsive, deracinating force of modernity and its dispersal of origin, with respect for bonds of blood and for ancient foundations. Thus the novel's opening scene is an archetypal ritual of leavetaking whose telos is not the autonomy of bootstrap striving but family reunion. Sam, "youngest child, lightest child" of the Delany brood, is sent off in a Jim Crow train car speeding toward New York to join his already thriving siblings. This is a quite different trajectory of modernity from the one that swept up Du Bois's John Jones a generation earlier. First exhilarated but quickly an outcast, Jones would soon be even more isolated back home in the South. Sam's is a city where page two of a New York newspaper features a large photograph of a scene from Eugene O'Neill's *All God's Chillun Got Wings*. In it "white actress Mary Blair knelt on the ground beside a seated, twenty-six year old Negro actor, Paul Robeson." And she is "kissing his hand!" announces an exultant young black poet, "did you believe you were ever going to live to see something like this in a paper" (36).

Race pride merges with a universalist consciousness when, at the dinner table in Harlem, two of the Delany sisters recall their protest against *Birth of a Nation* nearly a decade earlier. They ripped down the screen and slipped away before the police arrived, an event that the newspapers dubbed a "riot." "And I'd do it again today, if I had to," one says. "The lynchings went up all over the country in nineteen fifteen—because of that movie. That's probably why they're up now. Not a man or woman, black or white, Christian or Jew, with free-thinking ideas and care for his fellows was safe anywhere in the country while that movie was on" (51). When Sam interjects, "They don't lynch Jews," his sister tells him about Leo Frank and how, when the Jim Crow laws came in, some racists regarded it as a license to kill not only blacks but "anybody they didn't like" (51).

This scene suggests that the moral universe of the Delany family is grounded in solidarity with a transracial intellectual community where "free-thinking ideas" would flourish. Bishop Delany's St. Augustine was, of course, a model of such a community. That "kingdom of culture," somehow off-limits to lynch mobs, sponsored cosmopolitan freedom, evident in the staging, for instance, of a student production of *The Importance of Being Earnest*: "they had students of *all* colors, playing whatever part they did best. They just had to be able to speak the lines" (79). Here Sam rebukes Hart Crane, who had first laughed at the idea of Wilde done "in blackface." A chastened Crane apologizes and realizes that he would have loved the St. Augustine production—"it might even have been important." Sam recalls that one of the actors had "jazzed up the lines unmercifully, strutting and flaunting every phrase," making the audience roar. "Papa had said . . . it *wasn't* supposed to be funny in the way" the actor "had made it so. But now it was hard to think of the play any other way" (79).

Crane, albeit belatedly, grasps the importance of St. Augustine's version of Wilde as a mirror of his own aesthetic of unbounded appropriation. Indeed his earliest published poem was entitled "C 33," which he first tells Sam is the number of his Brooklyn apartment, but then admits (after hearing about *The Importance of Being Earnest*) was actually Wilde's cell number in jail. Just as the student actor did, Crane has "jazzed up" Wilde, has troped him for his own uses. And "jazzing up" is an apt capsule summary of how Crane and other modernists engage with predecessors.

The creative transactions between poets are a central topic of conversation between Crane and Sam. Sam's very name facilitates discussion: "Sam—now *that's* the name of a poet," Crane tells him, for it reminds Crane of the brilliant, tubercular, Viennese-born poet Samuel Greenberg, who died in 1917 at twenty-four. Though they never met, his short, impoverished, doomed life haunted Crane and Greenberg's urban lyrics influenced his own (83). When Crane discloses that he has taken some of Greenberg's imagery and diction, Sam asks, "Can you do that . . . if you write your own poems, can you just take words and phrases from someone else's?" In response, Crane tells him about T. S.

Eliot and how "The Waste Land" is "nothing *but* words and phrases borrowed from other writers." When Sam responds, uneasily, that "taking other people's poems . . . doesn't sound right to" him, Crane explains that "taking" simplifies his relation to Greenberg: "I'll link Sam's words to words of mine, engulf them, digest and transform them, *make* them words of my own" (91).

As he is talking, Crane's eyes wander to the bridge, "up to tangle in the harp of slant and vertical cables." This fleeting detail images a tense interplay of opposites, which crystallizes Crane's aesthetic (more precisely, his aesthetic as Delany has imagined him describing it). The radical originality of Crane's art arises out of the abandonment of any conventional grounds of originality. Turning from the dream of autonomous artistic control, choice, and intention, and from hope of undefiled, authentic origination, his poetry is committed to the reimagining of literary art as the act of making the words of others one's own. Here ownership is severed from a model of private property and reconceived more on the model of a public bridge or pathway inviting anyone so inclined to use, to jazz up, someone else's words. As incessant as traffic on a thoroughfare, creative appropriation is continual, limitless, and reciprocal. For those who are borrowing words of another are, in turn, having their words appropriated. Sovereign ownership is disowned in the kingdom of culture.

And it is disowned in the kingdom of Master Builders, as the father and son who built Brooklyn Bridge discovered. The surrender of the possibility of unfettered control, of achieved intention, is at the heart of the tale Crane tells Sam of the Roeblings, the men who sacrificed their lives in making the bridge. The father—John Augustus Roebling—had "already completed the plans" and was "surveying to start the work" when he suffered a foot injury in an accident at the waterfront and died of tetanus three weeks later. His son Washington took over but was soon permanently crippled by the bends and had to direct the building by peering through a telescope from the window of his room in an apartment house overlooking the bridge (the same apartment where Crane lived). Roebling's wife became his bridge to the bridge, going "down to the docks everyday to bring his orders and take back her report" (81). Moved by Washington Roebling's plight and his improvising of a logic of delegation, Crane imagines him "spying through his glass at the stanchions he'd raised . . . till new navigators remap those voyages to and beyond love's peripheries, till another alphabet, another hunt can reconfigure the word" (81). In the fate of the heroic Roeblings, Crane limns a parable of the unraveling of imperial, indomitable mastery and its remaking as an open, provisional web of dependencies soliciting future makers.

Atlantis: Model 1924 concludes by exuberantly declaring liberation from the dominion of origin and authority. But to reach that moment one must first examine those in which it is embedded. More precisely, one must walk across the bridge of Delany's novel, whose "slant and vertical cords" are wound together. Thus to examine one cord inevitably means looking at what interlocks with it. One central narrative cable is composed of Sam's recurring memories of boyhood adventures with his best friends John and Lewy, memories that nourish him in his early days in New York. These three black boys—a generic label which ignores that one is red-headed, one a bastard, and one "high-yellow"— are obsessed with science fiction and sword-and-sorcery tales of ancient quests and lost kingdoms. Their games are full of "codes and journals and secrets and cyphers" (16). With his knowledge of ancient lore, Bishop Delany is a great resource, especially for the brilliant and ambitious Lewy. When Lewy devises a homemade clock from a kerosene can he huddles with the bishop and comes up with an elaborately drawn dial that looks like a medieval compass. But mixed in are zodiac signs and Hebrew lettering "representing a special, ancient, mystic time scale, out of Africa from before the dawn of the West—which Lewy had just made up" (64). Sam's memory of Lewy's talent for fabricating origins breaks off here, to be resumed later.

Sam's musings occur as he enters the bridge's pedestrian walkway. Just as he encounters a "cable thick as an oil drum" lifting "slant and vertical cords toward the double vault of stone," the narrative breaks off and the page splits into two columns, as if miming the bridge's expansive walkway and its "miraculous suspension" (62, 67). The narrative of Lewy and his invented ancient clock is set on the right side; the narrative on the left is set down without any introductory or identifying context, save a title mentioned in passing, *The Poetry of the Negro*. With the title as a clue, one may deduce that the left column appears to be excerpts from letters (either actual or fictive) of Langston Hughes and Arna Bontemps regarding their 1949 anthology *The Poetry of the Negro*, which included work by white poets on black subjects. At the top of the double-columned page are a few unbroken lines narrating Sam's walk on the bridge.

The page, then, has a triple set of coordinates. One element that seems to connect them is a figure mentioned in the left column—Jean

Toomer. Like Lewy, Toomer is an extravagant inventor of origins who refused to be "limited to Negro" but instead took that as a starting point and from there "circled out" (qtd. Kerman and Eldridge 97). Toomer's shadowy presence threads through the novel: he is first mentioned as a friend of Clarice, Sam's brother's fiancée, and is later described at some length by his close friend Crane. Both Crane and Clarice remark Sam's physical resemblance to Jean. The anthologists mention Toomer's confinement to a nursing home and that "his literary disappointments after *Cane* were shattering. He tried desperately to repeat that artistic achievement (but not as a Negro) and failed" (63). Toomer's refusal to respect (allegedly) fixed origins and his mystical urge to be in touch with cosmic ones led to obscurity. His reputation was resurrected with the help of Bontemps's reissuing of *Cane* in the late 1960s. And Lewy, precocious artificer of origins, also reanimates Toomer's legacy, for he will keep circling out in Toomer-like expansiveness.

Late in the novel Sam recalls the context of Lewy's expansion. With Sam and John, Lewy had devised a game in which he cast himself as the "ancient Rabbi who understands the cabala's secrets and can speak them backwards." John protests that Lewy always wants to "take things back to the Jews": "Take 'em back to somewhere else, now—Egypt. Or Africa. You should take 'em back to Africa" (113). But rather than argue over whose origin should have priority, Lewy abruptly changes the terms of the argument:

> I'm going to originate everywhere . . . from now on. I've made up my mind to it . . . From now on, I come from all times before me—and all my origins will feed me. Some in Africa I get through my daddy. And my momma. And my stepdaddy. Some in Europe I get through the library: Greece and Rome, China and India . . . And I'll go on originating, all through my life too . . . Every time I read a new book, every time I hear something new about history, every time I make a new friend, see a new color in the oil slicked over a puddle in the mud, a new origin joins me to make me what I am to be—what I'm always becoming. The whole of my life is origin—nowhere and everywhere. You just watch me now! (114–115)

But John tries to puncture Lewy's bravado ("How you gonna stay a nigger . . . if you come from so many places?"), which prompts Lewy to grant that he cannot "stop anybody calling me a black bastard."

Lewy's joyous commitment to ceaseless originating crowns the intricately imagined effort of *Atlantis: Model 1924* to dismantle the rhetoric and ideology of authenticity, to cast off the yoke of provincialism and the proprietary. By dispersing origin everywhere, Lewy desacralizes it, or, more precisely, bastardizes it. Thus he deprives the logic of identity of metaphysical grounding and mitigates its capacity to foment violence. In undermining the authority of identity/difference, with its dogmatism and exclusions, Delany embraces an alternative aesthetic modeled on the democratic freedom of collage and the practice of troping. In this context, debate over authenticity and originality is made moot. For in collage, where all is borrowed and reworked, originality is never primary, but only derived. Cosmopolitan thievery (to recall Crummell's phrase) becomes the condition of creation.

For Delany, then, collage as the "kingdom of culture" suggests an ideal at once aesthetic and ethical. At the same time, he de-idealizes the kingdom, turning it from a distant realm beyond the veil to a living reality, as accessible and functional as Brooklyn Bridge: I sit with Hart Crane and he winces not. And in bringing the Du Boisian ideal down to earth Delany is very much his grandfather's grandson. Ironically, his Delany blood "tells" most strongly in the depth of his commitment to banishing the pernicious prestige of blood, of roots. And *Atlantis: Model 1924* is a tribute to the bishop's Du Boisian antirace race legacy.

Samuel Delany and Adrienne Kennedy powerfully culminate the black intellectual lineage that is the subject of this book. In escaping "The American Museum of Unnatural History," they build upon the commitment to complexity which informed the strategies of such earlier escapees as Du Bois and Locke, Hurston, Ellison, and Baldwin. But Delany and Kennedy are figures not only of continuity but of rupture. For, as we have seen, their freedom of invention and their exuberant fracturings of narrative and psyches initiate a crisis in representation that decisively reconfigures the tradition. Never ambitious to be public, representative intellectuals in the way their predecessors sought or were forced to be, Delany and Kennedy have evolved and prospered, not without difficulty, as experimental writers for largely an avant-garde audience.[23] Indeed, this fact itself is noteworthy for its rarity in the larger context of black literary history. Both Kennedy's recent *She Talks to Beethoven* and *Atlantis: Model 1924* possess a quality of serenity without a grain of complacency. This serenity may, in part, bespeak their pleasure in the fact of artistic endurance and maturity, achievements all the more striking when set against the fact that most black literary careers of this century has been severely foreshortened.

If serenity seems an odd quality to ascribe to the frenzied, insatiable, and compulsive worlds of Kennedy and Delany, another improbable but pertinent ascription is health. It resides in their poetics of the anti-proprietary, which sets in motion the "limitless interchangeableness of cultural goods" (Locke). Given the ample evidence of the destructive consequences, global and domestic, of reducing politics to identity, this democratic cosmopolitanism awaits a hearing that it has never really been granted. One reason may be that most of us play some form or other of the "supremacy game" and anchor ourselves to a local identity or construct a universal one. But cosmopolitanism demands "a balancing act," for "we live in between."[24] Delany and Kennedy have made the fraught and elusive balance of the cosmopolitan an ideal and found it fertile with metaphors for poetry. Their achievement is at the heart of the Du Boisian intellectual tradition with its genius for thriving amid double aims, unreconciled strivings, and warring goals. "The mind goes antagonizing on."

Notes ◆ Works Cited ◆ Index

Notes

Introduction

1. This is Naomi Wolf's blurb for Michael Eric Dyson's *Between God and Gangsta Rap*.
2. A measure of how rapid change has been is that as late as 1985 Cornel West issued a dire assessment of the "dilemma of the black intellectual" as suffering isolation and marginality owing in large part to the "racially separatist publishing patterns and practices of American intellectual life" which have deprived black writers of significant "institutional mechanisms" for building the necessary "infrastructure" that would preserve and transmit traditions and stimulate exchange. Yet within a half-dozen years after West described the "tragedy of black intellectual activity," a remarkable ferment of activity on both a collective and individual level occurred ("Dilemma" 133, 139–140, 134). By 1991, in a dialogue with West, bell hooks speaks of the "joie de vivre . . . of what it means to be Black intellectuals" now (*Breaking* 4). Five years later, hooks would receive the ultimate badge of New York intellectual celebrity with the appearance of a David Levine caricature of her in the *New York Review of Books*.
3. Although Habermas's remarks about the birth of modern intellectuals specifically concern the Dreyfus Affair, his depiction could also apply to the United States circa 1900. There two complementary and opposed projects of purification were at work: a WASP elite struggled to preserve the domain of culture from outsiders, while a technocratic vanguard of functionaries professionalized and rationalized politics and knowledge. Habermas calls Heinrich Heine Germany's first "protointellectual," for he violated the divide between culture and politics yet is not part of a group intervention. "Protointellectuals" in the United States prior to 1900 would include Emerson, Thoreau, and Margaret Fuller, transcendentalists who also practiced civil disobedience (in such causes as abolitionism) without coalescing into a collective. The cosmopolitan Fuller, whom Emerson described as "our citizen of the world," is a striking precedent for the type of "impure" and anti-organic, radically deracinated intellectual that Frantz Fanon exemplifies in Chapter 3. From 1847 to 1850 Fuller lived in Rome

and actively participated in the Italian Risorgimento, inspired by her friend Mazzini's vision of a unified Italy and an eventual world confederation of nations. Fuller made the struggle of decolonization her own, minimized contact with her homeland, and identified herself as Italian. And with a kind of apocalyptic cosmopolitanism worthy of Fanon and Du Bois (and Emerson), Fuller hoped that the revolutionary upheaval she had witnessed in Rome would herald radical severance from the past and the advent of a new culture and a new era of universal equality.

4. For my purposes here I will regard identity politics, cultural pluralism, and multiculturalism as synonymous, while granting that there are non-identitarian forms of each. These forms I associate with the cosmopolitanism found in Du Bois et al. One reason identity politics is being revised is that its main (and considerable) achievements are in the past. It emerged in the mid-seventies and helped foster the influx of women and minority groups into the university and countless other institutions and professions that had traditionally been dominated by white men. Apart from this incontestable political legacy, the intellectual credibility of identity politics has always been precarious. It emerged simultaneously with theory which critiques essentialism by putting identity, representation, and authorship under suspicion. As John Guillory points out in *Cultural Capital* (1993), the multicultural campaign to make the literary canon more representative was "quite vulnerable to certain elementary theoretical objections," since it depended, for one thing, on positing the "text's transparency to the race, class, and gender experience of the author." Thus canon revision "betrays an apparently unavoidable discrepancy between theory and practice, an incapacity as yet to translate theory into political practice." While granting that the precise relation of theory to practice is elusive, prominent left intellectuals ponder whether "practice is really condemned to invoke theoretical assumptions so manifestly deficient as those which govern" identity politics (Guillory 10–11). To mitigate the intellectual limitations of identity politics, certain theorists have sought to resolve the discrepancy between theory and practice: in the notion of a provisional "strategic essentialism" (Gayatri Spivak), or in a coalitional "politics of affinity, not identity" (Donna Haraway). Others make a double move of invoking and contesting identity, affirming it as both necessary and contingent so as to interrogate and revise the exclusionary procedures which constitute it in the first place (Judith Butler and Joan Scott). Later in this Introduction I note some problems with postmodern anti-essentialism.

5. Alexander ch. 1. Kristeva equates this ability to choose cosmopolitanism with democratic freedom, with the capacity to transcend the origins that have assigned to us biological and historical identity papers (Kristeva *Nations* 16). Analogously, David Hollinger in *Postethnic America* urges a cosmopolitan multiculturalism that prefers "choice over prescription" (13). And "to promote the act of choice," says Tobin Siebers, is to define the "principal task" of "cosmopolitan morality" (68). Anthony Appiah notes that "the cosmopolitan's high appraisal of variety flows from the human choices it enables." But he adds that it is not variety, ultimately, but the "autonomy that variety enables that is the fundamental argument for cosmopolitanism" ("Cosmopolitan" 635). Long stigmatized by the left as privileged and apolitical, cosmopolitanism (like universalism)

is currently being rehabilitated. For instance, rather than conceived as detached, it is now seen as multiply attached. See Bruce Robbins, "Comparative Cosmopolitanisms," in his *Secular Vocations* (180–211). A number of feminist thinkers defend a chastened universalism. They include Naomi Schor, who reaffirms a "differentiated" universalism, and Seyla Benhabib, who argues for one that is "post-metaphysical."

6. *Antirace race champion,* despite its inelegance, will be used not to replace but in conjunction with the more generic term *black intellectual.*

7. Because the effort to construct the aesthetic as an unraced category figures prominently in the notion of black intellectual that I argue for, I have restricted my discussion to literary authors and texts. For more historical accounts of black intellectuals see books by William Banks, V. P. Franklin, Kevin Gaines, and Joy James. The epochal study is Harold Cruse's *The Crisis of the Negro Intellectual* (1967). Chapter 1 touches on Cruse.

8. This absence is being remedied. George Hutchinson's pathbreaking *The Harlem Renaissance in Black and White* (1995) emphasizes philosophical pragmatism (James and Dewey) as a catalyst in creating the "interracial dynamics" of the Renaissance. Hutchinson and I share some interests—pragmatist aesthetics and Du Bois's and Locke's Jamesian legacy, for example—but examine them in different ways.

9. "Justice and humanity must prevail" is how Du Bois phrased the Niagara Movement's demand for equal rights in 1906. The Niagara Movement, which included black educators, lawyers, ministers, journalists, and publishers, was a forerunner of the NAACP (*Du Bois Reader* 369.)

10. A basic way to prompt a rethinking of literary history is to promulgate important but little-known facts of urban intellectual geography. Consider that in the late 1920s, to quote Thomas Bender, "within the bounds of a single two-block radius centering on Thirteenth Street, between Sixth and Seventh avenues," were the offices of *The Dial, The Freeman, New Masses,* and *Menorah Journal.* And around the corner on Fifth Avenue was *The Crisis,* under the editorship of Du Bois, who was also an advisory editor of the *New Republic,* a few blocks uptown (Bender 252). The suggestiveness of this one geographic configuration for a reconsideration of the culture of modernism is immense.

11. "Ellison's retreat from Marxism," a critic has recently claimed, "threw him into unsavory political stances . . . in which culture came to be a refuge of wish-fulfillment and democratic fantasy" (Lott "New" 134). This remark is made by way of endorsing the argument of Jerry Watts's recent book on Ellison and politics, a work which provides a striking and typical instance of how incoherent the contemporary invocation of "the political" can be. At one point Watts astutely defines the "importance of Ellison's example" for the Afro-American intellectual community as calling "blacks to a commitment to artistic/intellectual excellence." Moreover, Ellison's intellectual rigor "protects the fundamental freedom of the black artist and intellectual to be an artist/intellectual without apology." This protection is especially vital for a "besieged community like Afro-America" where "intellectual activity often assumes a utilitarian ethic" (114). Watts admires Ellison's commitment to the discipline and solitude the production of art requires, yet critiques Ellison time

and again for elitism, "obsessive-compulsive intellectual style," and "extreme . . . social and political disengagement" (115–116). But why does Ellison's protection of black intellectual freedom not count as a profoundly important political achievement? Watts's moralism leaves him with no cogent answer.

12. Thus noted Stanley Aronowitz in 1996, in the context of recollecting that, a dozen years before, when he tried to stir interest in Richard Wright's late works—among others *Black Power*, his account of Ghana's independence—he had met stony silence. African Americanists tended then to be hostile to these works, explains Aronowitz, because they were constructing a black tradition "along the lines of an ethnically based vernacular and folk culture" (224).

13. I am summarizing Christopher Lasch's critique in *The Revolt of the Elites* of the professional and managerial elite that Robert Reich extols as the new class of "symbolic analysts" of the "borderless global economy" who trade on information and expertise rather than on routine labor or " 'in-person' service" (34–35). Although his incisive assessment targets only a particular embodiment of cosmopolitanism, Lasch's moralistic tone unfortunately suggests a blanket indictment that ignores other constructions of cosmopolitanism.

14. Kant is quoted by Martha Nussbaum, who argues for the influence of Stoic cosmopolitanism on him ("Kant and Cosmopolitanism" 37). Kristeva has emphasized that in the scandalous *Republic* of the Greek Stoic Zeno, men and women "freely belong to one another" in a world "that makes a clean sweep of laws, differences, and prohibitions of established society and perhaps of sociality itself . . . an overstepping of the prohibitions that guarantee sexual, individual, and familial identity" (*Strangers* 60)

15. As I will note in Chapters 1 and 2, Locke's anti-proprietary view of culture as unraced is anticipated, less self-consciously, by Frederick Douglass, Alexander Crummell, and Anna Julia Cooper prior to Du Bois's epochal enunciations at the turn of the century. We shall see in Chapter 3 that Kelly Miller in 1905 offers a notably concise and incisive formulation of the view. Postmodern tribalism and relativism are inimical to the anti-proprietary view of culture. Ernest Gellner's powerful critique of postmodernism in *Postmodernism, Reason, and Religion* (1992) coincides with this point of view. "The single most striking, indeed shattering, fact about the world I live in is that real, culture-transcendent knowledge *does* exist . . . We happen to live in a world in which one style of knowledge, though born of one culture, is being adopted by all of them." Gellner is referring to a "cognitive ethic" that absolutizes procedural, formal principles of knowledge—impartiality, for instance—that tell us "we must proceed in a certain way in our inquiries; and this principle is then certainly transcultural—it is beholden to no culture" (77–78, 80).

16. Pragmatism is a philosophy of action; therefore it conceives identity not as a grounding term but inferentially, as an effect. As C. S. Peirce showed in his 1868 critique of Descartes, which inaugurated pragmatism, this commitment to action is a way to overcome the subject/object dualism of Cartesian rationalism and individualism. William James rejected consciousness as an entity (he called it "mere echo") and, in Dewey's words, whittled down the subject to a "vanishing point" whose existence is engendered in "interaction with environing conditions" (*Later* 12: 155–156). Dewey also pointed out that this

"behavioral theory of the self" coexisted in James's thinking, especially in his *Psychology*, with a traditional dualistic epistemology that set an autonomous, separate "mind" and "world" against each other (166–167).

17. Qtd. Hatch 163, 152. The incident involved Owen Dodson's 1949 Howard Players production of *The Wild Duck*, which the columnist Drew Pearson used to debunk Robeson's charge.

18. I borrow Etienne Balibar's formulation (175).

19. Be it Lincoln's successor Andrew Johnson of Tennessee, or William Dunning and John Burgess (leading historians of Reconstruction), or much of Du Bois's own audience for *Black Reconstruction,* they all treated "evidence of Negro ability" as the "stupid effort to transcend nature's law" (726, 280).

20. But, as George Fredrickson points out, it is unfair to say that Washington abandoned the cause of equal political rights. Like most nineteenth-century liberals, Washington regarded the ballot as a privilege for literate, responsible members of the community (34–36).

21. *Pragmata* is the Greek root of pragmatism, and the relation of pragmatism to politics, we shall see in Chapter 4, is intimately bound up with the capacity to cope with unsettlement.

22. Ivan Hannaford reconstructs these distinctions in *Race: The History of an Idea in the West* (1996; 21, 51). Drawing on Hannah Arendt, Hannaford's thesis is that ancient thinkers, principally Aristotle, invented a "paradigm of thinking politically . . . an archetype of politics *qua* politics. Seen in term of its postulates, political thinking was inherently and logically resistant to the idea of race as we understand it; it was more concerned with something called 'the civic' " (8–9). Race thinking, Hannaford shows, consistently depends on the "displacement of politics" (9). This antagonism is explained by the tendency of the political idea to "see people not in terms of where they came from and what they looked like" but in terms of membership and of "civic duty that was clearly differentiated from duty to family, clan, or tribe" (12).

23. The phrase is the title of Rustin's famous 1965 essay.

24. See Jervis Anderson's biography of Rustin, esp. ch. 18.

25. In "The Conservation of Races" (1897) and the final chapter of *The Philadelphia Negro* (1899) Du Bois urged the moral regeneration of the black masses. Wilson Moses has suggested that in these years, especially in 1897, Du Bois was attempting to win Crummell's "respect and affection" and to make a "declaration of solidarity with the man he had adopted as a father" (Moses "Conservation" 286). This seems very likely and explains the stridency of Du Bois's racialism at this time. It should be added that, in Moses's view, Du Bois remained throughout his career an "authoritarian mystic" in the Crummell mold and emphatically not a Jamesian pragmatist (289). For the suggestion regarding Du Bois's influence on James see Hutchinson (*Harlem* 36–37.)

26. Like Crummell, Henry James equates cosmopolitanism and the anti-proprietary. And, like Crummell, he racializes (but also nationalizes) this gift, ascribing the flair for seizure to Americans' "exquisite qualities as a race." In 1867 James declared: "To be an American is a great preparation for culture . . . we can deal freely with forms of civilization not our own, can pick and choose and assimilate and in short (aesthetically etc.) claim our property wherever we find

it" (*Letters* 1: 77). In Chapter 7 we shall see that James Baldwin equates America with the dream of cosmopolitanism but deracializes the link. Indeed, America's cosmopolitan potential resides in the fact that the nation (in theory) was situated to prove the "obsolescence of color." Chapter 1, note 7, further discusses the cosmopolitan and the American.

27. One reason Crummell's enthusiasm for cultural impurity did not extend to racial impurity was that he sought to publicize the intellectual achievements of dark-skinned "pure Negroes" (including himself) to disprove the popular mid-nineteenth-century prejudice propagated by some Northern whites that intellectual ability among blacks was restricted to mulattoes. Alfred Moss comments that Crummell, a foe of white racism, was himself entrapped in "complexional racism" (61). Crummell's defensive stance is a reminder that propagandistic vindicationism is a burden endemic to the race man, even to a staunch integrationist and universalist like Frederick Douglass. For instance, his 1887 trip to Egypt rekindled his abiding interest in ethnology and a desire, he said, to find "evidence of greatness under a colored skin to meet and beat back the charge of natural, original, and permanent inferiority of the colored races of men." Victory remained to be won against racist science, and Douglass hoped "to be of some service" (qtd. McFeely 330) even if it "undercut his own sense of the oneness of human experience," in the words of his latest biographer (McFeely 369).

28. In another essay Crummell speaks of "the progress of humanity" and "the yet untried possibilities of culture" as ideals that "no matter who or what you are . . . are the prerogative of no exclusive aristocracy of intellect. They belong to man!" (*Africa* 372).

1. After Identity Politics

1. Michel Feher remarks that postmodern "multiculturalism's blind spot" is its "repression—in a Freudian sense—of cosmopolitanism, which represents a perspective which is erroneously associated with a liberal position" of color-blind universalism. Feher describes cosmopolitanism as " 'color-curious' rather than color-blind or color-bound" (276–277).

2. So remarks Robert Penn Warren in *Who Speaks for the Negro?* (277). We will return to this passage shortly.

3. bell hooks (*Yearning* 23). Hooks is protesting the tendency to associate blackness with "concrete gut level experience" that is hostile to "abstract thinking."

4. John Higham has linked Kallen to his fellow Jamesian Du Bois. Higham argues that in "Conservation of Races" Du Bois strikingly anticipates the revival of ethnic pride in Kallen's cultural pluralism: "Like Kallen, Du Bois was fighting against the kind of assimilation that breeds contempt for one's origins" (211). But Higham makes an important qualification: that to call Du Bois a cultural pluralist "blurs a crucial distinction"—namely that, unlike Kallen, Du Bois never invokes a vision of America as a multiethnic federation but, instead, projects an "ultimate fusion—a city of man" (212) founded on "human brotherhood" (Du Bois's phrase).

5. This defect in the pluralist paradigm is evident long before Kallen. The first

cultural pluralist, the eighteenth-century philosopher Herder, was trapped in a similar paradox. As one recent commentator summarizes: "Herder's stress on the specificity of societies or cultures provided an important antidote to the tendency of Enlightenment *philosophes* to eternalise historical phenomena under the guise of universal law. But in arguing for the incommensurability of different societies, Herder discarded the common yardstick by which to gauge humanity." Against his intentions, the consequence of Herder's "particularist outlook was to encourage a racial viewpoint . . . Herder's *Volksgeist* became transformed into racial make-up, an unchanging substance" (Malik 79).

6. This formulation is borrowed from Joan Scott in a discussion that augments her essay in Rajchman (27). Charles Altieri has described the identity/difference paradox as the "incompatible paths" pursued by postmodern politics and theory. On the theoretical level, Enlightenment universalism is indicted for blindness to particulars—"to specific interests sustained by different local social organizations." Thus intellectuals are called upon to "help cultivate differences" and thereby extend participation in democracy to the marginal and heterogeneous. "But because social power in the United States depends on having large identifiable groups with claims on social resources, there have to be ways of locating specific representatives for that heterogeneity. However, then it seems impossible to avoid translating the need for such representatives into the terms provided by some version of identity politics, since the representative has to stand for a collective, even if the collective has its origin in the very process of resisting received ideas of identity" (771–772).

7. Because it is often said to favor hybrid identity, cosmopolitanism thus appears to be another post-identity rubric that is actually old (essentialist) wine in new (postmodern anti-essentialist) bottles. But the particular construction of cosmopolitanism I emphasize in this book is noteworthy because it resists identitarianism by grounding one's relation to culture not in a prior identity, however mixed or hybrid, but in an aptitude for practicing what Ellison calls the "appropriation game"—the "precious" freedom to improvise a self (*Territory* 28). Ellison, like James Baldwin and Henry James (who stresses the capacity to "claim our property wherever we find it"), regards this capacity for "freewheeling appropriation" as uniquely encouraged by the historical circumstances of America, which lacks "a usable cultural tradition" (29). Hence all three imply that the cosmopolitan and the American are (at least in theory) profoundly entwined. But however persuasive, this nationalist construction of cosmopolitanism runs its own risk of reinscribing identity. As later chapters will show, Ellison brilliantly attempts to avoid this reinscription, as does Baldwin. The cosmopolitanism I argue for functions as a conceptual (not a nationalist) corrective of a particular kind of intellectual, political, and aesthetic error—identity thinking. It would be difficult to argue for a cosmopolitan politics, since, as we shall see, it has sponsored a whole range of political practices—integration, segregation, support of and opposition to war.

8. I discuss Als in "Race and Responsibility."

9. One major locus of a discourse of authenticity was the vogue of black primitivism promoted by white "Negrotarians" (Hurston's word) in the Harlem Renaissance. For a particular historical episode in which the problematic status of au-

thenticity conspicuously emerged see Rena Fraden's book on the Black Federal Theatre Project funded by the WPA from 1935 to 1939. The project relied on a notion of the authentic as a way for planners, bureaucrats, critics, and politicians to make demands on behalf of a single, homogeneous entity (5). Fraden traces the paradoxes that emerged when a "race" of (allegedly) natural-born actors became stage professionals expected to portray icons of the authentic.

10. This generation spans Redding, born 1906, to Baldwin, born 1924. I include Rustin (1912–1987) because, though not a literary figure, he was a man of great learning, culture, and artistic gifts—singer, musician, art collector. Deeply influenced by Alain Locke, Rustin was part of Locke's gay artistic circle in Harlem of the late thirties. Owen Dodson (1914–1983) was an innovative theatre director, poet, and novelist, best known as the head of Howard University's famous drama department from 1948 to 1970. Gordon Heath (1918–1991) was a distinguished classical actor from New York who, after a considerable success on Broadway in the forties, chose to live and work mainly in Europe. His autobiography, *Deep Are the Roots,* imparts a vivid sense of lives (his own and his friend Dodson's) devoted to aesthetic experience in a white and black world suspicious of such devotion. Once, after Marian Anderson sang at Howard, Dodson mocked the passivity of his students, who had been intimidated by her singing of Schubert and Brahms but excited when she sang spirituals: "you didn't let her take you any further than you had already gone." This anecdote suggests Heath's and Dodson's dedication to breaking the grip of stereotype by, in Heath's words, "escaping into art . . . and rejecting the implied limitations of color and background" (69, 51). Like Rustin, Heath, Dodson, and James Baldwin each enjoyed his own interracial gay social and romantic life that was discreet in public since they also had other lives to lead. This cluster seems to confirm what the historian George Chauncey has concluded about gay New York, especially in the thirties and forties: that conducting multiple lives "was relatively easy for many men because they did not consider their homosexual identity to be their only important identity" (273).

11. Perhaps one explanation of the irrelevance of Baldwin's dialectic is that Johnson was a doctoral student in philosophy, concentrating on phenomenology and Eastern philosophy. Intense devotion to abstract thought would be likely to universalize one's relation to culture. "It's all a long conversation," notes Johnson of intellectual history (166). Significantly, accompanying Johnson's universalism is his conception of self as "palimpsest," as Chapter 8 will note.

12. This is how Michael Lind in *The Next American Nation* (1995) has described Toomer (300). In Lind's brief for a transracial "trans-American nationality," Toomer is at last given his due. Toomer's time has come because the United States has now achieved a "transracial *cultural majority*" that is growing ever larger than the "white *racial majority*" (277).

13. What complicates Toomer's coldness to the Harlem Renaissance's "trumpeting" of the Negro is that Toomer himself had made a pilgrimage in 1921 to rural Southern roots and had a powerful experience of his group identity (Kerman and Eldridge 83). But he regarded his sojourn of two months (which he repeated with Waldo Frank a year later for a week) less as permanently transformative than as discrete and as instrumental—fieldwork for composing *Cane.*

14. As George Hutchinson has noted, Toomer's sense of the "general inadequacy of language" about race helps explain why mysticism, "a route to knowledge 'beyond words' " would appeal to him ("Toomer" 231). In his essay "Jean Toomer and American Racial Discourse" Hutchinson analyzes Toomer's "entrapment in a racialist language."

15. Redding's disgust with the burden of race uplift took interesting expression in his 1950 novel *Stranger and Alone*. This portrait of a career black educator and administrator in the Southern black college system is an indelible portrait of an antirace man. Shelton Howden is a corrosively cynical self-styled "realist" and "white man's nigger" (136) who does the bidding of Southern racists and despises any free-thinking black people. What makes the novel chilling is the rigor of Redding's authorial reticence; he refuses to redeem or damn Howden or offer any resolution. This makes it difficult to recuperate *Stranger and Alone* as a cautionary tale that Redding writes as if to remind himself about the dangers of turning against uplift obligations.

16. E. Franklin Frazier, Abram Harris, and Ralph Bunche at Howard University were persistent critics of Du Bois's voluntary segregation program in the thirties, preferring interracial labor agitation. Their critique is the subject of the opening two chapters of James Young's *Black Writers of the Thirties*. I discuss Du Bois's segregation strategy in Chapter 4.

17. For another view of Du Bois's commitment to sacrifice and its wider cultural resonances see Susan Mizruchi's probing essay.

18. For instance, Shamoon Zamir in *Dark Voices* argues that William James was a negative, conservative influence on Du Bois. To defend this thesis requires him to dismiss a number of passages in Du Bois's autobiographical writings where he pays explicit personal and intellectual homage to James. See, e.g., Zamir, 11, 73, 98.

19. Du Bois's autobiographical writings represent his life "not so much as a linear trajectory but as a palimpsest in visible and continuous process," as Zamir aptly remarks (205).

20. Pragmatism's regard for creative action (i.e. "subject to little pressure to achieve unequivocal ends") decisively departs from utilitarian or instrumental models, as Hans Joas reminds us (21). This point bears emphasis because pragmatism has typically been equated with an ideology of social engineering and control. But, notes Joas, "for Dewey, pragmatism was nothing less than a means to criticize those aspects of American life 'which make action an end in itself and which conceive ends too narrowly and too "practically." ' " Joas is quoting from a 1931 statement of Dewey's.

21. This is the persuasive argument of L. W. Phillips in "W. E. B. Du Bois and Soviet Communism: *The Black Flame* as Socialist Realism."

22. Save for an unease with Du Bois's elitism, West's latest assessment of Du Bois seems at odds with his account in *The American Evasion of Philosophy* (1989). Largely absent from West's latest discussion is his earlier image of Du Bois the radical democratic pragmatist who corrects the "blindnesses and silences" about race and the poor that limit the Emersonian tradition of "self-creation and individuality" (146, 143).

23. This formulation adapts Pierre Bourdieu's construction of the figure of the

intellectual as a "paradoxical synthesis of the opposites of retreat and engagement" ("Corporatism" 101). Bourdieu's account of the genesis of the modern intellectual is discussed in Chapter 2.

24. Cruse and Rampersad have influenced my thinking about Du Bois's career, particularly his commitment to intricacy and doubleness, though I interpret and contextualize this commitment in different ways. For instance, I diverge from Rampersad's emphasis on synthesis; his Du Bois habitually seeks to reconcile, resolve, and balance liberalism, Marxism, and race work. Cruse, in a remarkable mix of exhilarating vituperation and richly detailed historical insight, castigates integrationists and nationalists alike for repeated failure to understand that "effective black revolution in the United States" requires black intellectuals to bind together economic, political, cultural, and imperialistic strands into a "meaningful critique" (475, 485–486, 540). While Cruse urges a sternly self-critical nationalism (542), his blind spot is any notion of a dialectical universalism. Instead, for Cruse universalism is a synonym for pseudo-universalism, a cover by which liberal integrationists, black and white, control black artistic production (282–283). His suspicions of universalism are grounded in the realities of his historical moment—the New York arts world, circa 1940–1965. Understandably, Cruse's nationalism is sympathetic to cultural pluralism. He salutes Randolph Bourne (who revered William James but derived his pluralism from Horace Kallen). In calling for a "complete democratization of the national cultural ethos," Cruse commends Bourne's critique of WASP hegemony. America, said Cruse in 1967, is a "nation of minorities ruled by a minority of one—it thinks and acts as if it were a nation of white Anglo-Saxon Protestants" and thereby has "crippled and smothered the cultivation of a democratic cultural pluralism in America" (456–457). Cruse's plea for pluralism was timely and was largely fulfilled in the next two decades.

25. Jameson is drawing on what he calls the "tragic sense of life" instantiated in the "great sociologists, from Weber and Veblen to Bourdieu," all of whom esteem "glacial disengagement" as the condition of sociological knowledge (278).

26. The authors whose essays are collected in *The Identity in Question*, ed. John Rajchman, pursue an internal leftist critique of identity politics. In addition to Jameson's essay, see Joan Scott's and esp. Wendy Brown's. Brown's Nietzschean analysis shows that identity politics is rooted in *ressentiment* (as is identity itself for Nietzsche) and thus "deeply invested in its own impotence," which it seeks to assuage "through its vengeful moralizing" (217).

27. But West's reliance on an "organic" paradigm of the intellectual is not his sole position. It coexists with other moments in his work when he eloquently pleads for recovering the universalism that animated the civil rights struggle of the sixties.

28. I am quoting from a passage in Hall's essay that is quoted by Isaac Julien and Kobena Mercer in their "Introduction: De Margin and De Centre" (5). Significantly, these British black intellectuals, along with Paul Gilroy, have led the contemporary critique of the black burden of being representative and of "ethnic absolutism." See Gates, "The Black Man's Burden."

2. The Unclassified Residuum

1. Dorothy West's remark recalls Dr. Johnson's famous remark about women preachers and, more particularly, David Hume's about a Jamaican Negro, reputed to be a "man of parts and learning; but 'tis likely he is admir'd for slender accomplishments, like a parrot who speaks a few words plainly" (qtd. Markman Ellis 54).

2. For a brilliant discussion of how "Douglass makes authorial revision a mode of revolutionary action," a revolt "against any form of mastery that he has not forged for himself," see Sundquist 88–101. The quotation is from 91.

3. Barrès's indictment "déraciné" recalls, inadvertently, the rootless mobility of the first group of self-consciously oppositional intellectuals, the Goliards. Emergent in the twelfth century, the Goliards were wanderers from various class affiliations, who severed their ties with home and abandoned the monastic, rural cloisters to move from city to city following the master currently in fashion. Jacques Le Goff calls them a fledgling urban intelligentsia, "escapees" from the High Middle Ages attempt to "put and keep everyone in his place, at his task, in his order, in his particular condition" (Le Goff 26). Deracination also marked the formation of perhaps the first class of cosmopolitan intellectuals. Gramsci notes that Julius Caesar sought to make Rome the center of learning by inviting intellectuals from all over the Empire to move to Rome and live as citizens. The result was the creation of a "permanent category" of "imperial" intellectuals, the earliest cosmopolitan class (Gramsci 17).

4. Habermas's important essay "Heinrich Heine and the Intellectual in Germany" tallies with Bourdieu's emphasis on the "paradoxical synthesis" of autonomy and engagement as the source of the modern intellectual's authority. Habermas argues that a half-century before Zola, Heine became the first German "proto-intellectual" not least because "he always defended the autonomy of art and literature, but he did not fetishize them" and thus "opposed the false alternative between fetishizing the mind and making art a political instrument." For Heine, "the autonomy of art and scholarship remains a necessary condition if the locked granaries that the intellectual wants to open for the people are not to be empty" (75, 88–89). Du Bois would concur, for he possessed a double commitment much like Heine's. Habermas notes that Heine, a Jew and cosmopolitan, suffered the same terms of abuse as would Zola and the Dreyfusards.

5. This generation, which succeeded Du Bois's, was full of former Harvard students and admirers of James, among them Walter Lippmann, Alain Locke, and Horace Kallen. There are numerous histories of this era of intellectual ferment. A good place to start is Thomas Bender's *New York Intellect*.

6. In his compelling study *Nietzsche and Modern Times*, Laurence Lampert stresses that Nietzsche, a master of philology, the science of interpretation, is an emphatic advocate of science but one who rejects its reigning Cartesian, mechanistic paradigm (300–301). James and Dewey share a similar attitude to science. In a strikingly Jamesian passage in *The Gay Science*, Nietzsche attacks William James's perennial philosophic foe, "that pedantic Englishman" Herbert Spencer (*Gay* 335). The grounds of James's and Nietzsche's critiques are the same: Spencer's arrogant confidence in the sovereignty of human reason as the tool

that will master nature completely by imposing categories it regards as preordained. Nietzsche, like James, urges that we learn to reason differently by attending to what lies "beyond," to the residues which escape reason's drive to categorize. Even today, amid pragmatism's contemporary renaissance, it remains necessary to stress its wariness of rationalism, for pragmatism still is shadowed by the simplistic critiques leveled against it in earlier eras.

7. In 1911 Du Bois paid tribute to Cooper in his first novel, *The Quest of the Silver Fleece*. Like Cooper, Du Bois's brilliant, urbane mulatto Caroline Wynn is a teacher at the M Street School. Caroline has grown cynical because racism has thwarted her chosen career in sculpture. For much of the novel she expends her artistry on sculpting the political career of Bles Alwyn, the novel's passive race man. Bles is overshadowed throughout by Caroline and the novel's other dynamic black female intellectual, Zora Cresswell.

8. Anderson's study is an invaluable history of how ordinary black men and women began to repudiate Washington's stranglehold. With some assistance from the philanthropist Julius Rosenwald, they created a building program that from 1914 to 1935 erected nearly five thousand mainly rural "common schools" (as opposed to training schools) in fifteen states.

9. Though it leaves Washington out, Phillip Brian Harper's critique of black masculinism in *Are We Not Men?* offers grim reminders of how enduring is Washington's legacy as it was reanimated in 1960s Black Arts and now in hip hop and gangsta rap. Harper observes that in "some African-American communities the 'professional' or 'intellectual' black male inevitably endangers his status both as black and as male whenever he evidences a facility with Received Standard English." A "too-evident facility in the standard white idiom can quickly identify one not as a strong black man, but rather as a white-identified Uncle Tom" and "probably a 'fag' " (11).

10. One might add that the James passage also supplied the terms for two other writers. The passage Wright quotes obviously informs Ellison's novel of invisibility and probably influenced Du Bois's famous image of caste segregation in *Dusk of Dawn* (1940). Segregation, says Du Bois, is tantamount to being entombed in "a dark cave in a side of an impending mountain" from which one sees the world passing by. But it is to no avail when one attempts to speak to those one sees, for they are sealed off as if by "some thick sheet of invisible" plate glass. Before long, those inside the glass start screaming in a "vacuum unheard" (*Writing* 650).

11. Paul Gilroy's chapter on Wright in *The Black Atlantic* decisively reorients Wright criticism. Gilroy detects in both those who support and those who critique Wright a suggestion "that he should have been content to remain confined within the intellectual ghetto to which Negro literary expression is still too frequently consigned" (173). In this view, his expatriatism subjected "his precious and authentic Negro sensibility" to "inappropriately cosmopolitan outlooks" (173).

12. Hopkins's use of William James was first discussed in 1992 by Thomas J. Otten: "In validating countercultural science, James also seems to validate those moments in black letters in which basic assumptions about identity become open to question" (242). See also Sundquist 570–574.

13. Although Griggs in *Imperium In Imperio,* like Hopkins in *Of One Blood,* concocts a black separatist fantasy (a black shadow government in Texas), he confines it to the United States rather than removing it to Africa. And the fantasy ends in disaster for the novel's hero. This fact, and Griggs's refusal to have his characters emigrate, suggests that though he breaks with strict verisimilitude he will not permit utopian impulses to dominate.

14. Walter Benn Michaels argues that John Walden's use of "new people" to describe his sister and himself intends (and succeeds) to disguise racial origin "as a question of class origin" (Michaels 53).

15. See also Moses *Crummell 7,* 96.

16. Yet this is the same review that Dunbar bitterly lamented as doing him "irrevocable harm." For Howells had singled out for praise his "dialect pieces," as if his poems in standard English, says Saunders Redding, were "ludicrous" efforts to "express in pure English the nice sentiments . . . the higher passions [that] blacks were assumed not to think, feel, and experience" (Redding *Scholar* 203). Howells privileged the "dialect pieces" because they captured poignantly, in his words, "the precious difference of temperament between the races which it would be a great pity ever to lose." In the dialect poems Dunbar delicately renders "the Negro's limitations" (qtd. Redding 203). Howells's slippage from unity to difference is analogous to Du Bois's double use "of one blood" as the "Credo" to *Darkwater* (1920). He uses the quotation to support his belief that "all men, black and brown and white, are brothers, varying through time and opportunity, in form and gift and feature, but different in no essential particular." He continues: "Especially do I believe in the Negro race: in the beauty of its genius, the sweetness of its soul . . . I believe in Pride of Race and lineage and self" (3). Howells and Du Bois both invoke "one blood" while affirming two bloods, though Howells's affirmation is racist and Du Bois's racialist. This move from one to two parallels Hopkins's effort at an Africanist and universalist synthesis noted earlier.

17. The contemporary instance of the problem is Jesse Jackson, who represents, for Reed, the chronic affliction of charisma in black politics. Because it subverts the norms of electoral procedures, charisma results in "authorization of an orthodoxy on discourse about Afro-Americans without consideration of either the ambiguities and complexities of political dynamics within the black community or the actual linkages of designated spokespersons to bases of legitimacy and support among blacks" (120–121). Reed's argument is also discussed in Chapter 5 in an analysis of Du Bois's anti-charismatic strategies.

18. One early scene in Chicago, where Helga is drawn "by the uncontrollable desire to mingle with the crowd," crystallizes her pleasure in flirting with oblivion: "The purple sky showed tremulous clouds piled up, drifting here and there with a sort of endless lack of purpose. Very like the myriad human beings pressing hurriedly on. Looking at these, Helga caught herself wondering who they were, what they did . . . What was passing behind those dark molds of flesh. Did they really think at all?" Yet as she moves into the crowd, a "queer feeling of enthusiasm" overtakes her, "as if she were tasting some agreeable food," and homeless Helga feels at home (30).

19. Yet many critics insist on domesticating Helga's primitivism by attaching it to

a redemptive telos. Thus they construct Helga as a "tragic mulatta," allegedly consumed by efforts to fashion an identity from her mixed blood. But her autotelic vagrancy neither pursues identity nor laments its lack. Important recent essays by George Hutchinson and Mary Esteve indicate that Larsen criticism is beginning to move in new directions.

20. But Johnson and Du Bois themselves had disagreements. See Du Bois's important review of Johnson's 1934 book *Negro Americans, What Now?* (*Book Reviews* 172–174).

21. But "casual whiteness" is achieved only after bitter experience. Freedom for Fauset's heroine Angela is not painless. Angela spends most of the novel misconstruing her late mother's legacy of passing. Rather than a programmatic policy that implied a flight from blackness, her mother's passing was context-dependent and based on her pleasure in the improvised "game" of "play-acting" (19). But Angela misunderstands because she has "codified" her mother's passing into a "principle" founded on belief that "joy and freedom . . . seemed to be inherent in mere whiteness" (14).

22. In suggesting that Thurman is committed to "Literature" as deracialized, I do not mean to imply that he was uninterested in race as a subject. In a 1927 essay he describes his journal *Fire* as "experimental," like Langston Hughes's poetry. "It was not interested in sociological problems or propaganda. It was purely artistic in intent and conception." To this aestheticism, Thurman then adds a Marxist twist: "Its contributors went to the proletariat rather than to the bourgeoisie for characters and material. They were interested in people who still retained some individual race qualities and who were not totally white American in every respect save color of skin" (Thurman "Negro" 109). His stance is close to "The Negro Artist and the Racial Mountain," his friend Langston Hughes's famous statement of 1927. Hughes favors the common folk as subjects because "they still hold their own individuality in the face of American standardizations." Although he insists on racial pride and derides the black bourgeoisie for desperately seeking to whiten themselves, Hughes's aesthetic is not one of simple uplift. Like Thurman, he combines Marxism and aestheticism: "We younger Negro artists who create now intend to express our individual dark-skinned selves without fear or shame. If white people are pleased we are glad. If they are not, it doesn't matter. We know we are beautiful. And ugly too . . . If colored people are pleased we are glad. If they are not, their displeasure doesn't matter either . . . We stand on top of the mountain, free within ourselves" (Hughes 306, 309). What provoked Hughes was efforts by the poet Countee Cullen and the journalist George Schuyler to make color "incidental" and to replace it with nationality and class as the crucial determinants of identity. A number of critics have discussed this debate. See Hutchinson (*Harlem* 220–223). Ann Douglas discusses and defends Cullen (340–344).

23. I have borrowed some phrases from George Kateb's "Notes on Pluralism" (522).

24. See Lewis 429–432.

25. Lewis suggests that Du Bois's "own private history of extramarital pursuits"

disposed him to be sympathetic toward Washington in his public beating (432). Lewis is referring to a comment that Du Bois made late in life.

26. This surrender is all the more striking given Du Bois's investment in powerful black masculinity in *The Souls of Black Folk.* In *The Souls,* Du Bois belittles Washington's masculinity, in effect rebutting the portrait of the educated Negro as foppish dandy in *Up from Slavery.* Du Bois portrays Booker's "counsels of submission" as lacking "true manhood." As an inveterate "compromiser," Washington falls short of the powerful "assertion of the manhood rights of the Negro" of such revolutionary black leaders as Douglass, Walker, and Nat Turner (394, 397). To accept Washington's program, warns Du Bois, risks forfeiting what is "worth more than lands and houses," namely "manly self-respect" (398). From the opening pages, when he declares that he will "wrest" the "prizes" of "dazzling opportunities" from white competitors, Du Bois contrasts his intellectual and physical prowess with those black youth stunted by impotent "sycophancy" or hatred. As Hazel Carby observes, "it is the process of becoming an intellectual in Du Bois's narrative that is posited as an alternative route to manhood, as a way to avoid gendered and racialized subordination . . . the practice of intellectual analysis . . . which, for Du Bois, conquers political impotence" (Carby 21; quotations are from Carby's book manuscript). But Carby wonders at the "cost" incurred by Du Bois's "gendered cultural politics." Not only did he "privilege a discourse of black masculinity" that is "still in place," but in *The Souls* he was "unable to imagine a community in which positive intellectual and/or social transformation could be evoked through female metaphors or images" (6, 10). But Du Bois imagines precisely this female community eight years later in his novel *Quest of the Silver Fleece.*

27. Sandra Adell in *Double-Consciousness/Double Bind* argues that a narrow preoccupation with race continues, regrettably, to dominate contemporary African American criticism (111–116).

3. Black Intellectuals and Other Oxymorons

1. "The kingdom of culture" has received surprisingly little critical scrutiny despite its prominence as the alleged goal of black Americans. Robert Gooding-Williams, one of the few to examine it, finds echoes of Josiah Royce in Du Bois's use of the words "co-worker," "death," and "isolation." In *The Spirit of Modern Philosophy* (1892), Royce described the Hegelian struggle for recognition as a "conscious appeal to others to respect my right and worth." If that appeal fails, says Royce, self-consciousness is "isolated," will "rot away," bereft of its identity "as brother, companion and co-worker" (qtd. Gooding-Williams 526). Royce was part of the illustrious Harvard philosophy department at the time Du Bois studied there. Though he was never a student in Royce's philosophy courses, Du Bois doubtless knew his work.

2. Shamoon Zamir astutely emphasizes Du Bois's penchant for simultaneously adopting conflicting roles and perspectives (98, 109). But, according to Zamir, Du Bois conceives the aim of the "talented tenth" as uplifting black folk "into

an acceptance of cultural values that are more or less identical to those of the white aristocracy" (151). This suggests that Du Bois's aim is to have high culture whiten blacks, when actually, as we shall see, Du Bois seeks to de-racialize culture.

3. The pairing of Du Bois and Fanon is not uncommon, but the way I am pursuing it here is. For recent instances see Holt "Marking" and also Zamir 140, 207–210.

4. Joan Cocks also makes this distinction (223).

5. "Uncolored" is how Du Bois describes the world his dead son enjoyed: "He knew no color line, poor dear . . . in his little world walked souls alone, un-colored and unclothed. I—yea, all men—are larger and purer by the infinite breadth of that one little life" (*Souls* 509).

6. "Yields him no true self-consciousness" revises "yields him no self-conscious-ness" from the earlier (1897) magazine version of the first chapter of *The Souls of Black Folk*. This revision suggests Du Bois's care in avoiding an essentialist epistemology.

7. According to Mead, "a multiple personality is in a certain sense normal" (142). The individual "enters his own experience as a self or individual not directly or immediately . . . only in so far as he first becomes an object to himself." Unlike the Du Boisian self, the deracialized Meadian self experiences itself "from the particular standpoints of other individual members of the same social group" or from the "generalized standpoint of the social group as a whole to which he belongs" (138).

8. The prominence of action and chance in the opening pages of *The Souls of Black Folk* suggests Du Bois's pragmatist perspective. In 1956 he noted that "Jamesian pragmatism" had encouraged him to value human action and to distrust any belief system, be it positivist or Marxist or theological, that held to "firm belief in unalterable Law." Such dogma devalued "the decisive action of human beings," he said, and changed "Man to an automaton" while "mak-ing ethics unmeaning and Reform a contradiction in terms" (*Correspondence* 3: 396). Respect for action and chance, the latter of which he linked to "in-explicable will," became the linchpin of his method.

9. Nostalgia also has a positive moment for Fanon. Native intellectuals appropri-ate the colonial production of nostalgic tribalism to help emancipate them from the supremacy of white culture and eventually to achieve a "universal stand-point" (*Wretched* 217–218).

10. The two most important discussions of Du Bois and black soul are found in Joel Williamson, *The Crucible of Race,* and Eric Sundquist, *To Wake the Nations.*

11. In this essay Sartre reduces Negritude to a transitional term in a dialectic whose synthetic moment is a society without races or memory of racism. Fanon pro-tests that "Sartre had forgotten that the Negro suffers in his body quite dif-ferently from the white man" (*Black Skin* 138). Sartre's reduction, in turn, elicited Fanon's famous pages in *Black Skin, White Masks* narrating his an-guished ambivalence to Sartre's Hegelian dialectic. It should be added that Fanon's commitment to a dialectic of universal and particular is in tension with what would short-circuit it—his Nietzschean leap of invention.

12. Two recent readings of Fanon—by Ato Sekyi-Otu and Edward Said—reflect

the current turn from identity politics. The former urges wariness of "post-modern readers of Fanon who would recruit him for the fashionable war against humanism" and universalism (21, 16). The Fanon that emerges from Said's *Culture and Imperialism* is anti-identitarian in his skepticism of nationalism and post-nationalist in his suspicion of national consciousness as anything more than temporary, until the colonizer leaves.

13. It is tempting to regard Creole culture as a particularly egregious instance of imperialist-mandated assimilation, a betrayal of a people's Africanity. But as Christopher Fyfe, a major historian of Sierra Leone, reminds us, the Sierra Leone situation runs counter to usual colonialist patterns. For one thing, the Creoles were not a conquered but a rescued people. Hence the British "did not appear to them as a machine of colonial oppression. They did not feel themselves in a 'colonial situation' " of racist paternalism. Instead, they identified with the British and felt loyalty (10–11). What else should they have felt, asks Basil Davidson. They were enthusiastic about "imperial Britain and its navy" because "without this power they or their fathers or mothers would have died in the infamous and stinking decks of slave ships" (29).

14. As commentators have noted, this situation of a European authority administering to natives reintroduced a colonial structure. See, e.g., Diana Fuss 36–38.

15. Though it seems Du Bois has banished race as an explanation, he then says "I felt myself African by 'race' and by that token was African." He dilates upon this when he ponders why his tie to Africa is strong: "On this vast continent were born and lived a large portion of my direct ancestors going back a thousand years or more. The mark of their heritage is upon me in color and hair. These are obvious things, but of little meaning in themselves; only important as they stand for real and more subtle differences from other men. Whether they do or not, I do not know nor does science know today" (639). In an influential essay Anthony Appiah reads this passage as Du Bois's retreat to the biologism he had previously learned to distrust. There is "pathos," says Appiah, in Du Bois's yearning for the argument he has prohibited himself from using and in his "unconfident certainty that Africa" is his "fatherland" (*Father's House* 41). But Appiah's deconstruction should not make us miss Du Bois's. Du Bois's retreat to biologism is strategic, an instance of his repeated destabilization of his own resolutions to the meaning of the race concept. His final response to his question (really Countee Cullen's) "What is Africa to me" is an anxious, open statement—"I do not know nor does science know today." Like Zora Neale Hurston's "who knows," which answers the question "How It Feels to Be Colored Me" (her words are the final two in the essay of that title), Du Bois embraces the equivocal as a way to defy the coercive demand of certitude. "Something always escapes," as William James was fond of noting. Priscilla Wald argues that Appiah ignores Du Bois's deliberate uncertainty about race throughout his career, and she rightly discerns an analogy between Du Bois's 1897 statement and Fanon's construction of national consciousness as provisional, a prelude to global vision (Wald 209, 338). For more discussion of Appiah see the essays in Bell et al.

16. In the last dozen years the critique of black authenticity has been largely a project of the left and often conducted by gay black critics and artists, among

them the late Marlon Riggs. They address the problem of homophobic masculinism, which remains a legacy of 1960s Black nationalism. But the critique also emerges from the right. For instance, the black neoconservative Glenn Loury begins his recent book, *One By One From the Inside Out*, by confessing that his desire, when younger, "to be regarded as genuinely black, to be seen as a 'regular brother,' " has "dramatically altered" his life. It narrowed the range of his intellectual pursuits and censored his political thought and expression. By "genuine" blackness Loury means Black Power political militants, and he defines his "intellectual maturity" as "largely a process of becoming free" of his need for their approbation (5–6). In short, Loury has come to terms with being a black conservative, a position that his radical brothers would have regarded as a disgrace to the race. In the last twenty years black intellectuals gay and straight, postmodern and neo-con, have emerged out of closets created by Black Power art and politics.

17. Lawrence-Lightfoot conceives her book as a rejoinder to Franklin Frazier's famous 1957 study *Black Bourgeoisie*, which portrayed the black middle class as deracinated, living "in a cultural vacuum," bereft of "cultural roots in either the Negro or the white world" (98). There can be little doubt that the more nuanced portraits gathered in *I've Known Rivers* decisively overturn Frazier's indictment of the black bourgeoisie for the sin of allegedly disowning and hating their roots. Yet what is most significant about Lawrence-Lightfoot's rebuttal of Frazier is that it stays entirely within his terms. The centrality of roots, of return, of the "journey home," remains the unexamined premise, firmly in place as the measurement of authentic blackness.

For another powerful statement, in the domain of literary criticism, of a commitment to the journey home as a measure of black psychic and moral health, see Houston Baker, *Workings of the Spirit*. Baker seeks to honor narratives (by Hurston and Morrison among others) grounded on a "return to a southern place" of "black southern vernacular energies" where the "communal expressivity of black mothers and grandmothers" is given voice (30, 35–36).

In a penetrating critique of Frazier, the important Afro-Trinidadian Marxist sociologist Oliver Cox exposes the unstated "nativistic yearning, a turning back to some mystical Negro folk culture" behind his animus toward the black bourgeoisie. Cox notes that Frazier and his school "labor under some vague atavistic impulse towards a Utopia constituted by an inherent Negro cultural pattern distinct from that of the larger society, and standing even in opposition to it" (16, 23). In effect, an important alternative to Baker, Lawrence-Lightfoot, et al. is found in the contemporary feminist critique of the yearning for home, conducted by Teresa de Lauretis, Bernice Johnson Reagon, and others. The political theorist Bonnie Honig surveys this critique in "Difference, Dilemmas, and the Politics of Home."

18. Wilson Moses reads Belton's masquerade as Griggs's way of "hinting at the fact that some black men have allowed themselves to be emasculated by racism" (*Golden Age* 186). Kevin Gaines concurs (114). I read his masquerade as exposing white blindness rather than black emasculation. Performing a mo-

bile improvisation, Belton's cross-dressing is made possible by white complacency and both images and exploits his invisibility to whites.

19. Miller, *Radicals and Conservatives,* is a retitled reprint of his 1908 *Race Adjustment.* The sociologist of culture Philip Rieff seems virtually alone among contemporary critics in recognizing Miller's importance. Rieff echoes Alain Locke: "A culture has no color; it belongs, as Miller insisted, to him who lives and enacts it. A high culture is a living and active faith. Blood cannot civilize" (228).

20. In Griggs's novel Belton Piedmont's views are congruent with those of Miller and Du Bois. By simply taking "possession of the great English language," the Negro "is thus made heir to all the richest thoughts of earth . . . we now can enjoy the companionship of Shakespeare, Bacon, Milton, Bunyan, together with the favorite sons of other nations adopted into the English language, such as Dante, Hugo, Goethe" (232).

21. While leaving William James unmentioned, Edward Said also links imperialism with identity thinking. He notes the "fundamentally static notion of *identity* that has been the core of cultural thought during the era of imperialism." This notion is founded on an unvarying idea: "that there is an 'us' and a 'them,' each quite settled, clear, unassailably self-evident" (*Culture and Imperialism* xxv). Said discusses the "epistemology of imperialism" in "The Politics of Knowledge."

22. Soyinka has been criticized as a deluded hybrid. The Kenyan novelist Ngũgĩ wa Thiong'o denies that Soyinka is an African writer, and instead groups him with a "hybrid tradition . . . that can only be termed as Afro-European literature; that is, the literature written by Africans in European languages." Ngũgĩ's solution is to write in his native Kenyan dialect and translate his work into English (*Decolonising* 27).

23. It is tempting to read *The House Behind the Cedars* as, on one level, Chesnutt's working through of emotional ambivalence that grants him psychic permission to leave the South. His working through involves a kind of psychic splitting: paying tribute (as tax and honor) to the past so as to be rid of it, he has Rena Walden perform the premodern, preordained sacrifice so that her brother can become an urban intellectual. But this formulation ignores that Warwick was first a Walden and that his home feeling with the past brings him back to Patesville in the first place. In other words, Chesnutt identifies not merely with John but with Rena. And, finally, with neither of them. Chesnutt was light enough to pass but chose not to. He neither stays (like Rena) nor passes (like John) but instead becomes a black intellectual, precisely in Kelly Miller's oxymoronic sense.

24. The black intellectual is invisible to those afflicted with procrustean vision, "those who see with one eye, speak with one tongue and see things as either black or white, either Eastern or Western." These words are the "dedication" and the only text of another blank book, "My Life Story—by Mustafa Said," the work of the fictive African intellectual and aesthete of Tayeb Salih's novel *Season of Migration to the North* (150–151). Once the toast of London and Bloomsbury in the 1920s, Said is an exotic hybrid nicknamed "the black Eng-

lishman" who returns to live out his old age in his village near Khartoum and leaves behind his sparse autobiography. In an uncanny echo of Chesnutt, Salih's empty pages also challenge readers to attain the requisite double vision—Du Bois would say "double consciousness"—to see the black intellectual in the margins, occluded by preordained categories.

25. The bleak fate of black womanhood envisioned by Chesnutt is mitigated by Du Bois in his first novel, *The Quest of the Silver Fleece* (1911), where powerful agency is depicted as inseparable from two conditions: being a black woman and being an intellectual. The novel narrates a return to roots without being a tragic mulatto tale. Instead, it is dominated by two black female intellectuals (Zora and Caroline) neither of whom is reduced to postures of noble self-sacrifice. Du Bois's novel functions as a bridge to modernity, reaching out to Nella Larsen's anarchic *Quicksand* and to Jessie Fauset's anti-tragic mulatta tale *Plum Bun*. By the fifties the modernist cult of expatriation had made deracination the virtual sine qua non of the intellectual. In the preface to *White Man, Listen!* (1957), Richard Wright proudly proclaimed: "I'm a rootless man . . . I like and even cherish the state of abandonment" (xxiv). In 1953 Fanon had written an admiring letter to Wright, stating that he was at work writing "a study bearing on the human breadth of your works" (Ray and Farnsworth 150).

4. The Distinction of Du Bois

1. Du Bois's refinement and aristocratic bearing were often remarked: "He was a man of distinction; the way he walked, settled his shoulders, and his voice . . . You had to pay attention to him," is how an Atlanta University student remembered him (qtd. Lewis, 216).

2. Some forms of Cultural Studies, ascendant in the academy since the mid-1980s, portray the aesthetic in this light. In "Reclaiming the Aesthetic," George Levine notes that "in the current critical scene, literature is all too often demeaned, the aesthetic experience denigrated or reduced to mystified ideology" (2–3).

3. Berlin's portrayal of J. G. Hamann in *The Magus of the North* recalls William James on a number of points. For instance, Hamann believes "the greatest error in the world is 'to confuse *words* with *concepts* and *concepts* with *real things*.' Philosophers are imprisoned in their own systems" (40). As we shall see in Chapter 6, James calls this error "vicious intellectualism." By his book's end, Berlin makes the comparison explicit. Noting Hamann's belief that the "kaleidoscopic metamorphoses of actual experience" "slip through the meshes of the most elaborate conceptual net," Berlin says: "Like William James more than a century later, Hamann is a champion of the individual, the complex and above all the unconscious and the unseizable" (115).

4. Schiller's aesthetic education (like pragmatism) has been appropriated by both the right and the left; indeed an aestheticized politics has often been associated with fascism.

5. The pragmatist, says Richard Poirier, regards the turning or troping of words as "in itself an act of power over meanings already in place." Such activity saves us "from being caught or fixed in a meaning or in that state of conformity

which Emerson famously loathed" (*Renewal* 17). Poirier, our greatest Emersonian critic, has shown troping, "acts of antagonism directed against the already formulated," to be central to the pragmatist imagination (176). See *The Renewal of Literature* and *Poetry and Pragmatism.*

6. Reed's recent book continues this narrow focus on the provenance of double consciousness (*Du Bois* 99–105). Not unrelatedly, Reed construes pragmatism reductively, as understanding "all human problems . . . as knowledge or information problems" (49). This more accurately describes the intellectualist error of James's opponents. David Levering Lewis and George Hutchinson acknowledge James's profound impact, but conclude that "in the end Du Bois hung on to a tenuous Idealism, strongly inflected by Hegel and Royce," to quote Hutchinson's summary of his and Lewis's views (456). Hutchinson discusses Dewey's and James's pragmatism in relation to Du Bois, Locke, and the sociologist Charles Johnson (33–61).

7. Du Bois would later look back upon his first book, *The Suppression of the African Slave-Trade* (1896), as limited in its historical understanding in part because of his Harvard training. Although he says that James's teaching liberated him from the "sterilities of scholastic philosophy," this liberation still promoted what Du Bois called "the New England ethic of life as a series of conscious moral judgments . . . I was continually thrown back on what men 'ought' to have done to avoid evil consequence . . . I still saw slavery and trade as chiefly the result of moral lassitude" (*Writings* 1315–16).

8. Reed has persuasively described Du Bois's Pan-Africanism as a modernization strategy for the Third World and thus dependent on "universalist, homogenizing assumptions of social engineering" and administration ("Du Bois" 440–441). But Du Bois's *domestic* strategies are far less unequivocally technocratic. He acknowledges that without "stern, unrelenting discipline," no "socialistic state is possible" (*Writings By* 4: 279). Yet Du Bois's vision of socialism, unlike that of Lenin, a fellow theorist of a vanguard party, could not be said to rest "in the end on the Promethean culture of capitalism" (Gouldner *Against* 44). Whereas Lenin was a great enthusiast of Taylorism, Du Bois distrusts technocratic ideology because it preaches efficiency as ascetic discipline. This distrust is derived in part from his pragmatist regard for improvisation and the incalculable but even more from esteem for the "gift" that black folk contributed to labor in the New World. Du Bois defines that gift as a "tropical" African product, an anti-Protestant "sensuous receptivity to the beauty of the world" that saved the black slave from being as easily reduced as the Northern European laborer to a "mechanical draft horse" (*Gift* 53). In *Roll Jordan Roll* Eugene Genovese concurs with Du Bois that slaves refused ascetic Protestantism. But he disputes Du Bois's claim that this refusal was uniquely African. Rather, says Genovese, the "general immigrant experience resisted the discipline of regularity" (313).

9. To be fair to Moses, he also says that Du Bois's stress on double consciousness "makes it impossible to neatly pigeonhole" him "in either the black nationalist or the radical assimilationist tradition" (*Golden Age* 136).

10. Dewey's statement here is remarkable in light of the faith he had in positivist science at the turn of the century. Indeed his remarks read as a veritable self-

indictment of his own naive scientism. Dorothy Ross observes the similarity between the Dewey of 1900 and the social control theorist Edward Ross. She calls Dewey "a leading advocate of Ross's central premise, that the social sciences would produce the kind of positivist knowledge that could establish rational control over society and history" (252). But she fails to credit Dewey for significantly altering his attitude, a change probably encouraged by Randolph Bourne's incisive critique in 1917. Bourne exposed Deweyan instrumentalism as a technocratic gospel that had deluded progressive liberals to imagine they could use war as a means of social reform. A more radical Dewey, one with close affinities to Marx, is depicted by Garry Brodsky.

11. For this "etymological excursus" I am indebted to Timothy Kaufman-Osborn's *Politics/Sense/Experience* (8–9), an exceptionally provocative work of political philosophy that begins by evicting pragmat*ism* from his pages to reinstate *pragmata*. Although Hannah Arendt does not invoke *pragmata*, her esteem of action (as the "spontaneous beginning of something new" whose consequences we are unable to control or foretell), her sense of its centrality to politics, and her argument that, starting with Plato, the Western philosophical tradition is uneasy and suspicious about action for exposing the "frailty of human affairs" and seeks escape from it in the concept of rule and in administration, strikingly parallel James and Dewey's critique of rationalism. All three thinkers could be said to urge that a free, democratic political life demands (to borrow Arendt's words) that we bear the "risks and dangers" of action, its "burden of irreversibility and unpredictability, from which the action process draws its very strength" (Arendt *Human Condition* 210, 198–202, 206, 209).

12. Ronald Judy's 1994 essay on Du Bois is a notable exception to the general neglect of "My Evolving Program for Negro Freedom."

13. For instance, Zamir (discussed below) and Robert Gooding-Williams choose Hegel against pragmatism. The latter makes an incisive critique of Cornel West's pragmatist account of Du Bois but at the cost of creating a nearly absolute gap between Hegel and pragmatism. But as Richard Rorty has noted, "once one starts to look for pragmatism in Hegel, one finds quite a bit to go on. In particular, one can capitalize on Hegel's remark that 'philosophy is its time apprehended in thought' " ("Dewey Between" 63). My pragmatist reading of Du Bois has little in common with West's and suggests that Dewey and Du Bois found points of compatibility between Hegel and pragmatism.

14. Twenty-six years later, in "Hegel and His Method," James would give a more sympathetic and less defensive assessment of Hegel, one that virtually inverts his earlier critique. James credits him with a "revolutionary" understanding of concepts. For, like James, Hegel conceived them not as the "static self-contained things that previous logicians had supposed." Hegel's "dialectic logic" superseded " 'the logic of identity' in which, since Aristotle, all Europe had been brought up." Hegel's error, in James's view, is his rationalism, expressed in his dogmatic insistence on possessing "*the* truth," single, eternal, "incontrovertible, binding on everyone" (James *Writings* 671, 675).

15. Zamir describes Du Bois as primarily a Hegelian, but one who does not "*adopt* Hegel" (as Williamson argued in *The Crucible of Race*) but rather "*adapts* him

to his own ends" (114; his emphasis). Those ends differ from the "upbeat" uses of the nineteenth-century American Hegelians (120). Du Bois's adaptation, says Zamir, recovers the negativity of Hegelian "unhappy consciousness" (rewriting it as "double consciousness") as a critical historicist psychology that places Du Bois in the company of Marx, Sartre, and Kojeve. This thesis is founded on Zamir's important discovery that in 1889–1890 Du Bois read the *Phenomenology of Mind* with his Harvard tutor Santayana and thus developed a more profound understanding of Hegel than James (who never read the *Phenomenology*) ever did. This is a provocative reading of Du Bois, to which Zamir brings considerable intensity. But it is unclear why the maximizing of Hegel requires, for Zamir, the minimizing of pragmatism, especially since the latter is not a philosophy replete with doctrine but a method. And it is a method that encourages precisely the distinction that Zamir makes so much of—the practice of creative adaptation rather than passive adoption.

16. Whites, said Du Bois, should fear rather than seek to evoke pride of race: "For the day that Black men love Black men simply because they are Black, is the day they will hate White men simply because they are White" (*Writings* 1194).

17. Certainly Du Bois minimized (or was not fully aware of) Stalin's totalitarianism and its hideous negation of democracy. But he was never a dupe of communism, Soviet or American, but rather used it as goad to unsettle American claims of having achieved democracy.

18. Du Bois revised his self-understanding in an Emersonian direction. A devoted reader of Emerson, he very probably read "Uses of Great Men," the pivotal chapter in *Representative Men*. We fail to "come at the true and best benefit of any genius," Emerson says, "so long as we believe him an original force," a "cause," rather than an "effect. Then he appears as an exponent of a vaster mind and will" (631). To understand a great man as an "effect" is to understand him as representative of larger forces. Du Bois appropriates this logic.

19. In his psychological portrait of Du Bois, the black social psychologist Allison Davis writes that "like many millions of educated Negroes later," Du Bois internalized bourgeois values of work and self-restraint and "learned to renounce the magnificent sexual vitality and sensualism of the underclass Negroes" (115). Lewis's depiction of Du Bois usefully complicates this.

20. This visit produced an epiphany: "efficiency and happiness do not go together in modern culture . . . as the world darkens it gets happier." Although he has been chided by critics for such primitivism, Du Bois himself is aware that he has romanticized Africa when he remarks playfully: "shall we all take to the Big Bush? No, I prefer New York. But my point is that New York and London and Paris must learn of West Africa and may learn" (*Dusk* 648).

21. Schiller's ultimate aim is political; by means of a "total revolution" in the "mode of perception"—from the instrumental to the "disinterested free appreciation of pure appearance"—he seeks to adumbrate an "aesthetic State" where "everything . . . even the subservient tool, is a free citizen having equal rights with the noblest" (132, 140). To achieve Freedom, Beauty must have precedence. It alone confers on man wholeness and a "social character": "to solve that political problem in practice" we must "follow the path of aesthetics,

since it is through Beauty that we arrive at Freedom" (27). For the German intellectual history of the concept of the "aesthetic state," see Joseph Chytry's book of that title.

22. Keith Byerman's study of Du Bois includes a reading of the essay. He notes Du Bois's "complex aesthetic position," which at one point he calls "pragmatic" in contrast to that of the "pure aestheticists" (101, 103).

23. Curtis Marez discusses the racist caricatures of Wilde in America (266–274). The black dandy, usually named Zip Coon, a much ridiculed social type and a staple of minstrel shows since the 1830s, was invoked by Booker T. Washington implicitly against Du Bois in his 1901 attack on the "educated Negro, with a high hat, imitation gold eye-glasses, a showy walking stick, kid gloves," who "was determined to live by his wits" (*Up* 92). At times Zip Coon was depicted in rivalrous combat with a black working-class figure, thus making intraracial conflict visible (Lott *Love* 133–134). Du Bois's distinction of personal style sparks similar conflict in 1920 with his working-class rivals, principally Garvey, for the leadership of black America. The next chapter touches on this.

5. Divine Anarchy

1. "I am becoming more and more an individualist and anarchist and believer in small systems of things exclusively," James confided to William Dean Howells in 1904 (qtd. Coon 71). "A New England kinship of patrician combativeness and superior culture" is how Lewis describes the affinity between Du Bois and Spingarn, and this kinship extends outward to William James (475).

2. See Spingarn's letter of Oct. 24, 1914, to Du Bois in *Correspondence* 1: 200–202.

3. This is the opinion of a number of commentators. See, e.g., Westbrook (196).

4. John Dewey, like Du Bois, links aristocracy and democracy. Because it "denotes faith in individuality, in uniquely distinctive qualities in each normal human being," democracy is "aristocracy carried to its limit." And the common enemy of true democracy and true aristocracy is "the habit of fixed and numerically limited classifications" that are "quantitative" and "comparative" (Dewey *Political Writings* 77–78).

5. Du Bois mentions anarchy, if not its "Divine" visionary version, in *The Souls* when he describes anarchy and hypocrisy as the two broad reactions among black Americans to their enforced "double life." And he correlates them, respectively, with the North and the South (502). In the South blacks rely on "hypocrisy"—flattery toward whites—to attain "compromise" and material acquisition. The practice of hypocrisy withers the inner life, as it demands vigilant self-effacement and sacrifice of "impulse, manliness and courage" (504). But the practice of anarchy results from the shock of freedom: "the soul, long pent up and dwarfed, suddenly expand[s] in new found freedom." For in the North the Negro is "intellectually quickened and awakened." This is John Jones's experience in New York, as is the bitter residue of balked hopes that sudden expansion leaves. As Du Bois explains, once the soul expands, "every tendency is to excess—radical complaint, radical remedies, bitter denunciation or angry silence." John's insistence on a radical remedy for Alta-

maha—to modernize immediately—dooms his chances for success, and plunges him into angry silence. In short, be he John Jones or Matthew Towns, the Du Boisian intellectual's anarchy of inner freedom is persistently shadowed by the destructive anarchy of embittered pessimism turned inward and outward.

6. Du Bois's thesis of a "double life" is a version of the "cultural lag" theory that was prominent in the sociology of his day to explain lack of black progress. Du Bois's particular use of the "cultural lag" thesis turns it toward the ways in which the dominance of group life thwarts aspirations to individualism and modernity.

7. Richard Wright, in *Black Boy,* makes his own version of Du Bois's point that the black American is stranded in a premodern provincialism: "Whenever I thought of the essential bleakness of black life in America, I knew that Negroes had never been allowed to catch the full spirit of Western civilization, that they lived somehow in it but not of it" (37). Regarding this famous passage, Ralph Ellison writes: "Wright is pointing out that Negro sensibility is socially and historically conditioned; that Western culture must be won, confronted like the animal in a Spanish bullfight" (*Shadow* 93). To win Western culture means, among other things, to win its esteem for individual rights. And to hold on to those rights becomes crucial even in a contemporary culture where postmodern theory is skeptical of the rights-bearing subject. "I am still evolving from being treated as three-fifths of a human, a subpart of the white estate." Thus the black legal scholar Patricia Williams explains her reluctance to join her white critical legal studies colleagues in deconstructing rights and replacing them with needs (147). For blacks to be without boundaries "has meant not untrammeled vistas of possibility but the crushing weight of total . . . intrusion" (164).

8. Frank Kirkland's "Modernity and Intellectual Life in Black" is a rich discussion of turn-of-the-century black intellectual discourse of modernity.

9. In *White Man, Listen!* (1957) Richard Wright extends the logic of Du Bois's resolute modernity by urging the spread of the European Enlightenment throughout the world: "what is good for Europe is good for all mankind" (64). And Wright calls imperialism a "boon wrapped in that gift of brutality that the white West showered upon Asia and Africa," the boon being liberation "from the rot of my irrational traditions and customs, though you [Mr. White Man] are still the victim of your irrational customs and traditions!" (61).

10. Rampersad acutely remarks that the memoir is a signal departure from the classic black self-narratives of Washington or Douglass, books that offer the narrator as the model of what "hard work, courage, discipline, confidence and faith" can accomplish. Whereas Washington and Douglass offer themselves as types worthy of emulation, Du Bois "deliberately depicted himself as atypical of the masses." He represents himself as a prophet, called to a mission (171–172).

11. Arraying himself in forbidding black, the color of negation, Baudelaire, the archetypal dandy, rejected identity with all existing classes, including the demimonde of Bohemia. His stylized austerity advertised a spiritual aristocracy. In this double refusal the dandy expresses the distinction of "haughty exclusiveness" grounded in hatred of the philistine bourgeois, the barbarian aristocrat, and the undisciplined, tawdry bohemian, as Baudelaire says in *The Painter of Modern Life* (1863). "The last spark of heroism amid decadence," with a

"burning need to create for oneself a personal originality," the dandy is precariously perched, about to be engulfed by the "rising tide of democracy, which invades and levels everything" (27–29). The dandy's love of distinction and his imperative of originality seemed to attract Du Bois, not least as one way, conscious or not, to evade the tyranny of stereotypes which operate by force of "nature's law."

6. Motley Mixtures

1. This phrase is Ann Douglas's. Without making this lineage part of her commodious tapestry, Douglas's *Terrible Honesty* enables one to discern it for the first time.
2. Murray in "The Alain Locke Symposium" (16). Henceforth cited as "Alain Locke." Besides Murray, the participants were Ellison, Nathan Huggins, Harold Cruse, and Archie Epps. Part of Ellison's contribution is reprinted in his *Collected Essays*.
3. For readings of Ellison's essay different from the one offered here, see Houston Baker *(Blues, Ideology, and Afro-American Literature)* and Henry Louis Gates *(The Signifying Monkey)*. Both discuss Ellison's essay as advocating a vernacular approach to African American literature.
4. Watts's book subtitled "Ellison, Politics and Afro-American Intellectual Life" is by turns critical and admiring, and finally exasperated by Ellison's choice not to be more like Langston Hughes, who devoted his energies to an "almost manic public intellectual life . . . In effect Hughes was too busy to write well . . . Hughes was a literal one-man black intellectual infrastructure" (112–113).
5. Besides Locke, Kenneth Burke, Ellison's close friend, was a prime mediator of a pragmatist politics and aesthetics. In *Counter-Statement* (1931), Burke refused to segregate the aesthetic from the social and political. More emphatically than Dewey, Burke and Ellison link modernist art and democracy, for both "play havoc with conventional ideas of order" (*Territory* 30).
6. Dewey's unease with the separatism that inhabits Kallen's pluralism inaugurates the critique of cultural pluralism that would be resumed, in different ways, in the seventies by Philip Gleason and John Higham, in the eighties by Werner Sollors, and in the nineties by Walter Benn Michaels.
7. Ellison's mention of Royce is also pregnant. Royce's notion of "beloved community" influenced Locke's construction of 1920s Harlem as "an augury of a new democracy in American culture" founded "on the fullest sharing of American culture and institutions" ("New Negro" 9).
8. "Dictatorship of Virtue" is the title of Richard Bernstein's book on multiculturalism.
9. The relation of pragmatism to radical empiricism (pluralism) remains a subject of debate. Richard Rorty, for one, is impatient with the radical empiricist turn in James and Dewey for (allegedly) violating the pragmatist taboo on epistemology and metaphysics. Instead of dropping the term "experience," as Rorty wishes he had, Dewey (like the James of *A Pluralistic Universe*) posited a kind of vitalism in the form of a prelinguistic immediacy of flux. But Rorty acknowl-

edges that the Dewey he prefers is a "hypothetical" construct, "a pragmatist without being a radical empiricist" (56).

10. For instance, Locke's "New Negro," according to Henry Louis Gates in "The Trope of a New Negro," is shorn of both racial and political identity (147–148). In contrast, Houston Baker finds *The New Negro* a black nationalist project and describes Locke's effort as an attempt to create an African-American nation "on the basis of RACE" (*Modernism* 79). A notable exception to this one-sidedness is Everett Akam's essay.

11. Thurman caricatured Locke as both a genteel aesthete worried about "decadence" and a "vindicationist" who sought to establish race pride by having writers return to their African "racial roots" and cultivate "a healthy paganism based on African traditions." Thurman satirizes Locke (as Dr. Parkes) in *Infants of the Spring* (quotation 235).

12. Jeffrey Stewart, in his valuable introduction to *Race Contacts,* pays particular attention to Boas's influence on Locke.

13. The capacity not "to dismiss the mystery of American identity . . . with a gesture of democracy-weary resignation" nor "attempt to dispel . . . the turbulence of the present" (25) requires a kind of Keatsian negative capability. This capacity of remaining in "uncertainties, Mysteries, doubts," in Keats's words, became for Lionel Trilling and others the virtual touchstone of literary value and spiritual worth. But Ellison's pragmatism has recontextualized negative capability as a mode of aesthetic and political engagement that American democracy requires.

14. In conceiving the aesthetic as a supple mode of conduct that thrives in, rather than being inimical to, democratic turbulence, Ellison reveals the influence of his friend Kenneth Burke, long recognized as a pivotal intellectual mentor for Ellison and Albert Murray. Particularly important was Burke's seminal *Counter-Statement* (1931). Its pragmatist aesthetics cut across the art-versus-politics dichotomy that structured both high-modernist aesthetics and the new criticism, and that would shape the liberal humanism of postwar New York intellectuals like Lionel Trilling. Defending the aesthetic amid Marxism's high tide, with its imperative that art be an instrument of social progress, Burke refuses to run for the cover of an idealist cloistering of the aesthetic. Rather, the aesthetic possesses social utility for Burke as a corrosive counter-statement to modernity's reign of practicality and efficiency, which encourages dogmatic action and static identity. For an excellent treatment of the Burke-Ellison connection see Tim Parrish's essay.

15. With her inveterate pugnacity and desire to outrage, Hurston once said that "the Jim Crow system works" (qtd. Hemenway 289). The remark was a counterattack on black critics who had criticized *Dust Tracks* for race disloyalty.

16. For a balanced assessment of Hurston's position on *Brown v. Board of Education* see Werner Sollors, "Of Mules and Mares in a Land of Difference; or, Quadrupeds All?"

17. For Dilthey's impact on Boas see Stocking (*Race* 152–154).

18. Summing up the links among Dilthey, James, and Dewey, James Kloppenberg writes: "If there is an essence of lived experience, its essence is its mutability.

That realization gave birth to a particular kind of historical sensibility, because when the conception of life as changing is coupled with the emphasis on praxis and the pragmatic theory of truth, history emerges as the empirical basis for knowledge about man" (*Uncertain* 109).

19. In 1936, writing of Hurston's first novel, *Jonah's Gourd Vine*, Nick Aaron Ford had lamented her missed opportunity to portray "the Negro . . . in a more favorable light . . . in his normal activities as an ordinary American citizen" (10). The irony of Ford's critique is that Hurston's "What White Publishers Won't Print" (1950) makes the same case for the importance of representing the average.

20. But predictably, the success of her move to a "raceless" space was equivocal. On the one hand, white liberals warmly greeted *Dust Tracks* and the *Saturday Review* awarded it a prize for its contribution to race relations. Hurston for the first time "became a recognized black spokesperson, whose opinions were sought by the white reading public" (Hemenway 288). But, on the other hand, this approval seemed to harbor some implicit condescension. Instead of confronting her book's critical force—the urging of a universalism committed to ending race—readers tacitly preferred to racialize Hurston's universalism, understanding it as an acceptance of culture as white. Universalism often elicits this containment strategy.

21. This focus was, perhaps, her way of answering critics and publishers who, she said, "think of the Negro as picturesque" and expect stereotypes (qtd. Hemenway 298). As we have seen, some black critics charged that Hurston had acceded to this demand. She, in turn, believed that leftist reviewers had practiced "intellectual Jim Crow" by making the burden of being representative the tacit criterion of literary value. In a 1944 letter she complained that reviewers "seek out and praise literary characters of the lowest type and most sordid circumstances and portray the thing as the common state of all Negroes" and conclude that "capitalist whites are responsible" (qtd. 299). Hemenway points out the "considerable irony" in her complaint, since some of Hurston's own work had overplayed the violence of "lower-class black folk" (299).

22. In the hands of others, a Toomer-like pan-humanism could be put in the service of a WASP hegemony. Consider Toomer's contemporary Herbert Croly, an architect of Progressive-era nationalism, which sponsored the melting pot as an ideal of social control and homogenized Americanism. In 1909 Croly called for an Americanism founded on a "religion of human brotherhood" inspired by Crevecoeur's famous declaration that in America "individuals of all nations are melted into a new race of men" (Croly 453, 9). By the mid-twenties Croly, like Toomer, fell under Gurdjieff's influence.

7. The Agon *Black Intellectual*

1. By the mid-1970s Baraka had moved from black nationalism to a Marxist internationalism. This widening of perspective, if not the particular ideology, was another factor that set him in the direction of Baldwin. In this light, note Baraka's remarks made in 1984: "if you are a modern artist who's not some

kind of cultural nationalist, you understand that you can learn from anything and anybody, see that the whole of world culture is at your disposal, because no one people has created the monuments of art and culture in the world . . . American culture is multinational. It's not just white" (qtd. *Baraka Reader* 249–250). This resembles a cosmopolitan, Du Boisian point of view that Baldwin had reached by the early 1960s.

2. Baraka clarified, in a 1981 interview, his use of the term "faggot," noting that "in the black community" it means "a weak, jive person." While adding that his use of the word "comes from the denigration of homosexuality," he also said he opposes "gratuitous attacks on homosexuals" (qtd. Riley 199).

3. As well, black nationalist poets had to worry about "their own possible estrangement from the very demands of everyday black life that they repeatedly invoked as founding their practice" (Harper *Men* 51).

4. In a 1965 interview Baldwin said: "in fact there are no whites and blacks in America, that all of us are mulattos or bastards. It is not a white country" (Standley and Pratt 50).

5. "What passes for identity in America is a series of myths about one's heroic ancestors." This is "dangerously infantile," notes Baldwin (*Price* 330).

6. The Caribbean writer George Lamming critiques this passage from another perspective: Baldwin's implicitly colonialist assumption of Africa as an embarrassing cultural void (30–33).

7. This is the summary observation of the political scientist Harold Isaacs, which is based on an interview he had with Baldwin around 1961 for a project on the attitudes of American blacks toward Africa. Isaacs notes: "by the time we talked of this [Baldwin's sense that he 'had no share of Chartres, Beethoven, or the Empire State Building'] he had forgotten he had ever cut himself off from these monuments of human achievement . . . He had stopped seeing himself as waiting, emptyhanded" (273).

8. Marcus Klein notes Baldwin's attachment to the word. Klein is impatient with Baldwin's elastic use of identity, and describes his ultimate understanding of identity as "theological" in its "purity"; identity is a "passion so pure that it is beyond all metaphors" (17, 27).

9. Baldwin's Jamesian inheritance is often discussed and is usually located in his predecessor's expatriatism, his technical innovations, his elaborate syntax, his representation of consciousness, his priesthood of art, and his fascination with the ambiguous relation of innocence and freedom. This last matter was something Baldwin himself eloquently addressed in his conversation on Henry James with David Leeming. Doubtless these aspects together compose much of the Jamesian legacy. But James's critical assessment of American culture in *The American Scene*, so remarkably congruent with Baldwin's, has been ignored, not least because too many critics still tend to rely on the received wisdom that caricatures James as a reactionary aesthete in flight from American modernity. Significantly, those who dismiss this image have included not only Baldwin but also Ralph Ellison and Albert Murray. See, e.g., Ellison *Territory* 313–314.

10. James's question, pondered at a pivotal moment in *The American Scene*, exemplifies the tradition of pragmatist pluralism. Henry James read his brother's *Pragmatism* (1907) and *A Pluralistic Universe* (1909). Of the latter he tells

William: "I am *with* you, all along the line . . . As an artist and a 'creator' I can catch on, hold on, to pragmatism and can work in the light of it and apply it." This eminently pragmatic response echoes his earlier enthusiasm for *Pragmatism,* which revealed to him the great "extent" to which all his life he had "unconsciously pragmatised." *The American Scene* embodies Henry's creative application of William's pragmatist pluralism. I elaborate on this in *The Trial of Curiosity.* Henry James's responses to his brother qtd. in Perry 1: 428.

11. W. J. Cash's is the classic formulation of how blacks and whites in the South are reciprocally entwined: "Negro entered into white man as white man entered into Negro—subtly influencing every gesture, every word, every emotion and idea, every attitude" (*Mind of the South* 51).

12. The affinity between Henry James and Du Bois has only recently been remarked on, and it is easy to understand why, given James's condescending and misinformed mention in *The American Scene* of *The Souls of Black Folk* as "the only 'Southern' book of any distinction published for many a year" (418). Du Bois was teaching in Atlanta when his book appeared, but he was a native of Massachusetts with a Harvard doctorate. Kenneth Warren regrets the missed opportunity in James's perfunctory mention, for the novelist's reading of *The Souls* "could have been one of the signal moments" in American literary history. As Warren notes, Du Bois's book might have suggested "an alternate trajectory" for *The American Scene* such that its cultural critique would have also become "a powerful brief against American racism" (112). My sketch of James and Du Bois's affinities is meant to suggest that *The American Scene* indeed possesses an "alternate trajectory."

13. In *Another Country,* Eric, the novel's bisexual hero, has loved black men since his Alabama childhood, and his sexuality and indifference to race are inseparable and equally scandalous in the community (197–206). I agree with Lee Edelman that in Baldwin's fiction homosexual relations tend to be valued to the extent that they reveal the permeability of identity, i.e. the ability to experience mutual penetration and passive receptivity "without experiencing a loss of integrity." In other words, Baldwin's homosexual lovers "reinterpret 'manhood' " by resisting the "phobic exclusions" inscribed in the "logic by which identity signifies a coherence linked to the unviolated integrity of the borders defining an autonomous self." Although in his last novel, *Just Above My Head,* the male lovers suffer internalized homophobia, which makes each unable to "survive his openness to penetration by the other," Baldwin is nonetheless committed to "the hope of dismantling the armored identities that keep self and other, inside and outside, resolutely, if arbitrarily, distinct" (70, 73–74). Cora Kaplan discusses Baldwin as an important protofeminist critic of masculinity.

14. This maverick mode of being depends, finally, on "doing things alone," on maintaining the category of the private as distinct, a realm always permeable but not absorbed by the public glare of Race Man. For Baldwin, then, on some level at least, the personal is not the political. Instead, he preserves a space between them, in his case Europe, a space that nurtures the distinction he makes between his "role" and his "place" (172). His role is artist (what he calls "witness"), while his place is spokesman or representative. It is a critical

truism that during his career this space steadily eroded, as Baldwin the artist was swallowed by Baldwin the celebrity voice of black anguish and outrage. But this received wisdom misses his consistent esteem for privacy. This esteem is puzzling to proponents of contemporary identity politics, who think it smacks of aestheticism. In this context, Baldwin's 1984 interview with Richard Goldstein is a classic collision. When Goldstein asks, "you never thought of yourself as being gay?" Baldwin responds, "No. I didn't have a word for it. The only one I had was 'homosexual' and that didn't quite cover whatever it was I was beginning to feel." "The word 'gay' has always rubbed me the wrong way." And, anyway, he adds, "one's sexual preference is a private matter." Like many of his generation, he had no interest in gay liberation movements. Baldwin tells an increasingly baffled Goldstein that he refuses "to make a life out of" homosexuality, which he regards not as a noun but as a verb (Troupe 174–184).

15. McKay had a notorious contempt for the African American intelligentsia that guided the Harlem Renaissance. As Harold Cruse notes: "Always apparent was a vague, undefined barrier between him—as a West Indian—and the American Negroes. He maintained much better rapport with the whites" (48).

16. Significantly, Horkheimer and Adorno add that the "intellectual is in the same category" as the Jew: he "appears to think—a luxury which the others cannot afford—and he does not manifest the sweat of toil and physical effort" (172).

17. Darryl Pinckney, as usual, is an exception. Like me, he reads both novels as concerned as much with black intellectuals as with celebrating black primitivism. See "The Outsider."

18. Samuel Delany's "pornotopic fantasy" *The Mad Man* can be read as a contemporary meditation on what, by now, is a trope of the (male) black intellectual coming-of-age saga: the Ray/Jake, mind/body self-division. The novel pushes the terms of that division to radically polar limits, as it discloses the sadomasochistic relation between an intellectual genius and a bestial sexual prowler, the "Mad Man" of the title.

19. In more general terms, Baraka reveres McKay for his hatred of the black bourgeoisie, his love of the working class, and his proto-Negritude affirmations.

20. Werner Sollors in *Populist Modernism* looks briefly at McKay's presence in "New-Sense" and *The Toilet* (169).

21. Houston Baker notes a tension in these concluding lines between "solipsistic artist" and "blues artist" (*Afro-American Poetics* 134).

22. "Sheep" is also the word Baraka uses in his memoirs to describe the "careerist Negro" who populates Howard—"prepared sheepdom of the readied-for-the-slaughter" (*Autobiography* 115).

23. Gouldner, *Against Fragmentation* (22). Gouldner argues that in its failure to "confront the issue of the *summoner*," the agent who will lead and educate the *"summoned"* (the proletariat), Marxism is hobbled by a "fundamental limit" on its capacity for "reflexivity" (22).

24. For this sketch of Cabral and Ngũgĩ I am drawing on Neil Lazarus (201–207).

25. Solo's loathing and jealousy of Modin's lover, Aimee, is the source of much of the misogyny that suffuses the representation of Aimee in the novel.

26. My reading stresses the need to see the full circuit of Solo's sensibility—the

rage which also contains the openness that makes "healing simplicity" impossible for him. Thus I diverge from the novel's most thorough analyst, Neil Lazarus, who finds *Why Are We So Blest* suffused with "reactionary manicheism," anti-intellectualism, "racial and sexual essentialism," and "sweeping dogmatism," all of which make the book a "novelistic failure" (147, 185). The novel certainly *dramatizes* these attitudes but also reveals the psychology—the frustrations, denials, jealousies, and rationalizations—that produces them and the social order that produces the psychology. In other words, I think Armah has some distance from his characters, whereas Lazarus tends to treat them and their attitudes as transparent, expressing the unmediated views of the author. Thus, for instance, I regard the novel's misogyny less as Armah's own attitude than as a product of Solo's competition with Aimee for Modin. See also Robert E. Fox's reading of the novel.

27. As many observers have noted, this depth of disappointment derived from unrealistic expectations, a confusion (or conflation) of independence and revolution.

8. Cosmopolitan Collage

1. The critic Greg Tate used to regard Delany as a problem. He admired his work but "figured Delany for if not an oreo then somebody who wasn't interested in being labeled black." Though his science fiction is full of nonwhite characters, their race "is not at the core of their cultural identity." This frustrated Tate, who expected a "more or less nationalist stance" from the best-known black science fiction writer. But upon reflection he realized that while Delany's characters are not proponents of Negritude, neither are they bourgeois. Rather they are usually writers who possess "social mobility within the dominant culture and the option of rejecting its values" (165–166).

2. In other texts, such as *The Mad Man* and the Neveryon cycle, Delany displaces race with slavery as a paradigm of sadomasochistic homosexual relations.

3. Johnson has called his characters "free-floating creative force[s]," "tissue[s]" of world experience." Their identity, he says, is "cumulative" in the sense found in Jean Toomer's poem "Blue Meridian," which celebrates the advent of "Universal Man" (Johnson "Interview" 162). Johnson's aesthetic universalism is an implicit corrective to what, in *Being and Race*, he views as the static provincialism of Negritude and Black Arts writing. He critiques them as forms of "kitsch," art that disguises its "retreat from ambiguity" with a confident belief that it possesses "an adequate image of man" (20).

4. William Demby's underappreciated novel *The Catacombs* (1965), an obsessively self-referential work set in Rome in the early 1960s, is a collage construction and experiments "with the theory of cubistic time" (40). More recently, Darryl Pinckney's *High Cotton* (1992) is constructed as a palimpsest upon which traces of prior figures exert a continuous pressure, creating an intricate architecture of allusion.

5. The groundbreaking discussion of the musical epigraphs of *The Souls* is Eric Sundquist's (468–490).

6. Patricia Leighten, in "Picasso's Collages and the Threat of War, 1912–13," discusses the milieu of anarchism out of which Picasso created his collages.

7. Kennedy's mastery of the opacity of postmodern irony is particularly evident in her prose work *Deadly Triplets: A Theatre Mystery and Journal* (1990). Kimberly Benston makes a probing assessment of the difficulty of evaluating authorial tone in this work and in Kennedy's memoir ("Locating" 129).

8. "Sarcasm, darkness, pride" is how Kennedy herself has explained her shifting use of quotation marks. "It has many meanings" (Diamond "Interview" 152).

9. Certainly another way to read *Dutchman* is that Lula's brazen imperialism does Clay a favor; she performs the valuable service of provoking his liberation from the hypocrisies of bourgeois assimilation. Urging him to dance, she implores: "Clay, you got to break out. Don't sit there dying the way they want you to die. Get up" (95).

10. Bell hooks links Kennedy to Du Bois in a way that both accords with and diverges from the link proposed here: "[Kennedy] acknowledges this obsessive fascination with Europe, with white people on the one hand, but on the other, she is politically aware, conscious of the importance of anti-racist struggle, of black tradition. In this way she reminds me of black intellectuals, like Du Bois, and even Martin Luther King, who though passionately devoted to the civil rights struggle were truly enamored of white culture . . . When I read Kennedy, I ponder how she could have such keen awareness of the politics of race and gender, globally and in the United States, yet sustain that fascination with all those artifacts of white cultural imperialism" (hooks "Critical" 183–184). Hooks's puzzlement may be a result of her racializing of culture, which is precisely what Du Bois and Kennedy make problematic. Because of her commitment to the "kingdom of culture," Kennedy would probably resist describing her love of writers and literature as "fascination with all those artifacts of white cultural imperialism."

11. Kennedy's translation is not the standard Charles Lam Markmann one, and she condenses the paragraph from Fanon she is quoting. In the following quotations I mix her version and Markmann's.

12. Jeanie Forte makes an interesting case for "Negro-Sarah" as a tragic mulatta who, like Clara Passmore in *The Owl Answers,* makes a "poignant cry for resistance" to the demand either to name herself "wholly African American or to ignore" her "white heritage" (161–163). I read *Funnyhouse* less affirmatively and try to show the differences between the two characters.

13. "I am only yearning for our kingdom, God" is a line that Kennedy repeats in *A Movie Star Has to Star in Black and White,* where the play's protagonist, the young writer Clara, is on stage typing her play and occasionally reading aloud from it (89). She describes it as "about a girl who turns into an Owl" (95) and what she reads is borrowed from *The Owl Answers.*

14. Sarah's lack of a face references her creator's lament that her face "will always seem to be lacking because it is not" her mother's "pale, luminous" face (*People* 51).

15. I concur with Marc Robinson that "Sarah's idea of whiteness transcends race. She doesn't merely long to be white. She seeks complete invisibility, a blinding invisibility that burns away all trace of her tortured birth" (129).

16. I share Marc Robinson's emphasis on the purgative power of *Funnyhouse* for Kennedy: "Through Sarah, she faced her own ambivalent feelings about race . . . She let herself be attracted to violence, and she played out persistent fan-

tasies. By welcoming such imagery, she inoculated herself, in a way, ensuring that she wouldn't be overwhelmed again by the darkest products of her imagination . . . Writing *Funnyhouse*, she learned she didn't have to choose one aspect of her identity over another—the student enthralled by *Jane Eyre* or the woman transfixed by the mysteries of African masks" (132).

17. This appears in the second (unexpurgated) edition of the memoir (513). References to *The Motion of Light in Water* in the text will be to the first edition.

18. Delany asserts that "class conflicts alone can explain the obfuscation, lies, and the unspeakable cruelties that are the oppressive system [of race] itself" (*Silent* 8).

19. For instance, in the trucks at the Westside docks Delany often joins over a hundred men who "were slipping through and between and in and out of the trailers, some to watch, but most to participate in, numberless silent sexual acts . . . I stayed perhaps six hours, had sex seven or eight times, and left, finally, exhausted" (121).

20. But, to be precise, Delany, at one point, in group therapy, presents himself as ill, in need of cure. Or at least he mimes that attitude, for he feels compelled to use the only language available to him in the fifties—the "public language" of abjection and shame—and thus to present himself (inaccurately) as a homosexual "victim" who is working hard to "get better." Delany inwardly vows to one day shatter the "public" discourse, which he considers "tantamount to silence," by finding his own language (245, 247–249). The memoir is one way he fulfills that vow.

21. For lack of a neutral term, says Barthes, homosexuality can become imprisoned in a binary form that reproduces heterosexual power relations of "active/passive, of possessor/possessed" (133).

22. Thus Yvor Winters was wrong when he accused Crane of "automatic writing," of giving in to his "linguistic impulses, rather than intentionally creating his ideas." All writing, Delany remarks, "is, in some sense, automatic" (*Longer* 193). Disconnected from consciousness and intention, the writing self is decentered: "I am always an animal excess to the intellectual system that tries to construct me" (150).

23. This restricted audience is perhaps truer in Kennedy's case. Her work is performed irregularly, and in 1995 she received her first New York production (which featured a season-long cycle of her plays) since 1976. Delany's science fiction sells well. By 1987 his masterpiece in the genre, *Dhalgren* (1975), had sold 700,000 copies, 100,000 more than *Gravity's Rainbow* (*Silent* 37). But his works discussed in this chapter are published for a far smaller market.

24. This is the observation of the anthropologist Paul Rabinow, who claims that "*Homo sapiens* has done rather poorly in interpreting" cosmopolitanism (56). See Fleischacker for a rich philosophical discussion of the ethics of culture that in some ways complements Rabinow's perspective.

Works Cited

Adell, Sandra. *Double Consciousness/Double Bind: Theoretical Issues in Twentieth-Century Black Literature*. Urbana: U of Illinois P, 1994.

Adorno, Theodor. "Reconciliation under Duress." *Aesthetics and Politics*. London: New Left Books, 1977.

Akam, Everett. "Community and Cultural Crisis: 'The Transfiguring Imagination' of Alain Locke." *American Literary History* 3:2 (Summer 1991): 255–276.

Alexander, Jeffrey. *Fin de Siècle Social Theory: Relativism, Reduction, and the Problem of Reason*. New York: Verso, 1995.

Als, Hilton. *The Women*. New York: Farrar, Straus, 1996.

Altieri, Charles. "What Is Living and What Is Dead in American Postmodernism." *Critical Inquiry* 22:4 (Summer 1996): 764–789.

Anderson, James. *The Education of Blacks in the South, 1860–1935*. Chapel Hill: U of North Carolina P, 1988.

Anderson, Jervis. *A. Philip Randolph*. Berkeley: U of California P, 1986.

—— *Bayard Rustin: Troubles I've Seen: A Biography*. New York: HarperCollins, 1997.

Appiah, Kwame Anthony. "Cosmopolitan Patriots." *Critical Inquiry* 23:3 (Spring 1997): 617–639.

—— "Identity, Authenticity, Survival: Multicultural Societies and Social Reproduction." In *Multiculturalism: Examining the Politics of Recognition*. Ed. Amy Guttmann. Princeton: Princeton UP, 1994. 149–163.

—— *In My Father's House: Africa in the Philosophy of Culture*. New York: Oxford UP, 1992.

Aptheker, Herbert. "Introduction." *Dark Princess*. By W. E. B. Du Bois. 5–29.

Arendt, Hannah. *The Human Condition*. New York: Doubleday, 1959.

—— *The Life of the Mind*. 1-vol. ed. New York: Harcourt, 1978.

Armah, Ayi Kwei. "One Writer's Education." *Black Literature Criticism*. 3 vols. Ed. James Draper. Detroit: Gale Research, 1992. 1: 47–49.

—— *Why Are We So Blest?* Garden City, NY: Doubleday, 1972.

Aronowitz, Stanley. "The Double Bind." *Transition* 69 (Spring 1996): 222–235.

Ayandele, E. A. *The Educated Elite in the Nigerian Society.* Ibadan: Oxford UP, 1974.

Baker, Houston. *Afro-American Poetics: Revisions of Harlem and the Black Aesthetic.* Madison: U of Wisconsin P, 1988.

—— *Blues, Ideology, and Afro-American Literature: A Vernacular Theory.* Chicago: U of Chicago P, 1984.

—— *Modernism and the Harlem Renaissance.* Chicago: U of Chicago P, 1987.

—— *Workings of the Spirit: The Poetics of Afro-American Women's Writing.* Chicago: U of Chicago P, 1991.

Baldwin, James. *Another Country.* 1962. New York: Vintage, 1993.

—— *Go Tell It on the Mountain.* 1953. New York: Dell, 1985.

—— *Notes of a Native Son.* 1955. Boston: Beacon, 1984.

—— *The Price of the Ticket: Collected Non-Fiction, 1948–1985.* New York: St. Martin's, 1985.

Balibar, Etienne. "Culture and Identity (Working Notes)." Rajchman 173–196.

Banks, William. *Black Intellectuals: Race and Responsibility in American Life.* New York: Norton, 1996.

Baraka, Amiri (LeRoi Jones). *The Autobiography of LeRoi Jones/Amiri Baraka.* New York: Freundlich, 1984.

—— *Home: Social Essays.* New York: Morrow, 1966.

—— *The LeRoi Jones/Amiri Baraka Reader.* Ed. William Harris. New York: Thunder's Mouth P, 1991.

—— *The System of Dante's Hell.* New York: Grove, 1966.

—— *Tales.* New York: Grove, 1967.

—— *The Toilet. The Baptism and The Toilet.* New York: Grove, 1967.

Barthes, Roland. *Roland Barthes.* Trans. Richard Howard. New York: Hill and Wang, 1977.

Baudelaire, Charles. *The Painter of Modern Life and Other Essays.* Trans. and ed. Jonathan Mayne. New York: Da Capo, 1986.

Bell, Bernard, Emily Grosholz, James Stewart, eds. *W. E. B. Du Bois on Race and Culture.* New York: Routledge, 1996.

Bender, Thomas. *New York Intellect: A History of Intellectual Life in New York City, from 1750 to the Beginnings of Our Own Time.* New York: Knopf, 1987.

Benhabib, Seyla. *Situating the Self: Gender, Community, and Postmodernism in Contemporary Ethics.* New York: Routledge, 1992.

Benston, Kimberly. *Baraka: The Renegade and the Mask.* New Haven: Yale UP, 1976.

—— "Ellison, Baraka, and the Faces of Tradition." *Boundary 2* 6:2 (Winter 1978): 332–350.

—— "Locating Adrienne Kennedy: Prefacing the Subject." Bryant-Jackson and Overbeck 113–130.

Berlin, Isaiah. *The Magus of the North: J. G. Hamann and the Origins of Modern Irrationalism.* New York: Farrar, Straus, 1993.

Bernstein, Richard. *The Dictatorship of Virtue.* New York: Knopf, 1994.

Bhabha, Homi. *The Location of Culture.* New York: Routledge, 1994.

Blyden, Edward Wilmot. *Black Spokesman: Selected Published Writings of Edward Wilmot Blyden.* Ed. Hollis Lynch. London: Frank Cass, 1971.

Boas, Franz. *A Franz Boas Reader: The Shaping of American Anthropology, 1883–1911.* Ed. George Stocking. Chicago: U of Chicago P, 1974.

Bourdieu, Pierre. *Distinction.* Trans. Richard Nice. Cambridge, MA: Harvard UP, 1984.

—— "The Corporatism of the Universal: The Role of Intellectuals in the Modern World." *Telos* 81 (Fall 1989): 99–110.

Bourne, Randolph. *The Radical Will: Selected Writings, 1911–1918.* Ed. Olaf Hansen. New York: Urizen, 1977.

Bredin, Jean-Denis. *The Affair: The Case of Alfred Dreyfus.* Trans. Jeffrey Mehlman. New York: George Braziller, 1986.

Brodsky, Garry. "Politics, Culture and Society in Marx and Dewey." *Context over Foundation: Dewey and Marx.* Ed. W. J. Gavin. Boston: Reidel, 1988. 77–118.

Brown, Wendy. "Wounded Attachments: Late Modern Oppositional Political Formations." Rajchman 199–227.

Bryant-Jackson, Paul, and Lois More Overbeck, ed. *Intersecting Boundaries: The Theatre of Adrienne Kennedy.* Minneapolis: U of Minnesota P, 1992.

Burke, Kenneth. *Counter-Statement.* 1931. Berkeley: U of California P, 1968.

Byerman, Keith. *Seizing the Word: History, Art, and Self in the Work of W. E. B. Du Bois.* Athens: U of Georgia P, 1994.

Carby, Hazel. *Racemen: The Body and Soul of Race, Nation, and Masculinity.* Cambridge, MA: Harvard UP, 1998.

Cash, W. J. *The Mind of the South.* 1941. New York: Vintage, 1969.

Chauncey, George. *Gay New York: Gender, Urban Culture, and the Making of the Male Gay World, 1890–1940.* New York: Basic, 1994.

Chesnutt, Charles. *Collected Stories of Charles Chesnutt.* Ed. William Andrews. New York: Signet, 1992.

—— *The House Behind the Cedars.* 1900. New York: Penguin, 1993.

—— *The Journals of Charles Chesnutt.* Ed. Richard Brodhead. Durham: Duke UP, 1993.

—— *"To Be an Author": Letters of Charles Chesnutt, 1899–1905.* Ed. Joseph McElrath and Robert Leitz. Princeton: Princeton UP, 1997.

Chytry, Joseph. *The Aesthetic State: A Quest in Modern German Thought.* Berkeley: U of California P, 1989.

Clayton, Bruce. *Forgotten Prophet: The Life of Randolph Bourne.* Baton Rouge: Louisiana State UP, 1984.

Cleaver, Eldridge. *Soul on Ice.* New York: Dell, 1970.

Cocks, Joan. "On Nationalism: Frantz Fanon, 1925–1961; Rosa Luxemburg, 1871–1919; and Hannah Arendt, 1906–1975." *Feminist Interpretations of Hannah Arendt.* Ed. Bonnie Honig. University Park: Pennsylvania State UP, 1995. 221–245.

Coon, Deborah. " 'One Moment in the World's Salvation': Anarchism and the Radicalization of William James." *Journal of American History* 83 (June 1996): 70–99.

Cooney, Terry. "New York Intellectuals and the Question of Jewish Identity." *American Jewish History* 80:3 (Spring 1991): 344–360.

Cooper, Anna Julia. *A Voice from the South.* 1892. New York: Oxford UP, 1988.

Cox, Oliver. "Introduction." *The Black Anglo-Saxons*. By Nathan Hare. New York: Collier, 1965.

Croly, Herbert. *The Promise of American Life*. 1909. Boston: Northeastern UP, 1989.

Crouch, Stanley. *Notes of a Hanging Judge: Essays and Reviews, 1979–89*. New York: Oxford UP, 1990.

Crummell, Alexander. *Africa and America*. 1891. New York: Negro Universities P, 1969.

—— *Destiny and Race: Selected Writings, 1840–1898*. Ed. Wilson Moses. Amherst: U of Massachusetts P, 1992.

Cruse, Harold. *The Crisis of the Negro Intellectual: From Its Origins to the Present*. New York: Morrow, 1967.

Davidson, Basil. *The Black Man's Burden: Africa and the Curse of the Nation-State*. New York: Times Books, 1992.

Davis, Allison. *Leadership, Love and Aggression*. New York: Harcourt, 1983.

Davis, Angela. "Discussion." Dent 325–331.

Delany, Samuel. *Atlantis: Model 1924*. In *Atlantis: Three Tales*. Hanover, NH: Wesleyan UP, 1995.

—— *Longer Views: Extended Essays*. Hanover, N.H.: Wesleyan UP, 1996.

—— *The Mad Man*. New York: Richard Kasak, 1994.

—— *The Motion of Light in Water: Sex and Science Fiction Writing in the East Village, 1957–1965*. New York: Arbor House, 1988.

—— *The Motion of Light in Water*. 2nd ed. New York: Richard Kasak, 1993.

—— *Silent Interviews*. Hanover, NH: Wesleyan UP, 1994.

—— *Triton*. New York: Bantam, 1976.

Delany, Sarah, and A. Elizabeth Delany. *Having Our Say: The Delany Sisters' First 100 Years*. New York: Dell, 1993.

Demby, William. *The Catacombs*. 1965. New York: Harper, 1970.

Dent, Gina, ed. *Black Popular Culture*. Seattle: Bay Press, 1992.

Dewey, John. *Art as Experience*. 1934. New York: Putnam's, 1980.

—— *Characters and Events*. 2 vols. New York: Holt, 1929.

—— *Experience and Nature*. La Salle, IL: Open Court, 1929.

—— *Freedom and Culture*. 1939. New York: Capricorn, 1963.

—— "From Absolutism to Experimentalism." *The Philosophy of John Dewey*. Ed. John McDermott. Chicago: U of Chicago P, 1981. 1–13.

—— *The Later Works, 1925–1953*. Ed. Jo-Ann Boydston. Carbondale: Southern Illinois UP, 1986. 14 vols. 1985–1990.

—— *The Political Writings*. Ed. Debra Morris and Ian Shapiro. Indianapolis: Hackett, 1993.

—— *The Quest for Certainty*. 1929. New York: Putnam's, 1960.

Diamond, Elin. "An Interview with Adrienne Kennedy." *Studies in American Drama* 9 (1989): 143–157.

—— "Mimesis in Syncopated Time." Bryant-Jackson and Overbeck 131–141.

Diggins, John Patrick. *The Rise and Fall of the American Left*. New York: Norton, 1992.

Douglas, Ann. *Terrible Honesty: Mongrel Manhattan in the 1920s*. New York: Farrar, Straus, 1995.

Douglass, Frederick. *Autobiographies.* New York: Library of America, 1994.

Drake, St. Clair, and Horace Cayton. *Black Metropolis: A Study of Negro Life in a Northern City.* 1945. 2 vols. New York: Harcourt, 1970.

Du Bois, W. E. B. *Against Racism: Unpublished Essays, Papers, Addresses, 1871–1961.* Ed. Herbert Aptheker. Amherst: U of Massachusetts P, 1985.

——— *The Amenia Conference: An Historic Negro Gathering. Pamphlets and Leaflets by W. E. B. Du Bois.* Ed. Herbert Aptheker. Millwood, NY: Kraus, 1986.

——— The *Autobiography of W. E. B. Du Bois: A Soliloquy on Viewing My Life from the Last Decade of Its First Century.* New York: International, 1968.

——— *Black Reconstruction in America, 1860–1880.* 1935. New York: Atheneum, 1992.

——— *Book Reviews.* Ed. Herbert Aptheker. Millwood, NY: Kraus, 1977.

——— *Color and Democracy: Colonies and Peace.* New York: Harcourt, 1945.

——— *The Correspondence of W. E. B. Du Bois.* Ed. Herbert Aptheker. Amherst: U of Massachusetts P. 3 vols. 1973–1978.

——— *The Crisis. Selections: 1910–1934.* Ed. Herbert Aptheker. Vol. 1. Millwood, NY: Kraus, 1983.

——— *Dark Princess: A Romance.* 1928. Millwood, NY: Kraus, 1974.

——— *Darkwater.* 1920. Millwood, NY: Kraus, 1975.

——— "The Dilemma of the Negro." *American Mercury* (Oct. 1924): 179–185.

——— *Dusk of Dawn: An Essay toward an Autobiography of a Race Concept.* 1940. Du Bois *Writings* 551–802.

——— *The Gift of Black Folk: Negroes in the Making of America.* 1924. New York: Washington Square P, 1970.

——— *Mansart Builds a School.* 1959. Bk. 2. *The Black Flame: A Trilogy.* Millwood, NY: Kraus, 1976.

——— "My Evolving Program for Negro Freedom." *What the Negro Wants.* Ed. Rayford Logan. Chapel Hill: U of North Carolina P, 1944. 31–70.

——— *The Philadelphia Negro: A Social Study.* 1899. New York: Schocken, 1967.

——— *The Quest of the Silver Fleece.* 1911. Boston: Northeastern UP, 1989.

——— *The Souls of Black Folk.* 1903. Du Bois *Writings* 359–547.

——— *W. E. B. Du Bois: A Reader.* Ed. David Levering Lewis. New York: Holt, 1995.

——— *Writings.* New York: Library of America, 1986.

——— *Writings by W. E. B. Du Bois in Periodicals Edited by Others.* 4 vols. Com. and ed. Herbert Aptheker. Millwood, NY: Kraus, 1982.

duCille, Ann. *The Coupling Convention: Sex, Text and Tradition in Black Women's Fiction.* New York: Oxford UP, 1993.

Early, Gerald, ed. *Speech and Power: The African-American Essay and Its Cultural Content, from Polemics to Pulpit.* 2 vols. New York: Ecco, 1993.

Edelman, Lee. *Homographesis: Essays in Gay Literary and Cultural Theory.* New York: Routledge, 1994.

Ellis, Mark. " 'Closing Ranks' and 'Seeking Honors': W. E. B. Du Bois in World War I." *Journal of American History* 79 (June 1992): 96–124.

Ellis, Markman. *The Politics of Sensibility: Race, Gender, and Commerce in the Sentimental Novel.* New York: Cambridge UP, 1996.

Ellison, Ralph. "Alain Locke." "The Alain Locke Symposium." *Harvard Advocate* (Dec. 1, 1973): 9–30.

—— *The Collected Essays of Ralph Ellison.* Ed. John Callahan. New York: Modern Library, 1995.

—— *Going to the Territory.* New York: Vintage, 1987.

—— *Invisible Man.* 1952. New York: Vintage, 1989.

—— *Shadow and Act.* 1964. New York: Vintage, 1972.

Emerson, Ralph Waldo. *Essays and Lectures.* New York: Library of America, 1983.

Esteve, Mary. "Nella Larsen's 'Moving Mosaic': Harlem, Crowds, and Anonymity." *American Literary History* 9:2 (Summer 1997): 268–286.

Fauset, Jessie. *Plum Bun.* 1929. Boston: Beacon, 1990.

Fanon, Frantz. *Black Skin, White Masks.* Trans. Charles Lam Markmann. New York: Grove, 1967.

—— *Toward the African Revolution.* Trans. Haakon Chevalier. New York: Grove, 1967.

—— *The Wretched of the Earth.* Trans. Constance Farrington. New York: Grove, 1991.

Feher, Michel. "The Schisms of '67: On Certain Restructurings of the American Left, from the Civil Rights Movement to the Multiculturalist Constellation." *Blacks and Jews: Alliances and Arguments.* Ed. Paul Berman. New York: Delacorte, 1994. 263–285.

Ferris, William. *The African Abroad; or, His Evolution in Western Civilization, Tracing the Development under Caucasian Milieu.* 1913. 2 vols. New York: Johnson Reprint, 1968.

—— "Darkwater." Vincent 342–348.

Ferry, Luc. *Homo Aestheticus: The Invention of Taste in the Democratic Age.* Trans. Robert de Loazia. Chicago: U of Chicago P, 1993.

Finkielkraut, Alain. *The Defeat of the Mind.* Trans. Judith Friedlander. New York: Columbia UP, 1995.

Fleischacker, Samuel. *The Ethics of Culture.* Ithaca: Cornell UP, 1994.

Foner, Eric. *A Short History of Reconstruction: 1863–1877.* New York: Harper, 1990.

Ford, Nick Aaron. "A Study in Race Relations—A Meeting with Zora Neale Hurston." *Modern Critical Views: Zora Neale Hurston.* Ed. Harold Bloom. New York: Chelsea House, 1986. 7–10.

Forte, Jeanie. "Kennedy's Body Politic: The Mulatta, Menses and the Medusa." Bryant-Jackson and Overbeck 157–169.

Fox, Robert Elliot. *Masters of the Drum: Black Lit/Oratures across the Continuum.* Westport: Greenwood, 1995.

Fraden, Rena. *Blueprints for a Black Federal Theatre, 1935–1939.* New York: Cambridge UP, 1994.

Franklin, V. P. *Living Our Stories, Telling Our Truths: Autobiography and the Making of the African-American Intellectual Tradition.* New York: Scribner, 1995.

Frazier, E. Franklin. *Black Bourgeoisie: The Rise of a New Middle Class.* New York: Collier, 1962.

Fredrickson, George. *Black Liberation: A Comparative History of Black Ideologies in the United States and South Africa.* New York: Oxford UP, 1995.

Fuss, Diana. "Interior Colonies: Frantz Fanon and the Politics of Identification." *Diacritics* 24 (Summer/Fall 1994): 20–42.

Fyfe, Christopher. *Africanus Horton, 1835–1883: West African Scientist and Patriot.* New York: Oxford UP, 1972.

Gaines, Kevin. *Uplifting the Race: Black Leadership, Politics and Culture in the Twentieth Century.* Chapel Hill: U of North Carolina P, 1996.

Garvey, Marcus. "What Garvey Thinks of Du Bois." Vincent 97–99.

Gates, Henry Louis, Jr. "The Black Man's Burden." Dent 78–83.

——— *The Signifying Monkey: A Theory of Afro-American Literary Criticism.* New York: Oxford UP, 1988.

——— "The Trope of a New Negro and the Reconstruction of the Image of the Black." *Representations* 24 (Fall 1988): 129–155.

——— "White Like Me." *New Yorker* (June 17, 1996): 66–81.

——— and K. A. Appiah, eds. *Zora Neale Hurston: Critical Perspectives Past and Present.* New York: Amistad, 1993.

Gellner, Ernest. *Postmodernism, Reason and Religion.* New York: Routledge, 1992.

Gendzier, Irene. *Frantz Fanon: A Critical Study.* New York: Pantheon, 1973.

Genovese, Eugene. *Roll, Jordan, Roll: The World the Slaves Made.* New York: Vintage, 1976.

Gilroy, Paul. *The Black Atlantic: Modernity and Double Consciousness.* Cambridge, MA: Harvard UP, 1993.

Gleason, Philip. *Speaking of Diversity: Language and Ethnicity in Twentieth-Century America.* Baltimore: Johns Hopkins UP, 1992.

Gooding-Williams, Robert. "Evading Narrative Myth, Evading Prophetic Pragmatism: Cornel West's *The American Evasion of Philosophy.*" *Massachusetts Review* 33:4 (Winter 1991–92): 517–542.

Gouldner, Alvin. *Against Fragmentation.* New York: Oxford UP, 1985.

Gramsci, Antonio. *Prison Notebooks.* Ed. and trans. Quentin Hoare and Geoffrey Nowell Smith. New York: International, 1971.

Griggs, Sutton. *Imperium in Imperio: A Study of the Negro Race Problem.* 1899. Miami: Mnemosyne, 1969.

Guillory, John. *Cultural Capital: The Problem of Literary Canon Formation.* Chicago: U of Chicago P, 1993.

Habermas, Jürgen. "Heinrich Heine and the Role of the Intellectual in Germany." *The New Conservatism: Cultural Criticism and the Historians' Debate.* Trans. Shierry Nicholsen. Cambridge, MA: MIT P, 1989.

Hall, Stuart. "What Is This 'Black' in Black Popular Culture?" Dent 21–33.

Hannaford, Ivan. *Race: The History of an Idea in the West.* Baltimore: Johns Hopkins UP, 1996.

Harding, Vincent. *There Is a River: The Black Struggle for Freedom in America.* New York: Vintage, 1981.

Harper, Phillip Brian. *Are We Not Men?: Masculine Anxiety and the Problem of African-American Identity.* New York: Oxford UP, 1996.

——— "Nationalism and Social Division in Black Arts Poetry of the 1960s." *Critical Inquiry* 19 (Winter 1993): 234–255.

Hatch, James. *Sorrow Is the Only Faithful One: The Life of Owen Dodson.* Urbana: U of Illinois P, 1993.

Heath, Gordon. *Deep Are the Roots: Memoirs of a Black Expatriate.* Amherst: U of Massachusetts P, 1992.

Hemenway, Robert. *Zora Neale Hurston: A Literary Biography.* Urbana: U of Illinois P, 1980.

Higham, John. *Send These to Me: Immigrants in Urban America.* Rev. ed. Baltimore: Johns Hopkins UP, 1984.

Hoffman, Katharine. "Introduction." *Collage: Critical Views.* Ed. Katharine Hoffman. Ann Arbor: UMI, 1989.

Hollinger, David. *Postethnic America: Beyond Multiculturalism.* New York: Basic, 1995.

Holt, Thomas. "Marking: Race, Race Making, and the Writing of History." *American Historical Review* 100 (Feb. 1995): 1–20.

—— "The Political Uses of Alienation: W. E. B. Du Bois on Politics, Race, and Culture, 1903–1940." *American Quarterly* 42 (June 1990): 301–323.

Honig, Bonnie. "Difference, Dilemmas, and the Politics of Home." *Social Research* 61 (Fall 1994): 563–597.

hooks, bell. "Critical Reflections: Adrienne Kennedy, the Writer, the Work." Bryant-Jackson and Overbeck 179–185.

—— *Yearning: Race, Gender, and Cultural Politics.* Boston: South End P, 1991.

—— and Cornel West. *Breaking Bread: Insurgent Black Intellectual Life.* Boston: South End P, 1991.

Hopkins, Pauline. *Contending Forces: A Romance Illustrative of Negro Life North and South.* 1900. New York: Oxford UP, 1988.

—— *Of One Blood, Or the Hidden Self.* 1903. *The Magazine Novels of Pauline Hopkins.* New York: Oxford UP, 1988. 441–621.

Horkheimer, Max, and Theodor Adorno. *Dialectic of Enlightenment.* 1944. Trans. John Cummings. New York: Continuum, 1972.

Huggins, Nathan Irvin. *Harlem Renaissance.* New York: Oxford UP, 1971.

—— *Revelations: American History, American Myths.* New York: Oxford UP, 1995.

—— ed. *Voices from the Harlem Renaissance.* New York: Oxford UP, 1976.

Hughes, Langston. "The Negro Artist and the Racial Mountain." *The Nation,* June 1926. Rpt. Huggins *Voices* 305–309.

Hurst, Fannie. "A Personality Sketch." *Modern Critical Views: Zora Neale Hurston.* Ed. Harold Bloom. New York: Chelsea House, 1986. 21–24.

Hurston, Zora Neale. *Folklore, Memoirs, and Other Writings.* New York: Library of America, 1995.

Hutchinson, George. *The Harlem Renaissance in Black and White.* Cambridge, MA: Harvard UP, 1995.

—— "Jean Toomer and American Racial Discourse." *Texas Studies in Language and Literature* 35:2 (Summer 1993): 227–251.

—— "Nella Larsen and the Veil of Race." *American Literary History* 9:2 (Summer 1997): 329–349.

Hutchinson, Louise. *Anna J. Cooper: A Voice from the South.* Washington: Smithsonian, 1981.

Isaacs, Harold. *The New World of Negro Americans.* New York: Viking, 1964.

James, Henry. *The American Scene.* 1907. Bloomington: Indiana UP, 1969.

—— *Henry James Letters: 1843–1875.* Ed. Leon Edel. Cambridge, MA: Harvard UP, 1974.

James, Joy. *Transcending the Talented Tenth: Black Leaders and American Intellectuals.* New York: Routledge, 1997.

James, William. *Pragmatism: A New Name for Some Old Ways of Thinking.* 1907. Cambridge, MA: Harvard UP, 1978.

—— *The Principles of Psychology.* 1890. Cambridge, MA: Harvard UP, 1983.

—— *The Will to Believe and Other Essays in Popular Philosophy.* 1897. Cambridge, MA: Harvard UP, 1979.

—— *Writings: 1902–1910.* New York: Library of America, 1987.

Jameson, Fredric. *Fables of Aggression: Wyndham Lewis, the Modernist as Fascist.* Berkeley: U of California P, 1981.

—— "On Cultural Studies." Rajchman 251–295.

Joas, Hans. *Pragmatism and Social Theory.* Chicago: U of Chicago P, 1993.

Johnson, Charles. *Being and Race: Black Writing since 1970.* Bloomington: Indiana UP, 1990.

—— "An Interview with Charles Johnson." By Jonathan Little. *Contemporary Literature* 34:2 (1993): 159–181.

—— *Oxherding Tale.* New York: Grove, 1984.

Johnson, James Weldon. *Along This Way: The Autobiography of James Weldon Johnson.* 1933. New York: Penguin, 1990.

—— *The Autobiography of an Ex-Colored Man.* 1912. New York: Penguin, 1990.

—— "Double Audience Makes Road Hard for Negro Authors." *Selected Writings of James Weldon Johnson.* 2 vols. Ed. Sondra Wilson. New York: Oxford UP, 1995. 2: 408–412.

Judy, Ronald. "The New Black Aesthetic and W. E. B. Du Bois, or Hephaestus Limping." *Massachusetts Review* 35:2 (Summer 1994): 249–282.

Julien, Isaac. " 'Black Is, Black Ain't': Notes on De-Essentializing Black Identity." Dent 255–264.

—— and Kobena Mercer. "Introduction: De Margin and De Centre." *Screen* 29:4 (Autumn 1988): 1–10.

Kahn, Michael. "An Interview with Michael Kahn." By Howard Stein. Bryant-Jackson and Overbeck 189–198.

Kallen, Horace. *Culture and Democracy in the United States.* New York: Boni and Liveright, 1924.

Kaplan, Cora. " 'A Cavern Opened In My Mind': The Poetics of Homosexuality and the Politics of Masculinity in James Baldwin." *Representing Black Men.* Ed. Marcellus Blount and George Cunningham. New York: Routledge, 1996.

Kateb, George. "Notes on Pluralism." *Social Research* 61:3 (Fall 1994): 511–537.

Kaufman-Osborn, Timothy. *Politics / Sense / Experience: A Pragmatic Inquiry into the Promise of Democracy.* Ithaca: Cornell UP, 1991.

Kempton, Murray. *Rebellions, Perversities, and Main Events.* New York: Times Books, 1994.

Kennedy, Adrienne. "Adrienne Kennedy." *Black Literature Criticism.* Ed. James Draper. 3 vols. Detroit: Gale Research, 1992. 2: 1149–63.

—— *The Alexander Plays*. Minneapolis: U of Minnesota P, 1992.

—— *Deadly Triplets: A Theatre Mystery and Journal*. Minneapolis: U of Minnesota P, 1990.

—— *In One Act*. Minneapolis: U of Minnesota P, 1988.

—— *People Who Led to My Plays*. New York: Theatre Communications Group, 1988.

Kerman, Cynthia, and Richard Eldridge. *The Lives of Jean Toomer: A Hunger for Wholeness*. Baton Rouge: Louisiana State UP, 1987.

Kirkland, Frank. "Modernity and Intellectual Life in Black." *Philosophical Forum* 24:1–3 (Fall–Spring 1992–1993): 136–165.

Klein, Marcus. "A Question of Identity." *Modern Critical Views: James Baldwin*. Ed. Harold Bloom. New York: Chelsea House, 1986. 17–33.

Kloppenberg, James. *Uncertain Victory: Social Democracy and Progressivism in European and American Thought, 1870–1920*. New York: Oxford UP, 1986.

Kristeva, Julia. *Nations without Nationalism*. Trans. Leon Roudiez. New York: Columbia UP, 1993.

—— *Strangers to Ourselves*. Trans. Leon Roudiez. New York: Columbia UP, 1991.

Lamming, George. *The Pleasures of Exile*. London: Allison and Busby, 1984.

Lampert, Laurence. *Nietzsche and Modern Times: A Study of Bacon, Descartes, and Nietzsche*. New Haven: Yale UP, 1993.

Larsen, Nella. *Quicksand*. 1928. *Quicksand and Passing*. New Brunswick: Rutgers UP, 1986.

Lasch, Christopher. *The Revolt of the Elites and the Betrayal of Democracy*. New York: Norton, 1995.

Lawrence-Lightfoot, Sara. *I've Known Rivers: Lives of Loss and Liberation*. Reading, MA: Addison-Wesley, 1994.

Lazarus, Neil. *Resistance in Postcolonial African Fiction*. New Haven: Yale UP, 1990.

Leeming, David. *James Baldwin: A Biography*. New York: Holt, 1994.

—— "An Interview with James Baldwin on Henry James." *Henry James Review* 8:1 (Fall 1986): 47–56.

Le Goff, Jacques. *Intellectuals in the Middle Ages*. Trans. Teresa Lavender Fagan. Cambridge, MA: Blackwell, 1993.

Leighten, Patricia. "Picasso's Collages and the Threat of War, 1912–13." Hoffman 121–170.

Levine, George. "Reclaiming the Aesthetic." *Aesthetics and Ideology*. Ed. George Levine. New Brunswick: Rutgers UP, 1994. 1–23.

Lewis, David Levering. *W. E. B. Du Bois: Biography of a Race, 1868–1919*. New York: Holt, 1993.

Lewis, Wyndham. *Paleface; or, The Philosophy of the Melting Pot*. London: Chatto and Windus, 1929.

Lind, Michael. *The Next American Nation: The New Nationalism and the Fourth American Revolution*. New York: Free Press, 1995.

Locke, Alain. *The Critical Temper of Alain Locke: A Selection of His Essays on Art and Culture*. Ed. Jeffrey Stewart. New York: Garland, 1983.

—— "Jingo, Counter-Jingo, and Us." *Opportunity* 16:1 (Jan. 1938): 7–11, 27.

Rpt. *The Critics and the Harlem Renaissance.* Ed. Cary Wintz. New York: Garland, 1996.

—— "The Legacy of the Ancestral Arts." Ed. Locke. *The New Negro.* 254–267.

—— "The New Negro." Ed. Locke. *The New Negro.* 3–16.

—— ed. *The New Negro.* New York: Atheneum, 1992.

—— *The Philosophy of Alain Locke: Harlem Renaissance and Beyond.* Ed. Leonard Harris. Philadelphia: Temple UP, 1989.

—— *Race Contacts and Interracial Relations.* Ed. Jeffrey Stewart. Washington: Howard UP, 1992.

Lott, Eric. *Love and Theft: Blackface Minstrelsy and the American Working Class.* New York: Oxford UP, 1993.

—— "The New Cosmopolitanism." *Transition* 72 (Fall 1996): 108–135.

Loury, Glenn. *One By One from the Inside Out.* New York: Free Press, 1995.

Lynch, Hollis. *Edward Wilmot Blyden: Pan-Negro Patriot, 1832–1912.* London: Oxford UP, 1967.

McFeely, William. *Frederick Douglass.* New York: Touchstone, 1992.

McKay, Claude. *Banjo: A Story without a Plot.* 1929. New York: Harcourt, 1968.

—— *Home to Harlem.* 1928. Boston: Northeastern UP, 1987.

—— *A Long Way from Home.* 1937. New York: Harcourt, 1970.

Malik, Kenan. *The Meaning of Race.* London: Macmillan, 1996.

Marable, Manning. *W. E. B. Du Bois: Black Radical Democrat.* Boston: Twayne, 1986.

Marez, Curtis. "The Other Addict: Reflections on Colonialism and Oscar Wilde's Opium Smoke Screen." *ELH* 64:1 (Spring 1997): 257–288.

Massa, Ann. *Vachel Lindsay: Fieldworker for the American Dream.* Bloomington: Indiana UP, 1970.

Matthiessen, F. O. *The James Family: Including Selections from the Writings of Henry James Senior, William, Henry and Alice James.* New York: Knopf, 1961.

Mead, George Herbert. *Mind, Self, and Society: From the Standpoint of a Social Behaviorist.* 1934. Ed. Charles Morris. Chicago: U of Chicago P, 1962.

—— *Movements of Thought in the Nineteenth Century.* 1936. Chicago: U of Chicago P, 1972.

Memmi, Albert. "The Impossible Life of Frantz Fanon." *Massachusetts Review* 14 (Winter 1973): 9–39.

Mencken, H. L. *Friedrich Nietzsche.* 1913. New Brunswick: Transaction, 1993.

Michaels, Walter Benn. *Our America: Nativism, Modernism, and Pluralism.* Durham: Duke UP, 1995.

Miller, Kelly. *Radicals and Conservatives, and Other Essays on the Negro in America.* Rpt. of *Race Adjustment.* 1908. New York: Schocken, 1968.

Mizruchi, Susan. "Neighbors, Strangers, and Corpses: Death and Sympathy in the Early Writings of W. E. B. Du Bois." *Centuries' Ends, Narrative Means.* Ed. Robert Newman. Stanford: Stanford UP, 1996.

Moon, Henry Lee, ed. "Introduction." *The Emerging Thought of W. E. B. Du Bois. Essays and Editorials from The Crisis.* New York: Simon and Schuster, 1972.

Morrison, Toni. "Introduction: Friday on the Potomac." *Race-ing Justice, Engendering Power.* Ed. Toni Morrison. New York: Pantheon, 1992. vii–xxx.

———— *Playing in the Dark: Whiteness and the Literary Imagination*. Cambridge, MA: Harvard UP, 1992.

Moses, Wilson. *Alexander Crummell: A Study of Civilization and Discontent*. New York, Oxford UP, 1989.

———— *Black Messiahs and Uncle Toms: Social and Literary Manipulations of a Religious Myth*. Rev. ed. University Park: Pennsylvania State UP, 1982.

———— *The Golden Age of Black Nationalism: 1850–1925*. New York: Oxford UP, 1988.

———— "W. E. B. Du Bois's 'The Conservation of Races' and Its Context: Idealism, Conservatism and Hero Worship." *Massachusetts Review* 34:2 (Summer 1993): 275–294.

Moss, Alfred. *The American Negro Academy: Voice of the Talented Tenth*. Baton Rouge: Louisiana State UP, 1981.

Murray, Albert. "Alain Locke." "The Alain Locke Symposium." *Harvard Advocate* (Dec. 1, 1973): 9–30.

———— *The Blue Devils of Nada: A Contemporary American Approach to Aesthetic Statement*. New York: Pantheon, 1996.

———— *The Omni-Americans*. 1970. New York: Vintage, 1983.

———— *South to a Very Old Place*. 1971. New York: Vintage, 1991.

Newman, Barnett. *Selected Writings and Interviews*. New York: Knopf, 1990.

Ngũgĩ wa Thiong'o. *Decolonising the Mind: The Politics of Language in African Literature*. London: James Currey, 1986.

Nietzsche, Friedrich. *The Gay Science*. Trans. Walter Kaufmann. New York: Vintage, 1974.

———— *On the Genealogy of Morals*. Trans. Walter Kaufmann. New York: Vintage, 1969.

Nussbaum, Martha. "Kant and Cosmopolitanism." *Perpetual Peace: Essays on Kant's Cosmopolitan Ideal*. Ed. James Bohman and Matthias Lutz-Bachmann. Cambridge, MA: MIT P, 1997.

———— "Patriotism and Cosmopolitanism." *Boston Review* 19 (Oct.–Nov. 1994): 3–6.

Otten, Thomas. "Pauline Hopkins and the Hidden Self of Race." *ELH* 59 (1992): 227–256.

Parrish, Timothy. "Ralph Ellison, Kenneth Burke, and the Form of Democracy." *Arizona Quarterly* 51:3 (Autumn 1995):117–148.

Perry, Ralph Barton. *The Character and Thought of William James*. 2 Vols. Boston: Little, Brown, 1935.

Petry, Ann. *The Street*. 1946. Boston: Houghton Mifflin, 1991.

Phillips, L. W. "W. E. B. Du Bois and Soviet Communism: *The Black Flame* as Socialist Realism." *South Atlantic Quarterly* 94:3 (Summer 1995): 837–863.

Pinckney, Darryl. *High Cotton*. New York: Farrar, Straus, 1992.

———— "The Outsider." *New York Review of Books*, Dec. 18, 1987: 15–21.

———— "Phantom." *New York Review of Books*, March 5, 1981: 34–36.

Podhoretz, Norman. *Breaking Ranks: A Political Memoir*. New York: Harper, 1979.

Poirier, Richard. *Poetry and Pragmatism*. Cambridge, MA: Harvard UP, 1992.

—— *The Renewal of Literature: Emersonian Reflections*. New Haven: Yale UP, 1987.

Posnock, Ross. *The Trial of Curiosity: Henry James, William James, and the Challenge of Modernity*. New York: Oxford UP, 1991.

—— "Race and Responsibility." *Raritan* 18 (Winter 1998): 120–136.

Rabinow, Paul. *Essays on the Anthropology of Reason*. Princeton: Princeton UP, 1996.

Rajchman, John, ed. *The Identity in Question*. New York: Routledge, 1995.

Rampersad, Arnold. *The Art and Imagination of W. E. B. Du Bois*. 1976. New York: Schocken, 1990.

Ray, David, and Robert Farnsworth, eds. *Richard Wright: Impressions and Perspectives*. Ann Arbor: U of Michigan P, 1973.

Redding, J. Saunders. *On Being Negro in America*. 1951. New York: Bantam, 1964.

—— *A Scholar's Conscience: Selected Writings of J. Saunders Redding*. Ed. Faith Berry. Lexington: UP of Kentucky, 1992.

—— *Stranger and Alone*. 1950. Boston: Northeastern UP, 1989.

Reed, Adolph. *The Jesse Jackson Phenomenon: The Crisis of Purpose in Afro-American Politics*. New Haven: Yale UP, 1986.

—— *W. E. B. Du Bois and American Political Thought: Fabianism and the Color Line*. New York: Oxford UP, 1997.

—— "W. E. B. Du Bois: A Perspective on the Bases of His Political Thought." *Political Theory* 13:3 (Aug. 1985): 431–456.

—— "What Are the Drums Saying Booker?—The Current Crisis of the Black Intellectual." *Village Voice*, April 11, 1995: 31–36.

Reily, Charlie, ed. *Conversations with Amiri Baraka*. Jackson: UP of Mississippi, 1994.

Rieff, Philip. *The Feeling Intellect: Selected Writings*. Chicago: U of Chicago P, 1990.

Robbins, Bruce. *Secular Vocations: Intellectuals, Professionalism, Culture*. New York: Verso, 1993.

Robinson, Marc. *The Other American Drama*. New York: Cambridge UP, 1994.

Rorty, Richard. "Dewey between Hegel and Darwin." *Modernist Impulses in the Human Sciences, 1870–1930*. Ed. Dorothy Ross. Baltimore: Johns Hopkins UP, 1994. 54–68.

Ross, Dorothy. *The Origins of American Social Science*. New York: Cambridge UP, 1991.

Ross, B. Joyce. *J. E. Spingarn and the Rise of the NAACP*. New York: Atheneum, 1972.

Rudwick, Elliott. *W. E. B. Du Bois: Voice of the Black Protest Movement*. Urbana: U of Illinois P, 1982.

Rustin, Bayard. *Down the Line: Collected Writings*. Chicago: Quadrangle, 1971.

Said, Edward. *Culture and Imperialism*. New York: Vintage, 1993.

—— "The Politics of Knowledge." *Raritan* 11 (Summer 1991): 17–31.

Salih, Tayeb. *Season of Migration to the North*. Trans. Denys Johnson-Davies. London: Heinemann, 1969.

Santayana, George. *Santayana on America: Essays, Notes and Letters on American Life, Literature, and Philosophy.* Ed. Richard C. Lyon. New York: Harcourt, 1968.

Sartre, Jean-Paul. "Black Orpheus." *"What Is Literature?" and Other Essays.* Trans. John MacCombie. Cambridge, MA: Harvard UP, 1988.

Scanlan, Robert. "Surrealism as Mimesis: A Director's Guide to Adrienne Kennedy's *Funnyhouse of a Negro.*" Bryant-Jackson and Overbeck 93–112.

Schiller, Friedrich. *On the Aesthetic Education of Man.* Trans. Reginald Snell. New York: Ungar, 1971.

Schor, Naomi. "French Feminism Is a Universalism." *Differences* 7:1 (Spring 1995): 13–47.

Scott, Joan. "Multiculturalism and the Politics of Identity." Rajchman 3–12.

Sekyi-Otu, Ato. *Fanon's Dialectic of Experience.* Cambridge, MA: Harvard UP, 1996.

Siebers, Tobin. "The Ethics of Anti-Ethnocentrism." *Michigan Quarterly Review* 32 (Winter 1993): 41–70.

Sollors, Werner. *Amiri Baraka/LeRoi Jones: The Quest for a "Populist Modernism."* New York: Columbia UP, 1978.

——— "A Critique of Pure Pluralism." *Reconstructing American Literary History.* Ed. Sacvan Bercovitch. Cambridge, MA: Harvard UP, 1986. 250–279.

——— "Of Mules and Mares in a Land of Difference; or, Quadrupeds All?" *American Quarterly* 42:2 (June 1990): 167–190.

Soyinka, Wole. *Art, Dialogue, and Outrage: Essays on Literature and Culture.* New York: Pantheon, 1993.

——— *The Man Died: Prison Notes.* New York: Noonday, 1988.

Spingarn, Joel. *Creative Criticism and Other Essays.* New ed. New York: Harcourt, 1931.

——— "A Question of Academic Freedom." Being the Official Correspondence between Nicholas Murray Butler and J. E. Spingarn. 1911 (no publisher). For Distribution among the Alumni.

Spitzer, Leo. *The Creoles of Sierra Leone: Responses to Colonialism, 1870–1945.* Madison: U of Wisconsin P, 1974.

Spivak, Gayatri. "Can the Subaltern Speak?" *Marxism and the Interpretation of Culture.* Ed. Lawrence Grossberg and Cary Nelson. Urbana: U of Illinois P. 271–313.

Standley, Fred, and Louis Pratt, eds. *Conversations with James Baldwin.* Jackson: UP of Mississippi, 1989.

Stewart, Jeffrey. "A Black Aesthete at Oxford." *Massachusetts Review* 34:3 (Autumn 1993): 411–428.

——— "Introduction." Locke, *Race Contacts.* xix–lix.

Stocking, George. "The Basic Assumptions of Boasian Anthropology." Boas 1–20.

——— *Race, Culture, and Evolution: Essays in the History of Anthropology.* Chicago: U of Chicago P, 1982.

Sundquist, Eric. *To Wake the Nations: Race in the Making of American Literature.* Cambridge, MA: Harvard UP, 1993.

Tate, Claudia. *Domestic Allegories of Political Desire: The Black Heroine's Text at the Turn of the Century.* New York: Oxford UP, 1992.

—— "Introduction." *Dark Princess*. By W. E. B. Du Bois. Jackson: UP of Mississippi, 1995. ix–xxviii.

Tate, Greg. *Flyboy in the Buttermilk: Essays on Contemporary America*. New York: Simon and Schuster, 1992.

Thurman, Wallace. *Infants of the Spring*. 1932. Boston: Northeastern UP, 1992.

—— "Negro Artists and the Negro." Early 2: 108–113.

—— "Negro Poets and Their Poetry." Early 2: 98–107.

Todorov, Tzvetan. *On Human Diversity: Nationalism, Racism, and Exoticism in French Thought*. Trans. Catherine Porter. Cambridge, MA: Harvard UP, 1993.

Toomer, Jean. *A Jean Toomer Reader: Selected Unpublished Writings*. Ed. Frederik Rusch. New York: Oxford UP, 1993.

—— *The Wayward and the Seeking: A Collection of Writings*. Ed. Darwin Turner. Washington: Howard UP, 1980.

Troupe, Quincy, ed. *James Baldwin: The Legacy*. New York: Simon and Schuster, 1989.

Vincent, Theodore, ed. *Voices of a Black Nation: Political Journalism in the Harlem Renaissance*. Trenton: Africa World Press, 1970.

Wald, Priscilla. *Constituting Americans: Cultural Anxiety and Narrative Form*. Durham: Duke UP, 1995.

Waldron, Jeremy. "Minority Cultures and the Cosmopolitan Alternative." *The Rights of Minority Cultures*. Ed. Will Kymlicka. New York: Oxford UP, 1995. 93–122.

Walker, David. *Appeal*. 1829. New York: Hill and Wang, 1995.

Warren, Kenneth. *Black and White Strangers: Race and American Literary Realism*. Chicago: U of Chicago P, 1993.

Warren, Robert Penn. *Who Speaks for the Negro?* New York: Vintage, 1966.

Washington, Booker T. *My Larger Education: Being Chapters from My Experience*. Garden City: Doubleday, 1911.

—— *Up from Slavery*. 1901. *Three Negro Classics*. Ed. John Hope Franklin. New York: Avon, 1965.

Watts, Jerry Gafio. *Heroism and the Black Intellectual: Ralph Ellison, Politics, and Afro-American Intellectual Life*. Chapel Hill: U of North Carolina P, 1994.

Weber, Max. *From Max Weber: Essays in Sociology*. Trans. and ed. H. H. Gerth and C. Wright Mills. New York: Oxford UP, 1946.

West, Cornel. *The American Evasion of Philosophy: A Genealogy of Pragmatism*. Madison: U of Wisconsin P, 1989.

—— "Black Leadership and the Pitfalls of Racial Reasoning." *Race-ing Justice, En-gendering Power*. Ed. Toni Morrison. 390–401.

—— "The Dilemma of the Black Intellectual." 1985. Rpt. hooks and West. 131–146.

—— and Henry Louis Gates. *The Future of the Race*. New York: Knopf, 1996.

West, Dorothy. *The Richer, The Poorer: Stories, Sketches and Reminiscences*. New York: Doubleday, 1995.

Westbrook, Robert. *John Dewey and American Democracy*. Ithaca: Cornell UP, 1991.

Wilde, Oscar. *The Artist as Critic: Critical Writings of Oscar Wilde*. Ed. Richard Ellman. New York: Vintage, 1969.

Williams, Patricia. *The Alchemy of Race and Rights.* Cambridge, MA: Harvard UP, 1991.

Williamson, Joel. *The Crucible of Race: Black/White Relations in the American South since Emancipation.* New York: Oxford UP, 1984.

Wright, Richard. *Black Boy. Later Works.* 5–365.

——— *Later Works.* New York: Library of America, 1991.

——— *The Outsider. Later Works.* 369–841.

——— *White Man, Listen!* 1957. New York: Harper, 1995.

Young, James. *Black Writers of the Thirties.* Baton Rouge: Louisiana State UP, 1973.

Zamir, Shamoon. *Dark Voices: W. E. B. Du Bois and American Thought, 1888–1903.* Chicago: U of Chicago P, 1995.

Index

Achebe, Chinua, 252
Adell, Sandra, 311n27
Adorno, Theodor, 174–175
Aesthetic, the, 169; and Du Bois, 2–3, 5–6, 14, 33, 35, 72, 100–102, 104–107, 110, 112–113, 116, 118, 133–145, 169–174, 183, 264; as unraced, 6, 29, 70, 82, 107, 299n7; and Alain Locke, 6, 141, 144; and Ellison, 6, 203; and Baldwin, 6, 220–221, 223, 231–232; and the political, 8–9, 88, 107, 112, 116, 118, 141, 144, 145, 148, 172, 183, 203, 220–221, 231–232, 252; and black identity, 22, 29, 32, 79; and pragmatism, 35, 113, 116, 133, 134, 144, 246; and "anarchy," 35, 133, 134, 264, 266; and cosmopolitanism, 152, 293; and cultural studies, 316n2. *See also* Complexity
Als, Hilton, 26
Ambivalence, 9, 86, 107, 262; and race representation, 37, 71; and Baraka, 44, 245, 248–249, 251, 255, 259; and Du Bois, 71, 105, 107, 112, 116–117; and Ellison, 77; and pragmatism, 116–117; and Baldwin, 233, 258
Anderson, Sherwood, 32, 163
Antirace race figure, 5, 8, 9–10, 12, 22, 70, 71, 85, 262, 293, 299n6; Du Bois as, 5, 6, 50, 69, 88; Locke as, 6, 195; Hopkins as, 50–51, 66, 69; Wright as, 69; Ellison as, 69, 77; Murray as, 202; Hurston as, 211–215. *See also* Black intellectuals
Appiah, Anthony, 3, 25, 46, 313n15

Aptheker, Herbert, 112
Arendt, Hannah, 102, 318n11
Armah, Ayi Kwei, 253–258, 259; *Why Are We So Blest?*, 253–256, 258
Authenticity, 3, 15, 27, 80, 86, 99–100, 104–106, 110, 253, 256–257, 303n9; critics and critiques of, 19–20, 26–27, 32, 63–64, 81, 88, 89–93, 96–98, 202, 313n16; ideology of, 21, 52, 53
Autobiography, 130, 215, 261, 285–286, 321n10
Ayandele, E. A., 99, 103

Baker, Houston, 314n17
Baldwin, James, 27, 28, 30, 48, 52, 70, 217, 232–235; and the aesthetic, 6, 220–221, 231, 232; and cosmopolitanism, 24, 29, 224, 226, 235–237; and "Jewish" identity, 55; and Baraka, 61, 220, 221–222, 223; and American identity, 223–225, 227, 228, 231, 235–237; and pragmatist pluralism, 223, 227; and Henry James, 227–228, 325n9; and homosexuality, 231, 233, 235, 326n13, 327n14; and ambivalence, 233, 258; and Elijah Muhammad, 233, 234; as intellectual, 234, 237, 281–282; and separatism, 234; and Delany, 280–282; *Another Country*, 233, 326n13; *The Fire Next Time*, 8, 224, 232–234; *Go Tell It on the Mountain*, 236; *Notes of a Native Son*, 224–226; "Stranger in the Village," 225–226
Baraka, Amiri (LeRoi Jones), 51, 247–248, 259, 269–270; as intellectual, 43–45,